CW00551725

Soldiers, Airmen, Spies, and Whisperers

Soldiers
Airmen
Spies
and
Whisperers

THE GOLD COAST
IN WORLD WAR II

Nancy Ellen Lawler

OHIO UNIVERSITY PRESS   ATHENS

Ohio University Press, Athens, Ohio 45701
© 2002 by Nancy Ellen Lawler
Printed in the United States of America

Ohio University Press books are printed on acid-free paper ∞ ™

10 09 08 07 06 05 04 03 02   5 4 3 2 1

Frontispiece: Drum Major Saidu Logos, Gold Coast
Regiment, Accra 1940. *E. C. Lanning*

Library of Congress Cataloging-in-Publication Data

Lawler, Nancy Ellen.
    Soldiers, airmen, spies, and whisperers : the Gold Coast in World War II / by Nancy
  Ellen Lawler
      p. cm.
    Includes bibliographical references and index.
    ISBN 0-8214-1430-5 (alk. paper)
      1. World War, 1939–1945—Military intelligence—Ghana. 2. World War,
  1939–1945—Secret service—Ghana. 3. Ghana—History—To 1957. I. Title.

  D810.S7 L325 2002
  940.54'86667—dc21

                                                                    2002017082

To Ivor,
who lured me over the border

Contents

Chapter Nine: Possible Futures

Illustrations

Maps

Preface

Following the collapse of the French Army in the face of the six-week German offensive in the spring of 1940, Afrique Occidentale Français (French West Africa) elected to remain loyal to the government of Marshall Pétain in Vichy. This left the four British West African colonies—Gambia, Sierra Leone, Gold Coast, and Nigeria—virtually surrounded on all but their Atlantic shores by potentially hostile Vichy territory. This was a worst-case scenario never conjured up by those who paced the corridors of power in Whitehall. No contingency plans existed to meet so unthinkable a threat. The plight was to last from the summer of 1940 to the closing days of 1942. This book tells of one of those colonies, the Gold Coast (or Ghana, as it has now become), and how it responded to the changed circumstances. Underlying this study are two fundamental questions. The first, and easier one to answer is, What was done to deter invasion? The second, and by far the more difficult to answer, is, had what was done not been done, would there indeed have been an invasion?

I have used the term Gold Coast to encompass the country's four constituent parts—namely, the Colony of the Gold Coast, Ashanti (or more correctly, Asante), the Protectorate of the Northern Territories, and British-mandated Togoland. The selection of this one territory, rather than the whole of British West Africa, was made for two reasons. First, the sheer volume of evidence available is such as to dictate a case study approach; and second, the profile of each of the four colonies is so distinctive, in terms of its material and human resources, that a general overview could only be undertaken at the expense of the particularities of the local scene. The choice of the Gold Coast as a case study virtually dictated itself. The general headquarters of the Royal West African Frontier Force was situated at Achimota College, near Accra; the Special Operations Executive, which established an active intelligence network aimed at French West Africa, was also based there; and, most important, a small airstrip at Takoradi was transformed into a vital Royal Air Force assembly and transit base for planes destined for the

The Gold Coast on the eve of war: Gold Coast Colony, Ashanti, Northern Territories, and British-mandated Togoland

North African and Middle East theaters of war. The importance of this last to the Allied war effort cannot easily be overestimated. Additionally, the Gold Coast possessed very considerable gold and other mineral resources of importance to the prosecution of war, and therefore presented the Axis powers with a tempting target for invasion.

The first part of the book has to do with the civil and military responses to the new circumstances arising from the fall of France. Chapter 1 looks at the efforts made in West Africa to persuade the administration of French West Africa to disown the collaborationist French government of Vichy and to continue the fight from Africa. An assessment of the overall military situation in the Gold Coast is presented. Chapter 2 deals centrally with the development of the West African Reinforcement Route operated by the RAF between Takoradi and Cairo, and considers the various measures taken to defend the Gold Coast against invasion. Chapters 3, 4, and 5 deal with the little-known saga of the Special Operations Executive (SOE) in West Africa. Its beginnings under the leadership of a Belgian banker are traced, its disastrous relationship with the General Officer Commanding, West Africa, is detailed, and the SOE's relations with Free French espionage and propaganda organizations are explored. On a very local level, an account of the conduct of the SOE's operatives in the Wenchi District of northwestern Asante is offered. In these three chapters, I have called attention to the extraordinary infighting between the authorities most crucially responsible for the defense of West Africa in general, and the Gold Coast in particular, specifically the general headquarters of the Royal West African Frontier Force, the West African Governors' Conference, and the West African section of the Special Operations Executive. As the war progressed, it sometimes seemed as if a perceived enemy "within" was assailed with as much vigor and enthusiasm as the real enemy "without." Nonetheless, beneath this level of upper-echelon feuding, there is singularly little doubt that the mass of the Gold Coast people were convinced that "Mr. Hitler" was not a good man and rallied rather splendidly to the British and the Allied cause.

Chapter 6 casts an eye on the propaganda techniques employed in West Africa by the British Ministry of Information. Its work included broadcasts directed at both the Vichy colonies and the Gold Coast home front, and the screening of patriotic films brought out to the bush by mobile theatres. Some account is also given of the so-called whispering campaigns—that is, the propagation of rumors that was to become a specialty of certain co-opted district commissioners. The rehabilitation of small-scale smugglers as special agents is also touched upon.

The concern of chapter 7 is with a major triumph involving the efficient collabo- ration of the British Colonial Administration, the SOE, and the Free French: the masterminding of the migration of the Gyaman from the Bondoukou area in the Côte d'Ivoire to Sunyani in the Gold Coast. Chapter 8 outlines the events that led to French West Africa rejoining the Allied camp and the fortunes of some of those spies, soldiers, airmen, and administrators who had played so important a role in the affairs of 1940 to 1942. The last chapter briefly explores several coun- terfactuals in order to assist the reader—and for that matter the author—in de- ciding whether the events described were a case of "suppose you had a war and nobody came" or whether, in the Gold Coast, these events helped deter any Axis operations against Britain's West African colonies. If some of these issues have been dealt with in a somewhat less than somber vein, the author must ask her readers' indulgence. One cannot fail to find humor, as participants undoubtedly did at the time, when dealing with, for example, propaganda campaigns called Hitler's Orchestra of Death, or members of the Home Guard requiring govern- ment to regard the treatment of venereal disease as part of the war effort.

To the best of my knowledge, the only full-scale study of this period in Ghana is the regrettably unpublished dissertation of Wendell Holbrook, "The Impact of the Second World War on the Gold Coast, 1939–1945" (Princeton Uni- versity, 1978). Holbrook's fundamental aim was to locate the war years in the un- folding development of a nationalism that was to result, in 1957, in the Gold Coast attaining independence as the new nation of Ghana. He was particularly concerned to explore how Gold Coasters "used the war years to: (1) continue many of their pre-war criticisms of colonial government; (2) seek a wider African par- ticipation in government; and (3) argue against economic policies which affected their real incomes." Holbrook concludes that, "in many ways, the government's decisions accelerated African grievances and built expectations for post-war re- wards" (423). Anyone seriously interested in the period should be encouraged to read this important study. David Killingray has written more generally on the military in West Africa, and his important dissertation, "The Colonial Army in the Gold Coast: Official Policy and Local Response, 1890–1947" (London Univer- sity, 1982), contains much useful material on the World War II era. E. C. Lanning is currently putting together a study of the Gold Coast Regiment in the East Africa campaign of 1940–41. This should be a definitive work and its publication is ea- gerly awaited. I am most grateful to him for the wealth of material on the regiment that he has shared with me, and for his support and encouragement in ways that are too many, unfortunately, to be listed here. Otherwise, I am much indebted to the many monographs, papers both published and unpublished, and chapters in books that have dealt with aspects of the Gold Coast at war, and these are, I trust, fully acknowledged in the endnotes and bibliography.

The present book has a somewhat different focus from the studies mentioned above. It describes, in considerable local detail, various aspects of the war effort in the Gold Coast, but at the same time attempts to locate these in the context of the global struggle. In my reconstruction of the period I have drawn heavily upon documents in the Public Record Office, namely, the archives of the Foreign Office, Colonial Office, War Office, and Special Operations Executive. I was most fortunate in that the last of these was declassified only in the course of my research, enabling me to offer for the first time an account of the extraordinary struggles between the SOE and the command of the Royal West African Frontier Force. I have also used collections from Rhodes House, Oxford, the Archives Nationales de la Côte d'Ivoire, the National Archives and Records Administration of the United States, and the Archives de l'Outre-Mer, Aix-en-Provence. I have also made extensive use of the vast collection of Africana materials at the Melville J. Herskovits Memorial Library, Northwestern University. Last but not least, I was able to locate much important material in the National Archives of Ghana at Accra, Kumasi, and Sunyani. Indeed, it was at Sunyani that my greatest stroke of fortune came when I discovered two bulky folders left over from the war years. Both had been marked, To Be Destroyed. Both had somehow survived, probably having been consigned for years to the inner recesses of the district commissioner's safe, whence, after Independence, it may be inferred that they were transferred to the National Archives. Special thanks must go to the staff at Sunyani, who arranged for the materials to be photocopied at the only working machine within fifty or more miles.

My initial fieldwork in Ghana was made possible by a grant from the American Philosophical Society, for which I am most grateful. Otherwise, this study has received no external funding. I am, however, deeply indebted to many individuals for having facilitated the research that went into the making of this book. Dan Britz of the Melville J. Herskovits Memorial Library was, as always, unflagging in his efforts to procure obscure documents and to identify useful archival sources. I am grateful to M. R. D. Foot for providing much needed information on Louis Franck. The late Sir Harry Hinsley kindly offered many useful suggestions toward untangling the threads of British intelligence operations in Africa, and Basil and Marion Davidson also provided many insights into the structure and operations of the Special Operations Executive, albeit their experiences were not in the West African theater of war. T. C. McCaskie, who has never ceased to express his enthusiasm for the project, shared with me memories of his father's tales of service in the Gold Coast Regiment. I am most grateful to Lynne Brydon, whose late father, Major Gordon Brydon, served with the Gold Coast Regiment in East Africa, West Africa, and Burma. She generously allowed me access to his personal diaries. Another veteran, H. C. Norman, not only spent long hours reminiscing about his war, but generously provided copies of his photographic record of the period. The Rev. A. C. Russell, the last British chief commissioner, Ashanti, let me peruse his diaries, and made available his recollections of the war years. David Killingray has long been a source of support and has assisted me in clarifying my ideas on a number of matters. I am grateful to W. R. Grigsby, J. Harris, and the late H. V. Wimshurst for taking the time to commit to paper their memories of the period.

Others who greatly assisted me by securing important information include Ivor Agyeman-Duah, Greg Mann, Amy Settergren, and Mike Tetelman. Nana Yaw Reynolds and Nana Osei Agyeman-Duah did much to make my field work in Ghana both exciting and productive, not least with their skills as translators. In Ghana, Côte d'Ivoire, and Britain, I was extremely fortunate to have been able to interview many who had directly participated in the events described in this book, and were generous enough to share their remembrances with me. Their help is fully acknowledged in the text and in the list of informants at the end of the book. It is sad to note how many of them are no longer with us. And finally, my thanks to Ivor Wilks, without whose critical appraisal of successive drafts of the text, this book would have been finished much earlier.

Abbreviations, Acronyms, and Code Names

AD	director of SOE staff—Overseas Missions
AEF	Afrique Equatorial Français (French Equatorial Africa)
ANCI	Archives Nationales de la Côte d'Ivoire (National Archives of the Côte d'Ivoire)
AOF	Afrique Occidentale Français (French West Africa)
bn	battalion
BNCO	British noncommissioned officer
Brig.	Brigadier
BSAP	British South African Police
C	Chief of SIS (MI 6)
CCA	chief commissioner, Ashanti
CD	executive director, SOE
CEO	chief executive officer
CO	commanding officer
COI	(Office of the) Coordinator of Information
COMDT	commandant
CQMS	company quartermaster sergeant
CSS	chief, Secret Service
DC	district commissioner
DCD	deputy chief, SOE
DCSS	deputy chief, secret service
DMI	director of military intelligence
DSO	Distinguished Service Order
FFC	Free French Committee

FO	Foreign Office
FRAWEST	SOE—French West Africa
GCC	Gold Coast Constabulary
GCR	Gold Coast Regiment
GHQ	general headquarters
GMC	Groupe Mobile Coloniale
GOC	general officer commanding
GOC-in-C	general officer commanding in chief
GSO 1	general staff officer, grade 1
GS(I)	General Staff (Intelligence)
HMG	His Majesty's Government
JIC	Joint Intelligence Committee
KAR	King's African Rifles
M	head of operations section, SOE
MC	Military Cross
MEW	Ministry of Economic Warfare
MI 6	alternative name for SIS
MP	member of Parliament
NAG	National Archives of Ghana
NCO	noncommissioned officer
Neucols	SOE—Neutral Colonies in Africa
OSS	Office of Strategic Services
PERO	Political and Economic Research Office
PRO	Public Record Office
PWE	Political Warfare Executive
SOE	Special Operations Executive
RAF	Royal Air Force
RAMC	Royal Army Medical Corps
RASC	Royal Army Service Corps
RPTS	Regiment Porte de Tirailleurs Sénégalais
RTS	Regiment des Tirailleurs Sénégalais

RWAFF	Royal West African Frontier Force
SIS	Special Intelligence Service
SLICA	Service de Renseignements et de Propagande sur la Côte Occidentale d'Afrique (Free French Intelligence Service)
W	Louis Franck, head of the SOE, West Africa
W.1	Francis Glyn, head of Gold Coast Section
W.4	(identity unknown)
W.7	(identity unknown)
W.11	Capt. L. J. Mothersill, SOE field officer, Gold Coast
W.13	(identity unknown)
W.29	(identity unknown), officer in charge, sabotage
W.30	Capt. Desmond Longe
W.32	Capt. R. J. M. Curwen
W.33	F. G. J. Roberts, head of Gold Coast Section (late 1942)
W.37	J. F. Scanlan
W.38	Meyer Fortes, Oxford anthropologist
W.44	Pilot Officer B. C. Stewart
W.45	(identity unknown)
W.46	(identity unknown)
W.52	Lt. F. G. J. Forbes
WAFF	West African Frontier Force
WAGON	West African Governors' Conference
WAPIC	West African Political Intelligence Centre
WE	Ronald Wingate, head of Frawest
WE.1	Braima Kamagate, SOE agent in Wenchi
WE.2	Mama Coulibaly, SOE agent in Wenchi
WF	Lt. Col. A. F. R. Lumby, head of Frawest, successor to Wingate
WP	Miles Clifford, deputy head of Frawest
W/T	Wireless/Telegraphy
X	Hugh Dalton, minister of economic warfare

Soldiers, Airmen, Spies, and Whisperers

1

The Fall of France and the British West African Colonies

INTRODUCTION

In early 1939, it should have been obvious that, despite the concessions to Hitler at Munich, war was imminent. The allied French and British armies braced them-selves for yet another confrontation with the Germans. They looked to their over-seas territories to continue to fulfill their well-established role in the imperial systems, for in war as in peace, the colonies were expected not only to support themselves, but to provide resources, both natural and human, for the good of the respective metropoles. In this context, neither France nor Britain envisaged the possibility that West Africa would become a theatre of war. Even more unimagin-able was the thought that their colonial frontiers would someday separate hostile nations.

Frontiers in West Africa had been carefully delineated by hard-bargaining and hard-working British, French, and German boundary commissioners in the late nineteenth and early twentieth centuries, and their recommendations had been accepted in London, Paris, and Berlin.[1] Britain and France had remained firm allies in World War I and carried out joint military campaigns to displace the Germans from their two West African colonies, Togo and Cameroon. This, of course, did not mean that there was complete mutual trust; indeed, the British and French in West Africa had cordially spied on one another throughout the

1920s and 1930s. Thus in the late 1920s, for example, Captain R. M. Hall had made a leisurely journey from Dakar to Grand Bassam, his mission to produce for the War Office in London a "Secret Report" on the state of the French colonial establishment.[2] Whatever conclusions the British had drawn about the level of military preparedness in Afrique Occidentale Français (AOF), it was such as to give them confidence in the security of West Africa as a whole, and particularly that of the land frontiers of their four West African possessions. Moreover, no one doubted that the Royal Navy commanded the South Atlantic shores.

France and Britain were at one in their resolve to oppose the territorial ambitions of the Third Reich. Both went to war on 3 September 1939. Indeed, in April 1940, one British observer made an extensive tour of West Africa and returned to the Gold Coast to report, optimistically, that the people of French and British West Africa together, "are in this war and want to be in it."[3] He did not foresee that, in the following month, the unimaginable was to happen. Germany launched its six-week blitzkrieg across northern Europe on 10 May 1940, and the French Army disintegrated in the face of the onslaught. The Germans marched into Paris, already declared an open city, on 14 June. Three days later, and only hours after being named premier of France, Marshall Henri Pétain announced that negotiations with the Germans for an armistice had begun. The next day, 18 June, a little-known general, Charles de Gaulle, broadcast a rallying call from London to the French people:

> It was the tanks, the planes, and the tactics of the Germans, far more than the fact that we were outnumbered that forced our armies to retreat. It was the German tanks, planes, and tactics that provided the element of surprise which brought our leaders to their present plight.
>
> But has the last word been said? Must we abandon all hope? Is our defeat final and irremediable? France has lost a battle! To these questions I answer —No! Speaking in full knowledge of the facts, I ask you to believe me when I say that the cause of France is not lost. The very factors that brought about our defeat may one day lead us to victory.
>
> For, remember this, France does not stand alone. She is not isolated. Behind her is a vast Empire, and she can make common cause with the British Empire, which commands the seas and is continuing the struggle. Like England, she can draw unreservedly on the immense industrial resources of the United States.
>
> This war is not limited to our unfortunate country. The outcome of the struggle has not been decided by the Battle of France. This is a world war.[4]

Soldiers, Airmen, Spies, and Whisperers

The vast majority of French men and women, stunned by the total collapse of Europe's largest army, either did not hear or did not heed this bold message of hope. On 22 June, in the same railway car in which the Allies had accepted the surrender of the German Imperial Forces in World War I, the French delegation, headed by Gen. Léon Huntziger, signed the Armistice with Field Marshall W. Keitel, representing Germany. Three-fifths of France would be under German occupation, no prisoners of war would be released, and the costs of the war were to be borne by the French. The French army was limited to a hundred thousand men in the unoccupied zone, now officially designated *l'Etat Français,* but to become widely known as Vichy France from the name of its new administrative center. This humiliating document had, perhaps, one bright spot. By Article 10, Pétain, now head of l'Etat Français, obtained what was widely construed as a concession, one giving him continuing authority over the overseas territories.

In Britain's West African colonies there was, inevitably, intense speculation about Germany's longer range imperial aspirations. It was assumed that the return of those parts of its former colonies, Togo and Cameroon, which were under French mandate, would be demanded as part of any final treaty signed with France. The matter received immediate attention in an editorial in British West Africa's leading commercial journal:

> Germany may demand that garrisons in French and French Mandated Africa should (a) give facilities to German and/or Italian troops to occupy by an overland route the territory demanded and (b) that in the meantime French garrisons should themselves take protective action against any move by the British Colonial troops to occupy neighbouring French territories. However the present situation is viewed, it has to be admitted that the terrible misfortune that has fallen upon France will have many severe repercussions throughout British Africa.[5]

For the Colonial Office in London, it seemed possible that the French colonies, so far from the reality of defeat and unable to witness the utter hopelessness that seemed to envelop the motherland overnight, might reject the Armistice and even respond positively to de Gaulle. As it happened, it was an unexpected occurrence in the Gold Coast Colony that forced the Colonial Office to cobble quickly together some semblance of a policy.

On 18 June 1940 a group of French officers arrived in Accra from Cotonou in Dahomey and offered their services to the British. The next day, Colonel Marguet, officer commanding troops in Dahomey and Togoland, also arrived there and managed to convince them to return to their posts. According to the official account of the matter, before leaving the Gold Coast, Marguet made clear "his intention to continue the fight in the event of French capitulation." He added that he believed that the commander of all French West African troops, General Barrau, would quickly proclaim the intention of the AOF to do the same. So enthusiastic for the fight was Colonel Marguet that he asked for assurance that, should his own military resources (described as considerable) prove inadequate, those of the British government would be made available.[6]

The Colonial Office responded, with remarkable speed. The governor of the Gold Coast, Sir Arnold Hodson, was instructed,

> to send Military Missions to the French territories surrounding the Gold Coast in order to implement the policy laid down by the Secretary of State; namely to encourage the French to maintain their territories intact and defend them as long as possible, but in the last resort to prevent military equipment or native troops from falling into enemy hands by encouraging any elements which showed such a desire to join the British Forces. These Missions are also designed to ensure that the French Colonial Governments received messages of British offers of financial, economic, and other help.[7]

As a matter of courtesy, the Colonial Office requested the approval of Pierre Boisson, governor-general of both the AOF and Afrique Equatoriale Français (AEF), in Dakar. He, however, was already mounting the fence he was to straddle the entire summer of 1940. He refused to grant the British permission to send the missions. It was, nevertheless, decided to ignore him.[8] Such was the confidence in information received from both Abidjan and Ouagadougou, and so great were worries about the vulnerability of the Gold Coast's northern and western frontiers, that it was decided to go ahead with the missions without Boisson's approval. Six missions were dispatched in all.

Between 22 June and 28 June, R. O. Ramage of the Gold Coast Colonial Secretariat, accompanied by an assistant district commissioner, A. Hughes, set out for Nigeria. En route they visited the capitals of French-mandated Togo and Dahomey, meeting with the governors of both colonies as well as with Colonel

Marguet.[9] Whether as a result of bad planning, or to add a sense of urgency to the talks, on 25 June, a Major Hamilton also arrived in Cotonou to meet with Marguet. Hamilton urged the colonel to consider the British government's offer to pay the wages and pensions of any anti-Vichy civilian or military officials who chose to enter British territory for their own protection.[10] Hamilton was, no doubt, much bemused when Marguet told him that his visit was quite unnecessary, as Ramage and Hughes were to meet again with him on their return trip from Lagos. No record of this second meeting has been found but, after the two reached Accra, they reported that the morale of French civil authorities, not surprisingly, was very low, and that effective power lay with the military. The mass of the people of Dahomey and Togo, they wrote, were widely expecting a British invasion, and indeed seemed prepared to accept it.[11]

On 22 June, the same day that Ramage and Hughes left Accra for Cotonou, two other officers of the Gold Coast Colonial Service traveled to Ouagadougou. These were W. J. A. Jones, chief commissioner of the Northern Territories of the Gold Coast, and R. A. M. McNicoll, assistant district commissioner. They brought with them a telegram from General de Gaulle for Edmond Louveau, lieutenant governor of Haute Côte d'Ivoire (formerly Upper Volta and today Burkina Faso). Louveau received them warmly, referring to Jones as his "old friend." Jones learned that Louveau had that morning already telegraphed his support, via the Gold Coast, to de Gaulle in London.[12] Jones first assured Louveau that he "could be certain that the British Empire would never fall, and, even if England was invaded and London taken, the Empire would continue the fight."[13] This was apparently the message Louveau wanted to hear for, in turn, he assured Jones that in the event of a German takeover of the Côte d'Ivoire, "many military and civil officers would cross into the Gold Coast bringing African troops with them." In his report, Jones also recorded Louveau's private opinion that any British invasion of French West African territories would receive much support.[14] Jones returned to his headquarters in Tamale on 24 June, having obtained Louveau's ready agreement to meet with a further British military mission. Following swiftly upon this visit, Lt. Col. G. H. Gibbs, a veteran of World War I, and currently a district commissioner who was to succeed Jones as chief commissioner in 1942, arrived in Ouagadougou on 26 June. Gibbs wanted, understandably enough, to know the sentiments of the local French community, civilian as well as military. He was reassured that all were prepared to answer de Gaulle's call to continue the war from the colonies, and he felt that he had been able to build upon the friendly relationship already well established between Louveau and Jones.

Another mission was headed by Maj. H. J. Le Mare of the Gold Coast Regiment (GCR). On 23 June he arrived in Abidjan to meet with the governor of Côte d'Ivoire, Horace Crocicchia, and General Schmitt, commander of French forces there. Le Mare was to stay in Abidjan for several weeks.[15] It may or may not have been a coincidence that, on 24 June, the governor of the Gold Coast received a telegram from the French Veterans Association of Abidjan: "All sections population wish to assure your excellency of our unshakeable will to continue the struggle together with British Empire until final victory is assured. Request you advise General de Gaulle London. Loyal sentiments."[16] And finally, the last of the missions left Accra, again for Cotonou, on 4 July. It was led by Lt. Col. Chandler and Capt. E. C. Neill, who obviously hoped to complete the work commenced by Ramage and Hughes.

Despite the coolness of Governor-General Boisson, throughout the early summer there some officials in the Colonial Office remained convinced that the AOF and AEF would join the British. Just prior to Pétain's call for the armistice, Churchill had, after all, made his proposal for a Franco-British Union, whereby not only would "every citizen of France enjoy immediately citizenship of Great Britain," but "every British subject will become a citizen of France." The text of the proposal concluded: "The union will concentrate its full energy against the power of the enemy, no matter where the battle may be. And thus we shall conquer."[17] Although the proposal, too little and too late, was never seriously considered by the panic-stricken French cabinet, in the summer of 1940 the Colonial Office still hoped that Churchill's message had made a considerable impact on the French colonies. The Gold Coast's missions appeared to be meeting with success in Abidjan, Ouagadougou, Lomé, and Cotonou, and the news from Britain's other West African colonies—Gambia, Nigeria, and Sierra Leone, who were also in contact with their French counterparts—could also be regarded as equally satisfactory.

The telegraph wires between the British West African colonies and the secretary of state in London hummed during the last days of June and the beginning of July 1940, as the governors attempted continuously to assess the mood of their respective French neighbors. Sir Bernard Bourdillon, governor of Nigeria, reported that young French officers in Zinder, Niger, were "restless and unwilling to remain passive." They were awaiting the order to continue the fight from their commander, General Aubert, who in turn had been cabling to Boisson in Dakar for instructions.[18] Apparently Aubert was willing to join the British, but only if he received orders to do so. The orders never came. Aubert, like the vast majority of other military and civilian personnel in French West Africa, feared for the

Soldiers, Airmen, Spies, and Whisperers

safety of his family in France should the Germans come to suspect his loyalty. In Dakar, Britain's consul general wired for instructions as to whether or not coups d'état, rumored to be hatching in Senegal's towns, should be encouraged. He was inclined to be cautious, and drew attention to the possible danger of inciting the "black population." They would, he thought, "back action, but lack their own leaders. I am exerting my influence, which is now tremendous, amongst them, to prevent their movement turning anti-French. Request early information as to whether strong naval force could be available in near future."[19]

The four British governors were in constant communication among themselves, and with Lord Lloyd, the secretary of state for the colonies, as to the best way of proceeding in the current circumstances. Lloyd could be quite indecisive. On 1 July, for example, he wired Governor Hodson of the Gold Coast: "I am still unable to authorise you to invade territories either in the name of General de Gaulle or on your own account."[20] On that very same day, by coincidence, the commander in chief, Royal Navy South Atlantic, cabled Hodson from Freetown informing him of a decision taken by, presumably, the War Cabinet that the AOF could not be regarded as friendly territory. He noted that "the fervent pronouncements of French African Colonies to fight on have evaporated," and that they seemed to have become "entirely subservient to whatever orders are issued from Bordeaux Government prompted by German and Italian influence." The admiral went on to suggest that "the French central system of government makes it extremely difficult for colonial authorities to break away from their normal attitude of looking to French Government for lead. And there is no doubt that German and Italian methods of propaganda will take full advantage of this weakness."[21]

The first of July was for Hodson obviously a very busy day. He had already been approached by the governor of tiny Gambia, W. T. Southorn, surely the British colony most exposed and vulnerable to invasion, who had been himself been sounded out by unspecified numbers of Frenchmen in Senegal to enlist in the British forces. On 1 July, Southorn cabled Hodson for advice. "Give them cordial encouragement," was all Hodson could think of replying, "and then ask the Royal West African Frontier Force if they could be of any use."[22] The governor of Sierra Leone, D. J. Jardine, having been informed on 26 June that the Gold Coast was considering the possibility of setting up some form of civilian defense force, was also to cable Hodson, not only to express his support for such a plan but his desire to emulate it if the Gold Coast could send someone to train the volunteers.[23] On 19 July, Governor Bourdillon of Nigeria also wired his endorsement, adding the suggestion that any such force should also be involved with cross-frontier intelligence. Ever mindful of the financial constraints besetting their administrations, Bourdillon estimated the cost of such a force for each of the four colonies to be £1,000. Obviously no large operation was envisioned and, indeed, Hodson in Accra was reminded by his Nigerian counterpart that absolutely no equipment except sporting rifles was available, and therefore no new organization could train very many men.[24]

THE LINES HARDEN: ORAN AND ITS AFTERMATH

On 4 July 1940 the Royal Navy virtually destroyed the French fleet, which had been at anchor off Oran, in the Mediterranean. The British government had been unwilling to accept Vichy assurances that it would never be used against them. The heavy casualties that resulted did much to rally the empire to the Vichy government.[25] Further naval action was taken on 8 July, when a British ship anchored off Dakar sent a patrol boat into the harbor to drop depth charges in an unsuccessful attempt to sink the thirty-five-thousand-ton French cruiser *Richelieu* docked there. A "slight list" was reported.[26]

Although the British missions at both Abidjan and Ouagadougou had reported that French officials recommended the British occupation of Dakar as "the best way to bring about a British-French bloc in West Africa," their patriotism was now being sorely tested. One by one, the British missions were asked to withdraw. Chandler returned from Cotonou on 5 July, and Neill on 7 July, at the request of Colonel Marguet, who had received news of Oran. Just prior to Neill's departure, Marguet addressed him. "Britain," he said, "was always making blunders, but that Oran was a bigger one than usual and should be retrieved immediately; meanwhile all that the French desired was to be left alone to continue as they were without interference, and that when Britain had become sufficiently strong to deal a decisive blow, it might be that the French Colonies would rise and help; the French would resist any attempt by the enemy to enter West Africa."[27] Marguet did not specify which enemy he had in mind, but we must assume it was Germany.

Whatever the case, the Colonial Office was aware of the problems caused by the sinking of the fleet off Oran. On 7 July, the secretary of state addressed the entire question, with particular reference to requests for British support from a pro-Gaullist faction in French-mandated Cameroon. The cardinal principle he enunciated was that any suggestion of "grabbing French territory" and thereby "giving the Pétain government a seemingly better pretext than Oran to declare

Soldiers, Airmen, Spies, and Whisperers

war," should be shunned. "There is, of course, as you have already been informed," he continued, "no question of transferring mandate. That must remain in French hands and our action will be directed solely towards maintaining orderly administration and integrity of territory in order to restore it to French Government as soon as a free and responsible Government is again in being on the soil of France."[28]

Five days later, on 12 July, the delicate problem of influencing the French West African authorities to throw their lot in with the British was further clarified. In a telegram to the governor of the Gold Coast, the secretary of state wrote, "If you consider action on these lines would be valuable in any or all provinces French Equatorial and West Africa with which you are in touch (and would help) definitely to crystallize the position where it is already favourable or to win over local authorities where they are wavering, you are authorised to proceed accordingly in consultation with G.O.C. [general officer commanding]." Hodson was further advised that he should "draw attention to offer of economic assistance to French conveyed in my telegram no. 505." The government, he was assured, is "fully ready to give effect in such assistance but they clearly could not be prepared to do so in the case of territories whose attitude remains equivocal." Furthermore, in case there was any remaining doubt about policy, Hodson was told to counter any impressions the French colonial authorities had, "that they can expect vital economic aid from H.M. Government without defining their own attitude. You should do your best to make position clear to them." If Hodson had any real confidence in his ability to influence the French authorities, and any chance of "making the position clear to them," it must have been severely undermined by the secretary of state's final paragraph: "I need hardly repeat that under present circumstances and for some considerable time to come we cannot send any assistance to West Africa."[29]

Captain Neill, who had remained at Cotonou until 7 July, withdrew. Immediately after his return, the Gold Coast military authorities deemed it prudent to station a small force of troops on the frontier with Togo, virtually on the outskirts of the capital, Lomé.[30] They were, presumably, there to turn back any sudden attack, rather than being the vanguard of any projected offensive action. In Ouagadougou, however, Lieutenant Colonel Gibbs continued to talk with Louveau. "What aid could you give us?" the lieutenant governor asked. Gibbs replied, presumably with regret but at least with honesty: "Nothing at the moment, all our troops are gone, but I will refer it to my government."[31] This time-honored diplomatic formula did little to dampen Louveau's enthusiasm. He and Gibbs apparently agreed that it was impossible for Haute Côte d'Ivoire to hold out against anticipated intervention from Dakar and that therefore those who wished to continue the fight should decamp to the Gold Coast. Sixty-five Europeans (mostly soldiers, but including twelve women and children and three civilians) and 467 African troops, crossed the border and entered the Gold Coast via the towns of Navrongo, Lawra, and Wa. Clearly this was what Governor Boisson had feared in refusing to authorize the British missions. He immediately ordered Louveau to terminate the talks in Ouagadougou, and Gibbs accordingly left on 8 July. Two days later Boisson closed the frontiers with the Gold Coast. Major Le Mare left Abidjan for Accra on 12 July.[32] Despite Boisson's increasing hostile attitude toward the British, the indomitable Louveau nevertheless made plans to keep in close touch with W. J. A. Jones, either by meetings on the frontier or by coded communications, and ordered his secretary, M. Helard, to join the chief commissioner at his headquarters in Tamale.[33]

Perhaps it was reports of Louveau's strongly pro–Free French and pro-British stance that led Governor Hodson to believe that the military in the Côte d'Ivoire might be on the verge of committing themselves to resistance. After the correspondence of the past week, Hodson presumably felt that he had brilliantly carried out his instructions to collaborate with the neighboring French authorities. Indeed, on 15 July he had asked the French consul in Accra to inform the governors of the Côte d'Ivoire and Togo that Britain's offer to provide economic and financial assistance remained on the table. He also suggested that a meeting might be arranged between himself and the two governors. The invitation was declined.[34]

At about this same time Hodson wired London with the news that he expected the imminent arrival of General Schmitt in the Gold Coast. Near panic seemed to grip the mandarins in Whitehall at this prospect. On 20 July the secretary of state wired,

> *Immediate Governor, Accra.* . . . I note you expect General Officer Commanding Ivory Coast and all his troops are likely to want to move into Gold Coast. Presumably this means that he and his forces do not accept French armistice and wish to continue war in association with us. If that is the case it seems that they might best serve our joint cause by not withdrawing into British territory but remaining in Ivory Coast and influencing administration to adopt a more friendly attitude. If all major military forces in Ivory Coast are in fact animated by these sentiments they should be in a strong position to bring such influence to bear. French G.O.C. and his officers are presumably aware of our offer to guarantee pay and pensions of French officials who stand by us. . . .

From point of view of security of our West African territories it seems most important that control of Ivory Coast and similar areas interlocking geographically with British territory should be in friendly hands.[35]

As late as 26 July 1940, Louveau could still inform Jones that the whole of Haute Côte d'Ivoire had come out in favor of de Gaulle. As it happened, this was the very day he was recalled to Dakar, supposedly having suffered a nervous breakdown. When he arrived in Dakar, he was immediately arrested for treason. Even as he despaired in his prison, Louveau was able to get a message through to Jones: "Am in prison in Dakar under terrible conditions by order of General Barrau [commander in chief, AOF] under instruction from armistice committee. I do not know when I shall be liberated. Sincerest regards. Still hope, suffer for our cause."[36] It is gratifying to be able to report that Louveau did survive his ordeal in Dakar. Although condemned to forced labor for life by a military tribunal on 12 October 1941, he was sent to a concentration camp in France.[37] There he managed to escape and join the Free French. It is sad, however, to note that after the war, as governor of French Soudan (now Mali), he became one of the most repressive administrators in the AOF.

The defections from Haute Côte d'Ivoire described above were by no means the only ones. At much the same time, on 6 July, Captains Bouillon and Champrosay had led a group of eighty Frenchmen from Bobo-Dioulasso into the Northern Territories of the Gold Coast. This apparently came rapidly to the attention of de Gaulle, who acknowledged their arrival with a telegram of welcome. He used this same communication to appoint Bouillon commander of French Troops in the Gold Coast and to give him his first orders:

> Please report on your position and that of French military elements in Colony or likely to arrive there. It is proposed to organise a French force on the spot which would be placed temporarily under the command of British Forces.
>
> Cordial greetings,
> De Gaulle[38]

Despite the borders between the Côte d'Ivoire and the Gold Coast having been closed on 10 July, there was continuing heavy leakage. The newly appointed commander, Bouillon, was surely much gratified to learn, on 11 July, that the entire garrison of Batié, a military district located along the Black Volta, had marched into the Gold Coast under the command of Lieutenant Bonnard. One artillery and one infantry company had, in fact, arrived in Wenchi during the afternoon of 10 July. The district commissioner there, A. C. Russell, estimated their numbers at about fifty Europeans and a hundred Africans. There were women in the party as well:

> The senior Madame was a real madam—as powerful as you can make them. I showed the group where they might camp, where the Rest House was, etc. I had six or seven to tea, several of them to drinks around 6 P.M., and then I invited Madame and half a dozen others to dinner. But, and this I found amusing, she insisted that I dine with them and be their guest. She insisted so I gave in, but then she asked if the dinner might be eaten in my house. "Of course," I said, "yes." Then she pointed out that my kitchen was better, so might the chicken be cooked in it, and by my cook? And so it went on. They came over for drinks and we had an excellent dinner in my house, but I'm sure Madame felt she made an excellent hostess.[39]

Another group of Frenchmen and women arrived in Wenchi on 14 July, Bastille Day.[40] Three days later Lieutenants Chevillot and Grandperrin moved an entire artillery battery, in training at Ouagadougou, across the border.[41] Apparently all these Free French groups converged on Kumasi, the railhead, where they were entrained and traveled to Accra. Those that had brought some vehicles with them into the Northern Territories were obliged to abandon them when boarding the trains. Certainly this proved to be an unexpected bonanza for the Gold Coast troops based in Kumasi, who had been so short of transport that they had been forced to hire trucks from local Lebanese and Syrian merchants. H. C. Norman, an agent for Paterson Zochonis who had been working in the Gold Coast for two years before his call-up, was now the company quartermaster sergeant (CQMS) in Kumasi. He remembers taking possession of, among other vehicles, a Renault truck, a huge Opel five-tonner, a staff car, and even one motorcycle.[42] T. E. Kyei, who was then a schoolteacher in Kumasi, remembered one group who had come down on foot through the Northern Territories:

> We saw some pathetic travelers, Europeans, coming from the North. Wearing ragged khaki. We saw they were tired, so tired. We were told they were Free French. I don't know [how many] exactly, they came in groups of ten, fifteen. On foot. Their khakis were dusty; they were really pathetic. We felt pity for them. We had heard that Pétain had given up and that De Gaulle was going on and that some white men were coming to join him. Pétain yielded. These men would never yield.[43]

It was not only potential recruits to the Free French forces that were important but, in some cases, what was brought with them. CQMS Norman was in the

Soldiers, Airmen, Spies, and Whisperers

hospital in Kumasi in July, recovering from a severe attack of malaria. Regimental Sergeant Major Tebbut paid a call, trying to determine if Norman was well enough to be discharged early. Evidently he was, for soon after Tebbut's visit, Norman was ordered to report with no delay to Fort St. Anthony, Axim, where a detachment of the Fifth Battalion GCR (5 GCR) was stationed under the command of a Rhodesian officer, Lt. Savile Eland. There he was surprised to meet a senior officer of the Gold Coast Police, Commissioner J. C. Piegrome. Norman was instructed to proceed to the Côte d'Ivoire frontier at Half Assini, where only a river fordable at low tide separated the Vichy colony from the British one. A platoon of the Fifth Battalion was guarding the crossing, under the watchful eye of a Sergeant Adamson. Members of the Preventative Police were there as well. Norman's instructions were to ensure the safe passage into the Gold Coast of a mysterious vehicle, the imminent arrival of which was clearly anticipated. Norman recalled,

> One day a covered truck came across. It was all very hush hush. There were lots of Preventative Police around. We were instructed that if there was any trouble, we should fire a Very Pistol [flare] to alert Axim. Axim was on a bluff and it would be seen from there. It was after the fourth of July, but only a few days after, I think. It was a pickup, but the back was heavily covered in canvas. One Preventative Policeman stood on each side of the cab. There may have been others in the back, but we couldn't see into it. I don't know if there was any European in there. We just couldn't see. . . . There was talk that it was bullion from the Free French in the Ivory Coast. Could it have been?[44]

Norman never did know who and what was in the truck, but the answer is supplied by a document in the Foreign Office. At the appropriate time, a French administrative officer from the southern Côte d'Ivoire, M. Stefanini, crossed into the Gold Coast at Half Assini, carrying with him the proceeds of a recent tax collection amounting to 1,680,740 francs (approximately $40,000 at the 1940 exchange rate), which eventually found its way into Free French coffers.[45] We may be sure that Norman had witnessed the arrival of M. Stefanini.

Some fifteen hundred Tirailleurs Sénégalais (Senegalese riflemen) had been at sea en route from the AOF to France when Pétain's armistice was signed. Their officers decided to reverse course and put into a Gold Coast port—presumably Takoradi.[46] They were subsequently moved to Accra, where many of the recruits to the Free French cause who had crossed the land borders joined them. In addition, other supporters of de Gaulle made their way to Accra from Cameroon via Nigeria.[47] It has not generally been appreciated that these men in a Gold Coast now surrounded by hostile Vichy territory formed the nucleus of de Gaulle's first army in Africa.

THE WAR OFFICE TAKES OVER

In 1935 a recommendation was made to the Committee of Imperial Defence that African colonial armies be greatly strengthened, and indeed returned to their pre-1930 strength. The committee also saw the need to bring the regiments in West and East Africa under joint command in preparation for any future role in defense of the empire. A necessary part of this program would be to transfer authority over African forces from the Colonial Office to the War Office. Not surprisingly, the Colonial Office found this an unpalatable intrusion on their bailiwick. It was one they strongly resisted, contending that the primary function of colonial armies was internal security.[48] Any decisions were, therefore, deferred. Thus, throughout the early part of 1939, the defense of British West Africa, and indeed of all other African colonies, was in the hands of the Colonial Office, although there appears to have been an understanding that the War Office would assume this responsibility immediately should war break out. In fact, at midnight, 31 August 1939, three days before war was declared, the War Office took operational control of all African forces. The colonial governors seem to have remained somewhat reluctant to yield up authority. In a classic case of bureaucratic compromise, the relationship between War Office and Colonial Office was thus defined: "In West African Dependencies forces will be directly under the control of the War Office for any operations against an external enemy or for reinforcing other theatres. Governors will still be empowered to re-form troops within these Dependencies for purposes of internal security, any such moves being reported at once to War Office by local commander."[49]

In the event, this new arrangement did not take hold immediately. Negotiations between the Colonial and War Offices continued throughout the rest of the year, and it was not until May 1940, when the situation in Europe had become catastrophic, that both departments finally agreed on the creation of the new post of general officer commanding. Following this, the War Office did take over, and Lt. Gen. G. J. Giffard was appointed to the post. He was not a stranger to Africa, having served with distinction in the King's African Rifles (KAR) in World War I. In 1936 he had been appointed inspector-general of the Royal West African Frontier Force (RWAFF) and the KAR, in effect becoming responsible for what were increasingly referred to as the African Colonial Forces. He served as military secretary at the War Office in 1939, and after a brief spell as officer commanding British forces in Transjordan and Palestine, he relinquished the post to take up the West African one. He arrived at Freetown, Sierra Leone, on 7 July 1940 and reached the Gold Coast several days later.[50]

Giffard quickly established his new headquarters in the spacious grounds of Achimota College, a few miles outside Accra. The initial strength of headquarters personnel was modest in the extreme, and he felt it could be accommodated with little disturbance to the normal activities of the school. He seemed, in fact, a bit vague about the size of the existing staff: "At present H.Q. [numbers] 38 only, about 7 or 8 officers, 5 B.N.C.Os. and a few African followers." Even when fully staffed, which might not be until the end of August 1940, he anticipated that only fifteen officers, fifty British NCOs and soldiers, and 250 Africans would be stationed there.[51]

Before his arrival in the Gold Coast, Giffard had been informed by Governor Hodson of General Schmitt's possible interest in moving his troops across the frontier into the Gold Coast, and of the Colonial Office's view that it would be better that they should remain in the Côte d'Ivoire and await the right time to bring that colony into the Free French camp. Giffard approved of the colonial secretary's stance and suggested that the lack of suitable accommodations for any sizable group of defectors might be used as an excuse for not encouraging Schmitt and his troops to cross over. However, he wired Governor Hodson, "If attempt proved unsuccessful, they should of course be welcomed into the Gold Coast. But though policy of attracting French troops into our own territory is desirable rather than let them pass under enemy influence we should be robbing ourselves of a valuable asset if we persuaded them to come over when by remaining in French territory they could secure that territory for us."[52] In other words, thanks but no thanks.

The *affaire Schmitt* seems to have rapidly resolved itself. On 21 July a Lieutenant Iehl from Abidjan appeared in Accra. He had been sent by Schmitt to demand the repatriation of all French troops in the Gold Coast, along with their equipment. Clearly the mood in the Côte d'Ivoire had abruptly changed, for Iehl made a veiled threat that should this demand not be met, "Schmitt would be reluctant to have to obey any order he might receive to use force to obtain the return of his men and material." Governor Hodson was not impressed and his rejection of the demand was subsequently endorsed by the secretary of state.[53] This was, it seems, the first overt threat directed by a Vichy French colony against a British one. With it, the Colonial Office initiative was at an end. There seem no way forward in terms of diplomacy. The question of whether or not General Schmitt had actually contemplated such a dramatic step remains unanswered. Either the report of his unhappiness with the armistice was exaggerated or his ardor for moving into the Gold Coast cooled by what he perceived as a lack of enthusiasm by the British. In any case, General Schmitt remained in the Côte d'Ivoire and further official communications between the two colonies virtually ended. As R. O. Paxton wrote, "in French Africa, a wave of animosity to London swept over circles which only recently had longed for a way to keep up the war alongside Britain."[54] The vast majority of colonial officials in the AOF, anticipating the imminent collapse of Britain and fearing for their families in occupied France, now came to accept the armistice and unflinchingly to serve the Vichy administration. Many who, like Edmond Louveau, had originally been responsive to de Gaulle's call for continued resistance now, unlike Louveau, closed ranks behind Pétain. The one exception to this generalization might have been *l'affaire Chichet* in the Côte d'Ivoire. Reports reached London that three civilians were planning a coup d'état. One was an engineering contractor named Chichet, one the head of the Railway and Harbor Administration, and the third, director of the Public Works Department. The incident is obscure, but apparently Chichet was contacted through unreported channels and given promises of British economic, but not military, help. Governor Crocicchia stepped in and quashed the plot. Chichet was arrested early in November and sent to Marseilles. His fate and that of the others is unknown to me.[55]

DE GAULLE, THE AEF, AND THE AOF: WIN ONE, LOSE ONE

By mid-August 1940, in the eyes of the British at least, the AOF had been lost to the Free French cause. Interest now turned toward the AEF, the vast area comprising Chad, Congo Brazzaville, Gabon, French-mandated Cameroon, and Oubangi-Chari. Chad was first to declare its support for de Gaulle. Félix Eboué, its governor, had been in telegraphic contact with de Gaulle since the middle of July and had declared formally for the Free French on 26 August at Fort Lamy. The matter of French-mandated Cameroon was, however, of much greater concern to London, for it shared a long and convoluted frontier with British-mandated Cameroon. The two mandates had together comprised the old German colony of Kamerun before World War I. It also bordered northern Nigeria. Anti-Vichy elements there included M. Mauclere, director of Public Works in Douala, who had made approaches to Lagos to request British military aid in overthrowing the Vichy regime. The request was transmitted to London. The secretary of state for the colonies apparently thought that it had merit, though the War Cabinet turned it down as conflicting with its plans for a future attack on Dakar.[56] However, de Gaulle had already given his support to a plan to attack Douala and had commissioned Comdt. René Leclerc and Capt. Hettier de Boislambert to pull together a small force in Victoria, British Cameroon, and from there to invade French Cameroon. De Gaulle had, however, done more. He knew that a thousand African "sharpshooters" had been sent from the Côte d'Ivoire to take part in the Battle for France. Too late to do so, they had been diverted to England and stationed there.[57] De Gaulle obtained British approval for a detachment of them to be put at Leclerc's disposal. They were sent to Accra to be placed under Free French command. British military officers, however—or so de Gaulle later claimed—admired their bearing and adopted them into the Gold Coast Regiment. Leclerc was thus deprived of their services. Nevertheless, he moved his small force into Victoria and prepared to cross the frontier. General Giffard in Accra became troubled about the effects of the projected invasion on the Vichy authorities in the AOF, thereby demonstrating openly for the first time his preference for coexistence with neighboring Vichy colonial regimes, a known quality, rather than with unpredictable Free French ones. He cabled an order to Victoria, insisting that the invasion of French Cameroon be abandoned. De Gaulle authorized Leclerc and Boislambert to proceed. The British in Victoria turned a blind eye to what was going on, and the Free Frenchmen crossed in local canoes from the one colony to the other. On 27 August, Douala declared for de Gaulle in what he described as a "coup de main."[58] Congo Brazzaville also joined the Free French on the same day, and Oubangi-Chari followed.[59] By the end of August the whole of Equatorial Africa, with the exception of Gabon, was under Free French control.

While all this was happening, the British government dithered. On the one hand, the governors of Nigeria and the Gold Coast had been urged by London to collaborate fully in encouraging the AEF colonies to rally to the Free French. On the other hand, London had refused to give de Gaulle any military support for his proposed coups in Cameroon and Gabon, sensitive that such might provoke counterattacks from the AOF on the British West African colonies. The adherence of Cameroon to the Gaullists was thus achieved by the Free French alone, albeit aided by the loan of a single British Blenheim bomber, which was used to attack the one Vichy ship lying off Douala, the *Bougainville*. Then finally, Free French air attacks on Lambaréné in November brought Gabon, if reluctantly, into the fold.[60]

The decision of the French administrators in the AEF to hear the siren song of de Gaulle, and to reject Pétain, finally gave modest substance to de Gaulle's claim to represent France. His apparent failure in the AOF did not, however, mean that he had given up hope in that quarter. He had, in fact, approached Churchill in late July with a plan to land Free French troops, supported by the Royal Navy, at Dakar, whereupon, the general assured the prime minister that Governor-General Boisson of the AOF would rally to the Allied side. Initially reluctant, Churchill was finally persuaded to approve the plan by overoptimistic reports from pro-British residents of Senegal, and, it must be said, by poor intelligence provided by the British West African colonies. At a meeting on 6 August 1940 at 10 Downing Street, Churchill's enthusiasm for the project, at least according to de Gaulle's memoirs, knew no bounds. The prime minister, de Gaulle wrote, painted a vivid scenario:

> Dakar wakes up one morning, sad and uncertain. But behold, by the light of the rising sun, its inhabitants perceive the sea, to a great distance, covered with ships. An immense fleet! A hundred war or transport vessels! These approach slowly, addressing messages of friendship to the town, to the navy, to the garrison. Some of them are flying the Tricolor.[61]

The reality was to be otherwise. A combined force of a few ships lay off Dakar, on 23 September 1940, in a very thick fog. In de Gaulle's view, the intemperate climate, more than anything else, accounted for the complete failure of the venture, having virtually destroyed the intended visual impact. To put it mildly, his optimism had been misplaced. Expecting to be welcomed by the populace and control of French West Africa eagerly handed over to him, de Gaulle's small flotilla was greeted by an outraged governor-general, Boisson, and a determined commander in chief, General Barrau. Heavy artillery fire from shore batteries caused considerable damage to several of the ships, and four aircraft from the *Ark Royal* were shot down. On the third day of the engagement, at de Gaulle's urging, the British commander, Adm. Arthur Cunningham, called off the attack.[62] The Dakar fiasco had the major political effect of converting the AOF's state of passive acceptance and uneasy neutrality into a virtual cold war.

INVASION SCARES: PERCEIVING THE THREAT

British fears were heightened in October 1940, when, at a meeting with Hitler at Montoire, Pierre Laval proposed that France take up arms with Germany in

Soldiers, Airmen, Spies, and Whisperers

Africa, against the British. Immediately afterward, Pétain announced his accept-ance of collaboration with the Third Reich in order to "maintain French unity."[63] By the end of 1940 the preeminent concern of London and the colonial capitals, with regard to West Africa, was to avoid any further provocation of Vichy, and certainly anything that might lead that regime to consider itself at war with Britain. One strand of official thinking about this matter was made quite clear in a Colonial Office telegram of 8 January 1941. Particular concern was taken to en-sure that "the slender thread" of communications remaining between Britain and Vichy France should not be severed. "H.M.G. [His Majesty's Government] did not wish the people of France to feel they were forgotten," the Colonial Office commented, adding that the Vichy government would be kept informed "of the successful development of our war effort."[64] Even direct appeals to French ad-ministrators and military personnel to break with Vichy, broadcast by the BBC and Radio Accra, were soon felt to be counterproductive. It was feared that the French would regard this as simply "British bribery."[65]

The view of the situation taken by the General Staff of the RWAFF is accu-rately reconstructed by Brig. F. A. S. Clarke. Clarke, a lieutenant in the Gold Coast Regiment during World War I, became one of the three members of the official RWAFF History Committee after his retirement. As such he had access to the regiment's official documents and to the recollections of senior serving offic-ers. "With the fall of France," he wrote, "and the assumption of power by a hos-tile government at Vichy, the potential danger of our West African territories caused considerable anxiety." He drew attention to the unfavorable geography of the British colonies.

> Thus, Gambia, surrounded by French territory, could be invaded overland or down the Gambia River. Though the approaches to Sierra Leone from the west and north were through difficult country with poor communications, and Freetown could only be approached overland down a narrow peninsula, the harbour was only two days' steaming from Dakar by fast ship and within range of French aerodromes. Both Gold Coast and Nigeria could be attacked from three sides by land.[66]

A "perennial" question, to follow Clarke, was whether the Germans might persuade Vichy to attack one or other of the British colonies. "It was fortunate, perhaps," Clarke writes, "that the Trans-Sahara railway had remained only a proj-ect."[67] Certainly, however, Clarke had no doubt that the RWAFF command was aware of the dangers in the situation:

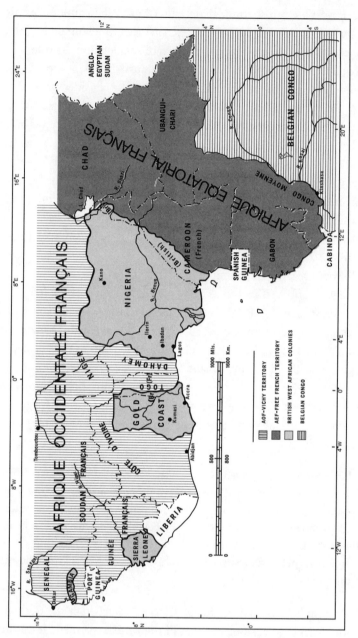

Vichy, Free French, and British territories, December 1940–November 1942
Adapted from H. R. J. Davies, *Tropical Africa: An Atlas for Rural Development*
(Cardiff: University of Wales Press, 1973).

Soldiers, Airmen, Spies, and Whisperers

There was speculation as to the possibility of an Italo/German force based on Tripolitania, carrying out a *blitz* with a mechanized column on one of the territories. Such an attack would be made down one of the main north and south routes in Nigeria or Gold Coast, and coordinated with French action to keep us occupied elsewhere. The thin orchard bush of the northern provinces would be little or no obstacle to tracked vehicles, and we had neither aircraft nor anti-tank guns. The tropical forest might constitute an obstacle if properly utilized, but it was far south of the northern frontiers. It looked as if we should have to go back to an obstacle, either one of the big rivers or the forest, but this would entail giving up country which produced ground nuts for export and native corn for home consumption, as well as being the main recruiting area for the infantry. It was clear that an attack of this nature would require a good deal of preparation and the backing of French African troops to operate on the flanks of the route used.

It was Clarke's view that if the Germans had really wanted to, they could have crossed into either Nigeria or the Gold Coast without a great deal of bother. In 1947, when Clarke wrote this, he knew that there were skeptics but argued convincingly that this scenario was not totally unrealistic. "The feasibility of a column crossing the Sahara," he commented, "was afterwards proved when General Le Clerc took a force from Lake Chad area to join the Eighth Army in Tripolitania."[68]

One must wonder if this concern about the safety of the Gold Coast and Nigeria, coming at a time when most "sensible" observers of the military situation in Europe would have been expecting a momentary German invasion of Great Britain, had something darker behind it. Is it possible that, stiff upper lips or not, some in the government felt it might be necessary, in the worst-case scenario, for Britain to continue the war from the colonies, rather in the fashion of de Gaulle? In any case, the safety of the West African colonies became of considerable concern. So much so, that in July, the SS *Accra* was dispatched with troops to reinforce the RWAFF, enemy actions against Nigeria in particular being feared. Regrettably the *Accra* was torpedoed two hundred miles west of Ireland, and only a few of its survivors eventually reached West Africa.[69]

Although the British probably had not understood it at the time, the attack on Dakar had led the Vichy authorities likewise to explore the possibility of an invasion of the AOF. Immediately after the signing of the armistice on 22 June, Germany had insisted that France reduce its forces in the AOF from approximately 118,000 men to 25,000.[70] By exploiting the attack on Dakar, and the "loyal" defense by Boisson, the French military was able to secure the German agreement to increasing the size of both the Armée d'Afrique in North Africa and the Coloniale in West Africa. Further concessions were obtained from Germany in November 1940, when Gabon fell to the Free French. Both General M. Weygand, commander in chief in North Africa, and General Barrau in West Africa were permitted to increase their armies further. In the AOF, troop levels rose immediately to 33,000 men, (and by mid-1942 had actually reached nearly 100,000 men).[71] The formation of a new regiment, the Regiment Tirailleurs Sénégalais du Côte d'Ivoire, was also approved.[72] Extraordinarily, only a few months later, one official of the British War Cabinet was able to argue that even this cloud had a silver lining. The growth of the military in the AOF would, he thought, remove the risk of any German invasion: "General de Gaulle's movement had served a most useful purpose (I was delighted to hear this) in that it had enabled General Weygand to regroup and re-arm the French forces in Africa on the pretext of guarding the unity of the French Empire against British machinations veiled under the de Gaulle cloak."[73]

This optimistic view was not immediately regarded by those on the spot as especially useful. For them, the effect of the abortive Dakar venture was to place the British colonies, now surrounded by openly hostile neighbors, in danger of attack. Indeed, it might even have seemed a position of extreme danger to those in Whitehall, who knew that Pétain was negotiating with the Germans about the repatriation of France's West African soldiers in Europe. Indeed, the situation was even more threatening, for Pétain was under intense German pressure to remove all black African troops from European soil. The return of tens of thousands of Tirailleurs Sénégalais to West Africa was, it is true, much hindered by the fact that the Royal Navy continued to rule the relevant waves. Nevertheless, a small but steady flow of battle-tested—albeit defeated—troops were disembarked in Dakar and dispersed to their home colonies. The numbers are virtually impossible to ferret out from the confused and incomplete records of that period, but some troops were reassigned to regiments in the Côte d'Ivoire and Togo. As such, they came under the Coloniale, the French West African army under the command of General Barrau, who was by this time known as the hero of the defense of Dakar in September 1940. A graduate of the elite French military college, St. Cyr, his career had been spent in the Colonial Infantry, serving in the Congo and Gabon. Wounded three times during World War I, and mentioned in dispatches six times, Barrau later served in Indo-China before returning to Africa. He was considered a formidable adversary should hostilities between the two colonial powers in West Africa break out.[74]

Soldiers, Airmen, Spies, and Whisperers

Barrau offered a simple solution to the AOF's manpower shortage: "the liberation of all the personnel of the Colonial Troops still held prisoner." On 1 December 1940, General Barrau presented his plan for the defense of French West Africa. To ensure that the AOF would not lose its access to the sea, Dakar was to be held at all costs. Its defense would be undertaken by an infantry division including field artillery, a line of coastal batteries (the majority of which were described as ancient), two fighter and four bomber squadrons, and an unspecified quantity of naval forces, which certainly included the cruiser *Richelieu*, fully repaired after being damaged in the September attack on Dakar. One battalion and one or two coastal artillery batteries would be permanently based there to defend the other principal ports, Port-Etienne in Mauritania, and Conakry, Abidjan, and Cotonou. Plans were also drawn up to defend the hinterland should attacks be launched from Gambia, Sierra Leone, or Nigeria, but the greatest concern was that forces in the Gold Coast were about to invade Haute Côte d'Ivoire, in the region of Bobo-Dioulasso. This action, it was feared, would cut the lines of communication between French Soudan and the eastern colonies of Dahomey, Niger, and Togo. General Barrau noted that the defense of the AOF rested on seventy-five thousand troops, including twelve thousand Europeans, thirty-one infantry battalions, eight field artillery batteries, and various specialized units, and that this force was superior to that of the British colonies. Nevertheless, he felt that the security of the AOF could not be guaranteed without reinforcements.[75]

There had always been a distinction between the attitudes of Britain and France about the role Africans would play in the military when war came. The British had no systematic method of military conscription. When men were needed, pressure was brought upon chiefs to supply the desired number of "volunteers." Their role was to provide internal security and, in imperial emergencies such as World War I, to fight, but then only on African soil. Indeed, this policy was strongly supported by the vast majority of those British citizens resident in the colonies. The missionary Dr. Walter Miller expressed his approval when, shortly before the outbreak of World War II, he wrote: "I can never think it an enlightened policy to train Africans as soldiers to take part in the quarrels of European nations; or to inflict upon them, beyond what may become absolutely necessary, the risk of all the ghastly concomitants of modern warfare in *our* defence."[76] The French had no such delicate scruples. They saw their West African colonies as a vast reservoir of soldiers for the defense of the motherland and North Africa. In the Côte d'Ivoire, as throughout the AOF, a system of general military conscription had been in place since World War I. The General Conscription Act of 1919 guaranteed a continuing supply of men for the French army. Even in peace-time, a tirailleur, whether conscript or volunteer, would usually spend two of his three years' military service in France or North Africa.

In the 1930s, some ten thousand recruits were taken from the AOF annually, by roving commissions that, district by district, culled the fittest of those judged to be twenty years of age. The Côte d'Ivoire was given a quota of around fifteen hundred men to be inducted into the ranks of the Tirailleurs Sénégalais. This quota was doubled in 1939, and in 1940 it more than doubled again. For the recruitment campaign of that year, 79,059 men appeared before the commissions in the Côte d'Ivoire. Of these, 11,658 were immediately inducted (the so-called first portion), and 14,993 were selected for later service (the second portion).[77] The men of the first portion were trained for combat in several camps, the largest of which were at Bouaké and Bobo-Dioulasso. Their numbers, however, were swollen by many inducted in adjacent territories, their movement throughout the AOF being unhindered by frontiers. To the recruits of the class of 1940 must be added those from earlier classes still undergoing training or awaiting assignment to combat battalions. Clearly, then, a sizable force of tirailleurs existed in the Côte d'Ivoire in 1940, and it was these whose numbers were swelled by the repatriation of seasoned soldiers from the European front. In that year alone at least thirty-five thousand tirailleurs returned from North Africa. Although transport difficulties, and the control of the seas south of Senegal by the Royal Navy, created huge bottlenecks in Dakar, most of the men were somehow moved back to their home colonies.[78] It has so far proved impossible to extract, from the military records of the period, the total of men who returned specifically to the Côte d'Ivoire, and of that number, how many were demobilized and how many stayed in the army. The exact number of men under arms in the Côte d'Ivoire must, therefore, remain a matter of speculation, although one must assume it was larger than the approximately fifteen thousand tirailleurs who were based in Dahomey and Togo alone in the summer of 1940.[79] It is known that recruitment continued in the following year. Approximately three thousand Ivoiriens were taken into the army in 1941, the only year of the war in which recruitment in that colony fell below ten thousand. Due to severe shortages of gasoline, guns, and other equipment, however, many of these men ended up not in combat units but in labor battalions, but, comforting as it might have been to the British authorities, this fact was not to emerge until much later in the war.[80] The experience of tirailleur Zio Soro may be cited as an illustration of many in the class of 1941:

Soldiers, Airmen, Spies, and Whisperers

I did my military service, but I never fought. I left here and went first to Bouaké. I did one year at Bouaké. From Bouaké we left for Abidjan. There I guarded the lagoons. I never left Abidjan. . . . When the army took me they said we were going to war, but I never fired a shot against the enemy the way you are supposed to during a war. . . . The year that the French and the English were at war, an English plane was downed and after that we waited at the barricades. We waited a week—on the bank of the lagoon—one week. We dug a trench and hid in it all day. The English planes came. They passed over us, but they didn't fire. There was one plane which came down over Abidjan, but no one was killed. They never told us why we were now fighting the English. When I started in the army we were fighting against the Germans.[81]

THE GOLD COAST REGIMENT BEFORE WORLD WAR II

At the signing of the armistice between Germany and France on 22 June 1940, the Gold Coast found itself surrounded by what was de jure neutral, but de facto enemy, territory on all its land frontiers. In it there were no regular British Army troops. Its defense was the function of the Gold Coast Regiment of the Royal West African Frontier Force. Unlike the Tirailleurs Sénégalais, who had been recruited, or better perhaps, conscripted, from all the colonies of the AOF, the RWAFF had four constituent parts, each of which had a history of its own. Throughout the nineteenth century, many small militia units had been raised in the British West African possessions to maintain their internal security and defense. They consisted, almost without exception, of African troops commanded by British officers. In the British Protected Territory of the Gold Coast, these locally recruited units were, when deemed expedient, reinforced by a garrison of the West India Regiment. Due primarily to the insalubrious climate, London was strongly opposed to using British troops in its West African possessions. This view was expressed in no uncertain terms in 1888 by Sir Garnet Wolseley in explaining the value of West Indian troops: "One of the great objects for which these negro regiments were kept on foot was for the purpose of finding garrisons for our stations on the West Coast of Africa. The climate there is abominable, and specially injurious to Europeans. We could not keep British soldiers there with safety for more than a few months at a time."[82]

The massive Asante invasion of the Gold Coast Colony in 1873, however, did make it necessary to deploy British troops in the territory. Soldiers of the Black

Watch, the Royal Welch Fusiliers, the Rifle Brigade, and the Naval Brigade were all moved there. Together with a further infusion of West Indian troops, two thousand in all, these regiments, along with colonial forces from Sierra Leone and Nigeria, and auxiliaries from the Gold Coast itself, mobilized for the campaign. The Asante campaign also necessitated an enormous expansion of the local forces available to Wolseley, its commander in chief.[83] With the end of the fighting, in 1874, all British troops were hastily withdrawn and it was decided that the local defense force must be placed on a more permanent basis than hitherto. Among the troops brought from Nigeria were those known as Glover's Hausas, who had originally been formed in the 1860s by Capt. John Glover (Royal Navy) to protect the new British colony of Lagos. Three hundred of these men stayed on in the Gold Coast and, together with a small and predominantly Fante militia hastily formed in 1872, became officially known as the Gold Coast Armed Police, but more commonly as the Hausa Constabulary. This was in 1875. In 1879 this force was renamed and reconstituted as the Gold Coast Constabulary (GCC). It now had a strength of sixteen British officers, three Native Officers, and twelve hundred Africans. By 1889 the constabulary had expanded slightly to include 437 Fantes, almost all of whom were assigned to civil police duties, and 870 "Hausas" whose role was defending the Protectorate from any further Asante incursions. Indeed, in 1894 the Fante police component was removed from the GCC and established as a separate force.[84]

The emergence of the Gold Coast Regiment from these earlier elements has been the subject of a number of studies, and most recently those by D. Killingray.[85] Each of these forces contributed something toward the development of the colonial army that was emerging and was soon to become part of the West African Frontier Force (WAFF). The story of the WAFF, which was to unify the four British West African colonial commands, begins not in the Gold Coast at all, but in Nigeria. The WAFF was formed in northern Nigeria under the aegis of Lord Lugard in 1897 and originally comprised two battalions of Hausas and Yorubas. The next year a third battalion was raised in Calabar, in eastern Nigeria.[86] In reality, most of the recruits were neither Hausa nor Yoruba. They were, however, generally northerners, by which sobriquet the British identified those peoples who lived in the vast region known to them as northern Nigeria. Although often Islamized in dress, they were not necessarily Muslim, and were commonly illiterate. But the British regarded them as "martial types" and for the next forty-odd years considered them to be the ideal recruit for the West African Frontier Force.[87]

The outbreak of the last hostilities in Asante in 1900 brought the three battalions of the new WAFF to the Gold Coast. There, along with the Gold Coast Constabulary, the Sierra Leone West African Regiment, and the Gambia Constabulary, they put down the rising. By the end of 1901, these three West African forces were joined to the three Nigerian battalions as components of the quasi-federal WAFF, which thus comprised the Nigeria Regiment, the Gold Coast Regiment, the Sierra Leone Battalion, and the Gambia Company. Despite the amalgamation, and unlike the regiments of Tirailleurs Sénégalais in the AOF, which had the advantage of contiguous territory, each of the four WAFF formations was largely autonomous. Movement between the four British colonies by their armed forces could only be accomplished by sea.

The early years of the WAFF were spent putting down rebellions, patrolling still uncertain frontiers with French and German territories, and suppressing the remnants of the internal slave trade.[88] Again in contrast to the tirailleurs, each of the WAFF units was expected to serve only within its own colonial borders, other than in emergencies. The outbreak of World War I was one such. In August 1914, in coordination with units of the Tirailleurs Sénégalais, the Gold Coast Regiment moved into German Togo and the Nigeria Regiment entered German Kamerun. Togo was surrendered on 27 August 1914 and in October elements of the GCR and the Sierra Leone Battalion joined the fighting in Cameroon. There the last German post in Cameroon surrendered on 18 February 1916. This campaign won the African soldiers of the WAFF many accolades for their courage and endurance.

In Europe, the French, suffering horrendous losses in the trenches, finally decided to bring to reality the dream of Gen. Charles Mangin, that is, to create the much-debated *force noire* to reinforce the Western Front. In 1916 and 1917 a mass recruitment campaign took place in the AOF.[89] The British expressed strong disapproval, regarding it as reckless on the part of the French to train Africans to kill Europeans. There was, however, an element of hypocrisy involved, for the British had no scruples whatsoever in using *their* African troops for operations against the Germans not only, as I have said, in West Africa, but also in East Africa, where the WAFF was thrown into the campaigns in German East Africa in what was then Tanganyika.

The Gold Coast Regiment sailed for East Africa in July 1916. The campaign itself has been the subject of many major studies, both contemporary and modern,[90] and is outside the scope of this work. Something of the esprit of the Gold Coast soldiers is conveyed in the memoirs of Jacob Dosoo Amenyah, regimental no. V124, who was selected for shipboard duties while at sea, being assigned to night watches. He was an Ada, from the area of the Volta estuary, but was nonetheless proud of one incident that occurred during the passage. The ship passed by the Seychelles en route to Mombasa. Some four decades later Amenyah, describing himself as the petitioner, remembered, in highly colored terms and inimitable prose, the special events of one watch:

> I was ordered to serve on, in the Navy every night (days exclusive) to hang in the cold always at the top of troop ship's masts voyaging on the Indian Ocean that would necessarily get him [Amenyah} to slumber for an occasion in order to leave room under the Army Code or Regulations and by that to be shot to death and body thrown into the sea for burial. This punishment indicated that the Petitioner to remain a watch-dog for submarines' movements at sea for detections and signallings as to what the torpedo boats might be for the Germans or Britain. With this, brought about the possibility for the Petitioner to flash out a message to Nana Kwaku Dua III alias King Prempeh I from the seas of Seychelles (the exile king of the Ashantis) over there that his subjects, the Ashantis were on the contingent of the Gold Coast Regimental Unit serving in the East African Campaign for Great Britain. And that the Gold Coast Regiment was stationed at Mpara via Kilwa-Kisiwani on the main African continent. The latter being the military landing stage for Mpara about 5 miles distance apart and onward for all British Army Units. Upon this, King Prempeh I had despatched some of his men from the Seychelles successfully to Mpara who had verified the truth of the Petitioner's message so sent to him (King Prempeh I).[91]

The men of the Gold Coast Regiment were in action almost immediately upon disembarkation. The difficulties of that campaign, and the subsequent honors won by the different units of the WAFF, consolidated that force's earlier reputation for courage and steadfastness. In recognition of its members' service during the war, in 1922 its battalions were awarded colors. A further increase in status was achieved in 1928 when King George V became commander in chief of what now became designated as the Royal West African Frontier Force (RWAFF).

Military life during the 1930s was peaceful. The Gold Coast Regiment was small, having been stripped down in a reorganization of 1933 to only two infantry battalions (1 GCR and 2 GCR), each comprising two rifle companies and one support company.[92] At full strength, then, the regiment consisted of less than a thousand men. Even this was considered more than adequate for the colony's needs. There was little necessity for frontier vigilance, as relations between the French and British colonies were decidedly amicable. Health and sanitary conditions had improved so much that Europeans no longer felt they were risking cer-

Soldiers, Airmen, Spies, and Whisperers

tain death by living in the Gold Coast, though, of course, they never ventured into the sun without their hats and spine pads! Europeans serving in the military in the Gold Coast could be put on a charge should they be observed hatless during the heat of the day. A gloss on this was provided by one of the many newcomers to Africa, Aircraftsman 2d Class William Grigsby, whose unit arrived in Takoradi in July 1940: "Steps had been cut down to our own private beach, which we were only allowed to use between dawn and 8 A.M. and in the afternoon after 1600, because between 0800 and 1600 topees [pith helmets] were obligatory, and none of us would have cared to be seen dead, swimming in a topee."[93]

Recruitment continued to be concentrated on men from the Northern Territories rather than from Asante or the Gold Coast Colony.[94] Underlying this preference were attitudes formed around the turn of the nineteenth century. They were unambiguously enunciated by Col. A. Haywood, who served in the WAFF in World War I: "The West African people may be broadly divided into Negro, or debased races, and the finer types. As a rough guide it may be said that the former inhabited the country south of 9 degrees North latitude, while the latter were located north of this, the dividing line being drawn approximately through Yola, Keffi, Jebba, Tamale, and the northern frontier of Sierra Leone."[95] By the 1930s, the racist element in this thinking ceased to be so openly expressed, but nevertheless the belief remained that northerners were truly "martial people" par excellence. One of those to reflect upon the matter was a young officer, Antony Read, who had been seconded to the Gold Coast Regiment from the Oxfordshire and Buckinghamshire Light Infantry in 1936. In a 1980 interview, Gen. Sir Antony Read (as he was then) made a pertinent comment:

The army had, I think wrongly on this, a very strong idea about the African in this particular case, in that they like as soldiers the Hausa speaking people from the Northern territories who had been, in their eyes, less rotted by civilisation. They were illiterate, they were very nice people. The savvy boys from the Coast who had been at Mission schools and that sort of thing, who had developed some of the various attributes of the white man, were slightly looked down on. They were good clerks, and they were used as clerks and signalers and that sort of thing.[96]

Interestingly, the "savvy boys" themselves could present the other side of the same coin. In 1994, for example, one of them observed that "in those days, to go into the army was a terrible thing. We had scholars in our school, not soldiers."[97]

Read, like most of the GCR's officers, had volunteered to serve in West Africa.

The word was out that the Gold Coast was an excellent place to work and to play. The attractions were many. The lure of double pay, two years' service credit for each year in Africa, unlimited low-cost polo, and responsibilities far beyond those likely to be given a subaltern in his home regiment proved irresistible to the twenty-three-year-old. One or two of Read's friends had highly recommended West Africa, he remembered: "Lots of polo, lots of very good soldiers to work with. It was a complete change from England, and I was young and green perhaps and said, 'Fine, Let's go.' . . . Do you remember Edgar Wallace and *Bones of the River?*[98] I had seen pictures of glamourous Hausa soldiers in their very smart uniforms—they used to wear a terribly smart uniform—and I just fell for it. There was glamour attached to it. . . . There was a slight pioneering spirit." Met at the coast by members of his new battalion, 2 GCR, he was taken to regimental headquarters in Accra. Introductions to other officers took place, and then, "one was told to get on with it." The next day, Read remembered, "one was introduced further and, you were posted to a Company, and the Company Commander said, 'Well, I am so glad you have arrived, because I am going on leave for six months in a fortnight's time and you can look after the Company.' This made one swallow a bit, but of course really, it was just what one wanted. So this was the greatest possible challenge."[99]

THE BUILD-UP TO WAR

The Italian invasion of Ethiopia in 1935 presented no immediate threat to Britain's East African colonies, but it did draw attention to their vulnerability. The idea was mooted of forming, from African colonial troops, an Expeditionary Force that could be deployed immediately should any serious threat materialize. Despite the Munich Agreement, the possible threat to East Africa (and therefore, of course, to the Suez Canal and the Middle East) seems to have been taken even more seriously, and £1 million was made available for the modernization of the King's African Rifles in East Africa and the RWAFF in West Africa. In Nairobi in December 1938, Inspector-General Giffard presided over a conference of officers from the two forces. The major item on the agenda was the deployment of the RWAFF in East Africa should, as seemed increasingly likely, war break out. That it seemed feasible to denude West Africa of troops in order to defend East Africa was, as Clarke points out, "based on two suppositions laid down by the Overseas Defense Committee; first, that we should retain command of the sea; secondly, that *France would be an Ally.*"[100] It was decided that both Nigeria and the Gold Coast would each contribute a brigade group to the proposed Expeditionary Force. Such a group consisted of headquarters and signals, three infantry battalions, a light battery, a field company, and a field ambulance, comprising between three thousand and thirty-five hundred men.

This all sounded fine in Nairobi, but in the Gold Coast at this time there was nothing approaching the size of a brigade. In 1938 headquarters, and two companies of the First Battalion, Gold Coast Regiment (1 GCR), were based in Kumasi, and the third company, which alone approached full strength, was stationed near Accra. The Second Battalion (2 GCR), in Tamale in the Northern Territories, was at about half strength. There was no Third Battalion, but its creation was projected.[101] In all, at this time, the GCR consisted of approximately twelve hundred men.[102] Rapid expansion up to brigade level began in 1939, when, in June, a new commander arrived, Brig. C. E. Melville Richards. He took over the mobilization of the regiment, then undergoing a major reorganization as it moved to a war footing. The very fact that the commander was now a brigadier indicated the wider role envisioned for the regiment. One of his first steps was to move regimental headquarters and 1 GCR from Kumasi to Accra on 29 August, although the main training center, known as the War Depot, remained in Kumasi.[103]

The build-up seems to have been rapid. On 26 August 1939 the strength of 1 GCR was seventeen officers, nineteen British noncommissioned officers (BNCOs), and 778 African troops. Full mobilization began the next day. By 1 October 1939, 1 GCR's numbers had increased to thirty-four officers, forty-four BNCOs, and 902 Africans.[104] Many of the officers and BNCOs were called up from the local forces and reservists. The increase in African soldiers was achieved, first, by beating the bush—principally the Northern Territories bush—for volunteers to serve as infantrymen. For the first time however, men from the Gold Coast Colony and Asante were recruited in fair numbers for a variety of semi-skilled jobs, including cooks, clerks, drivers, and medical orderlies.[105] Of these various categories, drivers were perhaps in the greatest demand. The RWAFF went to great lengths to "recruit" them. In 1994, K. Attakora Gyimah, a retired reporter for Kumasi's *Ashanti Pioneer*, described one mode of procurement: "At the beginning of the war there was compulsory service put out for drivers, licensed drivers. What we called compulsory service, into the army. An army officer would stop him a driver, look at his license, and take him to the army. Right at the beginning, until about '42—then they were recruiting volunteers."[106]

To deal with the growing shortage of officers and BNCOs in the regiment, men were seconded from British units, but also significant numbers of volunteers came from southern Africa. One BNCO, who had joined the RWAFF while working in the Gold Coast, had definite reservations about the wisdom of using men whose only experience of Africa came from the upper echelons of a settler colony: "The Rhodesians were brought into the Gold Coast regiment right at the beginning of the war. They wore the flash on their shoulders, BSAP [British South African Police]. Some were regulars and some were like me. They thought they were God Almighty. They were harsh towards the Africans. They didn't know how to get the best out of them."[107] This informant was not alone in his opinion of the Rhodesians—Southern Rhodesians for the most part. A former officer with the RWAFF who wishes to remain anonymous on this particular subject put the matter even more bluntly: "They [the Rhodesians] arrived in September or October 1939. They were posted to various battalions. They were very bad to the Africans. They were officers and NCOs and knew it all. To them, home was England, though few of them had ever been there. By joining the Gold Coast Regiment, they got ranks higher than were deserved in most cases. They didn't like us older people who were used to the Gold Coast soldiers. They referred to them as *munts*—bloody blacks. We were living in grass huts, and the Rhodesians didn't like that. A few of them stayed in Zimbabwe after independence. Most of them went to Thailand, Australia, and South Africa."[108]

Under the command of Lt. Col. I. R. G. M. Bruce, 1 GCR was now based at a new tent camp at Teshi, near Accra. It had some excitement in April 1939, having been placed on alert for a projected move into Togo. The occasion was a report that the Germans were about to make a preemptive strike to retake their old colony. The alert apparently only lasted a few days, but it served to convince many of those serving in the regiment that war was indeed imminent. Remaining at Tamale was 2 GCR, commanded by Lt. Col. J. W. A. Hayes, while the new 3 GCR, under Lt. Col. E. W. D. Western, enjoyed grass hut accommodations at Winneba, halfway between Cape Coast and Accra.[109] During the year, an engineers' company was formed at Akwatia, from Europeans working in the mines and the Public Works Department.[110]

When war was declared on 3 September 1939, Malcolm MacDonald, then secretary of state for the colonies, sent a rallying call to the empire:

I know while war clouds were hanging threateningly over us the people of British lands overseas were hoping fervently for maintenance of peace with all its blessings, and yet were preparing calmly and resolutely for the supreme test of war, if it should arise. Our knowledge of the feelings of sixty millions of our fellow citizens in the Colonial Territories has sustained us in Great Britain in our efforts for peace and steeled us in our own preparations for war. Unhappily work of peacemaker has been thwarted and we have been forced to enter into hostilities not only to honour our duty to our friend [Poland] but to secure survival of good faith and liberty among civilised peoples. We in the United Kingdom are prepared to make whatever sacrifice may be necessary in the course of this struggle. We shall be ever mindful that people in our Colonial Territories are sharing our task and our burden and our sympathy and sense of comradeship with you will be constant. In words of His Majesty the King, let us all "stand calmly firm and united in this time of trial."

The longed for and happy association of so many people of different races, and creeds is itself the best proof that ideal of peaceful and fruitful cooperation between diverse people, who are willing and respect each other, is attainable; and that knowledge will fortify us in our fight to securely establish that ideal in the wider world.[111]

Whether or not the Africans of the Gold Coast were counted among those happy millions who had longed for association with Great Britain is moot, although they must have been delighted to hear themselves referred to as fellow citizens. The secretary of state was considerably less forthcoming a week later, when, in response to queries from several colonial governors for guidance on the question of how to deal with the Soviet Union, signatory to the Non-Aggression Pact with Hitler. The answer was equivocal: "The question of attitude of H.M. Government towards U.S.S.R. is under consideration and meanwhile it is desirable to avoid references in press to Russia as far as possible."[112]

Throughout the summer of 1939, mobilization proceeded at full tilt, as reservists of the Gold Coast Local Forces were called up. These forces were made up of two formations, the Territorial Force and the Defence Force. The former was recruited from British subjects or British-protected persons born in the Gold Coast Colony, Asante, or the Northern Territories. To enlist, the recruit had to be under twenty-five years of age and be prepared to serve until forty. The new force was organized as an infantry battalion, with camps in Accra, Sekondi, and Cape Coast. Its officers—"gentlemen appointed by the Governor," it was hoped —were, however, for the most part drawn from the Defence Force, headquartered at Accra. So were many of its noncommissioned officers. Members of the Defence Force, who were subject to immediate call-up in time of emergency, had to be British subjects and of "pure European descent."[113]

One of these reservists was E. C. Lanning, then employed by a large gold-mining company at Tarkwa. He was to serve with the RWAFF throughout the war in Gold Coast, East Africa, Gambia, and finally in South East Asia. He explained why men joined the Local Forces:

> They went to camp for a short period once a year. Some were ex-servicemen, but most came from the trading firms, government departments, mining corporations and so forth. The annual get-together made a pleasant change from normal daily routine. In the larger centres they'd soon be encouraged to join the Local Forces. When the time came we were called up in turn, if not quickly enough. Gold mining was declared a reserved occupation so I panicked. One of our assayers managed to get away and beat me to it in joining up; then my friend Harry, on a visit to the Gold Coast, found himself posted to the 1st Battalion. Luckily as I was temporarily administrative, I was notified a week later, and found myself with the embryo 3rd Bn at Winneba. Naturally the 1st Bn got the pick of everything. Arms, equipment, the best African NCOs. Later, if we in the 3rd put up a man for promotion, it was a waste of time, for he would be immediately snapped up and transferred to either the 1st or 2nd Bns.[114]

A wide cross-section of the territory's European population went eagerly into the Local Forces. We have already met H. C. Norman, who was called up in late September 1939. Assigned to the 2 GCR, he remembered that the battalion was "near full strength when I arrived. All sorts of people had been pulled in to bring up the numbers. Reservists from the police, the constabulary, the preventative service and so forth. Some of them were veterans of World War I. There were some very seasoned men. I went up to Tamale for training. The battalion was pretty much at full strength."[115]

Some of the officers may have been described as seasoned, but certainly not all. The recollections of Lt. E. H. Jacques, 2 GCR, are much to the point. He had been sent to West Africa immediately after war was declared, was among those training recruits in Tamale, and expected rapidly to transform villagers into soldiers. He did not think that many of the highly likable recruits had the makings of trained killers, but he was impressed by their ingenuity. In early January 1940 a truck loaded with livestock passed the platoon on the road. "A little while after," Jacques reported in a letter to his uncle, "two of my men came up dragging a reluctant sheep with them which they asserted had fallen off the lorry." They were, of course, terribly anxious that it should be restored to its rightful owners, but, as Jacques commented, "I cannot help feeling that it probably arrived in the Company lines around dinner time yesterday night."[116] Training could clearly sometimes be a rather haphazard affair. A few days after this incident, Jacques and his commander, a Captain Criddle, set off from the camp in Tamale in the early hours of the morning for a three-day exercise in the bush. A point twelve miles out of town was reached. "All went well on the march," wrote Jacques to his sister, "except that at one of the hourly halts, Criddle, the company commander, went to sleep and forgot to move the company on until the company behind bumped into us."[117]

Potential combat troops had to be fed. This was a particular problem for the RWAFF, which had never had regimental cooks in peacetime, but relied instead upon the ability of the African soldiers to find women to provide this service for them. The British Catering Corps could be of little help, its personnel neither knowing the rudiments of African cuisine nor having the language skills to enable them to train African cooks. "The problem was solved in the Gold Coast," it was reported, "by getting the African lady contractor who dealt in jam and marmalade for the S & T [Supply and Transport] to provide teachers and run a school for a specified fee. She produced a collection of *mammies* and the local School of Cookery became a great success. On state occasions, Madam always appeared, dressed in a *Paris* creation from Dakar, ready to receive distinguished visitors."[118] Marmalade seems to have been somewhat of an obsession in the Gold Coast. In 1941 one district commissioner thought the subject important enough to mention it in his annual report. He informed all interested that a Mr. G. D. Egremont, owner of Venture Farms in the Bekwai District of Asante, and producer of the "finest poultry in West Africa," was presently supplying marmalade to the military. His production was only being restrained by the lack of suitable containers, so that he was being forced to ship the marmalade in gasoline cans.[119] That must have given it a rather exotic flavor! It may be noted in passing that this example of typical British muddling through was in sharp contrast to the practice in French territory, where the authorities, with a Gallic sense of priority, and decades of experience, took the question of feeding the tirailleurs extremely seriously.[120]

By February 1940 the War Office was convinced that Italy would be shortly joining the war and that Mussolini did have designs upon Kenya. Brigadier Richards was put on alert to have the Gold Coast Brigade Group ready to join the Expeditionary Force that had been prepared on paper in December 1938 at the Nairobi Conference. The next month the Gold Coast Brigade Group was redesignated the Second West African Infantry Brigade, the first being the Nigerian.[121]

Immediately after the officers were notified, the men were given the news that their destination was to be East Africa. "It was not exactly a matter of 'Gentlemen, we are going to war,'" Lanning remembered. "After all we were expecting it. The men were told immediately following an officer's meeting. The African warrant officers and NCOs were told, 'Here's some news. War begin; we go East Africa find Italian enemy man who be friend for Hitler.' The cheerful response was, 'Good, we go get machete ready and go tell men.' Soon the word spread and everyone was not only content but on their toes."[122]

Before they embarked, Richards led his full brigade on parade past Governor Hodson and other dignitaries in Accra. It was an impressive display of what had been achieved in a relatively short time. The regimental band under Drum Maj. Saidu Lagos, decked out in red Zouave tunics, playing the much-treasured silver drums and bugles, delighted the crowds that had assembled from all over the city.[123] And off they went. The Gold Coast Brigade began boarding the *Orion* and *Reina del Pacifico* on 30 May. They sailed on 4 June 1940, and the next day were at sea off Lagos, where the Nigerian Brigade joined them.[124]

It will be appreciated that, at the beginning of June, France, although in dire trouble, had not fallen to the Germans. It remained an ally. By the time France fell, the Gold Coast and Nigerian Brigades were still at sea. The planners in Nairobi eighteen months earlier had obviously not envisioned any such eventuality. Clearly, British assumptions that West Africa was not likely to become a theater of war had now become questionable. Moreover, with the German navy able to use French ports, and with the entry of Italy into the war, the vital supply route to the Far East through the Mediterranean and the Suez Canal was suddenly blocked. Thus it was of immense concern to London that the Royal Navy maintain command of the South Atlantic sea routes. The security of the Gold Coast's only deepwater port, Takoradi, second in importance only to Freetown in Sierra Leone, became vital. How then was this to be achieved, granted that the Gold Coast had been practically denuded of its troops? All that remained was the newly formed Fifth Battalion, led by Lt. Col. L. C. Whitcombe and composed mainly of men from the Local Forces.

The War Office made it clear that regular troops from Britain would be deployed in West Africa in any strength only in case of invasion. The RWAFF was expected to assume full responsibility for the defense of the four colonies. On 19 June 1940 the War Office agreed that three more West African battalions, two for the Nigerian Regiment and one for the Gold Coast, should be raised immediately.[125] The plan was to expand greatly the Fifth Battalion, using it not only for

Soldiers, Airmen, Spies, and Whisperers

the defense of Takoradi, but to train a nucleus of officers and both British and African NCOs. These would be used in the longer-range plan to create four new battalions that would ultimately constitute the Second Brigade of the Gold Coast Regiment. However this was to be accomplished, London made it clear that little material help would be forthcoming. Specifically, it was to be done "on the understanding that no (repeat) no infantry equipment or ammunition would be available from United Kingdom for six to eight months and that sufficient equipment could be found locally to justify a start on this basis."[126]

In a somewhat desperate telegram to Giffard, Governor Hodson pointed out that although London had agreed to provide three hundred thousand rounds of ammunition for battalion training, it had absolutely ruled out "any issue of even a small number of rifles." Hodson, however, was finding it almost impossible to acquire any new stocks of rifles. He went to the lengths of suggesting that all police not directly concerned with the colony's defense might be disarmed and their rifles redistributed to the RWAFF.[127] The first of the new battalions to be made operational was 4 GCR, formed in July 1940. To help it arrive at battle readiness, a large number of men from the Gold Coast Police were drafted into it, most of them quickly advancing to NCO rank.[128] Extraordinarily and unexpectedly, the battalion was dispatched to Bathurst (now Banjul) on 24 September 1940.[129] The timing was such that it is difficult to know whether it had been decided that, given the success of the Dakar operation, the presence of a larger force in the Gambia would be useful, or that in the event of the failure of the de Gaulle attack, Gambia would be much at risk. Indeed, there was an AOF plan to launch an attack on the Gambia on 28 October, and it may well be that the presence there of 4 GCR did much to convince the AOF military command to abandon it.[130] Be that as it may, 4 GCR was now in the Gambia; 1, 2, and 3 GCR were in East Africa; and 5 GCR was left as the only operational unit in the Gold Coast. The projected battalions —6, 7, and 8 GCR—were still only on the drawing board. The role of 5 GCR in the defense of the colony was to become increasingly important with the development of Takoradi as a major Royal Air Force base. Nevertheless, it was also required to train recruits as replacements for the battalions in East Africa and the Gambia.

By November 1940, then, the Gambia and Gold Coast were surrounded on all land frontiers by Vichy-controlled territory; Sierra Leone was exceptional only in that it shared an eastern frontier with neutral Liberia; and Nigeria, thanks to the Free French takeover of the AEF, had a friendly eastern border, although it still faced potentially hostile AOF countries to the north and west. General Barrau in Dakar, and General Giffard in Achimota, nearly fifteen hundred miles apart as the crow flies, warily assessed each other's strengths, and for that matter, weaknesses, and tried to determine the likelihood that the forces of the one would be launched against the forces of the other. Remarkably, at the end of 1940, General Barrau produced estimates of the military strength of the British West African colonies that were greatly exaggerated: "The permanent resources that are available in the British colonies are evaluated at 46 battalions, of which 6 are European —120 light tanks or armored cars, 2,000 trucks, 20 field batteries, 200 aircraft. The most import resources are to be found in the Gold Coast (15 battalions, 90 armored cars, 60 aircraft)."[131] It is unlikely that the general's intelligence was that bad. Rather, we may assume that he had decided to use scare tactics in order to convince the Germans to release the estimated ten thousand Tirailleurs Sénégalais languishing in the prison camps of occupied France, thereby ensuring the continuing military build-up in French West Africa. This, Barrau thought, would be a means of deterring not only any British advance into French territory, but also—perhaps even more important—of discouraging any designs the Germans might have had to move their troops into the AOF.

A much more realistic appraisal of the situation was held by officials of the colonial administration stationed in the border areas. One was H. V. Wimshurst, who was district commissioner of Wenchi in northwestern Asante during the critical period. Wimshurst remembered, "The war was going very badly for Britain. The Gold Coast was very isolated. All our trained troops had been sent to the East African campaign. The Gold Coast was the wealthiest Colony in the Empire and it was highly possible that the Germans were putting pressure on French African Military organisations to do us as much damage as they possibly could."[132] Wimshurst was, of course, right, in that the Gold Coast had indeed been denuded of most of its troops, and this at a time when the port of Takoradi was about to play a pivotal role in the battle for North Africa.

Soldiers, Airmen, Spies, and Whisperers

2

The Takoradi Ferry and Defense on the Home Front

BEGINNINGS OF THE WEST AFRICAN REINFORCEMENT ROUTE

The Italian occupation of Abyssinia in 1936 had alerted the War Department to the potential threat not just to Kenya, but to the entire Middle East. Thus, as we have seen, the decision had been taken at the Nairobi Conference in late 1938 to use RWAFF troops in East Africa should war break out. These plans were put into effect in the spring of 1940. They would not be reversed, whatever the potential threat to the West African colonies from, at best, an increasingly hostile France or, at worst, a German attack. British interests in the Middle East, and the Suez Canal as the gateway to India, were paramount.

The entry of Italy into the war, on 10 June 1940, was made evident in no uncertain terms. In the first twenty-four hours the Italian air force carried out nine raids on Malta. With the fall of France, a few days later, use of the Mediterranean was rapidly being denied to British ships and aircraft. Even had it remained an open sea, the continuing threat of a German invasion of Britain meant that very few supplies could be spared for the Middle East command. A true crisis loomed for the Royal Air Force in the region. The gravity of the situation is well described in the official history of the RAF:

Before June 1940, aircraft travelled to the Middle East either by sea, along the short Mediterranean route, or by flying in easy stages by way of southern France, French North Africa, Malta, and the Western Desert. But now to pass a convoy along the Mediterranean meant a major naval operation, and with France unfriendly only the longer-range types like the Blenheim and Wellington could make the trip by air. . . . Aircraft of shorter range, however, could only travel by sea; and this might mean the long, time-consuming journey around the Cape.[1]

The need for more planes was clear. The problem was how to get them to the Middle East. Flying them over Europe had become virtually impossible. Flying them across the Bay of Biscay and into the Mediterranean via Gibraltar was extremely dangerous. Two-thirds of one entire fighter squadron was shot down trying to reach Malta.[2] A solution had to be found. The RAF history may be cited again. "There was, however, an alternative which the Air Ministry was quick to explore. Valuable time and shipping space would be saved if the short-range aircraft could make at least part of the journey under their own power. Fortunately this was possible, for the pioneer flights undertaken by Squadron Leaders Coningham and Howard Williams before the war had forged a link between Egypt and the west coast of Africa."[3] This is where Takoradi came into its own.

As cocoa production had begun to dominate the Gold Coast economy in the later nineteenth century, the surf port of Sekondi became a major outlet for the export trade of the colony and Asante. A single-track railway line was pushed north from Sekondi in 1898, to reach Tarkwa in 1901. After Asante was declared a colony in 1901, it became possible to extend the line to Kumasi. This was completed in late 1903. By the 1920s, the volume of cocoa exports had developed to a point at which Sekondi and all the other surf ports could no longer handle it. The decision was made to construct a deepwater harbor near Sekondi, at Takoradi. It was ceremonially opened on 3 April 1928. Two years earlier, Squadron Leader Arthur Coningham of the RAF had pioneered an air route from Khartoum, in the Sudan, to Kano, in northern Nigeria, mapping the eighteen hundred miles. The opening of the port at Takoradi presumably encouraged the RAF to construct a small landing strip there. Squadron Leader Howard Williams must have been among the first to use it when, in 1930, he led a flight of Fairey Gordon IIIFs along Coningham's route to Kano, and thence south to Lagos, west to Takoradi, and so on to Freetown and Bathurst.[4]

In 1931, Imperial Airways, predecessor of British Overseas Airways Corporation, opened a scheduled London to Kenya route, and the following year regular flights to Capetown were initiated. In 1936, Imperial Airways created a West African link by inaugurating flights from Khartoum to Lagos via Kano.[5] The Gold Coast Public Works Department began construction of civil airports at Accra and Takoradi. By 1937, Imperial Airways was flying to Accra and in 1939 the service was extended to Takoradi.[6] The Takoradi airport by this time consisted of three one-thousand-foot runways (only one of which was metalled), an administration block, a radio station, one hangar, and mosquito-proof quarters for travelers.[7] It was this route from Khartoum to Takoradi that was about to become a lifeline for British forces in the Middle East.

Italy's declaration of war galvanized the Air Ministry in London into action. A decision was made to use the West African route to fly fighter planes and bombers to Cairo, for onward dispatch to the British forces in North Africa. Takoradi was chosen over Lagos primarily because of its better sea- and airport facilities, and because its somewhat less humid climate was felt to be better for the aircraft.[8] Three weeks after the fall of France, ironically on Bastille Day, a group of twenty-four officers and men, under the command of Group Capt. H. K. Thorold, took up their new posts at Takoradi. Thorold had been maintenance officer in chief in France, and it was felt he would have little difficulty in coping with any logistic problems encountered in West Africa.[9] On 24 August the rest of the party of three hundred fifty officers and men, including twenty-five ferry pilots, arrived.[10] Twenty-year-old Aircraftsman William Grigsby, whom we met in chapter 1, was in this second group, known as no. 17 draft. He recollected, "When our troopship, *Aska*, arrived at Takoradi harbor in late August 1940, we had to stay on board for a week because the ship carrying many supplies had been sunk on the way; so that it became necessary to manufacture beds and mosquito nets for us. Those primitive but essential items had to last us for quite a while."[11]

Thorold was faced with the task of converting a little-used civilian airport into a major RAF base. Its facilities had to be greatly expanded, allowing for the accommodation of substantial numbers of administrative staff, assembly line workers, pilots, and ground crews. One of the first problems encountered was the presence of a small hill at the end of the main runway. It was quickly dealt with by hiring African men to remove it with hoes and shovels, and African women to carry away the soil in baskets on their heads.[12]

Much of the responsibility for building the base fell on an African, Matthew Poku, building draftsman and surveyor in the Public Works Department. Nearly thirty years after the war, the kingmakers of Asante selected him the fifteenth Asantehene, that is, paramount of the powerful Asante people, to be known as

Otumfuo Nana Opoku Ware II. In 1994 he spoke of those early days: "A very interesting time. I was an engineer, working under the engineer in charge of Takoradi airport. I was a draftsman and surveyor. I arrived in 1941. The war was on and I was constructing the hangars for the airplanes. . . . They [the Europeans] were respectful, but they were surprised to see an African drawing, supervising the building. Everything then was secret. When you went over to the planes, they would say, Who are you? What are you doing here alone? Even the engineer. They would not allow you to go alone."[13]

The men of no. 17 draft found their living conditions reasonable, barring the frequent appearances of scorpions. "There was an officers' mess," Grigsby recalled, "and the NCOs and men were housed in very good premises: a technical school that had been built recently, but not yet put into commission. . . . We were interested on arrival to find that our buildings had no glass windows but wooden slatted shutters—for coolness, obviously. But when the tornado season started we soon found the disadvantage of the arrangement. The tornadoes are born in the Bight of Benin and rush westward along the coast—and thus right through our shutters." Many of those in no. 17 draft had been with the RAF in France. Having survived both that campaign and the perils of the convoy to Takoradi, they were to have a few moments of unpleasantness upon arrival. "The very day we went on shore at Takoradi," Grigsby added,

> "and as we opened those shutters, we spotted a plane coming in, flying very low. It was a Junker 52, and that caused considerable alarm and despondency amongst our people. We soon discovered, however, that the plane was a Sabena machine. We were fortunate enough to have three of these planes. . . . We had an array of aircraft, to bring back our ferry pilots, as well as, of course, for other purposes. We had those three Sabena planes, Hudsons, and also some really ancient Bombays."[14]

Some of the men did not have long to enjoy the bars and other delights of Takoradi, such as they were. Small maintenance parties were to be flown to what would be the staging posts for the ferry. The projected route that would be followed approximated that flown by the pioneers in the 1920s and early 1930s. From Takoradi, the planes headed for Lagos (reckoned at 380 miles), and continued from Lagos to Kano (525 miles), Kano to Maiduguri (325 miles), Maiduguri to El Geneina (650 miles), El Geneina to El Fasher (200 miles), El Fasher to Khartoum (650 miles), and Khartoum to Cairo (1,000 miles).[15] Provision was also made for emergency landings at various smaller airstrips. That nearest to Takoradi was Accra. The West African section of this complicated route was managed from

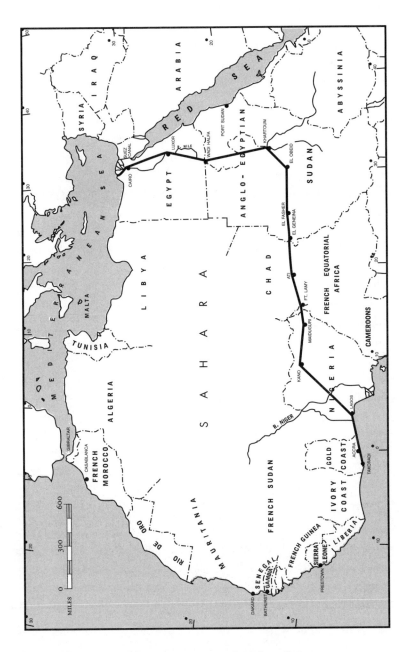

The West African Reinforcement Route—the Takoradi Ferry
 Based on Denis Richards, *The Fight at Odds*, vol. 1 of *Royal Air Force* (London: HMSO, 1953), facing p. 248.

The Takoradi Ferry and Defense on the Home Front   43

West African Ferry Control, Takoradi, while Number 2 Middle East Ferry Control, Khartoum, had jurisdiction over the ongoing route to Cairo.[16]

As Thorold and his team struggled to make what was commonly called the Takoradi Ferry, but was officially known as the West African Reinforcement Route, operational, the situation in North Africa was rapidly deteriorating. Italian air raids, on Alexandria and Haifa on 25 July 1940, for example, had shown that these naval bases were not secure. In the next month, Gibraltar and Malta came under heavy aerial bombardment. Then, in the second week of September, an Italian land offensive was launched from Cyrenaica in Libya. The Egyptian frontier was crossed and the coastal town of Sidi Barrani occupied. Meanwhile, the first ship carrying crated planes had docked in Takoradi, but not until 5 September. Its cargo included six Blenheim IVs, the most modern of the planes in the RAF Middle East command, and six Hurricanes. The next day, the aircraft carrier *Argus* arrived carrying thirty more Hurricanes. These last were completely assembled except for their wings and long-range fuel tanks.[17] The situation was not aided by the collapse of the main runway on 18 September. It was hurriedly repaired and, against all odds, the first flight of the original six Hurricanes and one of the Blenheims actually took off from Takoradi the following day.[18] On that first flight, only the Blenheim had a radio. The pilots of the Hurricanes were not issued maps—they followed the Blenheim, whose navigator alone had one. This was to become the general pattern of the air convoys—a mother hen followed by her chicks, as the bombers and fighters were known to the men who worked on them at Takoradi.[19] For Thorold and his team to have assembled and flight-tested these planes in so short a time was, by any standard, quite an accomplishment.

The next convoy was to dock in Takoradi at the end of the month, bringing eight crated Blenheims and one Caudron Luciole. Accompanying them were twenty-six Free French officers and NCOs who, as soon as the aircraft were fully assembled and tested, would fly the aircraft north to Maiduguri.[20] One obstacle, the long stretch over Chad, had been removed for these early convoys by Governor Eboué's declaration for de Gaulle. The air route could be modified accordingly to enable the planes now to land in Chad at Fort Lamy (now N'Djamena), before the long flight over the desert to El Geneina in the Sudan. Refueling at every stop, the first convoy from Takoradi, of 19 September, arrived at the RAF maintenance depot at Abu Suweir, near Cairo, on 26 September, having lost one of the six Hurricanes.[21] The West African Reinforcement Route was operational.

The logistics involved in getting the crated planes to Takoradi were manifold. The Royal Navy was already stretched to its limits protecting the vital North Atlantic convoy routes to North America. Nonetheless, so critical were North Africa and the Middle East becoming to the war that the aircraft carriers *Ark Royal, Argus, Furious,* and *Victorious* were all utilized to transport the crated planes to Takoradi. *Furious* alone made three such journeys.[22] On one, accompanied by *Argus,* it joined a convoy of ten troopships escorted by the anti-aircraft cruiser *Bonadventure,* destroyers, and corvettes that had sailed from Glasgow for Takoradi (en route to Durban) on 18 December 1940. The decks of the two aircraft carriers were completely loaded with crates of fighter aircraft. The convoy arrived at Freetown on 5 January 1941 and left for Takoradi three days later.[23] *Furious* had on board nine Fairey Fulmar fighter planes complete with RAF crews. They were rapidly assembled and flown almost immediately from Takoradi via Khartoum and Cairo to Alexandria in order to join 805 Naval Air Squadron in the doomed battle for Crete. Their commander was the brilliant flyer Maj. L. A. "Skeets" Harris, Royal Marines.[24]

As the Royal Navy continued to escort the convoys bringing their precious cargo to Takoradi, and as the Royal Air Force continued to assemble the planes and get them into the air, the security of operations there should naturally have been of utmost concern to the War Cabinet. The airport was just over a hundred miles from the Ivoirien frontier, a mere hundred and seventy miles from the airfield at Abidjan, and less than four hundred miles overland from the major tirailleur base at Bouaké. What, then, was the state of Takoradi's defenses? The answer is that they were virtually nonexistent. Governor Hodson was certainly alarmed, and he pleaded with London for artillery to protect Takoradi and other vital areas in the Gold Coast. The reply was tepid. The Colonial Office in particular seemed to feel that Hodson was exaggerating the situation and keeping back information about any extra equipment he'd managed to find for the colony's defense. On 18 July, Lord Lloyd, now secretary of state for the colonies, wired the governor granting him permission to use guns salvaged from the torpedoed merchant ship *Farndale,* lying off Takoradi. Lloyd also wished to know if any "ammunition, rifles, and gun spare parts which were on the ship were salvaged," indeed implying that the governor was holding out on him.[25]

Hodson's reply is unknown, and might well have been unprintable. The defense of Takoradi rested, then, upon one salvaged, but workable, four-inch gun placed at the disposal of the Fifth Battalion of the Gold Coast Regiment, which had been based there immediately after the fall of France. Under the command of Lt. Col. Whitcombe, A, B, and C Companies provided the guards for Takoradi harbor and airfield. The other, D Company, was stationed at Axim with "a tactical role of holding the line of the Ankobra River against any Vichy threat from the Ivory Coast."[26]

Hodson was not alone in worrying about the threat to Takoradi in particular, and the Gold Coast in general. In November, Air Vice Marshal A. W. Tedder had been appointed deputy to Air Chief Marshal Sir Arthur Longmore, commander of all RAF units in the Middle East, Egypt, Sudan, and Kenya. He decided to try out the Takoradi route himself, rather than attempt the direct flight from Lisbon to Cairo, in the course of which his predecessor's plane had crash-landed in Sicily. On Imperial Airways, as plain "Mr." Tedder, he flew to Takoradi via Lisbon and Freetown. Impressed by what he had seen in Takoradi, he continued on to Lagos, where he was entertained by Governor Bernard Bourdillon, who warned Tedder that a meeting with General Giffard, commander in chief of African forces, was scheduled.[27] Giffard, who had already taken a strong position on the necessity of building airstrips through West Africa, criticized the delay that, by the summer of 1940, had seen only ten of the projected thirty airfields built.[28] Giffard, so Bourdillon told Tedder, was extremely angry that the RAF had not seen fit to provide even one fighter squadron for the defense of both Lagos and Takoradi. Tedder admitted that he "saw no prospect whatever of any fighter defense being available," and added that he "could not regard the threat as being in any way a serious one." Not surprisingly, the subsequent meeting with Giffard did not go well. Giffard was convinced that a very real threat of invasion from Vichy AOF existed, and demanded a complete fighter defense system for the British West African territories. Tedder, according to his memoirs, informed Giffard as tactfully as possible that the idea was both unnecessary and unfeasible. Nothing, he said, could be spared from the Middle East and North Africa. Giffard's undoubtedly angry response to this dismissal of the threat to the Gold Coast and Nigeria is not on record.[29]

THE WEST AFRICAN REINFORCEMENT ROUTE: FULLY OPERATIONAL

As the West African Reinforcement Route became fully operational in late 1940 so, coincidentally, the news from North Africa and the Mediterranean began to look more optimistic. In the week beginning 9 December 1940, two British divisions forced seven Italian ones to fall back, with heavy losses, from Sidi Barrani. On 5 January 1941, Bardia in Libya fell, and seventeen days later the Italian garrison at Tobruk surrendered. Gen. F. M. Wavell's forces occupied Derna on 30 January. By the seventeenth of February, Benghazi and the whole of Cyrenaica were in British hands and Wavell was prepared to advance into Tripolitania. The tide, however, was to turn again.

On 20 January, probably unknown to Wavell, Hitler had decided to commit his Fifteenth Armoured Division to North Africa in the face of the Italian collapse. Gen. Erwin Rommel and elements of his Afrikakorps arrived in Tripoli during the second week of February. By then Wavell had slowed his advance, having been ordered to move many of his troops back to Cairo. They were being prepared for action in Greece, where the Germans had sent heavy reinforcements to shore up the crumbling Italian offensive. Most of the RAF squadrons in North Africa had also been sent to Greece, apparently leaving only one fighter squadron in Libya. This was to prove woefully inadequate when Rommel launched his counteroffensive at the end of March. Benghazi was retaken by the Axis troops on 3 April. By the second week of April, Tobruk was under siege. And by the end of the month, virtually all British gains in Libya had been lost and Rommel's forces were in control of the Halfaya Pass, on the Egyptian frontier.

A major factor in the British retreat was Rommel's control of the skies. At the beginning of 1941, Rommel's tactical air support already greatly outweighed that of the British. At his disposal were 107 Messerschmitts, including 42 long-range fighter-bombers, 84 Stukas, and just under twenty Junker 88s. When Crete fell to the Germans in June 1941, supplies of gasoline and ammunition could be regularly flown in from German bases by Junker 52s and Marchetti 82s, using planes recalled from newly occupied Crete and the Balkans. There were also more than two hundred fifty airplanes of various types belonging to the Italian air force. The British position was much weaker. Air Marshal Sir Arthur M. Longmore, commander of the RAF, Egypt, had two bomber squadrons, consisting of 68 Blenheims and 29 Wellingtons, and fourteen fighter squadrons with a total of 88 Hurricanes and Tomahawks. During one three month period in 1941, approximately a hundred and fifty aircraft arrived in Egypt via Takoradi, as compared with only seventeen through the much more dangerous, if shorter, Malta route. In the same period, while 172 new planes had arrived, the RAF lost 184 of its existing fleet.[30] The Takoradi Ferry became of critical importance. As Air Marshal Tedder was to write, "Thorold's men worked wonders there and Dawson's men worked wonders in the Middle East. Without them, I do not see how we could have mustered sufficient air strength to hold the Germans and Italians in 1941 and to defeat them in 1942 and 1943."[31]

The increasing menace of the U-boat wolf packs in the North Atlantic still constituted a major threat to the delivery of the crated aircraft to Takoradi. Circuitous routes had to be explored in order to try to outmaneuver the submarines. Fifty-five years later, former Sergeant Pilot Duncan Carmichael described his journey to Takoradi in 1941:

> The navy, the government, had commandeered two mailboats that sailed between Glasgow and Belfast—the *Royal Scotsman* and the *Royal Ulsterman.* We were put on the *Royal Ulsterman.* It was full of army [personnel], pilots, gunners going to Takoradi. We went in convoy. This was in August or September 1941. We went almost to America—a huge sweep to try to avoid the U-boats—then turned to the Azores—Ponta Delgado, where we met the convoy to Freetown. There were only a few Air Force people on board. We had a cabin—two pilots to a cabin. Then they came and told us: sergeant-pilots out! Give your cabin to a 2d lieutenant! Army! We said no. If they'd wanted to put two 2d lieutenants in our cabin, we wouldn't have protested—but only one! To replace two of us! We barricaded the cabins—had the water hoses ready to go. They said OK, the army officers will also double up.[32]

Brian Ellis, an RAF engine fitter who had been working on Bristol Beaufighters in North Weald, Essex, since his call-up on 1 September 1939, was also posted to Takoradi. He recollected:

> I came out on the *Highland Princess,* a refrigerator ship. They had wooden benches fitted into the large refrigeration containers; we used it as our mess. We hung our hammocks from the cooling pipes. After the ship dumped its people in West Africa, it would go to Argentina to pick up beef, then back to Britain, unload the beef, and become a troopship again. We left from Gourock [near Greenock] in Scotland. . . . The Germans knew that all the ships went straight across the Newfoundland Banks, then down the coast of America, then cut across.[33]

Ellis also recalled:

> There were very few escorts available to the Royal Navy in 1941 for convoy duties. So when the Americans gave us about forty World War I destroyers we had no option but to accept them. They were originally in shore vessels and their behavior in the open Atlantic was something to marvel at.
> Our convoy, sailing as Draft 4661, had two troopships and approximately twenty fast merchant ships. The troopships sailed in the heart of the convoy with a very sparse Royal Navy escort of an Armed Merchant Cruiser, one ex-

American four-stack destroyer, and two or three corvettes making a protective screen. The whole convoy entered Freetown, which had no merits whatsoever, but we left two days later on our own with a motor torpedo boat as escort.[34]

At first, most of the ferry pilots sent to Takoradi, were, like Carmichael, British. Later they were to come from all over the empire, as well as the occupied countries of Europe.[35] Many of them were Polish, so many in fact, that two flags always flew at Takoradi—the RAF standard and the flag of Poland.[36] Polish officers were also assigned to the Royal West African Frontier Force, seven of them being attached to 6 GCR on 29 October 1941.[37] Thousands of pilots from Australia, Britain, and New Zealand were being trained in Canada by the Empire Training Scheme. Nearly a year before Pearl Harbor propelled the United States into the war, 2,520 American volunteers were also being trained to fly in Canada.[38] Once qualified, the crews were given their first real flight assignments, to bring aircraft from North America to West Africa, and were then sent on the Takoradi run. By doing so, they could vastly increase their experience, at relatively little risk, before being thrown into actual combat.

Duncan Carmichael himself only did the Takoradi run once before being reassigned as a flight instructor near Khartoum. He expressed a certain amount of envy regarding the "regular" ferry pilots:

> When we left we were nine Hurricanes and one Blenheim. It [the Blenheim] had a Polish pilot and the navigator was a Scot. We had no maps—we followed the Blenheim. We flew from Takoradi. Went out to sea, skirted Togo and Dahomey—they were Vichy. Then we landed at Lagos. Spent the night there. Then from Lagos to Kano, then to Maiduguri, still in Nigeria. From Maiduguri to Ati to Fort Lamy. We refueled at every stop.
>
> Everywhere we stopped there were Nigerian sellers, everywhere selling snake skins, ivory. Those pilots made a bundle. They'd fill their planes up with snake skins, ivory, all sorts of things you couldn't get at home—then sell them in Britain, in Cairo for big money. Then they'd load their planes with silk and other luxuries for the return flights. A fortune. One poor bugger converted all his money to gold bars. He had mechanical trouble and had to land at Wadi Halfa—the only place along the route with customs officials. They took it all![39]

The pilots were given a few days to accustom themselves to the African climate. They would receive no special training—even those who were ordered to fly unfamiliar aircraft. Probably the most remarkable achievement of the entire operation would be that so large a proportion of the planes successfully made it to the Western Desert.[40] It became usual for flights leaving Takoradi to comprise never more than twelve planes—the chicks—following a two-engine bomber— the mother hen. While the bomber, usually a Blenheim, had a radio, the fighters did not. There was, therefore, no communication within the cohort, other than visual. Flight instructions were terse. According to Brian Ellis, pilots were "told not to think about bailing out, stay with the planes, go down with the planes. There were no radios of the necessary range, if they bailed out they could never be found. Go on in with it!"[41]

The pilots were, however, not entirely without help. I refer to fliers of a different sort, unsung heroes and heroines (but only the expert could tell which was which) of the RAF's operation. These were the carrier pigeons. Building improvements at the Takoradi base included the construction of a pigeon loft. A lifelong pigeon fancier, Sgt. Arthur Cogman was that rarity in the military, a man given a job he both knew about and wanted to do. He spent two years at Takoradi in charge of the pigeons. Once trained, their job was simple. They were carried on the ferry planes. Should a pilot be forced to land in the bush, the pigeons would be released, and the time it took them to arrive back in Takoradi was thought to give some indication of where the stricken aircraft might be. While not exactly a technically advanced means of rescue, and of doubtful efficacy, these birds must at least have provided some comfort and companionship to pilots making their long-distance journeys, often without adequate signaling equipment.[42] A year or so later, Jack Jones of the Air Sea Rescue Service sailed to Takoradi. He remembers three hundred pigeons, under the care of an RAF sergeant, the crates of which shared the deck of the *Carnarvon Castle* with those of the unassembled aircraft.[43]

Relations between the RAF and the RWAFF were occasionally strained, especially when questions of equal treatment of men in the two services arose. One such row, an example of pettiness carried to the extreme, erupted over rations. Brig. F. A. S. Clarke, then commander of the Gold Coast Area, wrote to General Giffard complaining that the RAF was receiving more and better food than that dished out to army personnel. Giffard had other, more important matters on his mind and was unsympathetic. He ordered Brig. H. Wood, quartermaster general of the military forces in West Africa, to settle the issue immediately. Of particular annoyance to Giffard and Wood was Clarke's complaint about the variety and abundance of the rations allotted to the RAF mechanics. After investigating, Wood was equally unsympathetic. "It is not agreed," Wood wrote, "that the work done by the R.A.F. mechanic can be considered equivalent to that carried out by Military personnel in Hospitals etc. R.A.F. mechanics are carrying out arduous manual labour for long hours in building aeroplanes." A slight concession was made to pacify Clarke, in that Giffard agreed that should any mechanics be admitted to military hospitals, their rations would be the same as those of equally sick Army personnel! Wood, recovering a modicum of dignity, pointed out that General Giffard was not about to enter into a dispute with the Air Force: "The R.A.F. authorities at Takoradi, who consider that their present scale of rations are the minimum with which the personnel can successfully carry out the work necessary to maintain the flow of aircraft to the Middle East, the maintenance of which is vital for the safety of that area. They only can be the judge of that." And just in case Clarke was still in doubt about the issue, Wood pressed the issue still further:

> It is the General Officer Commanding-in-Chief's policy that nothing should disturb the harmonious administrative arrangements between the Army and the RAF. The Air Ministry have agreed that the present scale of rations issued to the RAF are necessary, and the General Officer Commanding-in-Chief is not, at present, prepared to press the Air Ministry to order the R.A.F. at Takoradi to adopt the Army Scale. . . .
>
> In view of the facts set out above, the General Officer Commanding-in-Chief regrets that, for the time being, he cannot agree to take up the matter with the War Office.[44]

Matters of food supplies notwithstanding, the importance of the operations at Takoradi increased. Surprisingly, there seemed for a while almost a cavalier attitude toward security for a base that was, as I have noted, so close to the Ivoirien border. This changed on 8 April 1941, when Col. L. A. G. Dalziel and 2d Lt. M. Waltuch arrived from Accra to set up Fortress Headquarters at Takoradi to oversee and coordinate the coastal and anti-aircraft batteries, a signal section, and the 5 GCR guarding the base. Some excitement was generated a few days later when a three-engine flying boat with French markings was spotted over the harbor at eight to nine thousand feet.[45] On 1 May the Takoradi Fire Command was formed, consisting of HQ, three dual anti-aircraft sections, two 12 PDR sections, and CASL Battery. A few days later a program weightily titled the Preparation of Takoradi Defence Scheme was launched. The period appears to have been one of considerably heightened activity, as reinforcements from the Royal Artillery arrived, a searchlight section was formed, a cookhouse built, and, last but not least, proper latrines dug.[46] On 15 May, the main body of 7 GCR arrived to take over the defense of Takoradi and Axim from 5 GCR.

Despite this flurry, it was not until 11 June 1941 that even the most obvious precautions were taken to declare Takoradi a protected area. This meant the base was to be, in theory at least, off-limits to all but authorized personnel. Laborers and other local residents could no longer enter unless in possession of a special pass, in the form of a metal disk. The Gold Coast Railway was barred from issuing tickets from Kumasi to Takoradi to any passengers without the right papers.[47] It was, one suspects, rather like closing the stable door after the horses had gone. It is certain that the Vichy authorities in French West Africa were aware of what was going on, and one can presume that the Germans knew the part that the Gold Coast was coming to play in the war.

To this end, the British made strenuous efforts to impress the dangers of espionage and sabotage upon the men on the convoys en route for Takoradi. Duncan Carmichael remembered an incident when his ship, the *Royal Ulsterman,* docked in the Azores for supplies. "We were putting our baskets over the side, hauling up baskets full of fruit. We were ordered to throw the fruit overboard—told it had been 'poisoned by the German Fifth Column.' We'd die—of cholera or something. So we threw it over. Then we went down to our cabins, opened the portholes, and lowered our baskets again and brought up more fruit. Anyway, we finally got to Takoradi. The town wasn't blacked out. It was full of British NCOs coming to train the West African Frontier Force."[48] Men like Duncan Carmichael, having survived the Blitz, and leaving a Britain that had survived Dunkirk, did not seem terribly worried about the dangers to be faced in West Africa. Aled Jones of Air Sea Rescue put the matter in perspective: "In 1937 I joined the RAF. First I was in a fighter squadron, then in 1939, Home Defense. Driving and Balloon Barrages. Up and down from Bristol. Two years of it, the bombing. I loved Africa—it was like a holiday."[49] It may have seemed like a holiday for the pilots but, as Brian Ellis remarked, "there was a different point of view held by the engineers working in the heat and humidity for seven days a week. We didn't think it was much of a holiday!"[50]

All and all, the operation had been remarkably well organized. Holbrook has given figures for the number of planes assembled and flown out in 1940 and 1941. These are derived from a report by H. K. Thorold dated 1 January 1940.[51] From September 1940 to August 1941, over a thousand planes left Takoradi for North Africa and the Middle East. Ninety-four percent of them reached their destination intact. The pace picked up over the period and more fitters and mechanics arrived. By June 1941 the rate had reached two hundred planes a month, and a record was reached in November with 290 being assembled.

Soldiers, Airmen, Spies, and Whisperers

THE WEST AFRICAN REINFORCEMENT
ROUTE: ENTER THE UNITED STATES

The development of the Takoradi Ferry Operation, from pilots to pigeons, was obviously given high priority. It entailed the transfer of large numbers of skilled personnel and aircraft from the Battle of Britain to the Battle for the Middle East. In effect, they were redeployed to prevent the Axis forces in North Africa sweeping into Egypt and fanning out from there. Unfortunately, neither men nor planes were available in sufficient numbers from a Britain under heavy aerial attacks. Fortunately, however, both were soon to arrive at Takoradi from the United States by a new route: across the South Atlantic. The extraordinary story of how this happened has been unraveled by Deborah Ray.[52]

Britain had been recognized as a combat zone by the United States on 4 November 1939, and Congress asserted its neutrality. President Franklin D. Roosevelt felt a personal commitment to assist Britain, and this became stronger as his personal relationship with Winston Churchill developed. He was the moving force behind the passage of the Lend-Lease Act in March 1940, which permitted the export of war matériel even to combat zones, providing it could be shown that this was contributing to the security of the United States. American production of aircraft increased rapidly, and a large proportion were "lent" to Britain, the security of which had, indeed, been deemed essential to the security of the United States. The situation changed rapidly with the emergence of North Africa as a new theatre of war, and Roosevelt sought means of getting combat aircraft to that front. Sending planes to Britain was one thing, sending planes to North Africa was another. Unfortunately, at the end of 1939, the State Department, seeking to be helpful, had taken the step of defining the United Kingdom as not simply England, Scotland, Wales, and Northern Ireland, but as including "all British colonies, British protectorates, and Class B and C mandates under British Control."[53] Roosevelt's plan was to fly newly built planes to Takoradi. The problem arose now that it would be extremely difficult legally to declare that war supplies being sent to West Africa, for use in the Middle East and North Africa, constituted the defense of the Western Hemisphere.

A loophole in the State Department's written opinion, defining the United Kingdom, allowed a modification of that definition as the situation developed. Roosevelt had the State Department's grossly enlarged "United Kingdom" returned to the traditional one of the British Isles but excluding, of course, the Irish Free State. This was done in late May 1941. It had the seemingly paradoxical effect of prohibiting military personnel from flying Lend-Lease aircraft to West Africa. The new interpretation seems to have satisfied the opposition in a Congress that was still strongly isolationist. Few members of that august body appeared to have noted that there was nothing to stop civilian rather than military operators from doing so. Pan American Airways, already the leading air transport firm in the South American market, also flew a regular passenger route from Gambia to the Sudan. Pan American was "encouraged" to create a new subsidiary airline, Atlantic Airways, which was, in fact, no more than a cover for flying the new Lend-Lease planes to West Africa. Creating this cover would, it was hoped, be sufficient to assuage the suspicions of those in Congress who were concerned with any possible violations of Lend-Lease that would compromise American neutrality.

Atlantic Airways began operations on 27 May 1941, following the South Atlantic route to Africa, which had been pioneered in the mid-1920s by squadrons 45 and 47 of the Royal Air Force. It was this exploratory long-distance flight path that was to be the basis of the American supply route to Takoradi. The Gold Coast was ideally located from the U.S. point of view, in terms of accessibility to the new American Army Air Force base under construction on Ascension Island, one of the properties "leased" by the British. Planes were flown from the various factories in the United States—first, to West Palm Beach, Florida, thence to Trinidad, and so down the coast of Brazil to Natal, the extreme eastern tip of that country and the nearest point on the South American continent to Africa. From Natal, equipped with extra fuel tanks, they undertook the next stage, a thirteen-hundred-mile flight to Ascension Island. After refueling, the planes then went on to Takoradi, a further twelve hundred fifty miles.[54] This route had an obvious advantage over the only alternative, that of shipping crated planes via the Cape of Good Hope to Port Said at the Mediterranean terminus of the Suez Canal.[55]

Once the Americans committed themselves to the airlift, they had to assess the risk to Takoradi. Would the Germans attack the base, with or without Vichy assistance? During the summer of 1941, the proverbial carrot and stick was offered to Pétain, with whom, as a neutral, the Americans retained diplomatic relations. If Vichy resisted German demands to establish a military presence in French West Africa, then the Americans would continue to supply food and other commodities to the AOF and French North Africa. If Vichy did not, the British would undoubtedly blockade French ports on the Atlantic coast, thus cutting off vital American shipments. As if to reinforce the American approach, the British warned that they would indeed do so if this endangered, as Ray puts it, "the channel of communications through which the U.S. was giving assistance to British forces in the Middle East."[56]

By October 1941, Takoradi was playing two quite different roles in the airlift to Cairo and beyond. It continued to be an assembly base for planes arriving by crates from Britain. It had, however, also come to serve as a terminal for Pan American's African operation, the base where U.S. planes were overhauled and refueled before joining the ferry route to the Middle East. Little attention was given to the matter by the American press, and what was printed was generally favorable.[57] The short visit of Averell Harriman, Roosevelt's special envoy, to Takoradi on 17 June 1941 largely escaped journalistic coverage.[58] Clearly Roosevelt did not wish the venture, at this stage, to be extensively reported since America still remained technically neutral. As a result, the American public remained blissfully ignorant of their government's involvement in supplying British forces in the Middle East and North Africa. Not so the Vichy military authorities in West Africa. By some means, probably as simple as sending someone out with a fishing canoe, they were measuring the volume of air traffic arriving at and departing from Fortress Takoradi. A French report, probably written by General Barrau in late 1941, reads:

> As to aviation in particular, one notes the activity at the assembly base of Takoradi (Gold-Coast) and the importance of the movements of aircraft (British or American supplies) from West to East, of which the frequency observed is of the order of 8 to 10 daily. There is, therefore, in fact an ever present possibility of at least doubling [this number]. . . .
>
> The presence of regular American forces has not been observed in the vicinity of the AOF, but only that of specialized aircraft assembly personnel and pilots of Pan American Airways who are responsible for flying aircraft parts to the Near East. The importance for the British of the land and air imperial route, Lagos–Kano–Ft.Lamy–Khartoum, cannot be too strongly underlined.[59]

Barrau—if it was him—was quite correct. No regular American forces were in the Gold Coast, but on 15 October 1941, an advance party of Pan American personnel arrived, followed by another 190 a few weeks later.[60] They were to prepare a maintenance base for those planes being flown into Takoradi to begin their long flight to the Western Desert. By October 1943, over five thousand planes had either passed through or been assembled at Takoradi and sent to Egypt.[61] In 1941 the U.S. Army Air Force opened a base at Accra, no longer, it will be remembered, in what was officially a combat zone. The intention was to make that airfield their primary service area for planes being ferried across the Atlantic. In the meantime, Pan American continued its "civilian" service between West Africa and Khartoum —an excellent cover for conveying spare parts to West Africa for the air ferry operation.[62] It is reported that throughout 1942 and early 1943 between two and three hundred American planes landed daily at Accra for maintenance and refueling.[63]

NEW BLOOD: THE EXPANSION OF THE GOLD COAST REGIMENT

Duncan Carmichael's recollections, quoted above, of the *Royal Ulsterman* carrying British NCOs to join the RWAFF introduces us to a new phase in the war. The need to provide a better defense for the West African colonies was finally acknowledged. It will be remembered that in early June 1940 the Gold Coast and Nigerian Brigades had sailed to East Africa to join the Expeditionary Force. In the Gold Coast only the Fifth Territorial Battalion, with a total strength of just under seven hundred officers and men was fully operational and responsible, inter alia, to guard Takoradi.[64] At the War Depot in Kumasi, however, a new Fourth Battalion was being recruited and trained. The plan was to use these two battalions in order to create the nuclei of still further battalions that would assume both the tasks of guarding the Gold Coast and of providing reinforcements and replacements for the brigade in East Africa.

From the summer of 1940 onward, officers and NCOs from British home regiments began to arrive in the Gold Coast. They were known as Imperials, coming out to Africa as members of what were often referred to as Imperial Contingents. The term was probably coined to distinguish those coming from home regiments, who held the King's Commission, from those who had been recruited in the colonies and were commissioned by colonial governors.[65] The preponderance of the Imperials in this early stage of rebuilding the regiment can be seen on, for example, the roll of the Fourth Battalion GCR on 31 October 1940, the day it arrived in the Gambia. Of the twenty-seven commissioned officers, only twelve held GCR commissions, while the rest were Imperials, drawn from fourteen different regiments of the line. On 25 November, a further fourteen officers disembarked at Bathurst, drawn from eleven other British regiments.[66] Not all the Imperials were sent straight to West Africa to reinforce the regiment. At least two contingents sailed directly, via Durban, to Mombasa, where, after a short period of training in Nairobi, they were moved immediately to their units at the front.

The Imperials brought with them a wide range of new equipment. For the first time the entire regiment began to use the Bren gun rather than the older Lewis gun. One old hand, H. C. Norman, found some of the ways of the newcomers difficult to fathom: "All the new army people began to flood in the RAMC, RASC, and so forth. The Thirty-Seventh Field General Hospital was set up in Accra. All this to build up more battalions in the GCR. . . . These were new men who knew nothing about Africa. Many were roughnecks. We had to try to warn them about African women, not to treat them with disrespect. They would open a cigarette case for the African to take one. We never did this. We'd pass them the pack and say, Take one. We didn't really like the new men. We were the old army. By this I mean the original old army, the regulars, the Rhodesians, and those called up from the Reserve."[67] The quartermaster sergeant subsequently elaborated on this: "To keep the discipline and respect of the African soldier, we could not be familiar, and, as you know, we of the Colonial Army at the time and in peacetime, Europeans and Africans, respected each other—thus my illustration of the cigarette example. I'm sure you can understand someone coming straight out of UK had no idea of Africans and quick promotion to the lowest European Rank to be in line with the RWAFF was a little heady. The *old* African Soldier recognized this."[68] An officer with the regiment under combat conditions saw things rather differently. E. C. Lanning, for example, an old GCR hand then serving in East Africa, found that the newcomers presented no particular difficulties in working with African troops. "They went into what one might call the last of the Old Guard, . . . they mucked in well and did well for themselves."[69]

In order to recruit new soldiers, in effect to double the size of the Gold Coast Regiment, it was thought desirable to keep the general populace informed about the activities of their men fighting in East Africa. In July 1940 the GCR had arrived in Kenya. Governor Hodson received a coded telegram from its commander, Brig. C. E. Melville Richards, Nairobi, informing him that the Gold Coast units had arrived safely and that, despite some respiratory infections, in general the ranks were in good health.[70] This was just as well, because they were soon to be involved in heavy fighting against the Italians in Somalia and Ethiopia.[71]

Although the British had always had strong reservations about using Africans against European forces, the success of the Gold Coast soldiers against the Italians in battle had an immense propaganda value at home. It was deemed important for future recruitment, while having the additional value of assuring friends and families at home of the soldiers' indefatigable spirits. Brig. S. S. Butler had served as inspector-general of the RWAFF from 1926 to 1930. He visited the brigade soon after it had taken up its positions in the Northern Frontier District of Kenya, and returned to the Gold Coast with a firsthand account to report on the men's welfare. On 24 October 1940 he gave a stirring radio broadcast to the people of the Gold Coast. Having first assured his listeners that the men "are all looking extraordinarily fit and well," he added that he "was particularly struck by the cheerfulness and keenness of all ranks." He regaled the audience with accounts of the regiment's pleasure in the good army rations and free cigarettes, and spoke of their first engagements with the enemy. "A number of European Italian soldiers," the brigadier said, "have been seen in action. When asked to describe whether he had seen any European on patrol, one of our Gold Coast troops appeared puzzled and would not be definite. Eventually after much discussion he said 'Well I say they weren't white men, they weren't black men—what they were, were yellow men.'"[72] It may be inferred from Butler's inclusion of this little anecdote that he was more than a little sympathetic with the anonymous Gold Coast soldier as to whether or not Italians really counted as Europeans! His attitude toward the troops of the regiment was much more charitable. He went on to tell another story that had to do with "the gallant exploit of a private of the Gold Coast Regiment, who, after being taken prisoner by the Italians, escaped and without food or drink came back five days through the waterless bush and rejoined his unit." It was, Butler proudly announced, another "outstanding example of the bravery of the Gold Coast soldier."[73]

In the Gold Coast, recruitment for the new battalions followed the usual pattern. District commissioners went on trek to announce the glorious opportunity awaiting healthy young men. Chiefs were marshaled and told they were expected to encourage the appearance of suitable recruits at district headquarters. For once, the bushes of the *entire* Gold Coast—Asante and the colony, and not simply the Northern Territories—were beaten in the drive for soldiers. In particular, the army finally and totally overcame its reluctance to recruit Asantes as combat soldiers. There is a touch of paradox about this. On the one hand, the army had been schooled to think that the Asantes had never accepted their subject colonial status, and were likely, given the right circumstances, to rebel against their conquerors. On the other hand, it was believed that the Asantes had lost their martial spirit under colonial rule and were only fit to serve as clerks, drivers, and signalers, occupations for which literacy rather than weaponry was required. The change in attitude was signaled by the decision, in September 1940, to give

Asante its own infantry battalion, 7 GCR. Governor Hodson was enthusiastic, and reached positively lyrical heights when speaking about the fighting qualities of the Asante: "I cannot say how glad I am that a company is being organized consisting solely of Ashantis. I am sure the Ashanti people would have resented it very much if they had not their representatives in the Gold Coast Regiment. It is not necessary for me to refer to the fighting qualities of the Ashanti people, because they are so well known, and I feel certain, if they ever go into action, that they will raise their quills like the porcupine and drive off the enemy.[74] Some officers, however, remained skeptical. Lanning, for example, put it this way: "This was an idea of the new mob. We old hands always threw all the recruits together regardless of tribe."[75]

The headquarters of the Seventh Battalion was initially located at Kintampo. Meetings were held throughout Asante to discuss overall recruitment procedures, but an immediate decision was taken for the chiefs to have "gong-gong" beaten, thereby expressing their support for the new recruitment drive. In some areas, the Obuasi District for example, the chiefs were reluctant to proceed without assurances from the Asantehene, Sir Osei Agyeman Prempeh II, that he was backing the campaign. On 31 December 1940 they politely refused to begin allocating the district's quota of 143 men among the villages until they had their king's specific approval. But the Asantehene was ill and recruitment had to be delayed for several weeks.[76] On his recovery, however, he sent one of his spokesmen, or "linguists," to tour the area with Maj. C. O. Butler, DC Kumasi, thus giving the royal stamp of approval to the recruitment campaign.[77] In Bekwai, Acting District Commissioner G. E. Sinclair was able to report that recruiting was going very well, although he was somewhat disappointed that "most joined in search of adventure not a sense of duty."[78] Mampon was a particularly abundant source of soldiers.[79] Lt. W. N. Heaton of Eton and the Lancashire Regiment was among those to be stationed at Kintampo, specifically to train the Mampon recruits. One of them, he recalled, proclaimed, "We are all the bad men from our village."[80]

Among the first intake of recruits was young Kofi Genfi II from Kumasi, today a prosperous hotel owner there. He remembers:

Most of my friends were in the army, the WAFF, the West African Frontier Force. . . . I was posted to the Seventh Battalion, Gold Coast Regiment . . . It was only Ashantis. The British government requested from the Asantehene to form a full battalion. There are twelve hundred in a battalion—all Ashantis with the exception of the officers—and the senior NCOs. The senior NCOs were mostly from the north. [Before joining the army] I was keeping my own store. It was my friends. It was a drinking store, a bar. My friends used to call there, in uniform. I liked it [the uniform]. My mother didn't like it. I had to fight her hard to enlist in the army.[81]

Kofi Genfi went on to describe the general recruitment procedure.

We went to Kumasi. The man in charge of the recruitment was one Captain Sinclair, a DC, in charge of recruitment. He was allotted three trucks, to go to the villages. The Asantehene allotted every village chief, allotted a certain number of men. It worked like this: The Asantehene set a quota then he called the district chiefs and allotted each of them a certain number. Then the district chiefs called their village chiefs and gave them each a number of men that had to be ready on a specific day. It was the job of Sinclair, he had the list, he knew how many from each village there would be. He would take the trucks to each village and bring the men.[82]

As recruitment proceeded, 7 GCR was moved from Kintampo to the military camp at Cantonments, near Accra. According to its later commander, Lt. Col. W. B. Ponting, "after training and achieving battalion strength, the battalion had been given responsibility for the defense of Accra, and to be ready to repel any attacks by the Vichy French across the border with Togoland. For the latter task the battalion had to be ready to move at one hour's notice."[83] Apparently the commanding officer and his staff failed to bring the battalion up to par. Discipline was lacking, and morale was low. As a result, in the very beginning of 1942, command was to be transferred to Ponting, who had just returned from the Italian East Africa campaign. His staff was an eclectic mixture of officers, some from the Regular Army, some from the Gold Coast Local Forces, and some conscripted in the United Kingdom and Rhodesia, to whom were added six Polish officers. Instructed by general headquarters (GHQ) to have 7 GCR combat ready within six weeks, he took the immediate step of moving the battalion to a tented camp some ten miles from Accra, thus cutting the men off from the temptations of the capital. The battalion that Ponting took over consisted of 70 to 80 percent Asantes, and the remainder from the Northern Territories, as well as a few coastal recruits serving as clerks, drivers, and the like.[84] In July 1941, on the eve of his retirement, Governor Hodson had gone out of his way to give the Ashanti Battalion a further tribute. "For many years, it has not been the custom for recruits from Ashanti and the Colony to be accepted for the Regiment, but the people have proved that once the door has been thrown open to them there has been no lack of keenness to enter. The Chiefs, the people, and the District Commissioners deserve great

Soldiers, Airmen, Spies, and Whisperers

credit for the success of the recruiting campaign."[85] Ponting was not to agree with this assessment. He came to think the Asante, generally speaking, a poor soldier, lacking martial qualities. He hazarded the guess that the battalion had been raised by GHQ at the request of the Asantehene, and thought that the Staff, mainly recently out from Britain, had been too easily persuaded by him of the fighting quality of his subjects. He set about replacing Asante deserters, of which there were apparently many, with northerners, until the Asantes became a minority in *their* battalion. Holbrook has tabulated the percentage of deserters as of 30 November 1943 and shows that no less than 42 percent of Asante enlistees had deserted. This may be compared with 15 percent for all Gold Coast servicemen.[86] Interestingly, the Asantehene made known his embarrassment about the number of deserters, or those discharged as unsuitable. Ponting had an audience with him, and explained in great detail the deficiencies of the Asante soldiers. "I also told him," wrote Ponting, "that I was satisfied with those Ashantis remaining with the unit, but they no longer provided the largest number of men as was the case when I arrived. He seemed quite happy when I told him that we would continue to be known as the *Ashanti Battalion,* but I do not think I was able to convince him that his men did not make good soldiers."[87]

The army tried to increase popular enthusiasm for the nationwide recruitment drive by a variety of methods. K. Attakora Gyimah, a retired reporter for Kumasi's *Ashanti Pioneer,* remembered one of them:

In an attempt to recruit soldiers, those who had been trained—when they were trained—were marched through the streets. All in their uniforms singing:

Me ko soldier	I go to be a soldier.
Me ko soldier	I go to be a soldier.
Ako kyere Hitler	To capture Hitler.
Jolly	Jolly.
Adwuma nyinaa asa	There's no work
me hwehwe adwuma	for me to do
adwuma men y bi	but join the army.
Nye, yere ko a bongo	Yes, we are going to join the army.[88]

"Going to be a soldier" was one thing, but there was very little enthusiasm in any part of the Gold Coast for joining the Auxiliaries or the Pioneers, men who were essentially porters or laborers. So few wished to assume these onerous and distinctly unglamorous roles that it became necessary to send an officer from the

Infantry Training Center in Kumasi to launch a recruitment campaign in British-mandated Togoland.[89] The lack of success of these efforts is indicated by the figures: in a typical week, over a hundred privates would be recruited for the regiment, but only an average of three volunteers could be found to enlist as carriers.[90]

A recruit who was likely to go overseas was given an allotment card for his wife—for one wife only—which entitled her to a portion of his salary each month. The Asantehene provided another form of support for family values by ordering strict fines levied on any man committing adultery with a soldier's wife. To follow K. A. Gyimah again, "The Asantehene called a gong-gong to be beaten prohibiting those men who did not go to the army, forbidding them to have any relations with the wives of the soldiers. Anyone found to have had sex paid a penalty of £5 and one sheep. This money was for the soldier. The wives were somehow covered by this decree."[91]

In the Gold Coast Colony itself, the governor beat the drum for the RWAFF. Opening the meeting of the Joint Provincial Council at Saltpond, attended by twenty-five hundred people, Hodson directed his remarks to the fifty "Ahinfu" (i.e., Ahenfo, or chiefs) from the Western, Central, and Eastern Provinces. After praising the achievements of the Gold Coast Regiment in East Africa, the governor got down to business, asking the chiefs to take a vigorous part in finding many new troops for the regiment. He assured them that this would be a popular action as men were eager to join.[93] To make his case even stronger, Hodson pointed out that the gallant efforts of the GCR in blocking Hitler's path to East Africa might have the opposite effect of bringing the Germans to West Africa through the Maghreb. There were, the governor continued, already major concerns that the Nazis would insist that the long-delayed trans-Saharan rail link between Dakar and French North Africa be completed, so enabling such an invasion to take place: "As you know," he informed the Ahenfo, "Marshal Pétain had refused to agree to a German occupation of the French Colonies in Africa. But Pétain was an old man. Laval might come into power or the Germans might compel the French to let them do what they wished. We must look to the future, and that meant that we must recruit and organise new forces to defend West Africa and the Gold Coast."[94]

In urging the chiefs personally to attend to the matter of recruiting, Governor Hodson expressed his belief that they would assist him without any need for compulsion. Should their cooperation not be wholehearted, however, he reminded them that the new Defence Regulations gave him the powers of a "dictator." He would of course never abuse them, but, "the Spirit of the British Empire was one of sympathy; it detested brutality, oppression and cruelty. That is what had made the British Empire the greatest force for good that the world has ever seen. And

Soldiers, Airmen, Spies, and Whisperers

that is what we are fighting for, and will fight for, to the bitter end."[95] The response of the assembled chiefs was positive. Amanfi II, Omanhene of Asebu, speaking for all, dutifully assured the governor "that the chiefs and people would do their best in the common effort against their evil and snake-like enemy."[96]

There were, then, men eager to enlist, and the regiment needed them. Nevertheless, there were problems in procuring a sufficient number of recruits. The proportion of those rejected on grounds of being physically unfit was extremely high, reaching 75 percent in parts of the Gold Coast.[97] Despite these difficulties, by the end of 1940 three new battalions had been formed, staffed, and were undergoing intensive training to reach operational status as quickly as possible. At Accra, 6 GCR boasted 535 Africans, 42 British NCOs, and 17 European officers. At Tamale, 8 GCR, composed of men, drawn virtually exclusively from the Northern Territories, was being rapidly licked into shape. 7 GCR, the Ashanti Battalion at Kintampo, had its initial problems as we have seen above. Another seven hundred recruits were enjoying the pleasures of basic training at the War Depot in Kumasi.[98] Later, Sgt. William McCaskie was surprised to find out that these men were never to be issued with rifles and live ammunition at the same time! Whether this was ordained to preserve the lives of the men themselves, or of their officers and NCOs, or simply to conserve the dwindling stock of ammunition possessed by the RWAFF, was never made clear.[99]

Altogether, the strength of the GCR as 1940 drew to a close was 3,750 Africans, 375 British Other Ranks, and 213 officers. Though these were not exactly numbers to terrify an enemy, they were certainly a distinct improvement over those for men available to the Gold Coast in June 1940. The British officers, always delighted by the singing and dancing and joking of their men, had little hesitation in regarding them as "happy chaps." Sergeant McCaskie was one who never forgot how the boredom of garrison life was enlivened only by occasional musical reviews put on by British soldiers, although the sight of these amateur performers appearing in drag greatly astonished the Asantes in the audience. McCaskie was, in any case, too glad to be alive to worry much about being bored. His regiment, the King's Own Scottish Borderers, had been en route to India aboard the troopship SS *Anselm* when, on 5 July 1941, it was torpedoed and sunk some distance off the coast of West Africa. McCaskie was one of the few to escape with his life. His son recalled:

> He was in the water for two days, floating on a wooden bulkhead door. He only survived because he was from the Highlands, couldn't stand any temperature hotter than Edinburgh's. He used to sneak up on deck to sleep at

night. That's why he was saved, he was on deck when the U-boat struck. He was picked up after two days by a corvette, or an escort ship, and taken to the nearest naval base—Simonstown in South Africa! When he got there, he was threatened with being put on a charge, improperly dressed. By the time that was all sorted out, the regiment had already left for India. He spent two months in South Africa, then was seconded to the Royal West African Frontier Force.[100]

There was, it seems, some special concern for the morale of the Imperials. Col. T. R. Price was especially troubled that his noncommissioned officers were suffering in "this outpost of the Empire." He penned an emotional appeal to the British Press for donations of various sports gear. "We have no funds here," he wrote, "many of the men are scattered in small numbers in lonely 'bush' stations. They have no canteens or institutes and they feel keenly the disappointment of not being in the fight. For these reasons it is essential to provide them with bodily and mental exercise after their day's work. Money is no use to us, as there is nothing we can purchase."[101] Price's NCOs must have been professionals at wringing sympathy out of their officers, for most British veterans of the RWAFF, like Monty Norman, were generally content with their situation, feeling that they would enjoy the respite from battle as long as it continued. The Gold Coast in that period may not have offered a luxurious life, but it was far from being a penal colony.

A new sense of urgency seems to have taken hold of the Gold Coast by the spring of 1941. In June, Giffard reported that only 13 percent of his African troops were what he considered combat trained, despite many having had more than a year's service.[102] Indeed, in that month, the government stopped relying entirely on volunteers and those "volunteered" by their chiefs, and it passed the Gold Coast Compulsory Service Bill, which was to be invoked if voluntary recruiting faltered. It followed the lines and procedures of the British Conscription Act, and provided for the drafting of noncombatants for defense work as well as for the Gold Coast Regiment itself. Interestingly, it also contained a provision for conscientious objection, although the editor of West Africa felt this would never be invoked since it was "not an African institution."[103] He was, in a sense, right. One can scarcely imagine an Asante farmer, mobilized for the invasion of the Gold Coast Colony in 1873, informing Asantehene Kofi Kakari that he was a conscientious objector! Be that as it may, when the bill was presented to the Legislative Council of the Gold Coast Colony, no overt opposition was voiced to conscription. Nevertheless, it was noted in a high-level intelligence report that the speeches of certain African members displayed "a tendency to use the passing of the Bill to strengthen the native claim to a greater share in the administration of the Colony."[104] Such audacity! Whatever the case, the combination of volunteers and conscripts added up to the enlistment of twenty thousand recruits in 1941. They were drawn from all over the Gold Coast including, no doubt, a fair contingent of men who had slipped across the borders from northern Côte d'Ivoire to join the British forces.[105]

There was one other somewhat controversial aspect to recruiting, but it related to the recruitment of officers. In late 1940 the possibility of raising Africans to the heady ranks of the officer corps was entertained. The weekly magazine *West Africa,* hardly a radical civil rights publication, continually called for the recruitment and training of qualified Gold Coasters. Its editorials on this subject created a stir. The Gold Coast Government challenged the journal's assumption that there were no African officers in the regiment, and obliged the editor to issue a correction. "On the point, of officering African units with Africans as far as possible, an official of the Gold Coast Government has been able to correct a report which stated that there is no such officering, with the information that two Africans had been offered and had accepted commissions. Two is not an impressive number, in a country with over three million population, but it shows adoption of the right principle (which is not, of course, that a man should be commissioned in any of the Defence Forces *because* he is an African, but that he should not be excluded because he is an African—two widely different positions)."[106] Unfortunately the two were not named by *West Africa.* Killingray has pointed out that there were indeed two Africans on an Officer Cadet Training Unit (OCTU) in the Gold Coast in late 1940. Giffard rejected one, probably H. R. George, grandson of the chief of Anyako, but had the other proceed to an OCTU in Britain. This was Seth Anthony, who received an emergency King's Commission in April 1942.[107]

THE HOME GUARD

In the Gold Coast, recruitment for the Royal West African Frontier Force proceeded apace. It was highly successful, as always, in the Northern Territories, but less so in the Colony and Asante.[108] All parts of the Gold Coast, however, displayed great enthusiasm when a new line of civil defense was created. The Home Guard was inaugurated on 29 December 1940. Although officially modeled on its British counterpart, immortalized in the BBC's *Dad's Army,* the Gold Coast Home Guard was, of necessity, to be far smaller. It would also possess very little serious firepower. While theoretically its main goal was to defend the Gold Coast in case of invasion, in practice the Home Guard functioned more effectively to inspire loyalty, instill general vigilance in the population, and secure the involvement in the war effort of leading local dignitaries—teachers, businessmen, lawyers, chiefs, and the like.

The Home Guard appealed to men's patriotism as well as to their sense of adventure. In a broadcast on Gold Coast radio, the first African to have been appointed a Crown Counsel, barrister E. C. Quist, addressed his "fellow Africans" about the Home Guard:

> I need not tell you that by the establishment of a Home Guard in the Gold Coast Colony we have been afforded a grand opportunity of taking our part in the Empire War Effort and of helping to defend our Home Country, should it be necessary. You have all heard the news of Hitler's defeat of France, and that now, he is held up thinking and trying how to invade England. No doubt he is looking for what he can do next.
>
> His Excellency the Governor in his recruiting speech at the Adjabeng Lodge stated that Hitler at the moment was like the cornered Bush Cow which sought to break through the weakest link in the circle of hunters and that it was at least possible that he might try to break through in Morocco and from there attack the Gold Coast and other parts of West Africa. . . . To be ready for any eventuality is the primary reason for the establishment of the Gold Coast Home Guard. . . . Now let us all who are able bodied go to it and become Members of the Gold Coast Home Guard.[109]

There was, not surprisingly, an abundance of able-bodied volunteers!

From the Gold Coast Government's point of view, the Home Guard had two advantages. First, its costs were minimal, since the men were to be unpaid and were even expected to provide their own uniforms. Second, the Home Guard offered its recruits the opportunity of prominently displaying their enthusiasm for the war effort, while at the same time satisfying their bellicose tendencies in relative safety. Companies were organized in Accra, Bekwai, Bibiani, Cape Coast, Ejura, Koforidua, Kumasi, Mampon, Takoradi, Tarkwa and Abosso, Wiawso, and elsewhere, and all members given military rank. The original intention had been to create separate units for Africans and Europeans. This segregationist policy was soon scrapped, since it was only in a few areas that the local white population was sufficiently numerous. Depending on location, some units were all-African except for the officers, some all-European, and some mixed.

In Bekwai, a series of weekly lectures were held to promote the Home Guard.

By the end of March 1941, twenty-six men had volunteered and many others were expected to join once the company was officially formed. The only problem foreseen by the acting district commissioner there was the requirement the government had set, that all African volunteers be at least forty years old. One can only surmise that this minimum age was imposed by officials in Accra still nervous about arming and training younger Africans in modern military techniques. Bekwai's acting DC thought that this age barrier should be dropped. "I have considered the situation carefully and have come to the conclusion that it would be quite useless to form a Home Guard for Bekwai confined to people of say over forty. There are not more than a dozen intelligent and physically fit Africans of that age to my knowledge in the town. If it is desired to form a Home Guard Unit in the town, it could only be recruited from the intelligent and comparatively young members of the community employed by Government, Mission Schools and Firms."[110] Leaving aside this official's qualifications to judge others' intelligence, his point about the necessity of having fit men in the Home Guard is well taken, particularly since members were to be deployed in action should an invasion of the Gold Coast occur. In any case, no more was heard about a middle-aged Home Guard.

If the Asante had been reluctant to join the army, they eagerly signed up for the Home Guard. "The British Government had our full support," said the journalist K. Attakora. Gyimah, who had a much higher regard for the martial qualities of the Asante than had Lt. Col. Ponting: "Mostly the Asantes joined the army—more than any other group. The Asantes loved fighting. The Asantehene was in the Home Guard. He was the chief of the Home Guard for Kumasi. Because of that, almost all the chiefs joined the Home Guard. Everybody, all the chiefs."[111] One of the earliest Asante recruits was T. E. Kyei of Agogo, author and ethnographer but at the time a teacher in Kumasi. He joined soon after the declaration of war. His unit consisted of some thirty men: storekeepers, clerks, and teachers. In 1994 he recollected:

> We were informed of what was happening. They asked for conscripts to serve in the army. Many went in. There were some of us [i.e., certain professions] who could not join. Teachers could not. Some few did, but those who were left [at home] were asked to form a Home Guard. We had zones something like the areas today they have for polling. Kumasi was not so big then. We had quarters. The Asantehene was the Colonel in Chief of the Home Guard.
>
> Then, 1939–1940, we had Europeans—sort of officers. Each zone had a commandant. I enlisted as a soldier in the West African Home Guard. Pvt.

T. E. Kyei. No, no uniforms. Then, we had every evening, we had practice. I remember the UAC manager,[112] Mr. Backhouse, an Englishman. After school we had to go and practice. We would have some drill, drilling, to make us strong. We were warned we were faced with danger—the German Luftwaffe might bomb us.[113]

The Asantehene, Sir Osei Agyeman Prempeh II, was in fact appointed lieutenant colonel and zone commander in July 1942. This, if anything, set the final seal of approval on the Kumasi Home Guard. One of the Asantehene's senior *akyeame*, or "linguists," had already joined the Home Guard. This was Baafour Osei Akoto, who wrote of his experiences: "During the World War II in 1939, I was enlisted into the Home Guard Service. The then Colonial Government, expecting war in Africa beefed up our training schedule to make us combat ready for any possible German invasion in the Gold Coast. We used to report for daily training in the afternoon from 4:00 P.M. and 9:00 to 4:00 P.M. on Sundays. During the service time I rose through the ranks from Private to a Sergeant and retired as a Captain when the war was over."[114]

In 1994 former district commissioner R. J. Moxon (and the renowned "white chief" of Kitase in Aburi), talked about the early war period. I had spoken to him of the Gold Coast's vulnerability to attack, and of there being nothing to defend it at this time. He was quite offended and responded: "Not quite nothing. There was Captain Moxon of the Accra Home Guard. I was the captain of one company; Nii Amaa Ollennu, later a judge, of the other. We protected the Weija waterworks, the power station, electricity plant, and the post office. We had a very distinguished company. There was Pvt. A. G. Leventis, the Greek-Cypriot millionaire; there was the district mayor. Also, I remember Archie Casely-Hayford getting arrested. I had him arrested. He'd put his rifle up against the wall while he went around the corner. 'Under arrest!'"[115] Ollennu, later to be a justice of the Ghana Supreme Court, had just returned from London, where he had been called to the Bar of the Inner Temple. Leventis was a prominent businessman in Accra. District Magistrate Archie Casely-Hayford was the son of the famous Fante lawyer and Gold Coast politician J. E. Casely-Hayford and had been called to the bar after attending Dulwich College, London, and Clare College, Cambridge.

"Just about everyone" (who was anyone in Accra, Moxon implied), was in the Home Guard. They were drilled by one or two ex-sergeant majors and used Italian rifles captured in East Africa. Moxon recollected the strange case of the Koforidua Home Guard:

Soldiers, Airmen, Spies, and Whisperers

There was the young paramount chief of New Juaben, at Koforidua. He was so enthralled with us that he decided to join himself. He joined as a private. The elders were horrified. They didn't approve of him anyway—he was interested in music and dancing—thoroughly frivolous, they thought. Didn't approve at all. Word reached them that he had been seen, in the dress of a private, in the streets carrying sandbags. I was summoned to the palace. "What did I know about it?" they demanded to know. I didn't know anything. But I started to talk. Told them it was just his enthusiasm. As an Ashanti king he has fighting in his blood—he would be a general. However, we didn't have any vacancies for generals at the time, so I offered to make him a captain. They were delighted. Just think, he would be the same rank as their DC. The next day on parade, he appeared in his captain's kit, with the three pips on his shoulder and his Sam Browne belt. Made all the white subalterns salute him! First time they'd had to salute an African![116]

Private Kyei, the Asante, and Captain Moxon, the Englishman, were both members of what were so often described as warrior races. They did, however, have rather different attitudes toward the prospect of combat. "We were to prevent fires," said Kyei, whose unit was apparently not issued with arms:

We were told, warned that we were not soldiers. The Germans are not here—not coming here. They are coming to bomb. Forget about arms. We were warned, "What are you going to do if an incendiary bomb drops?" "What are we to do if a bomb comes." [There were] no lights. Blackout. Part of our duty as the Home Guard was to ensure a complete blackout. If we saw any sign of light, we would knock on the door and point it out. Tell them to put up some cloth and at the same time we had to hold ourselves in readiness [for any bombing]. We were told if an alarm sounded, an alarm from the Post Office, if the planes are coming, they will give an alarm. It was part of our training.[117]

Those in the Kumasi Home Guard, presumably due to the lack of arms, were not at all disappointed at the nonappearance of either the Germans or the Vichy French in the Gold Coast. "No," Kyei continued, "who wants to die? They told us about the incendiaries. You were at risk. Who wants to die? We always prayed that they didn't come. Once in a while they would give an alarm, but you were warned it was coming."[118]

Moxon's attitude toward the danger of an invasion was more cavalier. No one was worried about Vichy attacking, he claimed,

We were hoping they might—we were ready for them. You know, [Asante-hene] Prempeh II was in the Home Guard in Kumasi, he was a colonel. It was all a great thing. It was about the only place where we could mix. Social mixing in those days was impossible—the memsahibs, you know. A lot of them had come from India, and no mixing was conceivable. So, the Home Guard made it possible. A husband would come home at two or three in the morning, quite drunk. The wife would ask where he'd been. Reply: the Home Guard Institute. No further questions. They said they'd been helping the war effort.[119]

Fortunately for all concerned—whether a Kyei, who did not want to die, or a Moxon, who rather relished a fight—none of the Home Guard units in the Gold Coast was ever required to defend its soil of Ghana. It would be nice to think that the enemy had got wind of the resistance they might meet from the Home Guard, but, in all truth, it is quite likely that they knew nothing of it.

Not all units were as jolly as Moxon's. In Mampon, the failure of Acting District Commissioner P. J. H. Hornsby to join the Home Guard as was expected of him, plus his demands that its rifles and ammunition be removed from his office, provoked a storm. Heated letters over the issue flew among Hornsby; the commissioner of the Gold Coast Police, E. C. Nottingham; the chief commissioner Ashanti, E. G. Hawkesworth; and the Home Guard Organizer, Zone D, K. M. Vaughan. The atmosphere became so tense that a decision was finally made to disband the Mampon unit in 1943, although the chief commissioner's office felt it would "set a poor example to other places."[120]

Elsewhere the burning issue was the government's policy of insisting that members of the Home Guard supply their own uniforms. These consisted of khaki helmets, trousers, and shirt, a leather belt, puttees or gaiters, a Home Guard armband, and boots.[121] The costs, modest as they were by European standards, effectively served to exclude the vast majority of Africans, and all but assured that only the salaried classes and successful private entrepreneurs would join. It was the necessity of providing boots that provoked the most resentment. In June 1942 the *Ashanti Pioneer* published a stinging condemnation of the government's "buy your own" policy in a letter from a Home Guard member:

> The Home Guard training, unlike that of the local Boy Scout movement, is a vigorous one and a half hour's work sometimes in bushy places and on thorny grounds for practice. A complaint has been lodged with Platoon Commanders who in turn, have put it before the officers concerned, but the incessant complaints have not been seen to in any form.

Soldiers, Airmen, Spies, and Whisperers

I had only two pairs of shoes, one for business and the other for church. I had sacrificed the business shoes for drill and other practices; it now remains the other one to be used if I wish to continue: but seeing that my salary was 7/- a week I found that the purchase of a new one in a short time was impossible, and I was therefore compelled under the circumstances, to tender in my resignation.[122]

This created enough of a stir for the colonial secretary in Accra himself to become involved. Although the army was unable to issue the boots directly, the Home Guard was given the funds to establish a "shoe allowance" of 15/- per year to all members who attended 75 percent of the parades. "It is hoped," he wrote, "that this measure will overcome the difficulties which have been brought to notice."[123]

Boots and uniforms were not the only assistance requested from the government by Home Guard members. One Bekwai man informed the DC that he had been "seriously attached [sic] by a disease called 'genorrhea' since 1929." Having been treated unsuccessfully by twenty "Native Doctors" who had given him thirty-eight injections, he felt it was time to seek European medical assistance, and petitioned the DC accordingly.[124] Regrettably, we do not know how the official responded to this long-suffering individual.

By 1942 the strength of the Gold Coast Home Guard had reached twenty-three hundred men.[125] Whether or not the collective experience of such a considerable body of men brought them any lasting benefits is incalculable. One thing is certain, however. The Home Guard, stretching from the Atlantic Coast to the furthermost frontiers in the north, was the first civil organization to encompass the whole of what would become the Republic of Ghana. It is arguable that, in its distinctive way, the Home Guard contributed to the early development, among the peoples of the Colony of the Gold Coast, the Colony of Asante, and the Protectorate of the Northern Territories, of a sense of common interest transcending local ethnic identities.

INVASION AND COUNTER-INVASION: FEARS

Mid-1941 was obviously a period of heightened concern about the security of the British West African colonies, and their allies, the Free French Federation of Equatorial Africa. In April, Giffard had met with Generals de Gaulle and de Larminat to discuss a possible German threat to Chad that would in effect sever the Western

Reinforcement Route. His report reached the Foreign Office, where it was given careful consideration. "We have for some time been disturbed," Counselor W. H. Mack wrote to Col. L. C. Hollis at the War Cabinet, "by the danger of a German thrust southwards from Libya aimed at cutting the Takoradi-Khartoum air route; and with mechanized transport and troop-carrying aircraft at their disposal, it seems possible that the Germans may be able to launch an attack even before the end of the hot season. If the Chiefs of Staff confirm that the German threat is serious, it is, we should think, essential to supplement as soon as possible the present quite inadequate supply of anti-aircraft and anti-tank guns and aircraft in the Chad Territory."[126] This information, along with other recent reports from sources in Switzerland that Vichy was planning action against de Gaulle strongholds, came before the Joint Intelligence Subcommittee of the War Cabinet. They had to consider all possible targets. In a report circulated to the Chiefs of Staff, the subcommittee concluded that any attack on Fort Lamy across the Sahara from the north was unlikely until at least October, given the climatic combination of the hot desert summer and the rainy season in full spate throughout French Equatorial Africa. Fort Lamy had the additional advantage of being defended by six thousand Free French tirailleurs against an estimated four thousand Vichy tirailleurs. With Pétain and Boisson committed above all to the defense of Dakar, it was felt that virtually no air power would be available either to transport supplies and men to a Chad offensive, or to participate in any concentrated bombing of the AEF's towns and cities. Seaborne landings at the ports of Douala in Cameroon or Libreville in Gabon, were seen as far more feasible, given that Vichy probably had a surfeit of warships in Dakar. Should any such invasions take place, London admitted that they would be extremely difficult to counter, given first the paucity of military resources in British West Africa, and second the unwillingness to commit these to any defense of Gaullist territory. "We consider," the report of the Intelligence Subcommittee concluded, "that the greatest danger at present is of a sea-borne expedition to capture Duala, the administrative centre of the Cameroons. Unless early warnings were received, and the expedition intercepted at sea by us, such an operation might well succeed, and in that event the situation would be difficult for the Free French to restore without our assistance from Nigeria."[127]

It is difficult not to discern from the subcommittee's report the reluctance of the War Cabinet to provide any such "assistance from Nigeria." It must, therefore, have come as a great relief when the next day a report arrived from Washington. Robert Murphy, Roosevelt's envoy to Vichy, had met with Boisson, the

AOF governor-general, and also with General Weygand, commander of Vichy forces in Africa. The United States, still of course neutral, and continuing to trade with Vichy, was concerned to secure a promise from the two Vichy officials that any supplies of fuel delivered by American tankers to Dakar would not be used in offensive military operations. Weygand, Murphy reported, had categorically assured him that any attack on the Free French Colonies would be impossible before 1 September; that, in any case, he had no intention of ordering any such attack; and that if he did so, the majority of his officers would not obey. By 20 June 1941, however, further information had been received in London that an attack on Fort Lamy was indeed being prepared. The communication was accompanied by a Free French proposal to create diversions by minor operations against Côte d'Ivoire, Togo, and Dahomey, in the AOF.[128] In addition, Robert Parr, the British representative in Brazzaville, in the AEF, requested permission to allow de Gaulle's troops to position themselves along the frontiers of adjacent British territories in order to counter any such invasions from Vichy territory.[129] The reaction of the Chiefs of Staff was immediate and decisive. They were basically opposed to using any British troops in support of Free French operations, whether in the AOF or the AEF. This, they justified on the grounds that "(1) unlike Syria, there is no strategic reason for such operations, (2) British territories would be exposed to air attack with inadequate defences, and (3) we have no troops to back up the proposed Free French operations."[130]

There were, however, those who urged a quite different policy on the War Cabinet. One such was W. H. Grey. He had arrived in the Gold Coast in 1906 to take a post with Lagos Stores, but rapidly accepted a position as supervising agent for the famous trading company F. and A. Swanzy. His major commercial innovation was the importation of the first Ford light trucks in 1913, a venture that Sir Hugh Clifford, governor of the Gold Coast, characterized as having "wrought what amounts to a veritable revolution in the transport of the Gold Coast."[131] He served as an unofficial member of the Legislative Council of the Gold Coast from 1906 to 1918, although he was not physically present in that colony from 1915, when he was commissioned into the Royal Engineers. He served with them in Mesopotamia and attained the rank of major general by the end of the war. He returned to the Gold Coast as a director of Swanzy and Miller.[132] It was this distinguished businessman and soldier who emerged from his retirement to address a bellicose letter to Lord Hankey, chancellor of the Duchy of Lancaster and member of the War Cabinet on 16 May 1941. Claiming a knowledge of French West African affairs "extending over forty years," he wrote: "It would be an easy matter to make the natives in Dahomey, Ivory Coast, Haute Volta, and part of the French Sudan, rebellious against the French. It would only be necessary to send in agitators from Nigeria to Dahomey, and Gold Coast to the Ivory Coast, and let the Chiefs know they could get arms from our side, and I am sure they would give the French a lot of trouble. Actually, the natives in the Ivory Coast were fighting with the French up to 1914, and many of the Ivory Coast natives are akin to some of the Gold Coast tribes." Grey pressed his case a little further: "The French, years ago, cleared places for aeroplane emergency landings, all through Senegal, Ivory Coast, Haute Volta district, but those landings would not be much use if the local natives had arms."[133]

In June the Vichy administration in Togo and Dahomey went on full alert. They were presumably unaware of the Chiefs' of Staff opposition to any invasion of the AOF, and were quite oblivious to General Grey's plans for arming the "natives." They were, however, apparently expecting an imminent attack from either Nigeria or the Gold Coast, or both. British intelligence bulletins attested to the "panic" in Dahomey, and reported that two trains had been kept at the railway station in Porto Novo for several weeks, ready to evacuate French women and children to the interior when the invasion came.[134] General mobilization of African and European reservists occurred on 11 June, and Dahomey's endangered frontiers were sealed insofar as that was possible. Although the Europeans were stood down after several days, the frenzy of the administration's preparations had quite an effect upon the African population of Porto Novo, with rumors crediting Nigeria with an army of no fewer than seventy-five thousand men![135] In Togo, where a similar mobilization had taken place, African informants reported on "hysterical wives following tearful husbands to barracks."[136]

Meanwhile, back in Dakar, the SS *Scheherazade* duly docked with petroleum supplies from the United States, but these proved to be far less than reported, comprising only two thousand tons of low-grade gasoline, and kerosene, and lubricating oil suitable mainly for commercial purposes. With an almost audible sigh of relief, London concluded that "none of the material can be used by aircraft or motor vessels, and the petrol is also quite unsuitable for use in tanks."[137]

The Free French, not surprisingly, were unconvinced that Vichy had no immediate plans to take back the AEF. They continued to harass London with further reports of reinforcements of men and vehicles being sent to Dakar from North Africa, insisting that these formed part of the preparations for attacks on the AEF. London and Washington, demonstrating a seemingly unflinching belief in the veracity of Vichy officials, continued to disagree, stressing the low level of air power available to the French throughout West Africa. In October, Lord Halifax, foreign secretary and member of the War Cabinet, laid down what he obviously intended to be the last word. "Pro-Ally French officials secretly state that movement of equipment to Dakar has been engineered in order to get it away from German hands and point out in defence of this argument that a British or American landing at Casablanca or any point in Morocco would have the effect of outflanking and isolating Dakar from the Germans, even if they suddenly occupied it with air troops, rendering it useless to them. These French sources insist that the movement is to strengthen the French forces' morale by getting them out of the desert."[138] One must have sympathy with poor Parr in Brazzaville, who was charged with reporting this "good news" to General de Laminet and René Pleven.

In the Gold Coast, the comforting assurances given Murphy by General Weygand were not taken completely at face value. At long last, the defense of the colony was becoming a primary concern. In addition to the Compulsory Service Bill, the Colonial Office began to draw up a series of defensive measures against invasion. These have been succinctly described by David Killingray: "In June 1941 the Colonial Office asked West African governments to prepare 'denial' schemes. 'Scorched earth' policies were worked out in the four colonies although the War Council thought it inadvisable that Africans should know about these plans which entailed the total destruction of the gold mines and the demobilizing of the manganese mines at Nsuta. The formation of guerrilla bands in the Northern Territories was also discussed, but not proceeded with."[139] An Air Raid Warning System was set up first on the southwestern frontier guarding the approaches to Takoradi. In early August 1941 it was decided to extend it throughout the colony, with military observer posts to be set up in Kumasi, Kintampo, and Tamale. African plane spotters were ordered to report all aircraft movements immediately to Area HQ, West African Force, by telephone or radio. The use of code was dispensed with, presumably because any intercepted messages would be of no aid and comfort to the enemy, who already knew where their planes were![140]

Brig. F. A. S. Clarke, commander of the Gold Coast Area, prepared weekly reports for military headquarters at Achimota titled, "Appreciation of the Situation as It Appears to Comd. Gold Coast Area on. . . ." In these, Clarke evaluated which routes and which targets throughout the colony would be most at risk from any French overland, seaborne, and air attacks. Despite the existing wisdom that low morale and inadequate supplies would most probably keep the "enemy" —that is, Vichy in the AOF—from any large-scale action at that time, he drew up contingency plans to counter any invasion forces.[141] Underpinning the entire plan was the need to maintain the Western Reinforcement Route. Thus, Clarke wrote, "the retention of Takoradi is vital and its defence to the last man and the last round must always be regarded as the ultimate operation if it is impossible to stop and defeat the enemy further North and East."[142]

To this end, all available anti-aircraft and coastal defense artillery was concentrated at Takoradi harbor. Nevertheless, although the most "vital" installation in the Gold Coast, Clarke would not entertain the idea of stationing large numbers of troops around the port, on the grounds that "to close the bulk of our forces around Takoradi would be to lose such initiative as we possess, forfeit the power of manouevre and allow the enemy to advance through difficult country unimpeded. The garrison at the outset must therefore be kept to the minimum." And minimal it was. Takoradi's defense was to be in the hands of one section of the 197 Heavy Anti-Aircraft Battery, one troop of the 71 Light Anti-Aircraft Battery, First and Second Companies of the 5 GCR (to be relieved by 7 GCR in early May), and one platoon of European Voluntary Reservists. The Third Company of 5 GCR was "prepared to hold position already dug astride rd.[road] Newtown —Axim—Takoradi at R. Ankobra Ferry."[143]

Using such intelligence as it had on the Vichy Order of Battle, and the approximate strength and actual locations of the Tirailleurs Sénégalais, headquarters staff in Achimota drew up defense plans for the whole colony. In his "Appreciation of the Situation" of 11 April 1941, Brigadier Clarke summed up the geography of the situation: "as the land frontiers of the Gold Coast are entirely surrounded by their territory, the French, or hostile elements in their colonies, can invade from three sides. At present invasion from the North or West is the most likely course as the tps.[troops] in Togoland and Dahomey are of inferior quality and these territories are open to a counter-offensive from Nigeria."[144] Thus the Gold Coast Regiment was to prepare itself for a possible land attack coming across any of the colony's eastern, western, or northern borders, although it was generally felt that the most likely route of invasion would be from the west or north. Three reasonably good roads from Ouagadougou in Haute Côte d'Ivoire entered the Northern Territories near Tumu, Navrongo, and Bawku, and all converged at Tamale, from where a decent road (in the dry season) continued on to Kumasi. Detailed defense plans were drawn up to meet any possible invasion. District commissioners were issued the following instructions: "It will be necessary to stifle the activity of fifth columnists—amateur or otherwise—and to take steps against persons spreading alarmist rumours. The closest co-operation with military commanders in this respect is vital."[145]

Soldiers, Airmen, Spies, and Whisperers

By 21 July 1941 a complete demolition scheme was drawn up and distributed to military commanders throughout the Gold Coast. It was to be put into effect, "without delay," as soon as an invasion began. Responsibility for ordering and carrying out demolition was assigned by area. Selected units were to block the roads to any invading forces, to destroy bridges, ferries, drifts, embankments, and to fell trees and block certain narrow passes in order to halt the enemy at certain points along the projected invasion routes. Detailed surveys were made of each of forty targets. In each case the method of demolition was suggested, the amount and type of explosives needed, and an estimate made of how long the work would take. The tenth target, for example, was the important Yeji ferry on the main northern road between Tamale and Kumasi: "All steel pontoon; approx dimensions 75 feet x 25 feet. Estimated weight 60 tons. Not possible to remove from present site." The proposed action was: "Cut steel members of pontoon to submerge pontoon. Cut steel cables." The time and explosives required were: "1 sub-section; 2 hrs. 22 lbs. G.C.," and the responsibility for ordering demolition was placed on "Rear Guard Comd." To take another example, the fortieth and last target was the bridge over the River Bonsa on the road between Dixcove and Tarkwa: "Six 36 feet span bridge [i.e., six spans of 36 feet]. Six inch concrete deck on 6 R.S.J.s (22 feet x 7 feet). Water 200 feet wide." The proposed action was: "Cut 3 spans. Crater southern abutment. (Abutment to be prepared previously)." In this case the time and explosives required were estimated at "16 man. 200 lbs. G.C., and 350 lbs. Ammonal," and Fortress HQ at Takoradi was to issue the demolition order.[146]

A personal perspective on the demolition scheme was provided many years later by Sergeant McCaskie, whom we met earlier. It was during his posting at the War Depot in Kumasi that he learned that demolition sealed plans existed, that were only to be opened in the event of an invasion of the Gold Coast. His son remembered him saying,

When all the danger had passed the plans were opened. They contained detailed instructions about destroying all stores. They were not to be blown up, but "dumped" in various ways.... He had great and abiding memories of the sealed orders. They were to be opened if the Germans took Tobruk and crossed the Sahara. Before this there were certain preliminaries. If Tobruk fell, the RWAFF was to step up drilling and skirmishing. And this is what he [my father] remembered most.... There was also a huge list in the sealed orders—a list as long as the Encyclopaedia Britannica—a list of the order in which all the equipment and matériel that was to be destroyed before the Germans arrived.[147]

These dramatic preparations were given added importance when, in September 1941, intelligence reports were received from Colonel Adam, head of the Free French mission in the Gold Coast, detailing the recent arrival of military reinforcements in the AOF and of their movement eastward. Adam offered three possible explanations, first that an offensive against Nigeria was being prepared, second that the movement was defensive against a possible combined British and Free French action, or third that the situation was being prepared to allow German units to move into Dakar and French Soudan (today Mali), and thence to the coast. He favored the third explanation on the grounds that it followed the tactics of the Vichy authorities in Syria.[148] Reports were also coming in concerning the possibility of an AOF attack on Chad, this posing the danger of a disruption of the Takoradi Ferry route should Fort Lamy fall into Vichy hands. All this made sense, since in August a copy of an order by Colonel Avre, commandant of Vichy troops in Dahomey, had been obtained by British agents. It contained a direct threat to the operations at Takoradi. The British planes en route to Khartoum were to be shot down wherever possible, but German and Italian crews on authorized flights were to be given every facility at Vichy-controlled landing strips.[149]

These reports were followed almost immediately by ones of an unusual buildup of forces at Bobo-Dioulasso, in Haute Côte d'Ivoire, only ninety miles from the Gold Coast frontier. The first indications of this came in October 1941. By early November, the presence of a new force, the Groupe Mobile Coloniale (GMC), had become known to British intelligence. It was headquartered at Bobo-Dioulasso, with two battalions stationed at Ouagadougou, along with various elements of the Eighth Colonial Artillery Regiment. This base controlled all military units in French Soudan, Niger, and Guinea. British intelligence also had it that all Africans with experience of civilian motor transport—that is, drivers and mechanics—were being called up and sent to Bobo-Dioulasso for training. Large numbers of vehicles were being dispatched there. Seeing the GMC as a "mobile striking force that could be deployed in French Guinea, the Ivory Coast, Niger, Dahomey, and Togo in the case of any attack," intelligence analysts at General Headquarters, RWAFF, were particularly concerned by the fact that its commander, Colonel Montangerand, had served in Niger during 1936–37, and was regarded as a pioneer in the use of motor transport in the desert.[150] In the first week of January 1942 it was further learned that the infantry regiment of the GMC, the Porte de Côte d'Ivoire Nord, had been redesignated the Regiment Porte de Tirailleurs Sénégalais. There were also reports of a new battalion being formed at

Ouagadougou.[151] By the end of January, British HQ had learned that the First and Second Battalions of the RPTS at Bobo-Dioulasso and Ouagadougou each comprised between fifteen and sixteen hundred men and that each was under the command of the equivalent of a lieutenant colonel.[152]

The British military authorities in the Gold Coast were alarmed but had no clear picture of what the French were up to. In mid-July, British intelligence had been given somewhat more comforting information from a M. Savornin, head of the main palm oil extraction plant in Ebuinda, Côte d'Ivoire. Savornin, who apparently passed freely to and from Accra on his journeys to the Côte d'Ivoire, told the Free French Mission that the AOF military seemed to have an exaggerated idea of the strength of the British forces in West Africa, and were themselves preparing for an invasion. There was apparently an evacuation scheme to concentrate military and civil personnel around Bouaké, where the staff officers of the Third Brigade had already been relocated. Furthermore, whispers had it that Gov. Hubert Deschamps was watching developments closely and was said to peruse Free French propaganda with interest. Savornin also reported on Governor-General Boisson's visit to the Côte d'Ivoire early in July, and on the numerous arrests of suspected Free French supporters.[153]

Were these developments harbingers of offensive action, or were they defensive? In fact, the activity at Bobo-Dioulasso and Ouagadougou was, in part at least, a response to General Barrau's sense of increased threats to his territory from the British colonies. On 22 December 1941, Barrau had sharply revised his plan for the defense of the Vichy colonies, "in consequence of the worsening threats weighing upon the AOF." All efforts were to be directed, first, toward strengthening the defenses of Senegal and of its vital port, Dakar, which was to be held at all costs, and second, toward protecting the "*grande rocade*," the main route in the interior that linked Bamako, Bobo-Dioulasso, Ouagadougou, and Niamey. Protection of this line "from where," it was said, "the AOF pulls the majority of its resources," was clearly to be the task of the GMC.[154]

As for other seaboard colonies, the Côte d'Ivoire and Togo in particular, these were to be designated a *zone de manoeuvre*, where troops would not be expected to maintain fixed positions, but could, faced with superior forces, make a tactical withdrawal (i.e., a retreat) and prepare a counterattack. Drawing up the details of this plan was to be entrusted to the governor of Niger, Gen. Maurice-Emile Falvy.[155] Before his tenure as governor, Falvy had already established his credentials as a man who would brook no nonsense in the face of military necessity. When certain *évolués* in Senegal, French citizens all, objected to being conscripted into the Tirailleurs Sénégalais rather than the regular French army, Falvy had offered them a choice: conscription or the firing squad. Not surprisingly, they chose the former and were incorporated into the Seventh RTS. Captured in France, Falvy became an outright admirer of the German military, and was soon released from his prisoner-of-war camp and allowed to return to the AOF.[156]

Back in Africa, Falvy had no doubt that the Gold Coast, Sierra Leone, and Nigeria constituted a clear and present danger to the garrisons along the *grande rocade*. Should any attack take place, Falvy wrote in a communication that is somewhat hard to fathom, then "the majority of the forces covering the rocade —may, in maneuvering, retreat until the final line—Principal effort: region Bobo-Ouagadougou—Fada N'Gourma on one side, Bamako-Bougouni on the other. If the colonies of the south are not threatened, the forces that have been maintained there may be pulled to the rear, the flanks of the attack, or by raids in the colonies."[157] In other words, I think, the southern colonies were to be left undefended, and their garrisons pulled back to reinforce the *grande rocade* should the British attack. One British Intelligence report, received from the ubiquitous reliable source, claimed that a confidential circular from the Vichy government had been distributed among AOF officials, containing the orders to

> resist British Invasion for twenty-four hours, and surrender your forces, in case of British attack. Encourage natives to grow more food, such as rice, yam, corn, and if possible teach them how to plant potatoes. Store up your crops of cocoa, coffee, copra, raw cotton, palm and kernel oils. French soldiers to be withdrawn from Anglo-French frontiers when authorized.[158]

General headquarters in Achimota was, like its French counterpart, at this time far more preoccupied about defense than offense. While Giffard and his staff continued to increase the size of the Gold Coast Regiment, and awaited the return of the brigade from East Africa, they needed a constant flow of information about what was happening across the borders. This was becoming beyond the capacity of the army's intelligence-gathering operations, although its secret Weekly Military Reviews continued to be issued. This situation was to be radically changed by the appearance of another player on the scene, namely, the Special Operations Executive, to which we must now turn.

Drum Major Saidu Lagos, Gold Coast Regiment, Accra 1940.
  E. C. Lanning

Capt. E. H. Muldoon, MC, 1
GCR, August 1941, Abyssinia.
E. C. Lanning

First Battalion, Gold Coast Regiment, on parade at Accra, 2 August 1940, before embarking for East Africa. *Left to right:* R. S. M. Troth, Maj. C. F. J. Clifton (acting in command), Capt. P. M. Hughes (adjutant).
E. C. Lanning

Second (Gold Coast) Field Company of mining engineers, on route march in 1939. Lt. F. W. A. Timms *(left)* of the Consolidated African Selection Trust, Capt. C. W. Hooper *(center)* of the West African Diamond Syndicate, with NCOs and men recruited from diamond, gold-mining, and manganese-mining firms.

Brig. H. W. Baldwin

Sgt. Len Church *(top row, left)* and Lt. E. C. Lanning *(top row, right),* with men of D company, Third Battalion, GCR, Teshi Camp, Accra, 2 August 1942.

E. C. Lanning

Third Battalion, GCR, on parade at Winneba, led by Capt. E. M. Harper.
E. C. Lanning

Postcard commemorating
the first meeting of Gen.
Charles de Gaulle and
Félix Eboué, governor of
Chad, 1940.

Left to right: Sir Arnold Hodson, governor of the Gold Coast; Capt. W. D. Ponting; and Brig. C. E. M. Richards, commander, Gold Coast Regiment, reviewing the Gold Coast Regiment on parade, Accra, 2 April 1930.

H. C. Norman

CQMS H. C. Norman at demobilization, 1945.

H. C. Norman

Badge of the Welsh Male Voice
Choir at Takoradi, 1943.
Jack Jones

The Welsh Male Voice Choir of the Air Sea Rescue Section, Takoradi, 1943.
Jack Jones

Prewar official traffic at the frontier: Gold Coast postman exchanging mail with his Togolese counterpart, ca. 1937.
Gold Coast Government

Arrival of the first Imperial Airways flight at Accra airport, August 1937.
Gold Coast Government

"THE WAR WE SHALL WIN."

The Syrian - Lebanese Calling!

A GRAND EVENING DRESS DANCE
IN AID OF WAR CHARITIES.

AT PREMPEH HALL

ON SATURDAY AUGUST 31st 1940

Under the distinguished patronage of his honour

MAJOR H. C. STEVENSON C.M.G. D.S.E. M.C.
(Chief Commissioner of Ashanti.)
and
OTIMFUO SIR OSEI AGYEMAN PREMPEH II. K.B.E.
Asantehene

We are faced with the most atrocious events, ever known in the annals of
English History; yet we can easily over-come them by contributing our quota
however small it may be.

Attend this Dance and show your Patriotism.

MUSIC :- The Famous Accra Rhythmic Orchestra

DANCE STARTS FROM 9 P.M. TO 3 A.M.

M. Cs. *J. Sinclair Esq., E. O. Asafu-Adjaye Esq. B.L. & J. Colling Woode-Williams Esq.*

TICKETS Dancer 7/6 Spectator 2/-
Ladies By Special Invitation

Tickets can be purchased from M. Captan, Kingsway Stores, Bank of British
West Africa, Barclays Bank, K. Chellaram & Sons and Bardawil & Co.

BAR WILL BE OPENED.

6-K 2922

Poster announcing fund-raising event for war charities, Kumasi, 1940.

NAG-Kumasi

Spitfires Fund thermometer, Accra, 1940.

West Africa

3

The Special Operations
Executive in West Africa

THE FRANCK MISSION

ECONOMIC WARFARE AND THE
SPECIAL OPERATIONS EXECUTIVE

The Germans launched the blitzkrieg on 10 May 1940 with the invasion of Belgium and the Netherlands. The War Cabinet met in London late in the afternoon of the same day. Prime Minister Neville Chamberlain, who had—unbelievably, in hindsight—remained in office after the invasion of Poland in September 1939, and throughout the seven months of "phoney war," announced that he would tender his resignation to King George VI that evening. The foreign secretary, Lord Halifax, had already expressed his reluctance to assume the premiership, being a member of the House of Lords. Chamberlain, therefore, suggested to the king that Winston Churchill be asked to form a new government. Summoned immediately to the palace, Churchill eagerly accepted, and announced that he would form a national government and a war cabinet of five or six ministers.[1]

Hugh Dalton, Labour Party MP for Bishop Auckland, who had been acting as something like a shadow minister for economic warfare, set his sights on taking over that ministry from Ronald Cross. It was, as Dalton pointed out, a position that combined his interest in foreign policy with that in economics.[2] Churchill offered him the ministry on 14 May 1940 and he began work the next day. Dalton's conception of the role of the Ministry of Economic Warfare (MEW) was that it should create social unrest in the Axis countries and the occupied territories by cutting off the supply of commodities vital not only to the military but to the populace at large. To this end, three principal operational areas were identified: the blockading of supply lines, the destruction of production facilities such as factories and refineries, and the pressuring of neutral governments to limit trade with the Axis powers.[3] There were those in government, and particularly in the Foreign Office, who recommended caution. France was the main issue. Vichy France should be treated as a neutral country, they argued, and some sort of continuing relationship should be maintained with Pétain. Dalton opposed this view and carried the day.

On 25 June 1940 the Cabinet agreed to the blockade of both the occupied and unoccupied zones of France. The decision was of immediate relevance to West Africa, where, despite severe limitations in shipping capacity, the French colonies were able to continue exporting coffee, cocoa, rubber, groundnuts, and timber to North Africa, France, Germany, and indeed, to the still neutral United States. The real danger, in Dalton's eyes, was not simply that the defeated French could continue enjoying luxuries quickly disappearing from the shelves of British shops, but that these products would significantly aid the German war effort. Indeed, MEW already reckoned that four-fifths of French West Africa's exports were ending up in Germany.[4] Nevertheless, the idea of a naval blockade of French West Africa continued to meet opposition from both the Admiralty and the Foreign Office. For the navy it was more a question of strategy than an argument over the importance of French West Africa; they were incensed that some new upstart civil ministry should presume to order deployment of the Senior Service! The Foreign Office, for different reasons, also objected vigorously to the idea of a blockade. They feared such action would only increase the likelihood of land operations being undertaken against the British colonies in Africa.

The replacement of Halifax by Anthony Eden as foreign secretary in December 1940 turned the tide in Dalton's favor. Showing extraordinary foresight, considering how insecure Charles de Gaulle's future must have seemed in late 1940, and how dark the existing military situation was, Eden believed that a blockade was crucial. Whatever the inherent strategic dangers were, he argued, in the long run Britain would find it in its interest to have supported de Gaulle by making life as difficult as possible for the Vichy regime. Thus both the admirals and the mandarins in the Foreign Office were overruled, although the blockade was to prove ineffective for many months.[5]

Dalton was greatly to enlarge his power base and that of MEW by snatching control of the newly created Special Operations Executive (SOE) from what had seemed its natural habitat, the British Secret Service, that is, the Special Intelligence Service, or MI 6, headed by "C," Col. Stewart Menzies. The story of the various clandestine groups that were brought together into the SOE is outside the scope of this work, and has been extensively dealt with by M. R. D. Foot.[6] Ironically, Neville Chamberlain in his new capacity as Lord President of the Council, and a member of the War Cabinet, drew up the documents that brought the SOE into existence. He recommended that, on the prime minister's authority, "a new organization shall be established forthwith to coordinate all action, by way of subversion and sabotage, against the enemy overseas."[7] The War Cabinet endorsed what was to become regarded as the charter of the SOE on 22 July 1940. The SOE was not to be under the jurisdiction of Parliament, but responsible to the prime minister through Dalton at MEW. Its very existence was to remain top secret. It was, as Churchill succinctly put it, to engage in "ungentlemanly warfare."[8] The development was not one popular with Menzies. Indeed the core of the new organization consisted of the older Section D, which had been part of the SIS.[9]

Dalton's first appointment to the SOE was that of Sir Frank Nelson, who took the code name CD. He was a product of Bedford Grammar School and Heidelberg University, had served in the Bombay Light Horse in World War I, and then became chairman of the Bombay Chamber of Commerce. He served as Conservative MP for Stroud from 1924 to 1931, and had recently obtained experience of intelligence work as a British Consul in Basel.[10] Sir Charles Hambro was appointed Nelson's second in command. He was an old Etonian, a merchant banker, and a director of the Bank of England. Nelson and Hambro were in charge of the operational side of the SOE. Gladwyn Jebb, another old Etonian, was brought in from the Foreign Office as chief executive officer. Under the overarching control of MEW, Nelson and Jebb formed three sections of the SOE: SO 1, concerned with propaganda; SO 2, with conducting sabotage as well as other subversive activities; and SO 3, for overall administration.[11] At the War Office's insistence, Brigadier Willie van Cutsem took over SO 3 and, in Foot's words, "at once proceeded to strangle his sub-department in festoons of paper."[12] In January 1941, SO 3 lost its separate identity and was merged with SO 2. In August of the same year, SO 1 was split off to form the nucleus of a new organization, the Political Warfare Executive.[13]

Immediately after the formation of the SOE, a scramble for administrative personnel and suitable agents to conduct operations in both German-occupied and neutral territories began. Nelson and Jebb started recruiting. Nelson, in particular, was known to favor men of his own "sort." In casting around for the senior staff, he relied heavily on old-boy connections and preferred dons from Oxford and Cambridge, merchant bankers, lawyers, stockbrokers, and business executives from the City.[14] Clearly, in the SOE's view, while its sphere of operations was to be worldwide, its immediate priority was occupied Europe, and particularly France. Indeed, it was the SOE's concern with both occupied and Vichy France that was to lead it into an involvement with West Africa—one that has been virtually ignored in all existing works on British intelligence, with the exception, however, of several novels.[15] As we have seen, the region's role as a supplier of raw materials to Europe was a matter of grave concern to London. By November 1940, General de Gaulle's only notable success had been the rallying of French Equatorial Africa to the Free French cause, so deciding him to establish his base at Brazzaville. Nevertheless, on this basis, he began a campaign to induce Whitehall to take a more positive role in French West Africa. Some of the general's own admirers doubted the wisdom of this approach. One in particular, Gaston Palewski, was virulently opposed to the proposed policy.[16] He lobbied the Foreign Office and the War Office to help him set up a meeting with the general, whom he hoped to persuade of his folly. He intended to tell de Gaulle, with no respect for racial sensitivities, that "He would have to get away from the idea of a nigger kingdom and repair his damaged military prestige, for example, by a successful action against the Italians. The capture of Gaboon [sic] would be no good."[17] Despite, or perhaps because of Palewski, the debate was instrumental in drawing the SOE increasingly into West African affairs.

EYES ON WEST AFRICA

The British and French in West Africa, so we have seen, had cordially spied on each other in the period between the two world wars. With the outbreak of war, however, such activities were deemed unsporting in the face of the British-French alliance, and were apparently discontinued.[18] After June 1940, and the establishment of the pro-Axis Vichy regime in the AOF, such niceties and civilized methods of information gathering were no longer possible. Events were to move rapidly toward the involvement of an intelligence organization of Churchill's less gentlemanly kind.

The story begins on 4 October, when one Walter Fletcher had a meeting with Maj. Desmond Morton in London. Another old Etonian, Morton, who had long been a confidant of Winston Churchill, joined MEW at the outbreak of war. In May 1940, however, Churchill brought him into his private office and gave him special responsibility for secret service matters.[19] Morton had also been involved in the SIS although its head, Menzies, apparently held him in low esteem.[20] Walter Fletcher was a naturalized Austrian whose family name, Fleischl, had been anglicized. He was associated with a London firm of rubber dealers, Hecht, Levis, and Kahn. He lived, in Foot's words, "on the borderline between honest merchanting and smuggling."[21] Fletcher was later to join the SOE, and to operate very successfully in Japanese-occupied Dutch East Indies, French Indochina, and China,[22] and, in 1945, found his natural element as Conservative MP for Bury. In early October, however, Fletcher was probably unaware of the existence of the SOE. The substance of his talk with Morton has to be reconstructed from the letter Fletcher wrote to him on 5 October. Fletcher had presented Morton with a plan for action toward West Africa in light of the recent debacle in Dakar and the continued uncertainty over whether the Germans would wrest North Africa from Vichy control. His key proposal was to attempt rapidly to swing one of the AOF colonies into the British camp: "I would suggest, as a first move after the preliminary study here and the constitution of a mission, a concentration on French Guinea, using Sierra Leone as a base, at the same time, if it is found impracticable, working from Nigeria towards the main objective, which is A.O.F. via Bamako from either side."

The question of the status of such a mission was carefully considered. Fletcher asked,

> Shall it be an official body, whose activities must necessarily call attention to it, and, therefore, alert the points to be attacked, or an unofficial body which always meets difficulties as regards local government resistance to anything new, and increases the expenditure of time and energy of those concerned? There is, of course, in this case an added complication from the explanation you gave me yesterday.—If this is an official body on a "wooing" expedition to a French Colony, it must come under the De Gaulle regime. That will have definite drawbacks, not omitting the difficulty of maintaining the secrecy so essential to such a project, and may even make working conditions in British Colonies unnecessarily onerous. I believe, therefore, that a compromise should be found in the form of a mission ostensibly going to British West African Colonies for one purpose, such as the Cocoa Investigation Committee some years ago, but in reality for a totally different objective, which would, naturally, be explained to the powers that be.

Fletcher envisaged a situation in which a French colony would somehow secede from Vichy. For this to happen, he argued, it would be essential for them to appreciate the immediate economic benefits of their new status. They were to get a new currency, convertible to sterling and the dollar, as well as rapid access to shipping for imports and exports. "Taking a leaf out of the Italian and German book," the colony would be flooded with propaganda to counteract that of "the considerable number of die-hard pro-Vichy who will do their utmost to wreck or impede the swing-over." Fletcher declared his willingness to lead any such mission.[23]

Morton, who did of course know about the existence of the SOE, passed Fletcher's letter over to Jebb, who in turn brought it to the attention of Nelson ("CD") and others.[24] On 11 October, Nelson himself had a long talk with Fletcher, and thought him, despite his Austrian background, "the type of man with whom I am reasonably certain one can work."[25] As a result of this meeting, considerable changes in the design of the plan were made, most notably in selecting the Gold Coast as the base for the projected "economic" mission. Both Nelson's and Fletcher's accounts of the meeting survive. "I have come round," Fletcher noted, "from the idea of going for Guinee first as it seems to me that after Dakar it is too near what will clearly be the seat of suspicion and activity; the Cote d'Ivoire is the richest prize, is equally good as a political triumph and nearly as good as a jumping off place for AOF from the interior." Fletcher was opposed to sending what he called a "purely 'thug' underground mission," feeling that the best approach to the merchant class lay in convincing them of the "certainty of the economic revival" that would follow the Côte d'Ivoire's abandoning Vichy.[26] Nelson's comments on the interview were contained in a memorandum to Jebb. As he understood it, the plan was now that "a Trade and/or Economic Mission, composed of both British and French, but under a British Chairman, shall proceed to the Gold Coast." It would be impossible, he thought, to camouflage the mission. He felt it should be a small one, under a "tame" chairman of the SOE's choosing, but should also include three or four men of Fletcher's choice, including one "who is in every sense of the word a D. man"—presumably referring to Section D of the SOE.[27]

The truth of the matter was that the SOE had been taken unawares by Fletcher's proposals. The idea of a trade or economic mission was not one of great interest to Nelson, who was far more interested in setting off SO 2, the section of the SOE concerned with subversion, on a more aggressive course of action in West Africa. Cleverly, he pushed Fletcher's plan back to the Ministry of Economic Warfare, where Noel Hall was given charge of it. Hall was Professor of Economics at University College, London, director of the National Institute of Social and Economic Research, and had been co-opted into MEW in an advisory role. This done, Nelson appears to have galvanized SO 2 into producing its own plans for the SOE activities in West Africa. These appeared in a document of 24 October, classified "Most Secret." Of the eight copies of such documents routinely made,

Soldiers, Airmen, Spies, and Whisperers

five were destroyed, one was retained by Nelson, and one went into Jebb's files. The only copy to leave the SOE went to the secretary of state for the colonies, Lord Lloyd, whose cooperation was essential since the SOE's field offices were to be established throughout the British West African colonies. The document sought to initiate, within the charter of the SOE, subversive activities in a region where the British had neither policy nor personnel. This was French West Africa.

The author of the document—probably Nelson himself—offered a general comment on what would be SO 2's policy: "It is to institute a covert organisation in every country in the world whether or not an overt organisation exists. This policy is based on the fact that recently we have learnt from bitter experience in countries in Western Europe, and again in the Balkans, it is unwise to rely solely on official liaison with our Allies, in other words, when official liaison breaks down through failure on the part of such Allies to resist, there should exist a subversive organisation which can carry on unknown to official circles." The writer then turned to West Africa: "Our policy in regard to West Africa is of necessity vague and exists only in theory. We are, however, of the opinion that there should exist some machinery unknown to the de Gaulle movement which can operate, if necessary, should that movement in any way cease to function." The idea, Lloyd was informed, was that SO 2 should establish centers in each of the four British colonies, and from these bases should create cells within the neighboring Vichy territories. SOE personnel would require cover, either as businessmen or colonial administrators. Col. E. H. Grant, who had served as acting commandant of the Gold Coast Regiment, was being considered for appointment as head of the projected operation.[28]

Whether or not Nelson ever seriously considered appointing a regular military officer to so shady a post is not clear. In any event, Grant was shortly to be unavailable to the SOE, being posted to West Africa on unspecified War Office business. Within what can only have been a few days, the SOE selected the man who was to head the mission, a man not of the army, but more typically, from the City. This was Louis Franck; code name—W.

Louis Franck was born into a famous banking family in Belgium in 1908. He arrived in London in 1935 to join the merchant banking firm of Samuel Montagu and Company. Immediately after the declaration of war, Franck gave up his partnership at Montagu, although retaining some token managerial position in the firm. It seems that this bank was a prime hunting ground for recruits to the Ministry of Economic Warfare,[29] and it may be assumed that Franck joined the new ministry.[30] Among his other accomplishments, he was recognized as a top-ranking bullion expert.[31] This, of course, was of great interest to MEW. It was also of great interest to the prime minister. His decision to undertake the disastrous Dakar expedition of September 1940, intended to switch the AOF into the Free French camp, was undoubtedly motivated in part by the knowledge that great quantities of the Bank of France's gold reserves, along with those of Belgium and Poland, had been prudently transferred to Bamako before the military collapse. Accordingly, there is no surprise in learning that Louis Franck was attached to the expedition and in the course of this became well acquainted with General de Gaulle.[32] What may come as a surprise is that, despite the failure of the operation, Franck was able to maintain good relations with de Gaulle.[33] Whether Franck was officially a member of the SOE at the time of the attack on Dakar is unclear, but if not, he was rapidly inducted into that organization on his return and was given the rank of colonel.[34] More than anything else, his acquaintance with de Gaulle undoubtedly suggested to Nelson that Franck would be an ideal candidate to lead the West African mission.

In October, as Franck began laying his plans for a covert mission to West Africa, the irrepressible Walter Fletcher was still vigorously trying to convince Noel Hall of MEW of the virtue of his own ideas for an overt economic mission. Fletcher's activities were of some embarrassment to the SOE, since they threatened to compromise the setting up of Franck's organization. Nelson had an unsatisfactory talk with Lord Lloyd on the matter of the Fletcher scheme on 24 October. Their conversation ranged widely and never got down to the topic in hand. Lloyd promised to let Nelson have his views within a few days. "In the meantime," Nelson wrote to Jebb, "I have been trying to contact Fletcher to keep him quiet, for he is very impatient on what he naturally considers to be the usual Government dilly-dallying."[35] In fact Nelson continued on his devious path to abort Fletcher's economic mission. On 29 October he wrote to Hall, reaffirming that "the scheme now passes into your safe keeping," and informing him that he would appoint one of his, Nelson's, own officers to serve as liaison between them.[36] This turned out to be Horace Emery, who took the code name D/L. To complicate matters for Nelson, Hall invited Lord Hailey to head the economic mission. Hailey's monumental *African Survey* had appeared in 1938 and established him as among Britain's leading experts on the colonies.

On 4 November, the SOE received from Hall a new and revised plan for what was now termed the Economic Mission to Gold Coast, otherwise the Lord Hailey Mission. Although primarily concerned with trade and business, the notion of using it as a cover for intelligence agents was briefly mentioned.[37] At this

Soldiers, Airmen, Spies, and Whisperers

juncture, Nelson decided to use the services of Horace Emery to bring together Walter Fletcher and Louis Franck, confident that the latter's astute mind would find a way around all difficulties. Franck, drawing upon his personal experience with the Dakar expedition, was able to persuade Fletcher to reconsider his proposal, and to resubmit it at some future date. That Fletcher agreed was probably due as much to the hint that he would be asked to join the SOE himself, and so become a real spy, as to Franck's skills of persuasion.[38] In fact, questions of bureaucratic jurisdiction aside, it was generally felt that Fletcher's plans had been overtaken by events in West Africa. Had his economic mission been launched in July, right after the collapse of France, it might well have had an impact but, in the aftermath of Dakar, it had become impractical.[39]

The next day Nelson wrote to Hall to inform him that Fletcher had agreed to hold off. "The chief consideration," he explained, "which seems to have weight with Fletcher (after having heard Franck's views) is that surprising as it is to me, it appears to be a fact that both imports and exports of merchandise are taking place through Dakar, and that any deviation of this through or by the efforts of any kind of a Commission which might arrive out in that territory in the near future would tend to force the Dakar Authorities into action which might be inadvisable from all points of view."[40] Inadvisable was putting it mildly, for it must be remembered that Vichy AOF had tens of thousands of trained troops, at a time when most of the men of the Royal West Africa Frontier Force were in East Africa. Moreover, the AOF, as part of Vichy France, itself remained technically neutral, and there were strong voices, in London and in Washington, opposed to further provocation.

On 13 November, no doubt much to Nelson's dismay, Fletcher took the offensive once again: "I take it that the Prime Minister's determination 'to fight even upon the beaches,' must refer to those of Africa just as much as here, and that this firmness of purpose will not be so diluted in its trickle down through the various departments as to have become unrecognisable as part of the strong spirit which it originally was."[41] Fletcher more or less reiterated his faith in an economic mission, volunteered the services of his firm's office in New York, suggested that he and Horace Emery should travel to West Africa to carry out preliminary work there, commented that a dovetailing of his activities with those of Franck was essential, and ended by proposing a new scheme for using Zanzibar or Mombasa as a base for subverting Vichy control over Madagascar.

Despite Nelson's best efforts to bury the Fletcher scheme, it refused to die. Indeed, it came to the attention of Churchill himself. On 21 November the prime minister made his own assessment: "This is an extremely complex matter which appears to me to be quite outside the competence of SO 2 and more a matter for the DOT [Department of Trade] and MEW. I gather that they require certain intelligence and no doubt, Frank [sic] would supply that provided that it was made quite clear to him what was wanted. Perhaps though I have misunderstood the position."[42] Nelson undoubtedly agreed that Churchill had misunderstood the situation. He was relieved to receive a note from "AD." This was the code name for the Australian George Francis Taylor, who had been recruited early to take over Section D before becoming head of the SOE's Balkan Mission.[43] He had now returned to London. His advice was that nothing should be decided about the Hailey Mission until Franck had arrived in West Africa and reported back on the situation there. Should Franck recommend that some sort of "quite clean and straightforward" economic mission might serve a useful function, it should nevertheless be sent "with the idea of exploiting the legitimate trading activities of the mission for SO2 purposes—under the control of Franck."[44] With Taylor's support, Nelson had finally got the clearance he wanted. The Franck Mission was in business.

THE FRANCK MISSION AND WAGON

Throughout November, Louis Franck worked at breakneck speed on plans for his mission. On the nineteenth, Nelson took him to see Lord Lloyd. Lloyd told CD afterward that he was very impressed with the Belgian. Indeed, he even asked Franck to give him a memorandum on whether or not Bathurst, in the Gambia, should be defended. The Chiefs of Staff thought it should not, while Lloyd naturally regarded it as inalienable imperial territory, to be defended to the last African. In the view of the Colonial Office it was seen as pivotal to communications with the British West African colonies.

Franck drew up the terms of reference for his proposed organization in British West Africa. His intention was to establish sections in the four British colonies that would enable operations to be conducted in the neighboring Vichy colonies. These activities were to include the transmission of propaganda by word of mouth and printed pamphlets, the cultivation of "dissident elements" willing to cooperate with the British, and finally, the designation of specific targets for sabotage in French West Africa "if this should become the policy of the British Government."[45] As Franck saw it, "The policy as so far given to us is that the machinery created by the Mission should be used for the support of the Free French Movement

Soldiers, Airmen, Spies, and Whisperers

with the aim of swinging over all the French colonies within the defined area from Vichy to de Gaulle."[46] Franck was eager to meet with de Gaulle before leaving for West Africa, presumably to attempt to ensure that the hypersensitive general would not feel that the British were keeping him in the dark.[47] He also had Jebb plan a meeting with Lord Hailey, "in case he runs across him in West Africa."[48] This emphasis on anticipating ruffled feathers was to stand Franck in good stead on his arrival in West Africa. As Franck's departure approached, he and Jebb met with Dalton. Nelson, virtually purring, told Jebb that, "all the multitudinous details of this mission had been carried out in a really excellent manner by Franck himself. He has really done wonders." Nelson asked Jebb to ask Dalton to convey this sentiment to Franck, but the minister had, in fact, already seen Franck to wish him luck.[49]

By the end of 1940 Franck had already set up temporary headquarters in Lagos. Two officers of the Nigerian Colonial Service were assigned to him. One was V. M. Backhouse, a district commissioner, and the other, C. H. Ward, chief of Nigeria's Criminal Investigation Department. Both were immediately dispatched to northern Nigeria to open a station in Kano. It remained for Franck to set up the stations in the other colonies, namely, in the Gold Coast, Sierra Leone, and the Gambia. Although MEW was to be the sole cover for the mission, it lacked any facilities of its own in West Africa. Thus it proved necessary to secure the collaboration of the Colonial and War Offices. In point of fact the Franck Mission's London address was to be Room 055a at the War Office, located there since only that ministry was able to provide the essential coding facilities. The Colonial Office, in turn, agreed to provide mail and telegraph services, and all SOE non-coded communications were routed through J. S. Bennett of that ministry.[50]

Franck's initial team consisted of three officers, Capt. D. J. Keswick, yet another old Etonian and fellow recruit from Samuel Montagu; another banker, Capt. the Hon. J. E. Bingham; and Lt. V. Laversuch. They expected shortly to be joined by H. T. Bourdillon of the Colonial Office, son of Nigeria's governor.[51] The War Office took it upon themselves to inform General Giffard, the officer commanding British forces in West Africa, of Franck's activities. A cipher cable of 30 November read, "In order to co-ordinate propaganda, subversive activities, French West Africa, H.M.G. are sending Mission headed by Louis Franck which leaves for Lagos 6th December calling Bathurst Freetown on way. Mission will work close touch Colonial Governments and also with you to ensure that their activities are consistent with your policy."[52] This news could scarcely have delighted Giffard, who was already known by the SOE as an opponent of any activist policy toward French West Africa. Indeed, an SOE report of 24 October made that clear: "The War Office had the intention of despatching a Mission to West Africa for the purpose of organising irregular activities of an overt nature in the territories above-mentioned [i.e., the AOF]. General Giffard, however, has turned down the idea in view of the fact that he estimates this task should be entrusted to General de Gaulle and that he wishes to limit himself to a Military Intelligence Centre in British possessions in West Africa."[53] Over the whole of the Vichy emergency, nothing was to unsettle relations between Giffard and members of the Franck Mission more than the question of sabotage. One must wonder if Giffard's foreboding arose simply from the soldier's instinctive suspicion of civilian meddling, or whether he had also heard rumors of Nelson's own deep-seated distrust of "official circles" of the sort that certainly included generals.

Franck, whether aware or not of Giffard's views, was much more concerned to secure the confidence and cooperation of the governors of the West African colonies. He realized that it would be extremely difficult for his mission to set up its networks, and plan any actual operations, without their support, for the governors would be relied upon to provide most of the personnel and much of the logistical support without which the mission could not function. Certainly no Belgian banker, however knowledgeable about gold, could be expected actually to recruit field agents in colonies where virtually all European residents were civil servants, soldiers, or businessmen. To secure the necessary support, Franck attended the first session of the West African Governors' Conference to be convened since the fall of France.

This conference, with the telegraphic address WAGON, assembled on 18 December 1940. Three governors were present: Sir Bernard Bourdillon of Nigeria, who served as chairman; Sir Arnold Hodson of the Gold Coast; and Acting Governor Hilary Blood of Sierra Leone. For some reason the governor of Gambia did not attend, although this British "banana" pointing at the heart of Senegal would be party to all decisions taken. General Giffard was there, on an equal footing with the governors. There were also a number of senior administrative and military officers present. W. J. A. Jones, formerly chief commissioner of the Northern Territories of the Gold Coast, was appointed the conference's deputy chairman, Col. G. Miles Clifford its political advisor (code name WP—the P for *politics*), and R. de S. Stapledon its secretary.[54] Especially important, from the SOE's point of view, was the presence, as economic advisor, of Maj. R. E. C. Wingate (code name WE—the E for *economics*).[55]

The son of Wingate Pasha of the Sudan, and cousin to Orde Wingate, who was soon to find fame in Burma with the Chindits, this Wingate had been recruited into MEW by Desmond Morton immediately after the outbreak of war, and for a time had his desk in SO 2's office. Following the collapse of France, Wingate was summoned by Hugh Dalton, given a military rank, and told he was being sent on a hush-hush mission. He was ordered to report to Sir Edward Spears, Churchill's prime liaison officer with de Gaulle. The hush-hush mission was, in fact, the expedition to Dakar. His function would be, once the authorities in Dakar had seen the light and welcomed the opportunity to rejoin the war, to help organize the essential supplies that French West Africa would need. As to the supposed secrecy surrounding the mission, Wingate was less than impressed. At Euston Station, the regimental transport officer eyed him suspiciously. Asking a porter from which platform his train departed, the man, who seemed to know all about Wingate's travel orders, informed him no such train existed. Nonetheless, he found his way to the platform where just such a train did exist. There at least a hundred young Englishwomen were bidding tearful farewells to their French beaux. A truck pulled up to the train, loaded with bales of papers destined for one of the freight cars. "In the process of doing this," Wingate wrote, "one bale fell to the ground and burst open. There is always a wind in Euston Station, and within a second or so, sheets of paper were fluttering about the platform, obviously containing some sort of proclamation, the heavy type headlines of which it was possible to read. They were '*Aux Citoyens de Dakar*.'"[56] After the debacle at Dakar, Wingate was to spend two months with the Spears Mission in French Equatorial Africa before being summoned to Lagos to join the Franck Mission. He was, then, by no means unfamiliar with the West African scene.

Until 1940 the governors had not seen the need for new forms of cooperative action. They were, however, understandably perturbed at suddenly finding their colonies, on all but the easternmost frontier of Nigeria, up against potentially hostile Vichy territory. The gravity of the situation now clearly necessitated some form of closer collaboration. A Permanent Secretariat of the Governors' Conference was set up. It was to be "a means of co-ordinating the activities of the four West African Colonies in the prosecution of the war and ensuring identity of policy in regard to political and economic questions which result from and are connected with the war."[57] In principle this seemed eminently sensible. In practice both Hodson and Blood, as governors of the Gold Coast and Sierra Leone respectively, had doubts about ceding powers to this new bureaucratic body. A major change in policy seemed to them implicit in the creation of the secretariat.[58] The two, moreover, appear to have had reservations about the personal ambitions of Bourdillon, on whose initiative the conference had been convened and who had already forcefully expressed his displeasure with the War Office's decision to locate General Military Headquarters in the Gold Coast. As events were to show, their suspicions had substance. Only four months later, in April 1941, Bourdillon vigorously promoted a suggestion, first mooted by General Giffard, that a governor-general or high commissioner of British West Africa be appointed, and proposed himself, as governor of the largest West African colony, as first incumbent. This was to create another battle royal in London. The War Office, following Giffard, supported the idea, the Foreign Office strongly opposed it, and the Colonial Office was, to say the least, unenthusiastic.[59] The final minutes of the conference signaled the doubts about the idea of a super-governor for West Africa. "It should be clearly understood," the document read, "that, by agreeing to special measures of co-ordination now, individual Governments are in no way committed to the acceptance of such measures when the present emergency is over."[60] In the event, Bourdillon lost his bid for greater power. In April 1942, so we shall see, a resident minister for West Africa, Lord Swinton, was appointed from London to coordinate the activities of the four colonies.

In a cipher telegram to the colonial secretary of 20 December, Bourdillon, as chairman of the Governors' Conference, outlined the three major areas of the secretariat's projected work, as agreed upon by the three governors and Giffard. First, it was to coordinate relations between the political, army, and naval authorities at all levels of policy—that is, between representatives of the Colonial Office, the War Office, and the Admiralty in West Africa. Second, it would put together military and political intelligence and produce a regular information bulletin for high-level distribution in London, British West and East Africa, the Middle East, and the Free French governors in the AEF. Third, the secretariat was to be responsible for political and economic relations with both Vichy and Free French West and Central Africa. Bourdillon would, he said, deal with the matter of the Franck Mission in a separate communication.[61]

Louis Franck had, in fact, been in attendance throughout the conference and had addressed it. He spoke on political and economic intelligence and informed it, in no doubt the most general terms, of the nature of the activities to be undertaken by his mission. Bourdillon took up the matter with the colonial secretary on 21 December. Franck had been very helpful, he wrote, and he thought the mission would prove of great value so long as it collaborated closely with individual governors and WAGON. Franck had, it seems, agreed to work in each colony in combination with that colony's own political intelligence, and the combined organization would in turn work with the Free French Missions. Military intelligence would remain distinct and under the complete control of General Giffard. Wingate would continue to be responsible for economic operations directed toward the Vichy colonies, serving the Franck Mission and WAGON in a dual capacity. Bourdillon stressed that he had no desire to dominate the Franck Mission nor to dictate its policy, but thought that it was to the advantage of the Governors' Conference to have access, through Franck, to yet another ministry—that is, MEW. He believed that Franck was in agreement that setting up totally new organizations in the British colonies, rather than working with political intelligence, would unnecessarily duplicate efforts and perhaps produce policy conflicts.[62]

All this sounded wonderfully cooperative and clear cut, a perfect bureaucratic marriage. One might have thought, from his own report to Nelson, also of 21 December, that Franck saw the decisions made by WAGON in precisely the same way as Bourdillon. He virtually reiterated Bourdillon's interpretation of matters, adding only two further details. First, that relations with Free French Intelligence and Propaganda should be controlled by a central authority under de Gaulle's man Colonel Adam in Lagos, with whom he had established "most friendly relations," and second, but of considerably less significance, that the mission currently had £1,370 pounds left in its funds. Thus spoke the banker! It must be noted, however, that this communication to Nelson had been seen and approved by the governors and Giffard.[63] Over the next week Franck was to send further, and rather different, material to SO 2 in London that had not undergone the scrutiny of the governors and Giffard.

Nelson had seen Franck's first report and had noted on it, "So far, so good." By this time, however, Julius Hanau had been chosen to handle the Franck Mission from London. Bringing his code name, Caesar, with him from his knight-erranting, but unsuccessful, operations in the Balkans, Hanau was temporarily assigned as case officer for SO 2's new Africa missions.[64] Apparently, however much Franck had cultivated a warm personal relationship with Governor Bourdillon, he seems to have been economical with the truth about his intentions. He now gave Hanau ("Caesar") and through him Taylor ("AD") a more forthcoming account of the situation. "There is no doubt that the arrival of the Franck Mission was regarded in both civil and military circles here with considerable apprehension, based, I think, on a misunderstanding as to the role it was to play, and fear resulting from the experience of the military mission attached to General de G., and the unco-ordinated activities of the specialists of the type of Francis Rodd."[65] Franck pointed out that the Governors' Conference had now charged his mission with "co-ordinating political intelligence as well its original role in connection with the economic situation and propaganda." He was, he wrote, "more than satisfied with the present state of affairs. Now that the Gov. Conf. is in continuous session with a vice chairman and secretariat, and all the machinery for co-ordinating the policy of the four Colonies, it would have been quite impossible for us to achieve anything without their closest help and support." But Franck's view of matters was not quite so neatly in accord, as these opening comments suggest, with that of Bourdillon. "The question," he added, "was how to achieve this without losing our [SO 2's] independence, and how to avoid becoming part of the local machinery. This has been done by remaining an independent unit parallel to the Governors' Conference, linked only by bonds of personal liaison, and at the same time having a separate office in a different building for the conduct of our affairs."[66]

In early January 1941, for reasons that are not entirely clear, the mandarins of the Foreign Office stepped into the fray. A coded telegram classified most secret and dated 3 January was addressed to WAGON's chairman. It was signed by two first secretaries, H. L. d'A. Hopkinson and V. F. W. Cavendish-Bentinck, and initialed by R. A. Butler, parliamentary undersecretary of state in the Foreign Office. The arrangements for collaboration between the Franck Mission and WAGON were approved, but, it was noted,

> there appears to be some ambiguity as regards Franck's participation in intelligence work. As I understand it from your [WAGON's] telegram, intention is that items of political intelligence regarding Vichy colonies which come into the possession of the Franck Mission in the course of their activities should be passed on to political intelligence organisations in individual colonies and to Conference Secretariat for consideration and incorporation in periodical intelligence bulletins to be produced by Conference Secretariat. I have no objection to this procedure, which appears to offer many advantages; but I should hesitate to approve extension of functions of Franck Mission to include co-ordination by them of political intelligence in West Africa. . . . Authorities concerned here are in agreement that latter proposal would be undesirable as it would involve making Franck Mission virtually part of ordinary governmental machinery in Africa.[67]

War has its necessities, but clearly not such as to override bureaucratic fixations about jurisdictions.

It seemed, as the new year opened, that Louis Franck had succeeded in soothing everyone, not least by promising to provide the conference secretariat with all information gathered by the SOE's agents. By the end of the conference, indeed,

Soldiers, Airmen, Spies, and Whisperers

he had managed to secure its wholehearted approval for an even broader role for his mission than initially had been envisioned. Franck seemed in the course of a few weeks to have completely dispelled the worst fears of the governors, and for the time being at least, of General Giffard. Indeed, to some members of the West Africa expatriate British community, Franck was succeeding too well. Sir Hanns Vischer, who had been in Nigeria in various capacities since at least 1900, arrived in London early in June 1941 and met with Nelson. Nelson reported the conversation to "X" (probably Dalton). Vischer expressed "his frank [a secret punster?] admiration for the way in which Louis Franck has 'stolen the picture' in West Africa, and gave ungrudging praise to this young man's undoubted ability." However, Nelson continued, Vischer also had brought,

> rather grave news to the effect that he [Vischer] received what really amounts to a "round robin" from every one he saw (with the exception of Bourdillon) that he should approach Lord Moyne [now secretary of state for the colonies] and inform the latter that the presence of a Belgian at the head of an important Mission, such as the S.O.2 organisation in West Africa, and the extraordinary influence which Louis Franck seems to have obtained over Bourdillon, the Chairman of the West African Governors Conference, is not only unpalatable to the British Community generally, but is likely to prove thoroughly dangerous in the long run.

Vischer also informed Nelson that both the War Office and the Admiralty intended shortly to petition the Colonial Office to have a British subject appointed in place of Franck, a rather odd position for someone born, raised, educated, and married in Switzerland. He also informed Nelson that it was generally felt that the Franck Mission was tremendously overstaffed, a fact, he said, that "appears to be recognised by every one including all the members of the Franck Mission, with the exception of Louis Franck himself." While Nelson felt that the whole matter had to be brought before X, he did note that Vischer "is not a very clever man, and has spent practically all his life in West Africa, and thus believes, like all old West Coast hands, that he knows all there is to know about this part of the world."[68]

At the beginning of 1941 no one could claim that the intelligence situation in British West Africa was clear cut. Not least of the problems was that Free French intelligence had still to be slotted into the espionage landscape. Moreover, it was undoubtedly a matter of much surprise to all branches of Allied intelligence in West Africa when, so we shall see, a small American intelligence-gathering unit turned up in Accra at the very time that Franck was setting up the Gold Coast

Mission. And, underpinning all, was the problem of the Franck Mission's geographical jurisdiction. This may have been a matter that was afforded maximum secrecy, for fear of offending not so much Vichy France as various neutral powers. According to a later source the mission's "charter" empowered it to operate in the four British colonies, the seven Vichy colonies, the Spanish possessions of Río de Oro, Río Muni, and Fernando Po, the Portuguese colonies of Angola, Guinea, and the Cape Verde Islands, and the independent republic of Liberia.[69] A heavily censored document recently released by the Public Record Office summarizes the activities of the Franck Mission and deals, tantalizingly, with the question of cover: "The cover under which the Mission operated was as a branch of XXXXX [censored] with M.E.W. as a second string."[70] A branch of what? A bank? An economic mission? A commercial enterprise? One can only speculate, and wonder why the matter remains so secretive more than a half century later?

THE FRANCK MISSION: THE GOLD COAST SECTION

Obviously the Franck Mission's first priority was to find personnel to staff the fledgling outstations. One immediate benefit arising from Louis Franck's diplomatic success at the Governors' Conference was to arrange for some members of the Colonial Service to be seconded immediately to the mission. In each colony a few district commissioners joined the SOE. Finance, however, dictated that the Franck Mission should be able to call on the services of other DCs and civil service personnel without charge, as it were. This had been agreed at the Governors' Conference, and the decision had been passed down from governors to chief commissioners, provincial commissioners, and district commissioners. In March 1941, E. G. Hawkesworth, chief commissioner, Ashanti (CCA), immediately wrote to his DCs, instructing them to cooperate with the Franck Mission and to understand the nature of its work: "I must emphasize the importance of ensuring secrecy in respect to the subjects of such communications and of the fact that they are made."[71] Others to be co-opted in the Gold Coast included such men as L. Chapman, assistant superintendent of police (seconded to the Franck Mission in mid-February 1941),[72] and several preventive service [customs] officers and government medical officers. Even Capt. J. L. Stewart, director of veterinary services, was pulled into the work of the Franck Mission, not being required to interrogate cattle suspected of subversive activities, but assigned rather to monitor the health of beasts being smuggled into the Gold Coast (for which see chapter 4).

Capt. Francis Glyn was appointed to head the Gold Coast Section, with headquarters in Accra. A merchant banker of Glyn, Mills and Company, London, he had been called up at the outbreak of war. Commissioned in the Hertfordshire Regiment, in the autumn of 1940 he had been seconded to the SOE and assigned to the Franck Mission. He brought with him one of his bank's former employees, Lt. F. G. J. Forbes (code named W.52), who served the Accra station as secretary and accountant.[73] Glyn was also shortly to be joined by N. D. FitzGerald, a man whose background remains unclear but who was most likely another member of the banking fraternity.[74] An immediate decision was taken to open an outstation in the Northern Territories of the Gold Coast (NTs). This region was within the administrative jurisdiction of a chief commissioner whose authority also extended over the northern part of the former German colony of Togo, which had been placed under a British mandate by the League of Nations in 1922. On all sides, other than the south, the frontiers of this huge and sprawling region adjoined those of Vichy French territories. For purposes of the Franck Mission the NTs were divided into three sectors: first (moving clockwise), Bole, Wa, Lawra, Tumu; second, Navrongo, Bawku, Zuarangu, Gambaga; and third, Yendi, Kete Krakye. Each was thought to require its own SOE field officer, or "upcountry representative," as the official designation went, but requests for such had been turned down.[75] Thus, only one outstation was opened. Somewhat surprisingly, it was not located centrally but at Salaga, which was in the protectorate proper, but near the eastern boundary of the mandated area. In many respects nearby Yendi, which was in the mandate, might have seemed a more obvious location. Capital of the Ya Na, powerful ruler of the Dagomba, it was close to the French Togoland border and therefore well situated for carrying out covert operations. It may be assumed that there were those who thought that to place an espionage unit in mandated territory was in breach of international law. There were certainly those like General Giffard who, anxious not to provoke the Vichy authorities, thought it unwise to locate the station in a place of particular interest to the Germans, who had made clear their intention of taking back control of their former colonies. Be that as it may, the choice of Salaga seems all the more strange in that at some early stage in the planning it was decided that the areas of Western Ashanti bordering the Côte d'Ivoire should also be run from the northern outstation.

Capt. L. J. Mothersill was chosen to activate the SOE in Salaga. Born in 1899, he had attended Bedford School and had been commissioned into the Royal Scots from Sandhurst in 1918. From 1926 to 1927 he was attached to the Gold Coast Regiment. He applied to join the Gold Coast political service and in 1929 became assistant district commissioner in Ho, in British-mandated Togo. In 1931 he was temporarily seconded to the Gold Coast Police, as an assistant commissioner, but later in the 1930s returned to the political service and served as district commissioner in several stations in the NTs, including Gambaga and Navrongo.[76] He was attached to the Franck Mission in early February 1941.[77]

Accra and Salaga, with the telegraphic addresses Economy Accra and Economy Salaga, appear to have been the only SOE stations set up in the Gold Coast. Otherwise, civil servants, for the most part district commissioners based near the frontiers, had to be co-opted to work with the few full-time officers posted to the Franck Mission. In the autumn of 1941, FitzGerald toured the Gold Coast. He painted a somewhat discouraging picture of the operational reality: "as a result of my tour and interviews with the District Commissioners of Axim, Enchi, Bibiani, Sunyani, Wenchi, Bole, Lawra, Navrongo, Bawku, Salaga, Kpandu and Keta and the Chief Commissioners of Kumasi and Tamale and Dr. Saunders and others, I have come to the conclusion that the Franck Mission in the Gold Coast is at present hopelessly under-staffed and is in effect a head with only half a body. Various material and establishment requirements must be met also before any of the duties mentioned above can be seriously organised." The situation was made even more dismal by the fact that Mothersill was seriously ill in hospital and would be going on sick leave as soon as he was able to travel. Otherwise there were only three SOE officers actually in the field: W. B. McGee, D. G. Melville, and R. A. McNicoll. McGee had arrived in August 1941 and was posted to in Sunyani with responsibility for the districts of Sunyani, Wenchi, Bole, Wa, Lawra, and Tumu (with a "watching brief" over Goaso, Berekum, Pamu, and Sampa). Melville was responsible for the eastern border from Keta, on the coast, through Ho to Kpandu, fifty miles inland. The only other officer at that time, McNicoll, took over Mothersill's work temporarily but was due for leave.[78]

In early April 1941, Mothersill had laid down certain actions he required of the co-opted district commissioners. Each was to telegraph information judged of immediate importance, whether concerning civilian or military matters, to Economy Accra with a copy to Economy Salaga. Otherwise the DCs were asked to compile an intelligence report every two weeks, first copy to the colonial secretary in Accra, and second copy to Economy Salaga.[79] Mothersill's position vis-à-vis the co-opted DCs was a difficult one, though eased perhaps by the fact that he had himself been one of them—a matter surely not lost to those in the SOE who had arranged his recruitment to its ranks. The point was that a great deal of extra work was being unloaded on the DCs, who received no additional remuneration but only the satisfaction of contributing more to the war effort.

The attitude of the co-opted DCs naturally varied; they had no trade union

Soldiers, Airmen, Spies, and Whisperers

to coordinate their responses. M. M. Miln of Sunyani was one of those who displayed great enthusiasm. Unconcerned by matters so mundane as workload, he dashed off a letter to FitzGerald in Accra: "I make the following suggestion. If you consider it worthwhile, you should, I think, consult Government and the Military authorities. I, of course, shall take no action in the matter unless I am instructed to. That the roads hereunder be repaired and cleaned with as much publicity as possible. Sampa to boundary. Japekrom to boundary. Pamu to boundary. . . . This operation (which could be repeated at various selected points) would excite, anger and frighten the Vichy French. It would cause them to trouble their own people and go to some needless expense making roadblocks and moving troops." Remarkably FitzGerald found the plan so attractive that he sought and obtained the approval of both civil and military authorities, and asked the DC at Wenchi if he would like to "follow suit at any points in your district."[80] FitzGerald was perhaps unaware of the eccentricity of Miln, although Miln's activities were a source of continual astonishment to the people of Sunyani. In 1994, Nana Yaw Kran remembered him very well: "We were all afraid of him. The government had made an airport here. As soon as the war broke out, Miln saw a plane fly over. He immediately made all the people bring wood, stones, everything, to put on the runway. He thought it was an enemy plane and he wanted to make sure nothing could land."[81] And nothing could, including the RAF, until the government ordered Miln to clear the runway! A further insight into Miln's style of administration was provided by Kofi Adinkra, a RWAFF veteran of World War II: "Miln was not quite right in the head. He was a bit mad. He walked about the town and he would see a very pregnant woman carrying a very heavy load of plantain or whatever on her head. He would tell his policeman to take her load and arrest her. He would take her to court and fine her. But he would make her husband come to the court and pay the fine. The fine was for overloading. It was just like they do with lorries now."[82]

Other district commissioners were more realistic about their covert roles and voiced their concerns about the increase in their workload. When McGee arrived, they had hoped that he might assume much of the burden placed on them. Mothersill advised them otherwise: "It will be quite impossible for Mr. McGee to write the District Intelligence reports for he has such a large area to look after. This can only be done when the Franck Mission staff has been further increased. He will however do his best to take as much work off the shoulders of the local District Commissioner as he can."[83] Mothersill did, however, advise the co-opted DCs that McGee had limited funds at his disposal and that small claims for administrative expenses might be made direct to him. It was not much in the way of encouragement.

The rising discontent of the district commissioners came to the attention of FitzGerald when he made the extensive tour of the Gold Coast (referred to above) in the autumn of 1941. He addressed the matter in the memorandum he circulated to the DCs, among others, in October:

> *District Commissioner's Part in our Work.* This must be reduced. Complaints of the drudgery of typing and correspondence, the time taken by interviewing worthless agents and reporting thereon are general. In fact my visit came none too soon. There was considerable dissatisfaction with which I could but sympathise and promise to remedy. Therefore, subject to Government's consent, I have agreed with the D.C.'s that they no longer submit Intelligence Reports to F.M. [Franck Mission]. (I suggest they confine their reports to Internal for Gold Coast Government) but will hand over as and when received any material however rough or unreliable, to the area F.M. officer whose duty it will be to investigate, follow up and report direct to Accra.

The comments must have been much to the satisfaction of the DCs—until, that is, they came to the final paragraph: "This can only come into effect when our new organisation and increased personnel are functioning," and the memo was annotated, "Agreed by Colonial Secretary." This made matters much worse, for the colonial secretary in Accra was, the governor apart, effective head of the political service to which the DCs belonged.[84] Since any significant addition of SOE officers was unlikely, FitzGerald had done little more than notify the DCs that the status quo would be maintained. More than fifty years later H. V. Wimshurst, DC in Wenchi at the time, could still shudder at the memory of the work involved: "I can just remember questioning agents for hours in Ashanti, French, English, and trying to compose reports and type them with two fingers on a small portable typewriter. I never want to go through that again."[85]

THE FREE FRENCH

The officers of the Franck Mission had agreed, in principle at least, to work with both political and military intelligence. The broad nature of the cooperation had been discussed by the Governors' Conference, WAGON. There was, however, another group that had to be accommodated, namely, the Free French. As we have seen, de Gaulle's famous speech from London, on 18 June 1940, sought to rally

Soldiers, Airmen, Spies, and Whisperers

French patriots everywhere. Nonetheless, relations between the British and the Free French were seldom comfortable. Less than a week after the speech, Hugh Dalton noted in his diary: "Still no Frenchman blowing any trumpets anywhere except de Gaulle in London and his trumpet blasts are becoming a bit monotonous."[86] Churchill's pithy reference to de Gaulle will be recalled: "Everyone has his own cross to bear; mine is the cross of Lorraine." The war memoirs of Maj. Gen. Edward Spears, British liaison officer with the Free French Mission in London during the war, convey his constant need to reconcile a personal aversion for de Gaulle with deep admiration for the ideals he represented.[87]

The British government, committed to backing de Gaulle as the sole representative of the true France, against opposition from many factions, not least of all President Franklin Roosevelt, was often forced to resort to wry humor to defuse the tensions that de Gaulle inevitably created. Typical of this attitude was the comment of one Foreign Office official on the general's reaction to a message in the *Times* from French trade unionists—stating that de Gaulle was their representative and the representative of French people. "This news," the mandarin remarked,

> has had a tonic upon the General, and St. Joan of Arc is once more peeping over his shoulder. I fear that it will make him more troublesome to deal with and revive in him a desire to press claims which I have been at great pains to discourage. At all events, he said this morning that this should dispose of the false and mischievous stories put about by certain persons, that he is not the representative of France. We shall have to look out.[88]

However difficult de Gaulle and his representatives may have been, in mid-1940 the British had little choice but to welcome them as allies.

Within five days of de Gaulle's broadcast of 18 June, L'Union des Français Libres, the Free French Committee of the Gold Coast, had been formed in Accra. Its journal, *Le trait d'union: France libre et Gold Coast* was first published in 1941 and distributed around the world to other Free French committees.[89] By the autumn of 1940, an "official" Gaullist intelligence and propaganda organization had been set up in the Gold Coast. Like most fledgling patriotic movements formed at periods of high tension, it was to have several names over the course of its existence, reflecting changes in the breadth and depth of its activities. There are references to the French Missions, the Free French Military Missions, the Free French Missions, the Fighting French Missions, and to SLICA (Service de Renseignements et de Propagande sur la Côte Occidentale d'Afrique). *Fighting French* became more and more the term of reference used by the British, as they sought ways of not offending, more than was necessary, the Vichy French by implying that only de Gaulle's men and women were "free." Basic structure, functions, and objectives were outlined in a memorandum signed by de Gaulle in Brazzaville on 1 November 1940. The role of the missions, operating in all four British West African colonies, was to collect information on the AOF, to spread Free French propaganda, and to work toward winning over the Vichy colonies to the Allied cause. The missions came directly under the authority of Gen. Edgard de Larminet, commander in chief of the Free French forces in Africa, who was based in Brazzaville, capital of Gaullist French Equatorial Africa. There were to be five branches, two in Nigeria, one in Freetown, one in Bathurst, and one in Accra. Each was to have responsibility for adjacent Vichy territories, and that in Accra in particular for the Côte d'Ivoire and Togo.

The commander of what, for the sake of consistency, I shall call the Free French missions, was to be stationed in Accra, where he could be in close contact with General Giffard. In mid-November 1940 only two officers, Lieutenants Blondel and Rouillon, and one sergeant, G. Noirel, were manning the station.[90] They awaited the arrival of Colonel Adam, formerly of the Colonial Infantry, who had been appointed commander of the Gold Coast Mission,[91] and of Capt. G. L. Ponton, who had been named adjutant and also head of the Accra station.[92] While the Franck Mission had found it difficult to recruit personnel, men being in short supply in Britain, the Free French missions were in a quite different position. They were able to draw on the services of patriots unable to return to France. By the end of June 1941, there were eight Free French mission stations in the Gold Coast alone.

Ponton's second in command at Accra was Capt. B. G. A. Pallu, and the small secretariat comprised two NCOs, Adj. R. Prizac and Noirel, mentioned above. The propaganda section had three members: Lt. A. Kaminker of the infantry, H. W. Bernard, who served as chaplain to the mission, and Mlle. M. Girard, the stenographer. In addition, Baron J. de Koenigswarter, who held the rank of captain in the Colonial Artillery, acted as liaison with British general headquarters in Achimota. A second station was set up in Kumasi, capital of the Crown Colony of Ashanti, and also a city whose trading links extended deep into French territory. It was under the command of Lt. L. A. M. Blondel of the cavalry. The six outstations, moving clockwise from the southwest, were Sekondi, under 2d Lt. A. L. Schock; Berekum, under L. E. Bertin-Fournier; Lawra, in the extreme northwest of the Gold Coast, under Lt. R. E. Jobez of the Colonial Infantry; Navrongo, under 2d Lt. J. Bancel; Bawku, in the extreme northeast, under Sgt. A. Jaines, also of the Colonial Infantry; and finally Keta, in the southeast, near Lomé in French

Soldiers, Airmen, Spies, and Whisperers

Togo, under a Mr. Karam.[93] By the end of the year it was necessary to withdraw Bertin-Fournier to Brazzaville. He was replaced, temporarily, by an African, John Glover. From his name it would seem likely that Ponton had recruited him from southeastern Ghana, though he may well have been employed by one or other of the trading firms in the French colonies. Be that as it may, Ponton informed the CCA, Hawkesworth, that Glover was to be stationed at Berekum, and that he would present a letter to the DC Sunyani, M. M. Miln, who was working with the SOE. Glover, Ponton assured the chief commissioner, "will prove satisfactory to all."[94] There were, then, many ready to be recruited into the Free French Mission in Gold Coast. One might, however, suspect that Brazzaville took advantage of the situation to transfer some of its more troublesome and difficult followers to that country. Indeed, the first head of the mission, Colonel Adam, might be placed in that category.

From the moment of his arrival in the Gold Coast, the colonel was to prove a source of irritation to the British who worked with him. Extremely conscious of his role as de Gaulle's personal representative, he was quick to defend French interests in the event of any perceived British impingement upon French prerogatives. Adam's anger could be directed equally at French officials. He spoke, for example, "with some heat" of Free French General Georges Catroux, suggesting that "he was not a true Frenchman but a minion of the British."[95] During the first half of 1942, Adam was becoming intolerable to his British allies. "He is," wrote the newly arrived resident minister for West Africa, Lord Swinton, "an elderly Colonial official of immense self importance and conceit and very limited intelligence and views."[96] The Colonial Office sympathized with Swinton, agreeing that Adam was "a difficult man to work with," but adding that they "had not considered his position sufficiently important to make it desirable to approach the Free French and get him moved—always a difficult manoeuvre."[97] The SOE officers who had worked with Adam were even less flattering; and indeed, one of them described him as "tomato-like."[98] In the event, in August 1942 de Gaulle appointed Adam his personal representative in South Africa. The colonel could not resist one final flourish, on departure. "He was," he informed Resident Minister Swinton, "under orders to return in the event of a major crisis in West Africa."[99] Fortunately for all concerned, no major crisis erupted, and Adam's deputy, Ponton, took over the mission.

De Gaulle continued to keep a close eye on the Accra Mission, and, in a memorandum of mid-1942, stressed that its head, Ponton, would be responsible directly to his personal staff. At this time, the mission was divided into two distinct, but collaborating, sections. The first of these was the Central Bureau; Intelligence and Military Action, which (like Gaul), was divided into three parts: SR, or the Intelligence Service; AP, or Political Action and Propaganda; and AM, or Military Action. The other section was that for Reception—Rallying—Land and Sea Transport —Administration, which, despite its rather bewildering title, was basically concerned with the administration of the first section—if that makes it any clearer.[100]

One of the members of the Accra station was Baron de Koenigswarter, whose name is best remembered because of his wife, who accompanied him to West Africa. Baroness Pannonica "Nica" de Koenigswarter, a member of the English branch of the Rothschild family, stunned local society when she arrived with a lady's maid, and, there being no accommodation for European ladies' maids, the house boy and cook were unceremoniously ousted from their quarters to make room for her.[101] After the war, both moved to New York, where the Baroness was to gain a certain fame as a patron of American jazz musicians, including Thelonious Monk, Coleman Hawkins, and Charlie Rouse. Another, Charlie Parker ("Bird"), died in her apartment in 1955.[102]

The wife of another Free French official, Raphael Beretta, was likewise—but for different reasons—something of a problem. In March 1942, Brazzaville appointed Beretta to represent "the interests of the Jamanhene and his followers and any other Africans from Vichy territories who may seek asylum in the Gold Coast." Ponton made it clear that he did not consider Beretta a problem, but rather Beretta's wife. In an indiscreet but supposedly off the record conversation with an official in the colonial secretary's office, Ponton said that he had requested an unmarried man for the post, but had been given Beretta. Ponton's confidant could not resist conveying the information to the chief commissioner, Ashanti, in whose region the Berettas were to be stationed: "I gathered that the local Free French did not like Madame Beretta because she has the reputation of being an inveterate trouble maker. In the social sense—always wanting the best bungalow etc!! Also Ponton thinks she talks too much. I told Ponton that I would be prepared to support *Free French* representations that she should not be received in the Gold Coast. (There was nothing in his statements that indicated that the lady was in any way *politically* undesirable. Only that she was the type likely to be a bit of a nuisance to them, and one they would rather be without if practicable.)"[103] As it happens, Colonel Adam, then in Lagos, had already extracted a promise from Beretta, before the couple left there, that "his wife will behave herself and *not* be a nuisance.[104]

4

With Friends Like These . . .

THE SOE, THE SIS, AND THE ARMY

FROM THE FRANCK MISSION TO FRAWEST

How effective was the SOE in 1941? It is difficult to know, but in March of that year London received an encouraging summary of the activities of the Franck Mission. The staffing of the stations in Nigeria, the Gold Coast, and the Gambia was nearly complete. Relations between the mission and the Governors' Conference were "cordial and harmonious." The report went on to note that "definite communications have been established," presumably with people thought to have anti-Vichy sentiments, "in Dakar, St. Louis and Thiès in Senegal, and in Bamako in French Guinea" (and it is to be hoped that the location of Bamako in Guinea rather than in French Sudan was a mistake on the part of the summary's compiler rather than of Louis Franck himself!). Propaganda materials—newsreels, newspapers, periodicals, and so forth—had been sent out from London, on the assumption that the mission had already made arrangements for their distribution in the AOF. Moreover, a number of unofficial meetings had taken place with Vichy officials in border districts, including one that had been sanctioned by Dahomey's governor and perhaps by Governor-General Boisson himself.[1] Meanwhile, Louis Franck was preparing his organization for possible sabotage operations—including attacks by trained agents—on shipping, oil depots, and so forth. For this purpose dumps of "toys," presumably arms and explosives, were to be established.[2]

This was, obviously, an overview intended to obtain further support for expansion of activities in West Africa. The view of those on the spot provided a different slant on affairs. By February 1941, Francis Glyn had established the immediate major role of the Gold Coast Section as intelligence gathering. He laid down, for those working under him, the kind of information required from the Vichy colonies. Economic data was needed, first, on the matter of the availability and prices of commodities, both local and imported, in the marketplaces, and second, on the state of the livestock trade with particular attention to imports (on the hoof) into the Gold Coast. Political data should cover such questions as the morale of both Europeans and Africans, and the effects of propaganda, whether by radio transmission, leaflets smuggled across the frontiers, or orally transmitted rumor. Data was wanted on the attitude of the African population to the colonial administrations, on transport services, and on the sympathies of French administrative and military personnel, and traders.[3] A questionnaire devised by Mothersill in March 1941 followed Glyn's directive. It was prepared for the guidance of the district commissioners who had agreed to work with the SOE field officers.

Questionnaire—African

1. Name of Agent.
2. Date proceeded.
3. Date returned.
4. Places visited.
5. Route taken.
6. What did you see on the way going?
7. What towns and villages did you pass through?
8. What Chiefs did you meet?
9. What other persons did you meet?
10. Who are the leading Native chiefs in the areas you passed through and who is the most influential?
11. Did you meet any big native businessmen or traders?
12. What was their opinion about the international situation?
13. What had they to say about Native trade generally?
14. Are they selling any produce?
15. If so, what produce, and to whom, and at what prices?
16. What articles can one buy in: (a) European Stores. (b) Syrian and African Stores?
17. Is there anything you could not buy?

18. If so, what?

19. Is there plenty of money available?

20. Are there plenty of native foodstuffs available?

21. What is the political opinion of various persons you met enroute?

22. What is the attitude towards French Administration?

23. Are they pro-British, pro-de-Gaulle, or Vichy, or don't they care as long as they have their food and trade?

24. Did you meet any Native French Officials?

25. If so, what is their opinion about the War and things generally?

26. Has tax been paid and has there been any difficulty collecting tax?

27. What tax is paid per head?

28. Do women pay tax? If so, what amount?

29. Is there any sign of political unrest?

30. What are the French Officials telling the natives about the war generally, and the internal political situation?

31. Do the natives you meet know all about the war and are they being kept informed?

32. If they are being kept informed, what means is employed, i.e. Public lectures, newspapers, bulletins, etc. (Tell your Agent to bring back specimen of documents.)

33. How many francs can you obtain for £1 sterling at: 1. The Frontier [and other locations to be named]?

34. How many francs do you get for a shilling at: 1. The Frontier [and other locations to be named]?

35. Is there petrol and kerosene available for native use? Ascertain what stocks of petrol and kerosene are available generally.

In addition to these thirty-five questions, the operative was also asked to compile a list of the prices of some eighteen products, ranging from sugar and tea to wine and cigarettes, and from cooking oil to motor oil, matches, and milk.[4] The district commissioners were expected to obtain such information by the use of local agents for the payment of whom "plenty of money" was available. In March, Mothersill relaxed his demands on the DCs within the Salaga jurisdiction to the extent of having them submit intelligence reports on the seventh of every month,[5] but the respite was short, and by early April fortnightly reports were being asked for.[6]

The acute shortage of SOE officers, most of whom were being posted to European and Middle Eastern operational spheres considered more critical to the war effort than Africa, had—so we have seen—forced Louis Franck into a high degree of reliance on the cooperation of the colonial administrations. On 15 July 1941, Franck sent a report to SOE headquarters in London, enclosing a "most secret" memorandum of 12 July that spelled out in great detail plans for the reorganization of SO 2 in West Africa. These had been arrived at in consultation with Maj. R. E. C. Wingate and the heads of the Nigerian and Gold Coast missions, Capt. D. J. Keswick and Francis Glyn respectively. The current roles of SO 2 in West Africa, Franck wrote, extended over three areas. The first was that of political and economic intelligence, conducted with the cooperation of local officers of the colonial governments, analyzed initially by each colony's political intelligence unit, and then submitted to the Governors' Conference. Items of specific interest to the army were to be passed to the GOC-in-C and Military Intelligence, while all information would be shared by SO 2 and the Free French. The second area was that of propaganda directed at the Vichy colonies (which will be discussed more fully in chapter 6). The content of radio broadcasts and pamphlets designed for both British and French colonies was mostly supplied by London, and Franck did not see this activity as a particular burden on his mission. Verbal propaganda (i.e., rumor) was left to local officers in the field, who would again work closely with the officers of the Colonial Service. Third, and finally, Franck referred to sabotage and bribery of key individuals and, surprisingly perhaps, described these as "the main task" of his mission.[7]

Realistically, Franck acknowledged that his resources were overextended and recommended that both intelligence gathering and propaganda should be placed under the control of a colony's governor, to whose staff a Director of Intelligence (Political and Economic) and Propaganda would be appointed. This officer, who might replace the existing station head, would represent SO 2 and report to the SO 2 officer at the Governors' Conference, currently Wingate. Sabotage, however, would remain the major function of the Franck Mission as such. It was to be coordinated by an Officer in Charge, Sabotage, who would work in conjunction with Wingate in appropriate situations. Franck saw two main targets of sabotage, first, stocks of commodities in the ports and along railroad lines, especially oil, and second, ships docked at or lying off Vichy ports.[8] Implicit in Franck's reasoning was that these two activities, as forms of economic warfare, certainly fell within the scope of the SOE, for its charter of 22 July 1940 had defined unequivocally its role in economic warfare as being to "co-ordinate all action by way of subversion and sabotage against the enemy overseas."[9] Franck conceded, however, that targets of sabotage that were essentially military rather than economic should come under the direction of Giffard as GOC-in-C.[10]

Franck's proposal, then, was to divide the Franck Mission into two semi-autonomous organizations, the one headed by a Director of Intelligence (Political and Economic) and Propaganda, working as a member of the secretariat of the Governors' Conference, and the other by an Officer in Charge, Sabotage, working in conjunction with the GOC-in-C, West Africa. In his covering letter to Nelson, Franck seemed to imply that his proposals had the agreement of those he referred to as "the Military authorities." In this, he was to be proved wildly wrong. The basic assumption on which Franck had worked was "that Vichy Colonies are, to all intents and purposes, hostile territory," though he could scarcely have been unaware that Giffard persisted in regarding these territories as essentially neutral. Giffard, in fact, took his stand on the order given him by the government in July 1940, which was "to preserve the status quo in the areas under his command." This he interpreted as requiring him "to maintain absolute calm in the relationship between the British and Vichy Colonies in West Africa."[11] For Giffard then, there was no place for the SOE in West Africa, since the Vichy colonies did not fall under the rubric of "the enemy overseas." There were, moreover, strong advocates of this position in the seats of power in London. Gladwyn Jebb, chief executive officer of the SOE and well versed in the ways of Whitehall, put it thus: "S.O.E. wanted to stir up trouble, whereas the Foreign Office wanted to damp it down." Pimlott comments usefully on this: "The instincts in S.O.E.—like those of M.E.W.—were offensive; the instincts of the Foreign Office seemed to have changed little since peacetime. 'The impression in S.O.E. was that the Foreign Office wasn't really in the war,' comments one former SO2 officer [Robin Brook]. 'They were carrying on being the FO, seeking to maintain pre-war diplomatic standards through the crisis with their convictions undisturbed.'"[12]

We do not know precisely what happened when Franck's memorandum reached Nelson in London, for most of the relevant correspondence has been destroyed. We do know, however, that their recommendations were not accepted as submitted. The following month the mission was split in two, but not quite along the lines envisaged by Franck. Wingate, who had recently been in London, was to continue to work under the auspices of the Governors' Conference on political, economic, and propaganda matters, but would also cooperate closely with Giffard in the sphere of "major sabotage." One SOE sabotage school, already opened at Olokomeji in Nigeria, would continue to operate, and a second was shortly to be established in the Gold Coast. The other part of the original Franck Mission was to remain under the leadership of Franck himself, and to concern itself with what were unambiguously neutral territories, the Spanish and Portuguese West

African possessions and Liberia, to counteract German activities there.[13] Franck's organization was to be known as Neucols (neutral colonies), and Wingate's as Frawest (French Africa West), but code-named PERO—Political and Economic Research Office. Initially, both organizations were based in Lagos, but Frawest was almost immediately removed to the Gold Coast and relocated near GHQ, West Africa.[14]

INTELLIGENCE GATHERING IN THE GOLD COAST

It was about the time of the creation of Frawest that Glyn was replaced by FitzGerald as head of the Gold Coast Section. We do not know the reason for the change, but Glyn (with Keswick) was to become a member of the SOE group, code-named Massingham, that was active in Operation Torch, the November 1942 Allied invasion of French North Africa.[15] In the autumn of 1941 FitzGerald made his grand tour of the Gold Coast's border districts and was, as I have noted, disturbed by the shortage of SOE officers and sensitive to the complaints of the DCs on whom so much extra work had devolved. As a result of his talks with them, FitzGerald decided that the recruitment of high-quality, low-level operatives must be given priority. The only record of the discussions to have been found is in a report sent by H. V. Wimshurst, DC Wenchi, to his immediate superior in the political service—that is, to the CCA, Hawkesworth. At his meeting with the Frawest head of section in Kumasi on 28 September, Wimshurst disclosed, FitzGerald proposed "the formation of squads of specially selected men working under the Franck Mission." Wimshurst, who seems to have seen the squads as particularly useful for preventing Vichy agents from crossing into the Gold Coast, thought the idea a good one. The squads should, however, he suggested to Hawkesworth, be kept firmly under the control of SOE officers and the DCs. Wimshurst's reasoning was interesting: "I have not the slightest doubt that the Police and the Preventive Service [i.e., border control] would continue to give the utmost assistance and co-operation but it seems to me that to do this job efficiently a little less of the 'kid glove' is necessary. I am not sure that a Superior Police Officer would agree to his carefully trained men learning bad habits."[16]

FitzGerald decided to open recruiting for the new operatives—for his "squads"—on 1 November 1941. He invited DCs, the chief inspector of mines, and the general manager of the railways to recommend men they thought suitable. His initial plan was to have those selected spend a month at the Royal Engineers

Soldiers, Airmen, Spies, and Whisperers

depot in Teshi, "to show that they were fit for the honour to be paid them." There they were to be given basic military training to test their general fitness. They would have the same pay, one shilling a day, and the same entitlements, as an RWAFF private. Those showing themselves to be made of the right stuff would then be transferred to a special Home Guard—this was to be the cover—training depot and told that they were being prepared for special duties with DCs on the borders of the Gold Coast. They were to be put on a new pay scale of two to four shillings a day, backdated to the beginning of their training. These plans were outlined in a letter of 17 October 1941.[17]

Ten days later FitzGerald issued a revised plan that clarified the kinds of operatives being sought. He proposed to enlist five or six African "Courier-clerk Interpreters," to be attached to the SOE field officers. They were to be highly qualified and well paid, "the very best men obtainable." In addition he called for the recruitment of carefully selected African NCOs from the Gold Coast Regiment for special training and secondment to the SOE, namely, two sergeant majors, two sergeants, and two corporals. Their functions are not spelled out. Otherwise, FitzGerald planned to train some thirty to forty lower-level operatives ("village-men"), who would be equipped with motorcycles, bicycles, or horses according to local conditions. These were to be known as district messengers and would work along the frontiers. Finally, "agents," both male and female, were to be recruited, who would cross the frontiers and gather intelligence in Vichy territory. The women agents particularly would be expected, whenever possible, to "suborn" enemy troops. Precisely what was involved in suborning is unclear, but must have involved softening up tirailleurs and others working for the Vichy regime. The methods used may be left to the reader's imagination. Objections having been raised to the use of the Home Guard as a cover for training lower-level SOE operatives, FitzGerald decided instead to establish two permanent depots. One was to be at Anomabu Fort for those to be posted to the southeastern and southwestern frontiers, and the other at (provisionally) Pong Tamale, headquarters of the Gold Coast Veterinary Service, about fifteen miles from Tamale itself, for those who would work in the north.[18]

It was in this period that relations between FitzGerald's immediate superior, Wingate, and General Giffard were seriously disintegrating (as discussed more fully later in this chapter). It may have been this that obliged FitzGerald, on 17 November 1941, to make further modifications to his plans. Recruits were no longer be sent to the army for preliminary training, but would report directly to Anomabu Fort or (still provisionally) Pong Tamale. Those successfully completing training would be classified as agents, head district messengers, district messengers, or contact men. The district messengers were presumably those described in a later report as "prepared to cross the frontier and penetrate to a limited distance for a specific purpose"—that is, local men and women able to slip, inconspicuously, backward and forward across the frontier on a regular, almost daily basis. They were to be assured "that there is nothing to hide." They can, FitzGerald wrote, "be told quite truthfully and openly that they are required as 'District Messengers' to work with the D.C.'s, Native Chiefs and 'Government officials,' and make themselves generally useful. Those of good education can be promised immediate promotion to rank of 'Head District Messengers.' If recruiting is difficult they could also be told that the work is interesting." The agents, in contrast, were those to be used in deep penetration, and should, he directed, maintain secrecy about their training. All recruits, FitzGerald added, should have at least one "outstanding good quality." Among those to be looked for were courage, force of character, command of languages, and qualities of leadership. It is a measure of FitzGerald's concern about the DCs that he apologized for the extra work that recruiting operatives would place upon them, but expressed the hope that, once trained, they would effectively lighten the DCs' work load.[19]

No source has been found that describes in any detail the nature of the training given the SOE's agents and district messengers. In October 1941, FitzGerald briefly commented that male agents were "primarily to be instructed in observation and description of things seen. Accuracy in describing distances, numbers, etc. Spread of 'Buyers' news, rumours, suborning of troops etc." Female agents, FitzGerald wrote, had "similar duties. Particularly suborning."[20] The notion of buyers' news presumably involved the dissemination of price data for commodities in Gold Coast markets, as a stimulus to smugglers to move goods from Vichy into British territory. "Suborning of troops," we have assumed, means encouraging desertion and bribing French officials for information or even more direct participation in the Allied cause. "Observation and description of things seen" has obvious reference to the collection of political and economic data as instanced in Mothersill's Questionnaire—African of March 1941, reproduced earlier in this chapter. In October, however, FitzGerald also referred to, "any information of military interest which may come into our [the SOE's] hands being passed on to the Military Authorities."[21] This suggests that, at the time, SOE operatives might only acquire such material incidentally. Be that as it may, certainly a few months later they were actively engaged in collecting military data.

One document is of particular interest in this context. It appears to have originated from a military source, but survives in a Frawest file. The document is undated but is to be found with material from mid-1942.

1. Troops
    (a) How many are stationed at this place?
    (b) Are troops still arriving, if so, where from?
    (c) Are there any troops other than French in this area?
    Observe carefully the following details on the uniforms of N.C.O.s and troops.
    (d) Collar and shoulder badges, and any numbers on these.
    (e) Take note of the colour of the collar patches.

2. Armoured Vehicles
    (a) Are there any tanks or chenillettes (Infantry armoured tractors) at this place.
    (b) If so, how many such vehicles and where did they come from.
    (c) If any are seen, note any markings and numbers seen on them. (Other than registration number.)

3. Regional Defence
    (a) Are there any A.A. [anti-aircraft] guns, and if so, how many?
    (b) Are these fixed or movable?
    (c) A description of any other guns seen.
    (d) If the calibre of any guns can be ascertained such information would be of value.

4. Aviation Material
    (a) Are there any aircraft stationed there?
    (b) Note the number of engines on any aeroplanes that may be seen, and whether they have one or two wings.
    (c) Lastly, note carefully any markings on the wings and fuselages.[22]

The first intake of recruits to be trained at Anomabu Fort spent the whole of December and early January 1942 there, and the second course (apparently to be run by McGee) was to begin on 1 February. Evaluation of the quality and capabilities of the trainees led FitzGerald to spell out, in greater detail than hitherto, the work that might be expected of them:

1. To receive and report information, talks, rumours etc from over the frontiers.
2. To look out for, watch the activities of, and report any suspected foreign persons arriving in his district.

3. To spread abroad, orally, news as supplied by us and rumours or whispering campaigne [*sic*] items.
4. To hand out printed propaganda for distribution across the frontiers (not all the men—only certain individuals well placed and qualified to do this).
5. To suggest to us means, methods and men who could be employed to stimulate smuggling of gold, kapok and desertion of soldiers with their arms.
6. In isolated and rather rare instances to cross the frontier as agents.[23]

The matter of the reliability of the intelligence gathered was frequently an issue. Military Intelligence, seeing itself as faced with the problem of having to assess information often based "on the confused reports of uneducated Africans," developed an evaluation procedure.[24] The reliability of the informant as such was graded on a scale of A to D; the veracity of a particular piece of information on a scale of 1 to 3; and "Eur." was used to indicate that the informant was a European. A man who crossed into the Gold Coast from Ouagadougou in July 1942, for example, was thought not well placed to have a knowledge of military matters and thus received "a general grading of A.3 (Eur.)."[25] The evaluations of reports from the Côte d'Ivoire, in GHQ's "Intelligence Notes" for November 1942, ranged from A.2 to C.3:

Order of Battle.
B.2 Eur. One Pl[atoon] under an Aspirant is reported at Aboisso (3 17W—5 25N)
Comment. This is thought to come from 31 Garr[ison] Coy Abijan.
Movement of material.
A.2 255 coils of telegraph wire weighing 4,500 Kgs and belonging to Civil Post and Telegraph were sent to Bamako from Abijan.
Miscellaneous.
C.3 Two C.3 sources report that "beacons are to be lit in the Ivory Coast in the event of invasion from the Gold Coast. They have been installed on various hills near the G.C. Border."[26]

Very few reports earned an A.1. Those that did were for the most part derived either from photographic materials, for example: "A.1 *Kaolack*. Photographs show that the station in the town is linked up by rail with the water front and with a siding in a cul de sac W. of the town,"[27] or from the interception of official Vichy communications, for example: "A.1 Admiral Darlan arrived in Dakar on 21/10 and left again on 23/10. No report has been received of the purpose of his visit except for the announcement that a Governors conference was held at that time in Dakar. It must, however, be assumed that the policy of A.O.F. being more strictly

Soldiers, Airmen, Spies, and Whisperers

controlled by the Axis was a likely matter for his conversations."[28] Deserters were another major, and usually highly rated, source of information for General Staff Intelligence, known as GS(I). A very detailed account of the operations of No. 1 W/T Company of 41 (Radio) Battalion was, for example, obtained from a corporal who defected to the Gold Coast in May 1942 and who, under interrogation, listed the location of all the company's detachments including ones near the northwestern and northern borders of the Gold Coast.[29]

Army Intelligence drew upon long experience in the field. The SOE was never intended by its charter to be involved in intelligence gathering and had some difficulty in getting started. In West Africa each Head of Section appears to have been trying, but not always succeeding, to put together an efficient organization. In June 1942, FitzGerald informed the DCs working with him that he had been receiving complaints that PERO reports conveyed no idea of the sources—and therefore value—of the information it relayed. He proposed giving agents and district messengers code names ("symbols"), which would be used to tag the source of every report.[30] One of his staff, N. E. Hedley-Dent, took on the task of developing a method of evaluation, and produced what seems to have been a modified version of the Military Intelligence system. He communicated it to all the border DCs on 22 July 1942. Operatives were to be classified on a scale from A to E: "completely reliable," "usually reliable," "fairly reliable," "not usually reliable," and "unreliable." Each report was to be classified on a scale from 1 to 6: "confirmed from other sources," "probably true," "possibly true," "doubtfully true," "improbable," and "truth cannot be judged." Hedley-Dent also indicated that an E should be used for any information from a European source.[31] The identities of the operatives were, of course, to be "highly secret." A list started by Neil Ross, acting DC Wenchi, was abandoned after the third name, presumably for security reasons, but somehow escaped destruction:

List of Agents

1. Alasan
2. ?Assata? A woman informer (lover to Commandant's Registrar, Bonduku)
3. Akrah. Literate French.[32]

The nature of the political material passed on to WAGON by PERO, that is, to the Governors' Conference by the SOE's Frawest, may be illustrated by reference to a sequence of accounts about Ouagadougou, Haute Côte d'Ivoire, in the second quarter of 1941. It was reported in mid-April,

African discontent would appear to be intensifying and, if a recent report can be believed, may even take practical effect. The Moro Naba, Chief of the Moshis, had told his Council that he is not pleased with things as they are and that he would welcome British interventions. All indications point to the growing unrest of this numerous (three and a half million) and warlike tribe.[33]

Just over a month later the situation was updated:

Recent reports indicate that . . . forced labour is one of the principal grievances. In the Mossi country, the Moronaba . . . is said to be in trouble with the authorities on account of his openly expressed contempt for the present regime: this report is borne out by recent difficulties in making contact with him and by his request to the District Commissioner, Navrongo, to refrain from sending papers direct on account of the official surveillance to which he is subjected.[34]

By June matters were changing:

A report received in the Northern Territories of the Gold Coast suggests that the unrest which has been evident among the Moshis is giving way to a state of fear caused by administrative threats against anyone working in conflict with the present regime. This did not prevent the Moronaba from shutting his eyes to the escape into British territory of three French N.C.Os. . . . In a personal letter to the head of the Free French Mission at Accra the Moronaba says that he gave these men eight days to get clear before issuing instructions for them to be stopped. He adds, "At the moment Ouagadougou is a dangerous place for strangers. Most of the European officials are anti-de-Gaulle, especially the Commandant."[35]

The Moro Naba in question was Kom II. He was, not surprisingly, a particular focus of interest to Free French agents, who hoped that he would declare for de Gaulle.[36] Kom II also kept up his contacts with the British. In the summer of 1941 he had sent a personal messenger to the district commissioner, Navrongo. After the meeting, the DC was of the opinion that, "if we were to go into their country the Moshi would be one hundred percent with us." Further affirmation of the Moro Naba's discontent arrived when many Africans who were British subjects, but who had been working in various trading firms in the Côte d'Ivoire, were expelled. Clerks who had worked for the United Africa Company reported on a meeting between Kom II and Deschamps. The Moro Naba asked the governor of the Côte d'Ivoire if "the Ivory Coast was French or German? When the governor asked the reason for this question the Moro Naba replied, 'Have you not signed a pact with the Germans and changed the method of saluting?' It appears that both officials and schoolchildren saluted the tricolor Nazi-fashion at the Fete de Jeunesse on Joan of Arc's Day."[37] However encouraging this may have been to the British, Kom II had an agenda of his own. One of his stated ambitions was to see Haute Volta, the bulk of which had been attached to the Côte d'Ivoire since 1932, restored as a separate colony. In September 1941 he had petitioned Governor-General Boisson to this end, drawing attention to the thousands of Mossi soldiers recruited to the Tirailleurs Sénégalais through his efforts.[38] In November he even sent a message to the West African tirailleurs in French Somaliland urging them to be loyal to Vichy. British Intelligence, however, decided to attach no significance to the matter. "All previous reports," it was noted, "have indicated that pro-British sympathies were held by the Moro Naba and his tribe."[39]

The mass migration of Gyaman (or Abron) from the eastern Côte d'Ivoire into the Gold Coast in January 1942, treated in chapter 7, might well have inspired the Moro Naba to follow suit. That he did not may have had something to do with the fact that in late 1941 a third battalion of the Regiment Porte de Tirailleurs Sénégalais was being formed in his capital, Ouagadougou.[40] However that may be, Vichy radio announced his death on 14 March 1942.[41] There were rumors, perhaps put about by Free French intelligence, that he had committed suicide rather than continue to serve under Vichy tyranny. The Vichy French insisted that his death was due to natural causes, for he had suffered from heart trouble for many years. The Mossi said that he had suffered forever from the whites.[42]

The new Moro Naba, Saga II, continued to pursue the goal of a separate Haute Volta. He maintained quiet communications with the Free French while appearing to cooperate with Abidjan and Dakar. Like his predecessor, he kept his options open.[43] Behind all this posturing was the knowledge, on the part of both British and French, that the Mossi had long looked south to the Gold Coast for employment and, indeed, markets. "Gold Coast," one report had it, "seems to the natives of the old Haute Volta province by tradition a garden of Eden."[44] The SOE operatives constantly spread reports of the absence of forced labor in the Gold Coast, and the abundance of consumer goods there that might be obtained in exchange, particularly for cattle. Mossi drovers moved their herds toward the frontier. Vichy frontier patrols turned them back, sometimes executing herdsmen for smugglers. Chiefs near the Gold Coast border were threatened with life imprisonment if they allowed cattle to be driven across their lands.[45]

WEST AFRICA'S LITTLE WAR: GIFFARD AND THE SIS VERSUS THE GOVERNORS' CONFERENCE AND THE SOE

With the creation of Frawest and Neucols in mid-1941, the role of the SOE in West Africa might have seemed finally settled. It might have seemed also that the four West African missions were functioning satisfactorily, and certainly that in the Gold Coast appears to have been performing sterling service in the gathering of information. All of this was illusory, however. In late September or early October 1941 someone referred to as "the man S." appeared on the scene. He visited Freetown and Bathurst, continued to Accra, where he talked with Giffard, and then proceeded to Lagos to meet with Bourdillon, chairman of the Governors' Conference. He did not contact the Frawest officers. Wingate felt obliged immediately to retrace the steps of "S" to find out what was going on. He left Accra for Freetown and Bathurst, having placed his second in command, Col. G. Miles Clifford ("WP"), political advisor to the Governors' Conference, in charge, and having asked him to send an unofficial report on the situation to George Taylor ("AD") in London. Clifford did so. He wrote,

> The attitude of S. on his arrival gave a clear indication that something was toward and there is now no room for doubt that he has prejudiced the G.O.C. (Giffard) not only in regard to our value as a source of information but in regard to our other activities, actual or potential, as to which I suspect that a further attack will be launched. . . . This crisis, which has been so unexpectedly and so unnecessarily precipitated, is particularly stupid since with the collaboration and co-operation secured to us through our present organisation there is no doubt that we could play a most useful part in the critical days which undoubtedly lie ahead of us in West Africa; this is true whatever shape these developments may take.[46]

The truth of the matter soon came out. "S" was a representative of the SIS (otherwise MI 6), the old established Special Intelligence Service headed by Stewart Menzies ("C"). The function of the SIS was intelligence gathering, and Menzies was much disturbed by the intrusion of the SOE into this field.[47] Nowhere was this more annoying to him than in West Africa, where the SIS had no regular agents but where the SOE was building up an effective intelligence service with the cooperation of the Governors' Conference and the colonial governments.[48] Menzies's reasoning was logical enough: that insofar as Frawest was involved in intelligence, to that extent it should be responsible to him. The documentation has not been found, but Menzies must have had clearance from a very high source—perhaps from the prime minister, whose ear he had—to send "S" to West Africa with the authority, as it turned out, to inform the colonial governments, the GOC-in-C, and the Governors' Conference that henceforth the SOE—Frawest—was part of the SIS.[49]

Giffard, Clifford informed Taylor, had been prejudiced by "S" and was likely to launch a "further attack" on the SOE. He enclosed for Taylor's use a copy of a document prepared by Wingate and himself for the Governors' Conference, stressing that Frawest was responsible to, and only to, the SOE, "save and except the Governors and the Governors' Conference to such extent as these may find it necessary, in view of circumstances then obtaining, to modify or even to veto some specific operation designed to give effect to a general directive from the SOE of which they will, of course, be informed."[50] Clifford was obviously interpreting the challenge presented to Frawest by the SIS as a challenge to the powerful Governors' Conference. Shortly after, on 31 October 1941, Clifford himself drew up, though doubtless on the basis of conversations with Wingate and other Frawest staff, a memorandum titled, "The Role of S.O.E. Organisation in West Africa." It has no addressee, but was presumably also intended for the Governors' Conference. Two categories of operations were envisaged, Subversive A and Subversive B.

Subversive A were those actions to which the SOE was currently restricted by "the present state of dumb hostility." These included the more usual kinds of propaganda, and some less usual proceedings such as the burglary of the houses of Vichy officials in order to appropriate public funds. Subversive A also included economic warfare, ranging from comparatively modest goals, such as the encouragement of smuggling, to more dramatic ones, such as the destruction by fire or otherwise of produce and containers, of fuel dumps, of ship cargoes, and of railway lines. Subversive B activities would only be carried out in conjunction with the army, in the event of a Vichy French invasion of British territory or, conversely, a British invasion of Vichy territory. The targets would be determined by the military commanders, but in such circumstances, so the memorandum had it, "their specialised knowledge of affairs in A.O.F. must also make the service of S.O.E. personnel of particular value to military commanders to whom they [the SOE officers] would, wherever possible, be made available." The Frawest officers might have got away with it if Clifford had left the matter there. He did not. Area military commanders, he continued, "should themselves indicate what their requirements would be in hypothetical circumstances; we [the SOE] will then undertake the necessary preliminary investigations and subsequent detailed planning."[51] Nothing was more likely to infuriate General Giffard than a memorandum of this nature when it appeared on his desk, as it inevitably did. He had no doubt that Wingate was ultimately responsible for the document.

It may have been on Giffard's initiative that a meeting was convened, on 13 November 1941, at the War Office. It was chaired by Brig. W. A. M. Stawell. Giffard flew there in person. The SIS was represented by the deputy chief of the Secret Service, Col. V. P. T. Vivian, and the SOE by Julius Hanau. There were "some violent differences of opinion," particularly between Hanau and Vivian, having to do with the statement made by the SIS man, "S," to the Governors' Conference a few weeks earlier. Giffard waded in, in support of Vivian. The SOE, said the GOC-in-C, had been useless to the army, with the result that "at present the West African Colonies remained wide open to the enemy." He and Vivian agreed that the SIS should take over from the SOE. Giffard added that he himself had "sufficient control over the wilder activities of SOE," that is, over sabotage and subversion. Hanau, however, obliged Giffard to admit that he had received a letter from the SOE assuring him that no violent actions would be taken without his authorization.

Hanau immediately reported these proceedings to his headquarters on 14 November 1941, and on the following day, Charles Hambro, then deputy executive director of the SOE, obtained a meeting with Stawell. He found him not wholly sympathetic to Vivian and the SIS. Hambro confirmed that the SOE was willing to work with the SIS and suggested that an SIS man should be attached to Wingate as his second in command. The two, in collaboration with the chairman of the Governors' Conference, Bourdillon, and with Giffard, might then establish a modus operandi.[52] Menzies considered, "most earnestly," the SOE proposal and replied to Hambro on 29 November. Menzies was appalled by the idea that the senior position would continue to be held by Wingate, a man "whose experiences in the I.C.S. [India Civil Service] and the Indian Political Service I do not regard as qualifications, but rather the reverse, for planning and directing Secret Intelligence in our sense of the term. Nor, to be quite frank, do I consider that Wingate has shown the balance or the ability to rise above personal considerations, which would be essential in its head man if such a combined organisation were to have the faintest chance of success." The chairman of the Governors' Conference also invoked Menzies's ire. "I am anxious," he continued, "that Sir Bernard Bourdillon should be brought by his Secretary of State to a full realisation of the Imperial requirements of the situation and the desirability of falling into line with normal usage. He must comply with the Secretary of State's instructions and not continue to arrange the Intelligence system of West Africa."[53]

No doubt, to Giffard's dismay, but in accordance with Franck's recommendation of mid-July, an officer in charge, sabotage, had been appointed. Operating as W.29, his identity is at present unknown. Having apparently had no previous experience in West African, he arrived there on or around the beginning of August. On 1 December 1941 he reported to Hanau ("Caesar"), Wingate ("WE"), and Colin Gubbins ("M") then the SOE's director of operations. Decreasing exports from the Vichy colonies to Europe, he saw as his main goal. W.29 described what he regarded as the difficulties in carrying out sabotage, including the unreliability of "the native agent," and the efficiency of the French security system. He recommended attacks on shipping, railways, and road transport and stressed that efforts should be made to make these attacks look accidental. He requested "authority to prosecute a sabotage campaign under the guidance of W.E." and urged that it was essential to have "the blessing, if not the active co-operation, of the Army, Navy and Air Force."[54]

A new policy directive was issued by the SOE on 16 December 1941. It was put together by Hanau following the instructions of Taylor. It was predicated on the view that the SOE, first by its original charter, second by the terms of reference for the Franck Mission, and third by the terms of reference for Frawest, was set up to carry out acts of sabotage. The directive was skillfully crafted. First, with respect to land sabotage, it was pointed out that the Foreign Office had authorized acts of sabotage against factories in unoccupied France that were working for the Germans. There was, then, no reason why French territories overseas should be regarded as immune from attack. Taylor ruled that the SOE might proceed with plans to disrupt the groundnut trade "without reference to the F.O. or any other authority." Second, with respect to marine sabotage, it was argued that the Foreign Office and the Admiralty had already authorized SOE attacks on Vichy shipping, and that vessels carrying rubber, cobalt, groundnuts, or fuel oil had been identified by the Ministry of Economic Warfare as prime targets. The naval commander in chief of the South Atlantic was to be informed of the SOE's "free hand regarding shipping in A.O.F." Interestingly, no communication was to be had with "Military," that is, to Giffard. Nevertheless, Hanau, if Hanau it was, then drew up "Policy Directives to W.E.," which related to land sabotage and were therefore of concern to Giffard:

(a) Bribery, incendiarism, ca'canny [go-slow tactics], misdirection of transport and interference with machinery permitted in connection with minor sabotage intended to interfere with collection and export of goods. . . .

(b) M.E.W. anxious for interference with export of groundnuts from A.O.F. Wire what action possible to enable authority to be sought. . . .

(c) Consent given to a scheme for interference with locomotives and steam plants provided it acts as an effective deterrent to movement of groundnut crop. . . .

(d) Above action authorised as a means of interfering with transport of cotton and palm oil.[55]

The next day, Hanau wrote to Hambro and Taylor to alert them to his feeling that Wingate might be failing to adjust sufficiently to the pressures bearing down on the SOE.[56]

Misgivings about Wingate apart, Taylor was clearly prepared to risk a showdown with Giffard and hoped for support from the Foreign Office. In an internal memorandum of 19 December 1941, he wrote,

> I am wondering whether it would not be possible to get a general authority for endeavouring to interfere, by every means short of overt attacks by British personnel, on all transport, plant, or other facilities by which any commodities useful to the enemy are got from these Vichy colonies to France, and thence into enemy hands. My own impression as to the attitude which the Foreign Office takes to action against French West African colonies from the point of view of stopping supplies from getting to Germany, is such, that it seems to me quite likely that such a programme conforms with their views.[57]

On 5 January 1942, the SOE in West Africa received by telegram what was described as "both a charter on broad principles and a final instruction." It was unsigned but clearly originated from a very high level, possibly the War Cabinet. It went not only to the SOE and the SIS, but also to the Colonial and War Offices. It laid down, first, that the SIS should be responsible for intelligence gathering in Africa and should take over this function from the SOE, and second, that the SOE should be totally in control of subversive activities, sabotage, and propaganda of all kinds. Whoever drafted the "charter" was extremely cautious in addressing what was, in effect, essentially the problem of Giffard. Because the SOE would be using British territory as a base for its operations in the Vichy colonies, it would be necessary, the writer observed, "that your activities conform with wishes of local authorities military and civil."[58]

During this squabbling over what the SOE could and could not do, and where and where not they could do it, Neucols pulled off an impressive coup—Operation Postmaster. Captained by Graham Hayes, the *Maid Honor*, a Brixham trawler, docked in the Gold Coast in February 1942. Its objective was to seize two Italian ships lying off the Spanish colony of Fernando Po (now Equatorial Guinea). Upon reaching Takoradi, the SOE men asked Giffard for volunteers to join them.

Soldiers, Airmen, Spies, and Whisperers

Although twenty men had indeed expressed their eagerness to take part in the operation, Giffard refused point blank to allow it. Louis Franck, based in Lagos as head of Neucols, asked Governor Bourdillon for assistance. Bourdillon immediately allowed Franck to recruit volunteers from the civil service, and *Maid Honor* set off for the port of Santa Isabel. As the trawler approached Fernando Po, an SOE officer based there, Captain Lippert, turned up at the harbor and immediately invited all the port officials to a huge party. While the drink flowed and the music blared, the SOE volunteer "pirates" boarded the freighter *Duchessa d'Aosta* and the tanker *Likomba*, took over command and steamed them into British territory, a total haul estimated at nearly £300,000. The hijackings remained an official mystery. No accusations were made against the British, since that would have required the Spanish port officials to explain exactly where they were, and with whom, on the night of the incident. It was Neucols's major triumph in West Africa.[59]

Thus it seemed that the SOE was on a roll, so much so that in late February 1942 Wingate's orders, as originally laid down in the memorandum of 16 December, were now expanded to include three further charges:

(e) Scheme for smuggling cattle and horses out of Vichy territory finally authorised. . . .
(f) Scheme for interfering with coastal fuel oil traffic approved. . . .
(g) Bathurst project for rendering Senegal and Sudan unproductive by attacking transport and produce dumps approved, subject to concealment of British origin.

The revised memorandum, however, also contained a new conclusion concerning Wingate, showing that in early 1942 he was in a confrontational mood:

W.E. has recently telegraphed to London declaring that in his view an active sabotage policy against the Vichy colonies in West Africa is impossible owing to the prohibition placed upon it by the Service Authorities, and that a policy of subversion is equally impossible in view of the lack of definition in H.M.G.'s policy vis-à-vis Vichy, and owing to the position of the Free French. It is hoped that he will shortly be flying to London in order to take part in discussions aimed at securing an authoritative clarification both of H.M.G.'s policy and of the position of the Frawest Mission.[60]

It was perhaps on his journey to London that Wingate attended a meeting of the Governors' Conference in Lagos, and on 16 March entered into a written arrangement that the SIS should be responsible for secret intelligence, and the SOE in charge of economic and political intelligence. The relations between the SOE and the GOC-in-C remained a matter of high policy, and would have to be decided by London. At the same time, Wingate obtained permission from the governors to proceed there in person.[61]

The March arrangement only served to inflame Giffard further. He complained bitterly in a letter to the director of military intelligence (DMI) in London, stating that the SOE "were a menace to the safety of the Colony, and either they must be entirely disbanded or put completely under his command." This letter was brought to Hambro's attention, who protested to the DMI on 23 March. He reiterated that the SOE had assured Giffard that he would be informed and asked to authorize any actions against Vichy territory. However, Hambro pointed out that "we have been somewhat embarrassed by his [Giffard's] constant demand for inaction." The situation, Hambro continued, was all the more embarrassing because the SOE had recently received authority from the Foreign Office to disorganize Vichy shipping as much as possible, and from MEW, to interfere with the trade in groundnuts and other commodities. The matter was made even more ridiculous by the fact that the chairman of the Governors' Conference, Bourdillon, had made it clear that he thought that the SOE should assume a more aggressive policy. He felt it was time to make the Vichy authorities feel that they had more to fear from the British than from the Germans. As he put it, "it would pay us much better to make the French 'drink water' than to supply them with 'whiskey and soda.'" Hambro thus saw Giffard as having taken on the Foreign Office, the Ministry of Economic Warfare, the Governors' Conference, and indeed, the Chiefs of Staff.[62] Wingate tried to be helpful. "If I might make a suggestion," he wrote to Hambro, "as to how the General is to be handled, I would say with extreme firmness. He must be made to understand that S.O.E. and myself in particular, are just as much servants of the Crown as he is and that we act under instructions given by H.M.G. which instructions we obey. That it is not for him to impute action by S.O.E. in West Africa which is unsuitable or dangerous or wrong. It is for him and for me that suitable instructions are given by home."[63]

EXIT WINGATE

Frustration with Giffard's obstructionist policies toward the SOE was undoubtedly one reason why Wingate had decided to go to London. In March 1942, so we have seen, he obtained permission from the Governors' Conference to make the

Soldiers, Airmen, Spies, and Whisperers

journey and to attempt to sort matters out. "I feel that I alone can explain whole picture," he cabled optimistically.[64] But Wingate also had a hidden agenda. In January 1942 he had communicated with SOE headquarters in London by verbal message, carried by "W.45" (identity unknown). It had to do with developing a new initiative and was to the effect that Wingate was personally acquainted with Governor-General Boisson. Thus he was sure that he could get in touch with him "at any moment," and that a joint Anglo-American approach might succeed in swinging the AOF into the allied camp. Boisson, Wingate argued, was affected by the worsening economic situation in the AOF, by the apparent inclination of Vichy to collaborate closely with the Germans, and by the adverse reaction of the people of the AOF against Vichy French rule. Wingate thought that Boisson should be confirmed as governor of an AOF independent of Vichy for the duration of the war, and that the British and U.S. governments should be prepared to defend it in the event not only of Axis attack, but against any incursion of Free French forces unless with the governor-general's agreement.[65]

Wingate's antipathy toward the Free French much colored his views in this period. Professor René Cassin of de Gaulle's French National Committee later drew up an outline plan for the overthrow of the Vichy colonial regimes, envisaging a major role for the Free French. A copy was leaked to Wingate, who commented: "the Free French have no influence and no sympathisers in A.O.F. of any value whatsoever or who would be likely to sway the position in any way. . . . Once again I wish to emphasize that the Free French action directed from British colonies against the Vichy colonies must gravely compromise any action both vis-à-vis the Vichy French and the African. It has no hope of success, and we are inevitably associated with it."[66] Wingate was, however, walking into something of a trap. A conference was convened in London to address the SOE's problems. There was, apparently, little difficulty in resolving the matter of relations between it and the SIS. "An entirely satisfactory agreement covering the collection of intelligence was arrived at," it was reported, "by which S.O.E. works as the agent of S.I.S."[67] Relations with the army, however, proved less simple. Giffard had sent Brig. F. A. S. Clarke, his second in command (GSO 1), to represent him. Once again, much of the documentation is missing, but it seems that Clarke obtained a ruling, the substance of which may be inferred from an SOE memorandum of 9 May 1942: "As the G.O.C. in C. has been given the power of vetoing any S.O.E. operation in the area under his command none of the sabotage projects designed to bring about deterioration in the economic position of A.O.F. and to prevent the shipment of goods for the use of the Axis for which, with the agreement of the

Government Departments concerned, approval has been given in London, have been carried out. The G.O.C. in C. has in fact issued a comprehensive diktat ruling out of consideration all such projects."[68]

To synchronize with the London conference, Giffard arranged for General Hawkins, his area commander for Nigeria, to meet SOE officers there. Again, Hawkins ruled out acts of sabotage "until a state of war shall exist between France and England," but suggested that the SOE should make plans, and train operatives, to attack certain targets "in the event of hostilities"—but then only on the orders of the army, and under its command. Written proposals submitted by W.7 and W.32 (the latter, Capt. R. J. M. Curwen, on secondment from the Nigerian Political Service) were ignored. On 31 March W.29, Officer in Charge, Sabotage, wrote to Wingate, pointing out that Hawkins had effectively deprived the SOE of any role in West Africa and intimating that he would welcome a posting to some other area where he could carry out useful work. The next day Curwen, in his capacity as member of the Political Service, wrote to "W.33" expressing his dismay that Hawkins seemed quite unconcerned about defending Nigeria's frontiers from attack: "It is now clear that the Nigerian Government (in spite of the fact that the Governor is Commander in Chief) has been bullied by the army into dropping the scheme of defence bands controlled in any way by the administration. . . . An early attack on Nigeria may seem improbable but, quite apart from the now greatly enhanced value of the country's vegetable oils and tin, it must never be forgotten that recovery of the Reich's former West African Colonies is one of Hitler's war aims."[69] The situation had obviously become intolerable.

Giffard decided to go to London in person and it was rumored that he feared that Clarke was making too many concessions. He left West Africa by air on 2 April 1942. "A determined effort is being made," it was reported, "to obtain an authoritative policy directive binding upon both the G.O.C. and S.O.E. which will reconcile the claims of both parties." It is not clear which body determined policy in this matter. It may have been the War Cabinet, the authority of which transcended that of the warring parties—that is, the Foreign Office, the Colonial Office, the Ministry of Economic Warfare, and the War Office itself. No minutes of meetings have been located, but the general thrust of the decisions can be tentatively reconstructed. Giffard did not obtain control of the SOE in West Africa. The success of its intelligence gathering work, carried out with the support of the colonial governments and the Governors' Conference, was acknowledged. Thus, PERO would continue to operate as before, even if de jure but not de facto, under the auspices of the SIS. The propaganda section of Frawest, though still

Soldiers, Airmen, Spies, and Whisperers

"affiliated" to PERO in some undefined way, would function as an autonomous group serving as "distributing agent" for the PWE, that is, for the Political Warfare Executive that had been created in London in August 1941, out of SO 1. A third wing of Frawest was set up that was to train personnel—both SOE and army—for sabotage work, but this unit could only be made operational by the GOC-in-C himself, in the event of a Vichy French invasion of British territories or vice versa.[70]

Wingate was retired from his position as head of Frawest, and we may be sure that this was at the insistence of Giffard. It is unfortunate that Wingate's autobiography is so resolutely silent on these matters.[71] Giffard wanted him replaced by a man of his own choice, Lt. Col. A. F. R. Lumby, but Wingate nevertheless handed over Frawest to his deputy and ally, Miles Clifford, who was still, technically, political advisor to the Governors' Conference in Lagos. The War Office supported Giffard and informed him that Lumby would arrive in the Gold Coast on 15 June 1942. The SOE protested that this was impossible since, among other things, Lumby would have to attend various courses to familiarize himself with its work and could not be expected to leave until the second week of July at the earliest. The identity of the writer of this top-level SOE communication is unclear, but he went on to express his complete confidence in Clifford's ability to stand in for Wingate: "In this connection, I am a little disturbed at information which we have received from West Africa which seems to imply that the G.O.C.-in-C. anticipates that Lumby is going out in some sense as his man." The substance of this communication was conveyed to Giffard, who had returned to West Africa, by the War Office.[72] He responded angrily on 6 June in a "most secret" coded telegram to the War Office: "Present S.O.E. representative at Lagos is one Miles Clifford to whom I understand Wingate handed over when he left. I have no repeat no confidence in Clifford. The only qualification I ask for in Lumby is commonsense. As he has this he should not repeat not require further training but should be sent first ship."[73]

Whether such telegrams could be leaked or not, two days later Clifford sent a nine-page letter to CD—now Hambro, not Nelson[74]—giving his views on the prospects of the SOE in West Africa, and paying a stirring tribute to Louis Franck for building up an intelligence system where none had existed before. With regard to Clifford's personal situation, Giffard had made known his disdain for him in a recent conversation. "It has been made very plain to me," Clifford wrote, "that, as an incompetent and uninstructed civilian, I am persona non grata to Giffard and in consequence could be of little assistance to Lumby. . . . His [Giffard's] opinion of me leaves me entirely cold but since you are about to reorganise it seems desirable that you should rid yourselves at the outset of any possible source of friction and I shall therefore ask the Nigerian Government to recall me as soon as I have handed over to Lumby." This "incompetent and uninstructed civilian" had served in World War I in France and Flanders, among other duties in intelligence, and had then spent twenty-two years in the Colonial Service in Nigeria, where he had been "intimately concerned in the putsch which secured the Cameroons for the Free French."[75] Nevertheless, Clifford's work in the SOE in West Africa was over. The War Office made representations to the Colonial Office, and on 7 July 1942 the secretary of state for the colonies informed the Governors' Conference that Lumby had been appointed "Military Secretary to the Chairman of the West African Governors Conference"—though, significantly, "Military Secretary" was rapidly changed to "Economic Advisor."[76]

Giffard seems to have come out of the review process fairly well, and certainly so against Wingate. However, the latter could claim some successes. He had, he wrote, strongly advocated the appointment of a "supreme co-ordinating authority in West Africa who would have direct access to the War Cabinet." In this he claimed to have been supported by Bourdillon, who, if so, must have given up his goal of becoming governor-general of British West Africa. "My final visit home," Wingate wrote, which must refer to his appearance in London in the spring of 1942, "brought off the trick. A Minister of State was to be appointed. He was Lord Swinton, and from that moment West Africa, which had achieved wonders in the new role thrust upon it through the devoted efforts of its individual administrators, was in safe hands."[77] Obviously by "safe hands" Wingate meant out of Giffard's hands, and he presumably saw this as something of a victory. Frawest would henceforth be under the control not of the GOC-in-C but of a resident minister who would have "wide powers over all fighting services and the four colonial governors."[78] Lord Swinton, the former Sir Philip Cunliffe-Lister, had been secretary of state for the colonies in the National Government from 1931 to 1935 and, in his second year, had undertaken a major revamping of the entire Colonial Service.[79] This, combined with his tenure as secretary of state for air and president of the Board of Trade, must have made him an obvious choice to soothe the troubled waters of West Africa.[80] A broadcast he made from Accra testified to his concern to heal any breach between the governors and the GOC-in-C. "In our territories," Swinton announced, "I shall be working in the closest co-operation with the Governors, with all of whom I have worked before and with their civil Administrations. On the military side, we are fortunate to have

Soldiers, Airmen, Spies, and Whisperers

General Giffard as Commander-in-Chief. No one has a wider knowledge of Africa or a deeper understanding of African troops."[81]

With sentiments like these, Wingate may well have wondered whether Swinton's appointment would truly be one of his successes, but he probably felt less equivocal about his Boisson initiative. It is testimony to the respect in which Wingate was held in the higher echelons of the SOE that in April 1942 a modified version of his proposal was incorporated into a top-level SOE "appreciation" that was routed, inter alia, to Churchill's personal intelligence advisor, Desmond Morton. The current military strength of the four West African colonies was assessed at ten thousand British and seventy-one thousand West African troops, constituting seven brigade groups, and six thousand Free French in eight battalions. The closure of the Mediterranean and a possible Japanese threat to East Africa, so it was suggested, made absolutely essential the defense of West Africa. This was particularly so with regard to its role in refueling the Atlantic convoys and in operating the air ferry from Takoradi. Both these operations would also be threatened if the war continued to go badly for the Allies and, probably with Axis support, Vichy moved to the offensive. An immediate approach should be made to Boisson, via the U.S. government, to secure the "friendly neutrality" of the AOF, thus opening Dakar to Allied shipping. Should Boisson not respond to this overture, then immediate plans should be made for the occupation of the Vichy colonies. Some six weeks before military action was to be taken, the SOE would carry out an intensive campaign of subversion and sabotage. No specific role was assigned to the Free French. Indeed, it was commented that "the Free-French movement has ceased to exist as a force to rally the remaining Vichy colonies or as an inspiration to those that have already sided with the Allies." The writers of this "appreciation" asked that a clear directive be given to the SOE and, since "formal S.O.E. activities of subversion and sabotage have been greatly restricted and are now virtually forbidden by orders of the G.O.C.-in-C., the civil and military authorities notified accordingly."[82]

Although fundamental issues of authority were involved, the dispute between Giffard and Wingate clearly contained a strong personal element. Louis Franck had developed a great respect for Wingate and expressed the utmost confidence in his ability to run Frawest. "He has seen," Franck wrote, "the whole organisation grow, he has very wide administrative experience, he is absolutely independent of the various local governments, and has the temperament to keep a balanced and sensible control upon the whole organisation. He has also the full confidence of the Governors Conference as well as that of the Military authorities."[83] Giffard obviously did not share these sentiments. We can only ask why he, the professional soldier, so intensely disliked Wingate, the professional civil servant. Giffard no doubt, despite Wingate's distinguished parentage, considered him a novice on the African scene. After Rugby School and Sandhurst, in 1906 Giffard had been commissioned into the Queen's Royal Regiment, the First Infantry Regiment of the Line. Seconded to the King's African Rifles in 1912, the then Lieutenant Giffard commanded a company upcountry. When World War I broke out, his unit withdrew to Nairobi and from there took part in the East Africa campaign against the brilliant German, General Vorbeck von Lettow. In October 1916, Giffard, now a lieutenant colonel, was awarded the DSO for his actions at the battle of Nyangao. In 1936, as we have seen, he became inspector general, commander in chief of the KAR, and two years later, took command of all African colonial forces. An important clue to his personality was provided by Lt. Gen. W. Slim, Giffard's commander in the Burma campaign in 1943, with whom he served as general officer commanding the Eastern Army in India: "He abhorred the theatrical, and was one of the very few generals, indeed men in any position, I have known who really dislike publicity. . . . He understood the fundamentals of war—that soldiers must be trained before they can fight, fed before they can march and relieved before they are worn out." Giffard believed, Slim wrote, that "soundness of organization and administration is worth more than specious short cuts to victory."[84] Clearly Wingate had come to represent all that Giffard abhorred, especially "specious short cuts."

Wingate, by contrast, was the consummate political officer, born into a family with a strong tradition of service in India. His father, Wingate Pasha of the Sudan, spent most of his career with the Egyptian army, and it was in Cairo, in 1889, that Wingate was born. Sent to school in England at ten, he spent summer vacations at the new family home in Scotland, where visitors included such British heroes of the Sudan as Slatin Pasha and Kitchener. Wingate entered Balliol College, Oxford, in 1906 and joined the Indian Civil Service after university. Serving first in Baluchistan and Delhi, in 1917 he was appointed assistant political officer with the Mesopotamia Expeditionary Force. In mid-1919 he was made political agent and consul at Muscat and Oman. There he was to become friendly with another Indian civil servant, Henry Bourdillon. In November 1921, Wingate became assistant to the resident in Kashmir. He was to spend the remainder of his service on the northern frontiers of India, finally becoming revenue commissioner in Baluchistan, and agent there for the governor-general, in other words, de facto governor. He returned to Britain in 1937, took his leave entitlement, and retired from the Indian Political Service in 1939. Following the declaration of war, he was interviewed by Desmond Morton and found himself in a minor position in MEW. In August 1940 he was abruptly summoned by Hugh Dalton, commissioned, and, as we have seen, sent to accompany the abortive Dakar expedition. Assigned to the Franck Mission and the Governors' Conference, Wingate renewed his friendship with Bourdillon, now governor of Nigeria, and came to enjoy his strong support.[85] While it would be going beyond the evidence to suggest that Wingate deliberately pitted the Governors' Conference against the army, it is probable that Giffard was at least sensitive to this as a possibility. Whatever the case, Giffard's hostility to the SOE survived Wingate's downfall.

In June 1942, Julius Hanau ("Caesar"), on his way back to London from Durban, stopped at Lagos. As the London case officer for SO 2 in West Africa, Hanau not surprisingly paid his respects to the head of Neucols, who was based in Lagos. It so happened that Brigadier Clarke was on a visit there, and a meeting was arranged between him, Major General Hawkins (GOC, Nigeria), and Hanau. When Giffard learned of this from Clarke, he fired off a signal to the War Office, protesting that he had not been officially informed that an SOE officer had visited Lagos. He accused Hanau of having made a request that he, Giffard, "should in future not unduly obstruct S.O.E. projects." Hanau denied this, but agreed that he had tried to convince Clarke that minor SOE operations against Vichy targets ("of course given the approval of the G.O.C.-in-C.") were not likely to provoke reprisals from the Axis powers. But Giffard was also incensed about a further report that Hanau had stated, that on his arrival back in London, he intended to report directly to Lord Swinton. The general took this as a threat. In reply, Hanau said that he had merely expressed the hope that he could chat with Swinton, catching him before he left London for West Africa. CD (Hambro) wrote to the War Office to the effect that the misunderstandings could best be cleared up on the spot by Lumby—now designated WF. He had, remarked Hambro, applied for air priority as the new head of Frawest, but the Priorities Board had only given him a sea passage. Perhaps the War Office would be more successful if they chose to intervene, he added, with barely disguised sarcasm.[86]

The SOE, as part of its operations, had created the Y Radio Service for intercepting radio transmissions in the Vichy territories. They had assured the other services that all material gained would be shared with them. Notwithstanding this arrangement, the Y Service was taken over by the army, with disastrous results. The organization deteriorated badly, and the RAF, which relied on it quite heavily, made an official protest.[87] The SOE in London apparently decided to reestablish its interception operation, and obtained the services of an officer and six men from the signals corps. They arrived in June 1942, carrying a one-kilowatt and several smaller Y transmitters that had been consigned to PERO in West Africa. These were presumably to be put in the hands of SOE agents in the field. Unfortunately, the consignees had shipped the material via general headquarters, Achimota. Giffard learned of it and seized the equipment. His satisfaction in once again having thwarted the SOE was manifest in a coded telegram he fired off to the War Office on 1 July 1942: "I have for a long time been trying to curtail broadcasting receiving and general dabbling in military intelligence by P E R O who in this theatre act as part of S O E and regard it as their province to attempt para military activities in Vichy French territory. Have at last succeeded in withdrawing P E R O sets [transmitters] after some months struggle in view of imminent arrival of Lumby and probably Lord Swinton with whom I shall discuss whole question of propaganda."[88]

ENTER LUMBY

In the event, Lumby traveled to West Africa in the company of Lord Swinton. A curious sideline on the journey was that the latter wrote to Nelson to express his disapproval of Lumby's cover: "[he] should not be disporting himself in mufti as plain Mister."[89] They arrived in Bathurst on 10 July. Clifford, still acting head of Frawest, cabled headquarters in London in an effort to prevent Lumby from stopping in Accra and talking first to Giffard: "Hope you will advise W.F. to come straight to Lagos and not repeat not stop at Accra. Feel it is important that W.F. should obtain his first impression of West Africa lay-out from local headquarters S.O.E. You will be able to contact him at Bathurst."[90] He was too late. Lumby landed in Accra on 12 July and had talks with Giffard and his staff before proceeding to Lagos. Clifford had prepared extensive notes to help Lumby take over. In them he described the Gold Coast Section of the SOE as non-operational. He paid tribute to the founder of the section, "W.1," presumably Francis Glyn, but thought that the recently retired section head was a man of lesser caliber who had lost the confidence of the administration. Clifford suggested bringing "W.33" from Nigeria, "to put the Gold Coast Section back on the rails."[91] This may not have seemed very tactful, since W.33 was, as Clifford noted elsewhere, Wingate's "personal friend of long standing."[92] In fact, when Lumby returned to Accra from Lagos on 16 July 1942, he found himself in agreement with Clifford, that the Gold Coast Section was more or less moribund, and did send for W.33 to reorganize it.

Designated Economic Advisor to the Resident Minister, Lumby appears to have to taken over as head of Frawest quietly and efficiently. After talks with Giffard on 22 July 1942, he decided not to make sabotage an issue, but to focus on what PERO and Frawest had been doing well—that is, intelligence gathering. With the support of Giffard and Swinton, he began to work toward the creation of a Joint Intelligence Committee.[93] In late 1942 there were five agencies concerned with intelligence in the Gold Coast (and West Africa more generally), namely, the SOE itself; Military Intelligence (GS[I]); Free French Intelligence (SLICA); Menzies's Special Intelligence Service (SIS); and the American Office of Strategic Services (OSS). The SIS and the OSS were newly arrived in West Africa and neither had any capacity for collecting raw data. Indeed, the belated presence of the OSS came months after a preliminary mission consisting of two anthropologists sent out by its predecessor, the Office of the Coordinator of Information (COI), under the direct authorization of the White House. Jack Harris and William Bascom had arrived in the Gold Coast in February 1942 bearing letters from Roosevelt and operating under the flimsy cover of an anthropological expedition. "We were amateur bunglers in the field of intelligence," Harris wrote many years later. "We had no prior training except for brief instruction in a simple code for our reports. . . . In early 1942 the level of intelligence knowledge and operations in the U.S. was very low. I recall Ralph Bunche telling me at that time the files at U.S. Army Intelligence on West Africa were composed almost completely of clippings from *The New York Times*." Harris and Bascom rapidly concluded that it would have "been foolish for us to undertake setting up parallel sources of intelligence in the field and we did not." What they did achieve was, in Harris's words, "modest," the transmittal to Washington of a number of reports from British Intelligence on the general situation in West Africa, the content and quantity of which seemed to please U.S. intelligence.[94] In any event, the most significant conclusion reached by Washington was that they would base their intelligence efforts in West Africa at least on a close liaison with the British. Thus both the OSS and the SIS were dependent on picking up material from the other three agencies for transmission to their respective HQs in London and Washington.

The SOE—or, strictly, PERO—although technically now working under the SIS, was still the major source of political and economic data. This was organized and written up by PERO officers and was the mainstay of WAPIC, the fortnightly bulletin of the West African Political Intelligence Centre, put out by the Governors' Conference and distributed to the War Cabinet, colonial governors, and top military commanders. Inevitably, however, PERO agents acquired information of military significance and its reports were made available to GS(I). GS(I) itself had intelligence officers at all levels of command and also had its own "native agents" who operated in the Vichy colonies. The material gathered, after analysis, was presented in various secret reports, including: "West Africa Command Military Review" and "General Headquarters West Africa Intelligence Notes." SLICA appears to have worked more closely with PERO than with GS(I), and their field officers were paired with those of PERO whenever possible.

By the second week in August 1942, Lumby was already referring to a "new Joint Intelligence Committee" in a cable to Hanau.[95] "AD," (Taylor) expressed some misgivings that Lumby might run foul of the powerful C, head of the SIS, and instructed him scrupulously to observe the agreement between the SOE and the SIS that had been worked out in London.[96] He did so. On 21 August the existence of the Joint Intelligence Committee (JIC) was formally announced by the West African War Council (a body probably newly set up by Resident Minister Swinton). The JIC was to be located in Achimota. R. M. Makins of Swinton's office was to be chairman, and Lumby vice chairman. It would include representatives all three "Fighting Services," the Security Service (presumably military intelligence), the SIS, and the SOE.[97] Unlike its more high powered counterparts in Washington and London, the JIC would not, so it was minuted, "take in Intelligence from every source and then produce final appreciations for the use of the competent authorities, but on the contrary is strictly a co-ordinating and non-executive body. Its job is primarily to see that the Intelligence collecting bodies pool all their information and co-operate in every way (which they certainly did not do before), and settle any disputes which may arise."[98]

Although Lumby, in the months after his arrival in the Gold Coast, had focused his attention primarily on intelligence gathering, he had not ignored the matter of sabotage, nor could he. It had, after all, been generally agreed that the SOE should train saboteurs. This had not been the issue, but rather whether SOE saboteurs could become operational except on the orders, and under the command, of the army. Indeed, the Olokomeji Training School in Nigeria, about a hundred miles north of Lagos, had been functioning, with army and SOE cooperation, since February 1942, and was unambiguously designed to train saboteurs.[99] It was with reference to this institution that Clifford, in August, sent Lumby a copy of a syllabus designed for training Africans in the collection of information, but added, "Africans who have been trained in sabotage cannot, for obvious reasons, be employed thereafter on normal trans-frontier duties i.e. collection of information for our purposes, or on service demand, and effective distribution of propaganda, but must be held in reserve—and under close control—for special tasks. I have given explicit directions to this effect." If there were any doubts about the training of saboteurs, Giffard put them to rest in August. "Your general directive, as head of the Frawest Mission," he wrote to Lumby, "instructs you to make plans and preparations for acts of sabotage and subversion." Lumby, he said, should consult with the army area commanders about such matters but, the general added, "any plans which are made as a result of these consultations will not be submitted to the Resident Minister for his approval until they have been examined and approved by me."[100]

Lumby, with a new directive from SOE headquarters and apparent approval by Giffard, became quite enthusiastic about starting similar training schools in the Gold Coast and Sierra Leone. He moved rapidly in choosing a site for the first of these in Asante, and Nanwa Gold Mines, about eight miles from Konongo, which had been closed down in 1939 for the duration of the war, was taken over. PERO had already made use of one of its magazines as the central store for its weapons, ammunition, explosives, and other so-called toys. Staffing of the new training school proved remarkably easy, since there had been problems at the Olokomeji Training School in Nigeria resulting in its being placed indefinitely on a care and maintenance basis. This is fact meant that the Nanwa Training School in Asante became the only operational sabotage center in the whole of West Africa. Many of Olokomeji's staff were transferred to it. Among these was the invaluable Sergeant Quigley of the Royal Engineers, whose career history makes one speechless with admiration:

> *Sgt. Quigley R.E.* Previously a steward and chef on a Liner and more recently a Sapper Corporal in the Regular (pre-war) Army. *War Service.* He was a Party Sergeant at Ripon T.B.R.E. Demolition Instructor at one of the Scottish S.T.S. He knows his job very thoroughly. He had now had 2 months experience in Training Africans and has been very successful. His Regular Army training qualifies him as a Musketry and Drill Instructor. . . . Acting in capacity of Quarter Master, Camp Labour Officer also Instructor in Demolitions, Drill, Musketry, Intelligence Work, Patrol Work, and P.T. [physical training]. He also functions as Doctor.[101]

When Capt. Desmond Longe, "W.30," sailed from Nigeria on 19 September 1942 to take over command of the Nanwa Training School, he must have been delighted to have Sergeant Quigley there to greet him.[102]

Giffard made no attempt to close down the Nanwa operation, even though it remained under SOE control. In November 1942, on completion of its first course, Longe submitted a lengthy report to Lumby. Fourteen students had been enrolled and eleven completed the courses in unarmed combat, weapons training, demolition, map reading, observation, and fieldcraft. Longe thought the students by and large interested in the work, but made the sad comment that "they are a cheerful party and it has been an interesting, if almost heartbreaking, job training them. Although it seems unlikely that they will now be used for the purpose for which they are trained."[103]

AD (Taylor), who was, or was shortly to become, Special Emissary to SOE Overseas Missions, was in the Gold Coast in October and November 1942. He was impressed by the job Lumby was doing. In fairness to Lumby, Taylor wrote, "it is absolutely essential to make clear, what was certainly not fully appreciated by me till now, that when he [Lumby] came out here he started from well behind scratch. The Frawest Mission, as he found it, was not only moribund, but thoroughly discredited. . . . From the information which has been given to me, not by W.F. himself, but from innumerable outside sources, it is clear that it would be impossible to exaggerate the harm done by Wingate during the period in which he was in charge of Frawest."[104] This certainly put a different view on matters but, unfortunately for the historian, Taylor did not go into detail. As he himself wrote, "I do not want unnecessarily to go back on the past and disinter ancient scandals," and, from the point of view of the SOE in late 1942, Wingate belonged to the past but Giffard still very much to the present.[105]

Asantehene Sir Osei Agyeman Prempeh II in his uniform as lieutenant colonel of the Home Guard.
Nana Opoku Ware II

The Empire Training Scheme: pilot trainees marching at their base in Borden, Saskatchewan.
War Illustrated, 14 February 1941

Kwadwo Bosompra in 1994, an eyewitness to the arrival of the Gyaman in Sunyani.
Author's photograph

T. E. Kyei—author, broadcaster, anthropologist, and Home Guardsman.
Author's photograph, 1994

Fuselages for RAF Hurricane bombers being uncrated at Takoradi and carried to the assembly buildings.
  War Illustrated, 14 February 1941

The Light Battery, GCR, 1937.
  Gold Coast Government

The Light Battery, GCR, on the march, 1937.
Gold Coast Government

The dilapidated remains of District Commissioner M. M. Miln's house, Sunyani, where the "red carpet" of mats was laid out for the French commandant in 1942.
Author's photograph, 1994

Takoradi airfield, 1963, showing the general layout of the base.
Gold Coast and Ghana Forces Association (GCGFA)

RAF Blenheim IV bombers in front of the control tower at Takoradi, ca. 1941.
Tony Blythe and GCGFA

RAF Hurricanes lined up after assembly at Takoradi, ca. 1941.
GCGFA

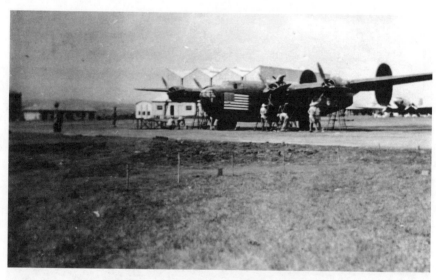

U.S. B-24 Liberator bombers on loan to the British government. Takoradi, ca.
1940–41.
GCGFA

Douglas Dakota transports outside their hangars at Takoradi, ca. 1942.
GCGFA

Lt. E. C. Lanning, GCR, in tropical dress, including slouch hat with RWAFF hackle (feather from a domestic rooster), 1942.
E. C. Lanning

Men of the Ashanti Battalion (7 GCR), in or about December 1942.
E. C. Lanning

5 The Special Operations Executive at Work in the Gold Coast

A WINDOW ON WENCHI

The secrecy surrounding SOE procedures, resulting in the massive destruction of files, makes it very difficult to know what was happening at the local levels. This generalization, as the reader may already have realized, breaks down in the case of the Wenchi district in northwestern Asante. Several files marked To Be Destroyed were, in fact, not destroyed but, to my complete astonishment and delight, had been preserved in the National Archives of Ghana at Sunyani. They had obviously been stored in the district commissioner's safe and had escaped further attention until the creation of the new branch of the National Archives there. Such good fortune must be attributed to the oversight of either H. V. Wimshurst, who was DC, Wenchi, at the time, or his replacement, Neil Ross. It has been possible to communicate with both men, although it seemed tactless to ask whose failure it was to carry out the destruction order. Wimshurst, after a quarter century in the Colonial Service in the Gold Coast, retired and found his way via Southern Rhodesia (now Zimbabwe) to South Africa, where he died in 1995. He was most generous in sharing his wartime experiences with me. Ross left the Colonial Service after the war and, after serving in local government in Scotland, took a well-deserved retirement and now lives in Edinburgh.

In July 1942 the structure of the Gold Coast Section was laid out by Clifford, then acting head of Frawest, in a memorandum to the designated permanent re-placement, Lumby. The headquarters were, of course, at Accra. Its SOE personnel consisted of the section head and secretary. The former, FitzGerald, was replaced by W.33 in mid-1942, and the latter, who also doubled as accountant, was F. G. J. Forbes. There were posts for seven field officers. One of them served as subsec-tion head in the Northern Territories, with his base at Salaga. This position was filled by Mothersill, who was assisted by two other full-time field officers and the district commissioner of Navrongo, who had been seconded to the SOE on a shared-time basis. Two other field officers were stationed on the western frontier. One of these was McGee, who was temporarily assigned to direct the Training School for District Messengers and Agents at Anomabu. There were also two more field officers posted to the eastern frontier. This seems to have been the sum total of SOE operatives in the Gold Coast at this time, and to make matters worse, Mothersill was on sick leave. Thus the section was grossly understaffed when Clifford wrote. However, an SOE man from Nigeria, Pilot Officer B. C. Stewart ("W.44") had just been transferred to the Gold Coast; the Colonial Ser-vice had agreed to return Mothersill ("W.11"), assuming his recovery, and "W.13" (unidentified) to the SOE. It was further hoped that the section might also se-cure the return of A. Hughes. Hughes, it will be remembered, accompanied R. O. Ramage on the unsuccessful mission in June 1940 to bring Dahomey and French Togo into the Allied camp and was temporarily seconded to the resident minis-ter's office. In addition, there was a certain W.46 who had not impressed Clifford very much, and who had asked to be transferred to the SOE's propaganda sec-tion. Finally, there was a matter of reopening the training school at Anomabu, which was opposed by General Giffard. Notwithstanding this, Clifford thought it would require the recruitment of a demolitions expert, and two good NCO in-structors, as well as a director. He noted, however, that "W.29," who may have been McGee, did not himself regard Anomabu as a very suitable site. And it may be that he thought it should be reestablished at the Nanwa site in Asante. In view of all these considerations, Clifford did not think that the Gold Coast Section could be truly operational before the end of November 1942.[1]

Other than its regular field officers, the Gold Coast Section of the SOE relied heavily on the services of the DCs. Wimshurst was one of these. He was co-opted into the Franck Mission, subsequently Frawest or PERO, and was involved in building up a network of agents. According to Wimshurst, "these were not diffi-cult to obtain. International boundaries cut through tribal lands and local fami-lies crossed to and fro at will. I paid agents to travel and pass on the rumors as

Soldiers, Airmen, Spies, and Whisperers

supplied to me by P.E.R.O. . . . I naturally recruited the most intelligent locals that came forward."[2] His task was much facilitated by his good fortune in procuring the services of Cpl. R. Quarshie, a member of the Gold Coast Escort Police, who turned out to be an indefatigable gatherer of information and a writer of many lucid, if somewhat oddly worded, reports. Wimshurst stationed Quarshie at Sampa, on the Gold Coast-Ivoirien border, and the main crossing from western Asante to Vichy Bondoukou.[3] There Quarshie worked together with Awuah-Barmeh, the Free French agent also posted at Sampa.[4] Quarshie, whose name indicates his southern Ghanaian origins, was nevertheless well known on the frontier and was, according to Neil Ross, a "special" individual.[5] The war had put him in the unusual position of handing out money for information, rather than collecting it to smooth the passage of travelers.

The funds at the disposal of the district commissioners were not overgenerous, as Ross testified many years later. "They were trifling sums—from [CCA] Hawkesworth's office. . . . They [the agents] volunteered. Got paid for it. Not much —really a trifle. Once they brought news that foreigners had come to Bamako— probably Germans—but nothing ever came of it. They were local Brongs. They would go as far even as Bamako, and bring back information. We paid them, of course, but it was only a very small amount. Then I would send on whatever information was valuable to the chief commissioner of Ashanti in Kumasi. . . . No, never used code."[6] In contrast to British parsimony, Ross had noted in 1942 that the Free French tended to be more lavish in their payments to informants, but added that the price of information had quite recently gone up "owing to recent killing and maltreatment of agents by the Vichy French Administration."[7] Wimshurst remembered being "supplied with thousands of French Equatorial francs (of no value elsewhere)," that were at the disposal of the Free French, and used by their agents.[8] Whatever the sums involved, Quarshie dispensed them. Lacking cover, he spent most of his time policing the border on the Gold Coast side, in order to intercept both smugglers and Vichy agents.[9]

Quarshie also controlled a number of "secret messengers," presumably district messengers, who crossed into the Côte d'Ivoire. Not all these were imbued with a strong sense of duty, as Quarshie discovered. One, a certain Adama, was found to be taking PERO money from Wimshurst in Wenchi, and SLICA money from Bertin-Fournier at Berekum, and was suspected of also working for the enemy. Another stayed in Sampa and simply reported gossip from travelers. He admitted that "he daren't go across," and it turned out that he had escaped from jail in Bondoukou, where he had been serving a three-year sentence.[10]

Others, however, carried out their duties as expected. One, for example, a certain Alasa, crossed the border to Bondoukou on 15 March 1942. He was probably the source of the detailed list of commodities and prices in its market that Quarshie wrote up nine days later—noting, inter alia, the unavailability of tea, cooking oil, kerosene, gasoline, motor oil, flour, corned beef, and so forth.[11] Alasa proceeded deeper into the Côte d'Ivoire, and another agent was sent to Bondoukou. He returned with information about a meeting between the commandant and the imam, having to do with the *impôt*, or head tax. He also brought specimens of imported goods that could only be purchased with a permit from the commandant. Quarshie sent them on to the acting DC in Wenchi, Ross (who could be forgiven if he failed to forward such delights to his superiors). "Sir," wrote Quarshie, "I am sending to you per one of the Secret messengers Mama Kurubari or No. W.E.2, one small wooden box sealed containing 2 small bottles of Rhum Saint-Esprit @ 75 francs each, one bundle (25 packets) of French National Cigarettes value 100 Francs, and 2 boxes of matches value 5 francs, all to the total value of 255 francs."[12] Something of the background of this messenger is known, for he was among the first intake of the Training School at Anomabu Fort. On 21 November 1941, Wimshurst had selected two people for training as operatives. Both had previously been working with him, and one with the Free French as well. Wimshurst gave their names as Braima Kambagarty and Mama Krubarli—that is, Quarshie's Mama Kurubari. Their patronymics, more recognizable as Kamagate and Coulibaly, indicate that both men belonged to the local (Muslim) Dyula community. More complete dossiers on them were sent to Accra on 23 November:

Braima Kambagarty.
Lives in Sampa, Wenchi District. Mother and father both live in Sampa. Father formerly in [Gold Coast] Regiment and has many medals. Speaks following languages:—Wangara, Mfantra, Nkorang (Jaman), Hausa, Ashanti, Grunchie, Banda, and a small amount of Moshie, English and French. Has done some work for me and for Free French.

Mama Krubarli.
Lives in Sampa. Mother and father both dead but from Sampa. Speaks:—Mfantra, Wangara, Nkorang (Jaman), Hausa, and Jimini. Small English and Ashanti. Has been working for me through Cpl Quarshie.

Both were accepted by FitzGerald for district messenger training and sent to Anomabu Fort. They arrived there on 25 November.[13] Two other recruits recom-

Soldiers, Airmen, Spies, and Whisperers

mended by Wimshurst, both apparently southern Ghanaians working in Wenchi district, Kofi Jarko and J. E. Ankama, failed to arrive on time, having been stranded for some unknown reason in Sekondi. McGee, who was running the course, hoped this latter incident would not deter Wimshurst from sending further recruits, and expressed his hope that the two under training would be returned safely just after Christmas.[14] On 14 December, Wimshurst did in fact send another recruit to McGee, an Asante named Kodjo Amankwa, who had served in the Gold Coast Regiment as a driver and apparently settled in Wenchi after his discharge.[15]

Braima Kamagate and Mama Coulibaly both passed their training course and were to be paid two shillings a day with bonuses for "meritorious work." The money would come from PERO funds. In token of their new status they were given the code names WE 1 and WE 2, respectively—that is, first and second Wenchi graduates from Anomabu Fort. They were back in Wenchi by the beginning of 1942, and it seems likely that they were used as long-range operatives. With the cooperation of its district commissioner, Wenchi was being used as a base for dispatching agents, through Bondoukou, to the important garrison town of Bouaké. Thus in early June 1942, Neil Ross, then running Wenchi District while Wimshurst was on secondment to Kumasi, requested extra funds from FitzGerald at Accra. He needed them, he explained, in part because, "I am sending men through to Bouaké and their expenses are heavier than for more local informants."[16] In one Wenchi file that escaped destruction there is a handwritten sheet, undated but from early to mid-1942, that contains instructions for an agent who was, it seems, to travel to Bobo-Dioulasso and thence, perhaps by train, to Bouaké. He was being asked to find out

1. How many railway engines at Bobo?
2. How many soldiers at Bobo?
3. How many aeroplanes come to Bobo?
4. How many times does train run to Bouaké?

There were also specific questions relating to Bouaké.

1. How many soldiers?
2. How many tanks?
3. How many armoured cars?
4. How many Germans visited Bouaké?
5. Are there many European soldiers?
6. What tubes [tires] makes?
7. How is the Groundnut trade?

Are much bought? Price? (Used to be 25 francs per kerosene tin)
Where are they sending the groundnuts?[17]

The collection of intelligence from the Côte d'Ivoire was the principal, but not the only, function of the DC, Wenchi. Wimshurst, who presumably knew of Giffard's opposition to subversive acts, nevertheless used his own initiative to devise minor acts of sabotage. He directed an operation to have a firing pin removed from an artillery piece in the French post opposite his district. Decades later he explained how the idea had come to him: "I saw the native mammies walking so freely back and forth. I was able to get the whole plan of the fortress just by asking the 'mammies' about it when they returned." After the success of this bit of chicanery, Wimshurst then expanded his original plan:

> Having some knowledge of military equipment, it occurred to me that rifles without bolts and artillery without firing pins in the breach are not much use—so?? . . . No, I did not go across the frontier—I just offered large sums of useless French Equatorial francs to anyone who produced a rifle, or easier still, a rifle bolt. When I heard that a battery of mountain artillery had been stationed nearby I asked PERO to send me diagrams of the workings of the breach-block and spent hours showing agents how to extract the firing pins. I doubted they [the French] had much ammunition to waste and if they ever did fire a gun after I left the district, they probably put it down to dud shells![18]

No reports other than Wimshurst's remain as to the success of his firing pin sabotage, but one is tempted to think that blacksmiths in the Bonduku-Wenchi area had a mini-boom, as orders for firing pins to present to the DC must have been flooding in! In any case, in July 1941, Wimshurst received fifteen hundred francs from PERO to help finance the operation.[19]

FREE FRENCH OPERATIONS

The quantity of the intelligence from Bouaké suggests that other agents, presumably run by SLICA, must have been active there. These no doubt involved the use of members of L'Union Franco-Britannique. Formed in January 1940 at Bouaké, the organization's goals had been to promote the Anglo-French alliance. It had, curiously, evolved out of the local sports and music club.[20] After the armistice, the union's president, M. Lebouath Cayssekand, became a devoted adherent to the Free French cause. He and his followers were regarded as a major threat to security, and there can be little doubt that the group was in contact with PERO or SLICA agents, or both. Ultimately Cayssekand and several other leaders were caught by the Vichy secret service, stripped of their property, tortured, and sent to Dakar for judgment. Fortuitously, their trial was interrupted by a Boisson become suddenly prudent after the Allied landings in North Africa in November 1942.[21] Information was also coming from a small, but active cell of Free French sympathizers in Abidjan, which apparently included some employees of the commercial firm Aero Maritime.[22]

Another source of information, but one so far barely explored, may have been the workers on the Abidjan-Niger Railway which, despite its name, at that time terminated in Bobo-Dioulasso in Haute Côte d'Ivoire. These workers had already demonstrated an impressive level of organization in their strike against the colonial administration in 1938. This won them the right to form their own hard won union, but this was disbanded by Vichy racial legislation. The railway workers' contributions to army intelligence in Achimota can be inferred from the detailed information in its files, not only on the construction of the new Ouagadougou section of the line, but also on the movement of commodities between Abidjan and Bobo-Dioulasso. In May 1942, for example, British Intelligence was able to report an A.2 (i.e., highly reliable) source on supplies en route for the tirailleurs in Bobo-Dioulasso:

Movements of Material

Bobo is to get shortly from Abijan for R.P.T.S.

> 50 Mattress covers
> Pillows
> Mosquito Nets
> Sleeping Bags
> 500 Kgs. bed stuffing.[23]

The railway workers certainly lost none of their hostility toward colonialism during the Vichy (and indeed the succeeding Free French) period, for in 1947 they walked out for three months.[24] The bitterness of the strike is still remembered.

The quality of the intelligence received from such sources, however, varied greatly. Army analysts gave only a B.3 rating to material received in May 1942:

The garrison at Bwake [Bouaké] is stated to consist of:

> 1 Colonel
> 2 Ch. de Bn [*chefs de bataillon*]

16 Subalterns

9 Officiers sans troupes

85 Sous officiers

1000 Tirailleurs.

Another item from the same report earned a creditable A.2: *"Movement of Tps. [Troops].* From Abijan 29/5 [29 May] for Bwake 119 tirailleurs (28 for RT.S.C.I.S.)"[25] In September the following information was collected and also graded A.2:

> *Movement of Tps.* To Bwake from Bobo, 2 Officers, 104 O.Rs [Other Ranks] and 5 tons luggage 2/9 [2 September]. . . . *Equipment.* Regt. Bwake may buy 4 new Peugeot m/cs [motorcycles] which are available at Abijan. . . . *Movements of Materials.* To Bwake from Abijan 20 tons of cement 1/9 [1 September].

Of a different character, but graded A.2 in the same report, was the item: "Vichy wireless reports that Gov. Ivory Coast (M. Deschamps) has moved to Bwake from Abijan." The comment on this piece of information read: "It is not known whether he will make his residence permanently there or not. . . . Bwake is thought to be growing in importance, and it is not impossible that an alternative site for administration is being organised there."[26]

It has been remarked that the Free French had a relative abundance of available personnel, such were the number of anti-Vichy French men and women unable to return home. Recruitment into the Free French Mission presented far fewer difficulties than those being experienced by the SOE. With people stationed in Accra, Kumasi, and six outstations throughout the colony, the French were in excellent shape. The nature of the linkage between Free French officers in the outstations and their colleagues in the SOE is nowhere made explicit. We have pointed out that Wingate had a very low opinion of the Free French in West Africa, but this attitude does not seem to have percolated down to SOE operatives in the field. We have seen, for example, that, until he was withdrawn to Brazzaville at the end of the year, Bertin-Fournier, then at Berekum, worked closely with one of the SOE field officers for the western frontier, McGee, at Sunyani.

Virtually nothing is known about the identity of the lower-level field officers of SLICA, the relevant files having disappeared. According to Jean Rouch, who in the early 1950s interviewed Malam Ansa, one of SLICA's men, the organization had as many as forty "secret agents," including "five Zerma, five Songhai, four Hausa, two Peul, two Mossi, and two Bambara" (but no partridges in pear trees!). They were sent regularly to the Côte d'Ivoire, Niger, and French Soudan to gather information on French military establishments, to make contact with those in

Soldiers, Airmen, Spies, and Whisperers

the AOF thought to sympathize with the Gaullist movement, and to distribute Free French propaganda.[27] In fact, many of these people had always been regarded as mere smugglers by the British, but were now elevated to the status of secret agents. Had SLICA's records survived, much more light might have been shed upon such matters. The organization recruited agents from among those accustomed to crossing the Gold Coast border: traders, cattle dealers, and the like. Migrant Mossi workers in Accra joined the Union Africaine de la France Libre, contributing one shilling a month for the Free French cause.[28]

Giffard, we have seen, exercised a virtual veto over the SOE, preventing it from putting into operation any of the proposed sabotage and subversion plans. If the SOE were to launch incendiary attacks on the AOF's stockpiles of raw materials destined for Europe, mostly located at the ports of Abidjan, Lomé, Conakry, and Cotonou, the real fireworks would come from Giffard in Accra, whose main goal was the avoidance of provocative action against the Vichy French. Giffard, however, had no comparable control over the sabotage activities of SLICA, even though the latter were technically guests in the British territories. Indeed, General de Gaulle continued to take a close interest in the Free French Mission in West Africa. In a letter of 7 July 1942, for example, to General Sir Alan Brooke, chief of the Imperial General Staff, de Gaulle stressed that, in his view, the Free French personnel were in a superior position to carry out operations in Vichy territory. This, he wrote, was "a result of their knowledge of the people and locality and their experience of French Colonial Administration." He enclosed detailed notes on their organization and duties. The head of the mission in Accra was to receive instructions directly from de Gaulle's personal staff and was to report to him on all operations. This, of course, was not calculated to please Giffard. General Brooke informed de Gaulle that he would have to refer the matter to Giffard, and this was done in collaboration with the Foreign Office. Giffard was uncharacteristically slow to reply. The War Office, no doubt correctly, inferred "that General Giffard's reactions are likely to be adverse."[29]

While Colonel Ponton, unlike his much-detested predecessor Adam, was proving himself amenable to the authorities, being polite to Giffard did not deter him from what was his primary goal, the deliverance of the AOF from Vichy hands into de Gaulle's. His agents faced extreme danger, for they would not be merely spies, but traitors who would be shot if captured. The Free French believed that the only way to resolve the situation was to take direct violent action against the Vichy authorities. And no member of Ponton's staff was more enthusiastic about this than M. Raphael Beretta.

Beretta, it will be remembered, had been assigned to the Free French Mission in the Gold Coast in March 1942 and had caused considerable alarm due to reports from Brazzaville regarding his difficult wife. This, however, looked unimportant when it became known that he had secret instructions from Médecin-Général Adolphe Sicé, the high commissioner of the AEF, to "study the possibilities of forming armed bands for raids into Dahomey and the Ivory Coast with the object of creating such confusion as to enable those colonies to be taken by military action." Reactions to this unwelcome bit of news were swift. Diplomatic necessity clearly dictated that Giffard exercise a much greater degree of tact with the Free French than in his dealings with the SOE. He was, nevertheless, outraged that such actions were being even contemplated by some obscure Frenchman obviously sent specifically to the Gold Coast to try him. Everyone concerned was informed, in no uncertain terms, that forming armed bands of this nature was "entirely contrary to policy," and that M. Beretta and other members of the Free French Missions should not engage in subversive activities of this kind.[30] Although the Free French were playing a vital role in the intelligence gathering in the Gold Coast, their potential for more aggressive operations undoubtedly caused Giffard even more anxiety than the SOE had.

As chance would have it, Beretta was posted to Sunyani with the overt task of managing the affairs of the Gyaman refugees, whose exodus from the Côte d'Ivoire will be the subject of chapter 7. He was thrown into close collaboration with the district commissioner there, M. M. Miln, some of whose eccentricities have been mentioned above. The two were within the administrative purview of Chief Commissioner Hawkesworth in Kumasi. Reports he received of Beretta's activities made Hawkesworth fear that a serious frontier incident might occur. For someone like Hawkesworth, who clearly accepted Giffard's line of nonprovocation, this was an eventuality much to be feared. Adding, no doubt, to the CCA's discomfort was the nature of the clarification he had sought on the actual position of the Free French Mission in the Gold Coast, for he had been informed by no less than two brigadiers that SLICA was not under British military control.

Beretta was determined to boldly go where few Frenchmen had ventured recently—that is, across the border into the Côte d'Ivoire. There he proceeded to set up an active spy network and to attempt to convert as many members of the French administration to the Gaullist cause as possible. Miln wrote a secret note to Hawkesworth on 28 July 1942, after having had a rather exciting tour of the border in the Frenchman's company: "I remain of the opinion that M. Beretta is loyal, vehemently and bitterly anti-Vichy. I consider that he might have some difficulty in restraining his emotions if he were to come across a Vichy official (he himself would employ a term at once more colourful and more violent) by chance, some day, on the frontier."[31] Reports reaching Hawkesworth from his district commissioners contained worrying details of SLICA's operations. It was not only that Beretta's projects were ones completely distasteful to Giffard, but they were also ones Hawkesworth thought specifically designed to further sour relations between British and Vichy administrations.

One such planned operation was to disrupt the vital harvesting of wild rubber in the Côte d'Ivoire by organizing a smuggling ring. This was a material critical to the Axis war effort, for most of it was being exported into France and thence into Germany. Beretta sent African agents across the border who, armed with SLICA money and messages from Ivoirien refugees, encouraged men to bring their harvest across the frontier into the Gold Coast. There they would be assured of a better price than the French paid, as well as the opportunity to purchase cloth and other consumer goods in such short supply in the AOF.[32] In this operation, Beretta did, in fact, enjoy the close cooperation of the SOE, and of one agent whom we know of only as W.33, but who, it will be remembered, was a close associate of Wingate. Lumby, now in charge of Frawest, once again seems, despite Giffard, to have approved. In August 1942 he wrote to Hanau ("Caesar"): "We hope we have found a way of helping in a rubber smuggling scheme. W.33 has helped in the working out of the scheme which involves smuggling rubber over the south-eastern frontier of the Gold Coast, and we are putting up £100 to start the ball rolling. It will go to buy cotton goods which go to pay for the rubber which is sold for cash which repays the £100, and so on."[33] By one of those not infrequent confusions in directions, Lumby wrote "south-eastern," when he obviously meant northwestern. Rubber smuggling from Togo across the Volta seems extremely unlikely.

SMUGGLING

In the course of 1942, smuggling had become a major preoccupation of the SOE. An undated memorandum shows that it was viewed as a form of "Economic and Financial Subversion," which would distort the balance between supply and demand in the Vichy colonies and thus depress the value of the AOF franc. Basically SOE operatives would send "travelling agents," including women, into Vichy country to spread the news that goods could be sold at frontier villages at advantageous prices, and that a good market existed for livestock, gold, silver, diamonds, and a wide range of other products. "In order to make a starting incentive," sellers of such goods were to be paid at least one-third above prevailing frontier prices. If this proved an inadequate incentive, buyers were instructed to increase the differential. In the same document, it was also suggested that further attempts be made to induce tirailleurs to desert with their arms, offering a thousand francs to any soldier with a rifle, and correspondingly higher bounties for those with machine guns, tommy guns, and so forth.[34] The price for a tank was not noted.

In fact, the payment of desertion bounties was not immediately sanctioned, but efforts to increase the smuggling of vital consumer goods were given priority. In June 1942 the anthropologist Meyer Fortes, a fellow of the International African Institute and a lecturer at Oxford University, who had been working in the Northern Territories for several years, was recruited to the SOE as W.38. His appointment came despite his long having been the target of suspicion in the colony as both a "left-winger" and a Jewish South African. Perhaps these alarming defects were regarded as unlikely to affect his work, which was to "increase the supply of cattle which was being smuggled into the Northern Territories by the Moshi tribe, the cattle breeders of the North Ivory Coast."[35]

The eleven-hundred-kilometer border between the Gold Coast and the Côte d'Ivoire could not, in any case effectively be sealed. A new Vichy force of armed border guards, ironically known as partisans, was formed, probably in early 1941. They were recruited from ex-tirailleurs and retired militia men, gardes-cercle. Enlisted locally, and thus well informed as to both the topography and the population of the area, they were estimated to be approximately two thousand strong and were strung out along the Ivoirien borders.[36] The Gold Coast countered with a new Preventive Patrol. Clashes between the two were infrequent, but not unknown.[37]

It should be realized that the trade routes that ran between what had become on the one side, the Côte d'Ivoire, and on the other, Western Ashanti and the Northern Territories of the Gold Coast, were very ancient and much-used ones. Control over them became more rigorous in the colonial period, but their importance hardly diminished. By the 1930s smuggled goods and livestock from the French colony were an essential component of Gold Coast markets, despite the best efforts of border police on both sides. Even during the war the traffic continued. Cattle, tobacco, and spirits were the most desirable commodities, and the great risks taken by the smugglers were deemed worthwhile in light of the possible profits. Elderly traders can remember in great detail their youthful adventures as smugglers. In 1986, Mamourou Camara of Bouna, in northeastern Côte d'Ivoire, spoke of the general nature of the trade:

I bought livestock from the Lobi—in their villages. We then sold the cattle in Ghana and bought that old kind of jewelry there.[38] The jewelry made by the whites, and salt, which we sold to the Lobi. . . . In those days we had a lot of bother with *colons* [the French]. The seller needed a pass to go into Ghana. . . . There were many who crossed illegally. They would buy the cattle from the Lobi and continue directly into Ghana. When they caught a smuggler they put him right in jail. Despite that you couldn't stop doing it. There was too much profit in it. As to the goods we bought—salt, pearls [glass beads], cloth, and kola. If we couldn't sell it here—if there was too much for here—we would go to Burkina [the former Haute Côte d'Ivoire] to sell the rest. . . . The commerce was general. If you had the means, you were in it. If you were ten or fifteen, you would choose the oldest man as head of the caravan. One group of fifteen persons would have one chief. But once you got to the village, everyone did his own trading. Some would buy one or two animals, others fifteen. After the purchases, you'd regroup. There were often great problems in this region—robbers, bandits who would barricade the routes. We were all armed as well, so we were usually all right. We protected ourselves. We were our own soldiers.[39]

Kwadwo Bosompra was living in Sunyani when World War II broke out. He also had difficulty with the French border patrols:

We brought things from Bondoukou all the time during the war—we smuggled them. We were taking bush routes. . . . We bought things here [in the Gold Coast]. The French soldiers did not want us to cross the border. We brought salt, cutlasses, cloth, lanterns, sandals, and rubber. It was French police. [If you were caught] all your goods would be confiscated. They had one soldier, Tano. He was very very bad. He was not a white. If he arrested you, he would bring you to the white. If you tried to bribe him, he would not take it. He would take all your goods. This was Soko on the French side of the border.

I was arrested once. There were seven of us in the group, two were arrested. I was the first [in line and arrested]. We decided amongst ourselves who would be arrested first—it would be the person leading. We went single file. I was leading the seven. We knew that if one gave the alarm, the others could get away. If anyone catches you, you give an alarm and all the others come together to assist you. I heard, at my back, a soldier saying stop. The sun had set. Now, he said. I called my group. I knew we couldn't continue the walk. By this time, the others had all slipped into the bush. Then someone was calling out: "They're killing me." But there was no one there. I had a clock watch on my head. It was ticking. That's how they found me. It was like this. The time we got to the place where the soldiers were, one of the soldiers went into

the bush. One of us bit his finger. He started yelling, "Someone's killing me."
This all happened before the Hitler time.[40]

"The Hitler time," as Bosompra called it, saw a considerable reduction in the
traffic, but in no way eliminated it even before the Gold Coast government had
officially sanctioned it.

Smuggling had always been regarded as a major problem. Before the war the
Kumasi chamber of commerce was so incensed by the volume of smuggling that
Capt. Angus Durham MacKenzie, comptroller of customs, was moved to make a
personal inspection of the permeable borders. He concluded that smuggling was
uncontrollable. There were three major reasons: first, French customs duties were
lower than British; second, the depreciated franc had reduced prices for Asante
traders buying in the Côte d'Ivoire; and third, there was virtually no effective
Customs Preventive Service in Asante. "The longer the war lasts," MacKenzie
wrote, "the harder it will be to get cigarettes and tobacco. As long as there is a profit
to be made, smuggling will continue."[41] Adding to the incentive for the traders to
bring in contraband were new taxes imposed in the Gold Coast. Anticipating
financial stringencies that were bound to arise with the outbreak of war, Governor Hodson had already cut the budget sharply. To try to replace revenues that
would surely drop given the necessary reduction of cocoa exports due to lack of
shipping space, the governor had, in 1939, raised import and export taxes.[42]

MacKenzie's assumption that smuggling was bad was made before the fall of
France turned it into a valuable instrument in the prosecution of the war. The
Gold Coast government and the SOE became promoters of the clandestine traffic.
For quite obvious reasons, rubber and other strategic goods had to be prevented
from reaching Germany. The smuggling of cattle, however, was encouraged for
another purpose. Beef was needed to feed the rapidly increasing numbers of
men in the RWAFF.[43] Oddly enough, an SOE report emanating from London
headquarters in September 1942 offers a very wry comment on this matter, considering that its agents had already been actively engaged in smuggling activities:

> A scheme for promoting the smuggling of cattle from A.O.F. into the Gold
> Coast is at present under consideration by the Head of Mission. It was origi-
> nally advanced by the local administration. A number of other projects, ini-
> tiated by the Mission, for interfering with the supply of materials useful to
> the Axis powers and derived from A.O.F. have been authorised and encour-
> aged by the interested Government Departments in London. For some of these
> preliminary plans based on the intelligence available have been worked out,

but permission to execute them has in every instance been withheld by the G.O.C. in C., West Africa.[44]

One may speculate that this is one case where Giffard did not want to know what the SOE was doing, since its activities were backed by no less than the Gold Coast government, which itself had encouraged the district commissioners to aid and abet the smuggling of cattle—and all this with the approval of the Colonial Office! Obviously this particular means of economic sabotage did not cause anyone in the Gold Coast many sleepless nights.

TO FRATERNIZE OR NOT TO FRATERNIZE

If no less than the Colonial Office had approved of smuggling cattle, then Beretta's involvement with contraband rubber could scarcely be regarded by Giffard or Hawkesworth as contravening the rules of engagement they had attempted to lay down. Much more controversial, however, were Beretta's activities aimed at urging French soldiers, civilians, and civil servants to desert and join the Free French cause.[45] The basic problem was that no clear definition of the role of the Free French had been worked out. Hawkesworth, on the receiving end of complaints and questions from his district commissioners, sought enlightenment from Accra, and ultimately from the Governors' Conference. On the basis of the responses, he sent the following memo: "M. Baretta of the Free French Mission will be stationed at Sunyani and his duties are confined to looking after the interests of the Jamanhene and his followers and of other Africans who may seek asylum in Ashanti. He may not undertake any subversive activities in adjacent Vichy territory without my permission."[46] But could Hawkesworth issue such a decree? Beretta, clearly thought not, and had no patience with bureaucratic minds concerned with avoiding conflict rather than inflicting damage upon the enemy. Even Hawkesworth realized that he had taken a somewhat indefensible position. "Members of the Free French Mission frequently visit Ashanti," he acknowledged, "but I assume they form part of the military intelligence system, and are therefore of no concern of mine. . . . If Beretta is using these men for espionage and smuggling purposes I feel that there is always a risk of a frontier incident. . . . I have nothing against him personally but I am rather vague as to the position of the Free French Mission generally and would be happier if it could be defined."[47] In the event, Beretta continued to make mysterious visits across the border.

Only a few days after Hawkesworth's plea for clarification, Miln was invited by Beretta to join him at Pamu, near the frontier. Somewhat to Miln's surprise, a French priest living at Berekum, Father Mondé, was also present. Miln accompanied them to the frontier. He reported the proceedings to Hawkesworth at some length:

> We went first to Kofibadukrom, but shortly before reaching that village a Free French Agent stopped our car and, as I believe, informed M. Beretta that two French soldiers were in Kofibadukrom and that they might possibly wish to come into British territory. I at the time thought they were Frenchmen. We proceeded into the village and M. Beretta and Father Mondé held a prolonged conversation with the two African frontier guards that we met there. I, personally, beyond waving them good-morning and having a good look at them took no part in the proceedings. The actual meeting took place at the boundary pillar. The men behaved themselves very quietly and in an orderly manner. Their uniforms were extremely shabby and they were armed with rifles, whips and rope. After a while I retired to a chair some 30 or 40 yards within British territory and waited until M. Beretta and Father Mondé had finished their negotiations. About an hour later the two frontier guards left and M. Beretta and Father Mondé—who were elated as the result of their conversations—informed me that both men intended to come into the Gold Coast with their families, to-day.

The small party then proceeded to another border village, Gonokrom, where, on either side of the boundary marker, three young African guards held a lengthy conversation with the two Frenchmen while Miln retired to the chief's compound, about a hundred yards from the frontier, safely in British territory. Beretta and Mondé felt certain they would be adding these three to their catch as well.[48]

Once back in Pamu, Miln went about his usual duties, not returning to Sunyani until 25 July. The next morning, in a rather mischievous mood, he telephoned acting DC Ross in Wenchi:

> I asked him to outline to Your Honour [i.e., Hawkesworth] M. Beretta's programme for to-day and to ascertain whether or no I should accompany him back to the frontier. Yesterday (27/7/42) I told M. Beretta that I proposed to do so and I immediately sensed that he felt disturbed at the suggestion. His attitude was courtesy itself and correct in every detail. In these circumstances I telephoned to Your Honour in Kumasi and suggested that perhaps it would be as well if M. Beretta went to Kofibadukrom without me. The situation as I write is that M. Beretta has just left for the frontier. I shall be mildly surprised if, when he returns, he brings many Vichy personnel with him.[49]

It was about this time that a most embarrassing incident occurred when two French soldiers deserted the Vichy forces, crossed the border, and gave themselves up. Instead of being welcomed, they were taken into custody by the police in Sunyani and held until Miln returned from a tour up-country. Beretta, furious, demanded that the police turn the men over to him. The police refused. On Miln's reappearance in Sunyani, he passed the buck to Hawkesworth in Kumasi, who ordered that the men be put in the custody of the military authorities for questioning. Not surprisingly, Beretta protested that "such action was interfering with his work." And that again was the problem. What was Beretta's work? The colonial administration continued to maintain, publicly at least, that he was simply a liaison man, sent to deal with refugees from Vichy territory.

The only solution possible, Hawkesworth felt, was the removal of Beretta from the Ashanti region, and the immediate imposition of some kind of military control over the Free French Mission.[50] Two weeks later, after intensive discussion as to their exact policy toward the Free French, Accra was able to reassure Hawkesworth with the following information. Chef de Bataillon Ponton had summoned Beretta to Accra and given him a "final warning that if he does not abide by his instructions he will be returned to Brazzaville."[51] This aside, Ponton did try to make his allies realize that Beretta's activities, presumably in a common cause, had achieved some results, including the disruption of the wild rubber harvest in the Bondoukou region, achieving a sharp reduction in the yield.[52]

Hawkesworth, thwarted in his efforts to control Beretta, turned his wrath on Miln. He told him in no uncertain terms that he was never again to attempt communication with French officials on the Vichy side of the frontier.[53] It is unclear why the CCA had taken such a hard line against Miln's enthusiastic advocacy of fraternization. In the Northern Territories of the Gold Coast it had occurred intermittently without drawing any censure, despite the involvement of Free French operatives. The commandant of Batié, in Haute Côte d'Ivoire, Captain Alby, for example, had maintained regular contacts with the Free French Mission in the Gold Coast. When he went on leave, his replacement, a Lieutenant Ibos, kept these up. Ibos apparently was convinced that Generals Weygand and Barrau were just waiting for the right moment to take up arms again. Until then, Ibos felt, he could never join the Free French Mission. He admitted to admiring its ideals, but would never put himself in a situation that might lead to Frenchmen fighting Frenchmen.[54]

Whatever the cause of Hawkesworth's negative attitude toward Miln's initiative, that was far from the end of the matter. Miln put in reports, not only to his superior in the administration, but also to Lumby, at SOE headquarters in Accra.

One of the latter contained a more revealing account of Miln's adventures in Pamu. First, he conveyed information that he thought would be of interest to the Governors' Conference, then proceeded to make a proposal of his own to Lumby:

> During a recent routine trek, I heard rumours both in Berekum and Pamu with regard to a very remarkable speech said lately to have been made by M. Deschamps. His Excellency seems to have stated that (a) the Forces of the United States of America will shortly occupy Dakar and (b) it is quite uncertain whether the Government of the Ivory Coast is in fact pro-Vichy at all. It might even, he is reported to have said, turn over to the British at any time.
>
> I now ask permission after full consideration to adopt a policy of fraternisation towards the French authorities at Bondoukou and Abengourou. Nothing, I feel, can be gained by further hostility and bitterness. Indeed, the spirit of "perfide Albion" will be increased whereas if the French can only be convinced we do not intend to deprive them of their colonies and so forth, and that it is not our custom to turn on fallen comrades, perhaps then they or some of them might be persuaded to adopt a more helpful attitude. I take it that the Fighting French will have to be consulted. I see no reason why whichever way future events may turn a policy of hostility on M. Beretta's part and a policy of fraternisation on my part should not be prosecuted side by side, with of course, the full knowledge of the Fighting French Mission.[55]

Hawkesworth, already alarmed by Beretta's conduct, obviously objected to the good cop–bad cop technique advocated by Miln. Lumby, however, took a different view of things. He was clearly interested in developing a fraternization policy. He also had before him an extract from an intelligence report from the district commissioner in the western district of Gonja also having to do with the same matter:

> Unfortunately, owing to a letter being delayed and consequent confusion of dates, the [Vichy] Administrator, Gautier, did not come to meet me at Saru on July 15th as arranged. It is unlikely now that we shall be able to meet until after the rains. I was accompanied on my trip to Saru by Mr. Mead of the F.F.C. [Free French Committee], who came down from Lawra specially for the purpose at my request.
>
> Whilst at Saru, Mr. Mead wrote a long letter containing all the latest news to the Administrator, and I enclosed this in a letter of my own. These two letters, literature, and a parcel were all received and duly acknowledged.
>
> Presents of sugar, tobacco, money, bicycle pump, and various other trifles to the Partisan Frontier Guards have now made them so friendly that the African Adjutant in charge of the stretch between Tantama and Vonkoro now

personally supervises the expeditious carriage of letters and parcels between M. Gautier and myself.[56]

Additionally, Lumby had also learned from the DC at Lawra that a party of American and British missionaries from Bobo-Dioulasso had been repatriated at the frontier. The French official who accompanied them showed every sign of being willing to fraternize, but only with the British officials. He would not do so while an agent of the Free French was present.

Lumby was much inspired by these developments. He put together a memorandum outlining the various cases and went on to suggest that a clear policy about fraternization should be evolved and made known to all the DCs in the frontier districts. He recommended that every advantage should be taken of any contacts, "to try and make the Vichy French realise that their only hope lies in friendship with us," and that British officials should actively seek such contacts, and try to restore "the system of periodical meetings to exchange views on local frontier problems which I understand prevailed before the fall of France."[57] And indeed they had, including the staging of football matches between schools in Ouagadougou and those in the Northern Territories. One such event was attended by chiefs from the Gold Coast and other from Haute Côte d'Ivoire, including the Moro Naba himself. Lt. Gov. Edmond Louveau reported to his superior Governor Crocicchia of the Côte d'Ivoire that the occasion "showed the natives of these lands the ties which unite the two great empires in the fight against the Third Reich."[58] As we have clearly seen, these ties did not survive the fall of France, at least among the Europeans. Now, two years later, fraternization had again become the order of the day. Lumby, however, was of the opinion that any such policy would be at this stage compromised should Free French officers be involved. The point was that while the Vichy French were prepared to welcome overtures from the British, who while technically enemies, were at least former allies, they would have no truck whatsoever with the Free French, who they considered traitors. The Free French, of course, insisted that it was *Vichyistes* who had betrayed the motherland.

Lumby was clearly something of a politician. He had, after all, succeeded where all other SOE personnel had failed, in sustaining good relations with General Giffard. Lumby now discussed his views on fraternization with both Resident Minister Swinton and the new governor of the Gold Coast, Sir Alan Burns, on 24 August 1942, and obtained their approval of it. Two days later, he approached Ponton, having what he called "the dirty task" of telling him that the SOE did not wish the Free French Mission to be involved in this initiative. Ponton took the news well, and "made no fuss at all." It was only on 27 August that Lumby informed Julius Hanau in London of all that had transpired, fraternization being a virtual fait accompli. Lumby added a further piece of information, that in that very week section head W.33 had returned from a tour of the north to report on a very satisfactory opening for contacts with Vichy officials on the eastern frontier of the Côte d'Ivoire.[59]

The policy of fraternization, pioneered by Miln and other frontier DCs, had received the support first of Lumby, then of Swinton and Burns, and was made official on 31 August 1942. The colonial secretary in Accra dispatched a "most secret" memorandum to the commissioners and chief commissioners stating "that a policy of fraternisation should be generally adopted. . . . British administrative officers should not only take full advantage of every opportunity which arises of making contact with Vichy officials, but should themselves take whatever steps may be possible to create such opportunities." Guidelines for these opportunities were set down:

(i) That Britain wishes to remain the friend of France, and that we have no territorial or other designs on France or her colonies. In fact we stand by our pledge to see her re-established.

(ii) That Britain realises that the present hostile attitude to Vichy France is forced upon her by the Germans.

(iii) That the main reason for the continued estrangement of relations locally is the fact that French Colonies continue to produce goods which find their way to Germany.

(iv) That practical common sense demands that the present unjustifiable and intolerable impasse should be ended and a solution found to restore real friendship.[60]

The colonial secretary, however, went on to confirm the ban on Free French officers being present when overtures to Vichy officials were initiated. They would only be allowed to participate in subsequent meetings with the agreement of the latter.

In a little more than two months the entire situation was to change radically. On 8 November 1942, Operation Torch, the American and British invasion of French North Africa, was launched. Four days later, the colonial secretary, Accra, wired all frontier district commissioners that "no hindrance to be given to Fighting French officers who wish to contact people in Vichy territory. Any help wanted should be given."[61] Within days of that new instruction, Miln was reporting on a

Soldiers, Airmen, Spies, and Whisperers

Free French agent who had crossed the border carrying a letter from Beretta to the commandant of Bondoukou, advocating an end to hostilities and a declaration for the Free French. Although received courteously at first, this agent soon found himself physically assaulted by diehard French supporters of Vichy. The commandant, realizing that the wind was blowing from a new direction, rescued him and gave him a bed for the night. In the morning, the commandant and the Free French agent met with a French army officer to discuss Beretta's message. The meeting was, Miln reported, "heated." Although no decision was reached, the SLICA man returned to Sunyani bearing "an expression of the Commandant's compliments."[62] Letters between Sunyani and Bondoukou continued their flow and, with each passing day, official relations at least grew warmer until, at the end of 1942, the AOF had moved, almost imperceptibly but surely, toward the Allied side in the war. With the advantage of hindsight, it might well seem that General Giffard's dogged attempts to block anything he regarded as tending to escalate the conflict between the Vichy and British colonies had the justification of history on its side.

6

Propaganda

THE HOME FRONT
AND BEYOND

SPREADING THE WORD: WARTIME
BROADCASTING IN THE GOLD COAST

War demands much of its participants, even the humblest of whom is expected to support the cause. It is essential to secure the backing of the populace at large. In World War II, the importance of the wholehearted devotion of the British Empire, with its vast human and natural resources, cannot be underestimated, a matter that was to be formally set out in the Colonial Development and Welfare Act of 1940. At the outbreak of war, then, a major thrust of British propaganda was toward securing the support of its African peoples. Special emphasis was put on the German threat to West Africa that arose from the Nazi determination to regain the colonies lost during World War I. For the Gold Coast, the obvious threat was to British-mandated Togo, which was administered as part of it. Between September 1939 and June 1940, official propaganda stressed the contributions the empire was making, in men and materials, to the war effort. For West Africa, much of the effort was concentrated on the exploits of the Royal West African Frontier Force in the East Africa campaign. Examples of "the bravery of the Gold Coast soldier" filled the airwaves and the local newspapers.[1] It was a theme that was to recur in much subsequent military propaganda, one that undoubtedly fostered a sense of commonality between the different peoples of the

Gold Coast—between Fantes, Asantes, Dagombas, and so forth. The Gold Coast Regiment was presented as a national institution in which all civilians should take justifiable pride. The contribution of African soldiers to the grand task of winning the war was a primary focus of British propaganda, particularly during the recruitment drives for both the RWAFF and the Home Guard—defenders of the ideals of Great Britain and its empire.

Concentrated efforts were made to involve as wide a range of the people as possible in the war. The Gold Coast had a particular advantage, thanks to Governor Hodson's initiative in setting up a radio network capable of beaming programs not only to the entire Gold Coast but to the neighboring French colonies. This was in place before the outbreak of war. Indeed, there were sixteen radio relay stations that not only picked up BBC transmissions but could also be used for local broadcasts. Hodson had become a firm believer in the power of radio communications as the best way of conveying information to a largely illiterate African population and had managed to extract considerable funds for the project. Early in the war much of the programming was taken straight from the BBC, with a heavy emphasis on entertainment, although a certain amount of local news from towns and villages throughout the colony became a regular feature.[2] Soon, the medium's potential for educating and inspiring Africans with its patriotic broadcasts was recognized. The main obstacle was the dearth of private radios in the Gold Coast. There were fewer than seven hundred, of which only an estimated 147 were in African hands. This was partially overcome by an expansion of the prewar rediffusion network, a system that issued, to the homes of subscribers, loudspeakers wired to a central receiver. By 1941, over five thousand people had signed up for the service, and thousands more would doubtless gather at the homes of friends and relatives to hear the broadcasts.[3]

The thrust of all military propaganda directed at the Home Front was that the men of the RWAFF were fighting, not for Asante, not for the Protectorate, not for the Colony, but for the whole Gold Coast—Britain's faithful ally. In December 1939 and January 1940 programs on the history of the Gold Coast Regiment met with popular success, although not without causing a few feathers to be ruffled. Word had reached the Ministry of Information that the chief commissioner of Ashanti, Hawkesworth, had disapproved of the programs devoted to the regiment and had refused to allow them to be broadcast. This provoked an aggrieved response from the producer of the series, John Duncan of the colonial secretary's office, whose creative sensibilities had been severely affronted. He fired off a letter to Kumasi, wanting to know if "this information, (which reached me at third or fourth hand) is accurate." "If it is accurate," he continued, "would you please let me know what the objection is? As you probably realise, producing a full length news bulletin from a few none too interesting scraps of news—in addition to doing a lot of other stuff—is no sinecure and I have no desire to waste time producing anything which is utterly useless." Duncan pointed out that the series had proved popular with both African and European listeners, as well as having the stamp of approval of the Gold Coast Regiment, where it was felt important that Europeans now serving in the regiment learn something of its history. "I am puzzled," he wrote, "to understand why, if it was so popular in Accra and received the Regiment's official blessing, it should be disapproved of in Kumasi, which has closer associations with the Regiment than has Accra. Nevertheless as I am only in my first tour in the country and have had no service in Ashanti I realise that I may unwittingly have been dropping some colossal brick."[4]

W. A. Stewart-Cole, at the time secretary to the CCA, replied virtually by return mail, soothing the fevered brow of Duncan by assuring him that the story was a complete fabrication, and that the entire series, "with the exception of one or two extracts which it was impossible to read," had been broadcast with the local news from Kumasi.[5] It is a shame that the scripts of this series have never surfaced. They were broadcast in English and had as a target audience both Europeans and literate Africans. It was soon recognized, however, that to reach the mass of the people, programs had to be transmitted in African languages. A call went out to district commissioners to recruit "reliable and well-educated Africans" who not only spoke English and their own languages, but had a command of others that enjoyed wide currency: Twi, Ewe, Hausa, and Dyula for example.[6]

Among the educated Africans recruited were such men as Christian Baeta and T. E. Kyei. They were directed to translate and present programs in the languages of their people. In 1994, Kyei, whom we have already met in the context of the Home Guard, reminisced about his days as a broadcaster: "We now had the radio station and the news had to be broadcast to people. I was a teacher at the government school. They wanted someone to translate the news in Ashanti. I was asked to be a news reader at 6 P.M. in the evening. We had [in charge] Ken Harrison, somebody [some name] like that. There were the technicians, but before 6 P.M. they would send the news to me. I would translate, then go to the room to broadcast. There were two lights—red and green. Green meant get ready to read. Then red comes on. In Twi, I would read the introduction and so on and so on. It was much—it was edited for the Kumasi people. All things not relevant were cut out."[7]

Soldiers, Airmen, Spies, and Whisperers

Christian Baeta's broadcasts were aimed not only at the Ewe of the south-eastern Gold Coast but also at those across the frontier in Vichy-controlled Togo. "It was a half an hour broadcast every day, in Ewe," he recalled. "They [the British] desired you to say certain things, a script, but I was old enough to consult myself before I translated it and read it out. There was war news—it was all designed to keep the affection of the people. We told them the Vichy French were bad. We told them all the time how bad Hitler was and now, how the Vichy French had linked up with the Germans." Baeta considered that the propaganda work directed at Togo also had an important effect in the Gold Coast. Its impact would be, he felt, to "explain the situation to our [Gold Coast Ewe] people. So that they would know who were their friends." Before the broadcasts from the Accra studio, he and the other announcers were given the transcript in English. They did the translations. He continued,

> I was doing some of the broadcasting. A half an hour a day in Ewe—the Ewes on the Togo side were keenly interested in the war. The French, in Togo, were operating for Vichy. We had a lot of fun. . . . We were not short of news. We would say that the British had beaten the enemy severely in such and such a place. Losses? No, they would put it this way: They [the British] had to withdraw for tactical reasons. [8]

James Moxon, whom the reader will remember as Captain Moxon of the Accra Home Guard, had as his first assignment in the Gold Coast the production of newscasts, both in English and the vernacular. When an immensely powerful new transmitter was put into service in 1941, the Broadcasting Service was faced with the necessity of filling up the air time. This they did by increasing the number of programs in Ewe, Twi, Fante, and in both standard and *bariki* ["barrack"] Hausa. The French soon persuaded the service also to hire Mossi speakers for broadcasts to Haute Côte d'Ivoire. This proved somewhat of a project. "We went to Navrongo," Moxon remembered, "to the DC, and said we wanted two good, well-educated Mossi announcers. He went to the bishop to recruit two of his best. Two genuine mission boys. They were sent to us in Accra. The DC in Navrongo used to monitor the broadcasts in the car park. All the Mossi gathered there to hear them." The DC was seemingly less than impressed with the content of the programs, explaining that once the novelty of hearing their own language on the radio wore off, the listeners departed. "He told us we needed more local gossip and spice—not just war news. These mission boys had no idea of 'spice.' We told them to go to Makola Market and listen to gossip. They did and after the next broadcast we got a telegram from the DC: 'Superb. The crowds are really gathering.' The same day we got another telegram from the bishop. 'Return my boys immediately. You are corrupting them.'"[9]

Some propaganda campaigns seem to have been rejected by the Gold Coast administration as either too ridiculous or too implausible for the people. For once the administration was absolutely right. One such scheme dreamed up in London, entitled the Orchestra of Death, was designed to promote the idea of Adolf Hitler's death having been forecast by astrologers. The "fact" sheet assured all potential propagandists that this prophesy was "based on accurate astrological information." The prophesy was as follows:

> During April and May (Hitler's birthday is April 20th) Neptune is in the house of death, which makes for a mysterious fate and soon the progressed ascendant will be in a place where Neptune was at the moment of Hitler's birth, and during this summer Uranus will bring the birth constellation into effect with grave consequences for Hitler. . . . This is the authentic astrological view, and we are arranging for our representatives in a great many parts of the world to encourage astrologers, soothsayers, fakirs etc to cast Hitler's horoscope and to announce that this [1941] is to be the year of his death. We are sending a special man to America to organise the campaign there.[10]

It is a tribute both to the administration's respect for the intelligence of the people of the Gold Coast and to its own foresight in predicting the effects of such a campaign should Hitler not die in 1941, that the Orchestra of Death did not play. Equally, some tidbits of propaganda emanating from the colonies did not play in London either. R. L. Speaight of the Foreign Office dismissed out of hand one story, reported in the weekly West Africa Political Intelligence Committee (WAPIC) Bulletin. It claimed that confirmation had reached the British regarding the construction of a secret camp in Abidjan, built to treat Tirailleurs Sénégalais. These, so the story went, were men "returned from France who bear traces of barbarous mutilations inflicted on them by their German captors." They were, however, the lucky ones, for "some Africans were shot as an example to others who dare fight against Germany."[11] Speaight discounted the whole matter: "As you know, we keep a record of all really authentic German atrocities. This story is too vague to be regarded as authentic, although useful for propaganda purposes."[12] But Speaight was seriously misinformed. African veterans of the European War like Tuo Lielourou, held in a German prisoner-of-war camp for three and a half years, would have disagreed with his smug assumption. The Ivoirien *ancien combattant* said,

There were a lot of deaths. The Germans killed many prisoners. Because in 1914–18, the French had killed many Germans. They lined them up and shot them. It was the Germans who told us about that. They said they were going to settle the debt. So in camp, when morning came, they would pick a portion of the men—we were still in bed—and put them in a trench and shoot them. Others had their ears chopped off and their eyes taken out. This happened at the beginning. Of course they killed the French too. Why just us? . . . It was terrible. They had forced the Africans, those with ["tribal"] scars to scrub their scars with soap and not to stop until they came off. We suffered so much. It was the old one who stopped it. They had forced the Africans to scrub their scars until they came out. So many suffered.[13]

The story rejected by Speaight never became a subject of Gold Coast propaganda; indeed, typical nightly fare on the radio was generally restrained on the subject of Vichy atrocities. Broadcasts consisted mainly of translations of various speeches and news commentaries designed to hold the interest of their African listeners. In one week in February 1941, the people of Asante were treated to such daily broadcasts as the reading of "Rumour, Wild Rumour," extracted from the weekly broadsheet produced by the Ministry of Information, *The Empire at War,* and translated into Twi by T. E. Kyei; "The Life of an Infantry Soldier," translated by C. E. Osei from a broadcast by a Colonel Dickinson; and a translation in Twi by K. O. Agyepong of General Giffard's speech of 3 January.[14] The Asantehene was an enthusiastic advocate of the radio transmission of news and features in the vernacular. This is not to say that friction did not arise when it came to the actual allocation of air time. Mr. Henry Prempeh, a "prince" of the Golden Stool and an active member of the Kumasi Broadcasting Committee, was very concerned about the quality and quantity of news broadcasts in Twi. "Mr. Prempeh expressed his opinion," the committee chairman reported, "that the announcer (Mr. Frimpong) spoke too fast. The delivery of the announcer in Hausa was much slower and clearer, and he had the impression that the Hausa News contained less than the Twi News. He thought that more time ought to be allowed to the News in Twi in order that it could be read without haste."[15]

Other African leaders were less enthusiastic. Nana Sir Ofori Atta I, Okyenhene of Akyem Abuakwa in the Gold Coast Colony, left the governor in little doubt as to his objections. "Just one word with regard to broadcasting. There is no doubt, Sir, that your efforts in that regard will ever remain a monument for years and years to come; but let me say that until the new transmitter has arrived and it has been put into full use when the whole country can have access to radio and listen in, it should not be considered that the radio is the proper medium for communication to the people of this country." After registering his complaints that announcements about cocoa and other matters could not be heard away from the cities and larger towns, he came to the point: "Until you are satisfied that everybody can hear from Accra what is being said by Government, the old system of getting the Chiefs informed of any new proposal should not be allowed to die."[16] In effect, a powerful chief was letting the government know that while radio might be seen by them as invaluable to the propaganda campaign, rallying the people to the war effort still required the cooperation and direct intercession of traditional leaders. However, Nana Sir Ofori Atta went on to soften his stance: "Sir, in regard to the war; the struggle for justice against injustice, for freedom against oppression. I should like again to assure Your Excellency that the whole country is solidly behind you in whatever efforts you make towards its successful prosecution; and I can further assure Your Excellency that though we may have reverses, nothing will affect the complete confidence which the people of this country have in the ultimate issue. We are perfectly certain, Sir, that His Majesty's Government and its Allies will win the war, and some of us who will live to see that end, will be free in their aspirations and will live to breathe freely in that their freedom is secured once and for all."[17]

While most of this activity was controlled by the administration through the Gold Coast Broadcasting Service, the Franck Mission was also busily setting up its own programs. These were aimed at Africans from French territory who had slipped across the border to trade in the Gold Coast. A daily broadcast in Mole, the language of the Mossi of Haute Côte d'Ivoire, was arranged. It was hoped that the Mossi, whose growing discontent with an administration headed by a socialist-turned-Vichyiste, Governor Hubert Deschamps, would prove a fertile field for British propaganda. The theory was that the traders, once business was completed, would bring the news back to their homeland, and help spread, as the SOE so fervently hoped, disaffection among the African population. The main obstacle to this wonderful plan, however, appeared to be the reluctance of local district commissioners to add the task of spotting Africans from French territory to their already increased workload. "It is of no use," a frustrated Mothersill wrote from Salaga, "making this special Mole broadcast unless the audience is organised to hear it and I should be most grateful if District Commissioners would have all their outgoing French natives (kola traders and others) who happen to be in the station each day gathered together to hear the broadcast. If this is not done, then, of course, the whole object of the broadcast is lost."[18] One must have a certain degree of sympathy with government officials throughout the country who, in drawing up the broadcasting schedules, had to cope with the delicate feelings of so many diverse interests.

INFORMATION BUREAUS AND CINEMA VANS

In towns and cities from Accra to Navrongo, official information bureaus had been and were being set up. That at Kumasi was officially opened on 22 April 1940. Constructed by the Public Works Department for a grand total of £40, the new building contained pictures, posters, magazines, and overseas newspapers, and would soon serve as a place for the townspeople to listen to Gold Coast radio broadcasts. Its curator, B. A. Addo, described the opening in his weekly report to the CCA:

> The keen interest which the public evinced at the pictures exhibited on the four blackboards outside the bureau can better be imagined than described; for hours and hours they lingered and only reluctantly dispersed when the boards were taken inside at the close of the day . . . there is no elbow room as the crowd vie with each other for a sitting space. With avidity they peered into the papers and while the literate classes enjoyed themselves silently, the illiterate and more inquisitive lot invaded the curator with an array of questions which he answered as best he could, to the satisfaction of all.[19]

The Kumasi Information Bureau was a great success. Its display boards of war photographs and clippings were of such great interest that they were displayed for two weeks at a time. "So eager is the crowd in pressing forward," Addo wrote, "that to preserve the pictures from being touched or destroyed some railing should be erected on which the crowd will comfortably lean to look at the pictures."[20] The demand for the broadsheet, *The Empire at War*, continually outstripped the supply that Accra had for distribution. Whether or not this reflected the quality of the publication or simply the opportunity for literate Africans to receive free reading material is not known, but in any case the propaganda and news contained within its pages were being devoured in Kumasi. The Asantehene, Sir Osei Agyeman Prempeh II, showed his support for the bureau by paying it an informal visit on 9 May 1940. He was followed that next morning by the governor of the Gold Coast, Sir Arnold Hodson, and the chief commissioner of Ashanti, E. G. Hawkesworth.[21]

On the next day, 11 May 1940, the CCA's secretary, W. A. Stewart-Cole, delivered a transcript of the previous night's BBC news broadcast to the Kumasi Information Bureau. It was to the effect that the Germans had invaded Belgium, Luxembourg, and the Netherlands the day before. According to Addo, within a short time of the notice being posted on the bureau's bulletin board, "everyone about town was shaking fists at Hitler for trying to steal victory overnight." Week after week, Addo assured his superiors of both his and Kumasi's total devotion to the cause of Great Britain, no effort being spared by him to explain the progress of the war and the justness of the cause: "We, in this part of Africa, are firm and resolute in our loyalty and attachment to the Allied Cause and we therefore hope and reverently pray that the day may not be far distant, when Prussian Autocracy and Nazi domination will be forever crushed to atoms under the grinding wheels of British Justice, Fair play, and Equity."[22] A week later he reported, "The public are breathlessly watching the trend of affairs as they can be seen wending their way to the Bureau, each day, to be informed of the movements of the enemy and when they are told that the united forces of the Allies present an impenetrable and impregnable front to the enemy, they clap their hands and shout that by God's help victory will soon crown our efforts."[23]

Having established the success of his efforts at the information bureau, Addo complained, politely but firmly each week, of the government's failure to keep its promise to supply him with Boy Scouts to move the extremely heavy bulletin boards. He was also affronted by the appearance of the bureau's building, for not only did it need painting but was in the throes of an all-out attack by white ants.[24] The carefully worded announcement of France's capitulation, and the evacuation of the British Expeditionary Force at Dunkirk, dampened neither Addo's enthusiasm for his post nor his insistence that the government should provide him with more assistance. The facts of the complete collapse of the Anglo-French campaign, however, forced Addo to alter somewhat the tone of his reports regarding the unswerving confidence felt by the Asantes toward the success of the British war effort. In what can only be described as prose worthy of any bureaucrat forced to give unpalatable news to his superior, Addo reported that "the imagination of the public has been captured and there is no doubt they are championing the British Cause, through all the changing scenes of the war, until victory shall finally time our song. The few unthinking individuals, especially among the literate classes, who appear to be pro-Germans, should be round [sic] and brought up for summary punishment."[25] A week later, Addo was back in full voice. His report to the chief commissioner's office read: "Allied cause is simply infectious and it is abundantly clear that the voice of the people is, really, the voice of God in that whatever be the odds against us, in the end, Jehovah shall triumph and we shall win a great and glorious victory that will ring down the ages. Britain that stands for Justice, Righteousness and Fair play never, never, shall be slaves."[26] By way of a digression, it may be noted that Addo's faith in God's support for the Allied cause contrasted sharply with that of other African soldiers serving in France's colonial forces. One of them, Nanlougo Soro, who was in the Tirailleurs Sénégalais during the war, was asked about the matter. "We did hear about Hitler," he replied. "Hitler said that his God wanted war. The French wanted to stop the war, but Hitler said, 'No, God wants war.' It must have been another God; ours doesn't make war."[27]

Such theological matters aside, however, pending Jehovah's triumph, it would be necessary for the Gold Coast government to reshape its modus operandi, which, as one can gather from Addo's one-man operation at Kumasi, was designed more to secure the support it felt was properly due than to confront the very real possibility of invasion. In any case, Addo's isolation was little improved by the arrival in 1941 of the British Council. This purveyor of British culture to the world, although not officially part of the wartime propaganda effort, established its headquarters in Accra, where its library and reading room proved extremely popular, as did the novelty of lectures, art classes, and other experiments in adult education.[28]

In addition to radio, the use of another mass medium became widespread during the war. The Ministry of Information understood the power of films to influence and to inform, and gave the development of its use high priority at the very beginning the war. They set up a Colonial Film Unit, charged with the production of short sixteen-millimeter films designed to enlighten Britain's colonial subjects about the war. The project was welcomed throughout the four West African colonies, but all shared the common logistical problem of how to get the message into the crucial rural areas, ones without movie theatres and, indeed, generally even without electricity. The solution was economical and practical: the mobile theatre. In the Gold Coast, the Information Department operated four cinema vans, which traveled far and wide bringing a selection of newsreels, feature films, short subjects, and the ever-popular Charlie Chaplin movies. In many ways, the bill of fare was not unlike that being offered to British and American audiences, since during the war years few films were made without an eye to their propaganda value, no matter how remote the connection. In this context, one only has to remember the decision of Laurence Olivier, when asked to make an inspirational film for the war effort, unhesitatingly chose *Henry V*, with its depiction of a tremendous British victory against overwhelming odds. "Once more into the breach," seemed particularly apposite after the disaster at Dunkirk.

Film after film depicted various military units fighting bravely against heavy odds, triumphant even in defeat. The royal family was another element in the campaign, as it was thought that no audience could ever have enough of them. Set up on playing fields and in markets, the free shows attracted huge audiences, sometimes of between two and three thousand people. It was estimated that by 1941, in the Gold Coast alone, over half a million people had attended film sessions in the towns and villages of the country. Attendance was boosted by an efficient publicity system. Local chiefs and officials were notified of the dates to expect the cinema vans and competed among themselves to turn out the largest audiences. Little prodding was needed. The novelty of a colonial government providing something desirable at no cost to the recipient would have almost been enough in itself. The fact that it was free entertainment, at a level all could appreciate, made it irresistible. The vast majority of the audience had never before seen moving pictures and it was an experience not easily forgotten.[29]

It is, of course, difficult to measure the actual impact of the cinema on the average African movie-goer. To what extent they believed the propaganda messages implicit in all they saw, and explicit in most of the fare, is anyone's guess. It would, however, be difficult to imagine that African interpretation of and responses to the films did not mirror that of more sophisticated audiences in Great Britain and the United States—involving, if not total belief, then certainly the suspension of disbelief. Whether or not this faith in the veracity of what was being presented to them translated into the kind of wholehearted support for the war effort exemplified by the reports of government employees like B. A. Addo is debatable. Negative evidence, such as the lack of any open resistance to the war effort, to army recruitment, to labor recruitment for the mines, railways, and public works departments, to enlistments for the Home Guard, or to various war-related fund-raising efforts, is always unsatisfactory. What can be said without qualification, however, was that the programs increased enormously the people's awareness of the war and left no doubt that they mightily approved the government's benevolence in providing them all with wonderful entertainment. There is little doubt that the Gold Coast's propaganda machine, the most extensive in West Africa, greatly advanced the government's efforts to mobilize the colony behind the war effort.[30]

The radio broadcasts, the information bureaus, the pamphlets, journals, and newspapers distributed throughout the colony, apparently all met with consider-

Soldiers, Airmen, Spies, and Whisperers

able popular approval. Requests from district commissioners and chiefs for more of everything poured into the various government offices. Those from the former were much concerned with assuring the colonial secretariat that all such materials would be put to good use. When the elders of Wam Pamu, near the Ivoirien border, expressed their desire that a radio be installed there, M. M. Miln, DC Sunyani, strongly supported the idea. "The Native Administration clerk at that town," he wrote, "knows how to operate a set and is not likely to tune in to enemy stations." Cautious for once, however, Miln added, "I cannot ensure that he does not."[31] Miln also reported the popularity of the broadcasts in Sunyani, though he continued to complain about the apparent difficulties of finding anywhere to charge its sole battery and the lack of a spare. "I have not noted any undesirable tuning in," he stated, but pointed out in one of his more self-evident pronouncements that, "listeners tend slightly to be over-dejected when there is news of a reverse and perhaps a little over-elated at news of a British advance."[32]

The administration never lost its respect for the power of the spoken word and was most circumspect about allowing members of other unofficial groups to broadcast even messages of support for the Allied cause. In Kumasi, when a Mr. P. Zacca of the Syrian community wanted to give a speech in Arabic about the evils that Vichy France had wrought in the Levant, permission was denied. The news officer, W. A. Stewart-Cole, had received the script, which certainly was pro-British in the extreme:

> Excepting the vexed and complicated Jewish problem in Palestine, the Arabs know and appreciate the help given to them by the British in their fight for self-independence and organized rule. They know that it was the British who crowned Feisel I, that great Arab leader, to be a king of Iraq and helped him to raise that country from poverty and strife to prosperity and peace. . . . It was the British who built the dams in Egypt and so revived and encouraged the cotton trade. . . . The Syrian, with his business-like qualities, cannot but appreciate these facts existing in the neighbouring Arab countries and cannot but contrast them with conditions prevailing in Syria.

Despite Zacca's text, Stewart-Cole did not trust him and thus wrote, "I have no person whom I can trust to check his Arabic translation. I do not propose to allow him to broadcast on this subject in Arabic."[33] Obviously no Syrian (or Lebanese) could be trusted with such an important propaganda weapon as the radio!

Sometime in 1941, the elders of Effiduasi petitioned the chief commissioner's office in Kumasi, "soliciting a special favour of His Majesty's Govt." They wanted a radio in their town, "to broadcast news of the War, and to know the varied success being achieved by the Allies, and our brothers and Sons in Gold Coast Regiment fighting in the far East [of Africa]. That . . . people in this Division will be aware of whatever condition we stand and feel the necessity of joining 'The Colours' by readily responding to the call."[34] H. Millar-Craig, acting DC of Asante-Akyem, requested a radio set for Juaso, site of a government school containing a "large number of school children of whom the eldest are quite advanced enough to take a considerable interest in the affairs of the world." He also pleaded for a set in Agogo, pointing out that "more men have gone to join the colours from this town than from any other town in Ashanti, and several very generous contributions have been made towards various War Charities by the people of the town. It seems to me obvious that Agogo has a very prior claim to any Government benefits with regard to the better understanding of the world situation by the Africans."[35] The placement of a radio set in every town and in every information bureau became a matter of priority, although the paternalism behind the reasons for so doing was scarcely disguised. One memorandum of unclear provenance is indicative of the attitudes that prevailed: "The news must be brought to the African, he will not walk a mile to hear it. The danger of the set being tuned in to enemy broadcasts in English can be eliminated by setting it at the middle wave band line and then removing the switch which operates this setting. Enemy broadcasts can then be only obtained on these metre bands at night when Africans usually sleep."[36] How typically African—to sleep at night!

After the Fall of France, the emphasis of the propaganda shifted—portraying Britain as the last bastion of resistance to the Nazi onslaught. Throughout the four isolated British colonies, Africans were repeatedly reminded that should Germany conquer and occupy Britain, all of them would fall under German (mis)rule. No opportunity was lost to hammer home the undesirability of such an eventuality.[37] Straight news increasingly gave way to propaganda, to the considerable distaste of many officials, who felt it demeaning and even ungentlemanly. But, as had been signaled by the creation of the Special Operations Executive, the age of gentlemanly warfare was over.

PROPAGANDA, THE FREE FRENCH, AND THE SOE

By August 1940, the Free French were being allowed to relay broadcasts in order to inform "all French people in the Gold Coast" of the progress of the war. Almost immediately, the content of these broadcasts became an issue of great concern to the Colonial Service. The original understanding between the Free French Mission and Governor Hodson had been that the former were not to engage in direct attacks on the Vichy colonial administrations, but to "follow the BBC line."[38] That "line" was decidedly nonprovocative in regard to Vichy. It was, of course, to show the flag, to present the British case, but in no way should broadcasts, or any other form of propaganda go so far as to cause any further deterioration in relations between the Gold Coast and its neighbors. There were already concerns, indeed strong feelings that initial Free French propaganda was dysfunctional, and that the attempt to build up de Gaulle's reputation in the AOF was disastrous. In particular, Dinan has argued, material containing personal attacks on Boisson was not well received, and the language used in leaflets destined for the French colonies was disapproved of by both the British and the French authorities. The phraseology came very close to inciting the "natives."[39] By default, therefore, much of the themes of the propaganda being sent out by London concentrated on the economic hardships suffered by the French and the extraction of food and raw materials, not only from the empire but from France itself, to strengthen the German war machine. The contrast between the plentiful consumer goods enjoyed by Africans in British territory and the dearth of such staples in French West Africa was also given wide currency. The Free French, however, did not see it in the same way, and after a year of what the British regarded as typical Gallic insouciance, a memorandum was issued from the colonial secretary's office in Accra trying to clarify the nature of what the Free French ought to be saying to their compatriots across the frontier. Two guiding principles were enunciated—and highly contradictory ones at that:

I. That such steps are taken as are likely to weaken and undermine the French Administration so that German infiltration (if and when it occurs) will be as unproductive as possible to the enemy; and
II. That in present circumstances no action must be taken which might lead to so serious a deterioration of relations with the Vichy Colonies that active operations, either local or general, might result.[40]

The discrepancy can be seen when, in March 1941, General Edward Spears, Churchill's liaison with de Gaulle, proposed that it would be important to work on "native" opinion in the AOF. Robert Parr, currently attached to the Governors' Conference at Lagos, reacted strongly against the suggestion. "I should observe," he wrote to the Foreign Office, "that all my experience of French colonies inclines me to think that the policy apparently suggested, apart from its problematical short term advantages, would tend to impart an embarrassing complication into our relations not only with Vichy administration but with Free French, at present time, and with France after the war."[41] One can understand the problem. On the one hand, propaganda had obviously to convince Africans in the British colonies that their war was just, and that the Vichy French were on the wrong side. On the other hand, however, there was a danger that, in turning Africans in the AOF against their Vichy overlords, a chain reaction might be created and lead British subjects to become increasingly dissatisfied with *their* colonial masters.

The situation was further complicated by the developing involvement of the SOE in a field that had previously been controlled by the administration. The Gold Coast government was inclined to emphasize the nobility of the British cause and strove to impress Africans in the surrounding territories with the superior economic and political circumstances being enjoyed by British subjects. In contrast, the SOE and the Free French were less concerned about holding up the British territories as models, but rather with directing propaganda deeply into the Vichy colonies and thereby seeking to raise the level of disaffection. If, for many in the Gold Coast administration, propaganda aimed directly at the French colonies was considered distasteful and even dangerous, then the SOE officers had no such reservations. In December 1941, the head of the Gold Coast Section, N. D. FitzGerald, informed border DCs, "We are anxious to compile and *up-date* list of Europeans and African Literate Notables to whom you are still, at this date, in spite of the strict Vichy Police controls, in a position to send propaganda with a more than 50/50 chance of it being delivered. Kindly furnish us with the names, Habitat, Functions of any such individuals."[42]

Infighting seemed to be developing between the Colonial Office and the Governors' Conference in West Africa over the question of propaganda. It appears that the mandarins in London had virtually discounted any possibility that pro-British, anti-Vichy propaganda would have any significant effect upon French citizens or literate Africans. The French, according to a Colonial Office memo, only believed what they heard on Vichy radio, and the African elites generally followed the anti-British line of the whites. Of the latter, only "Greeks and Lebanese" could be counted as pro-British, and there were hardly enough of them to make a propaganda campaign cost effective. The main target of propaganda must be, the memorandum concluded, the illiterate masses who were seen as passively pro-British. The problem was to work on their latent sympathies. "There is one important consideration, however, at present," the colonial secretary wrote from

Soldiers, Airmen, Spies, and Whisperers

Accra, "which is that the measures adopted to that end must not be such as are liable to lead to open revolt against French authority. The result of such an occurrence would almost certainly be that the French would crush disturbances with great severity, which would not merely render it impossible to look for further support in that area, but would tend to weaken potential support in any area."[43]

Having established, or failed to establish, the rules of the propaganda game, it became necessary to consider methods of delivery. Radio broadcasts beamed at the AOF were generally discounted, although by 1941 they were apparently having an impact on Europeans in the Côte d'Ivoire. A certain M. Reinach, a French coffee planter, spoke with the Englishman J. A. Bolton of the United Africa Company just before he was released from custody and allowed to enter British territory. Reinach, described as a man with Free French sympathies, explained that enough people were listening to Radio Accra to have caused the Vichy administration to print a notice in *La Côte d'Ivoire Française*, the government's mouthpiece, stating that listening to foreign broadcasts was forbidden. Reinach also had some criticism of the content of these broadcasts, namely, that more Frenchmen would be convinced if the appeal was made to "continue the fight for France and Liberty rather than France and de Gaulle."[44] Despite the ray of hope offered by Reinach, Africans in the Côte d'Ivoire were little affected, for like their opposite numbers in the Gold Coast, few of them possessed radios and fewer still would have had sets powerful enough to be able to receive programs from either the Gold Coast Broadcasting network or the Free French Brazzaville transmissions.

The Free French Mission produced and broadcast a fifteen-minute morning newscast, but despite Reinach's assurances, relatively few Europeans in the Côte d'Ivoire, for example, dared or cared to listen to them. This did not stop the Free French station in Brazzaville from continuing to beam propaganda toward the AOF, often thereby incurring British displeasure. In March 1941 de Gaulle ordered a M. Kamenkraus to assist the Gold Coast propaganda department in the production of French language broadcasts. Governor Hodson received a coded telegraph from Nigeria's Governor Bourdillon, warning him that Kamenkraus was "not likely to prove a success. [Louis] Franck knows him well and so does Desjardins, Controller of Brazzaville broadcasts. He is a quarrelsome and opinionated political journalist and I fear that Ponton, who has been warned by de Larminet, will have difficulty in controlling him."[45]

Written propaganda, such as broadsheets, pamphlets, or fliers, was seen as inappropriate for the target population, although sometimes it did end up in strange places. An agent in the Côte d'Ivoire reported that one of the French administrators found "a neat little pile of pamphlets on the only seat in a very private room in his own bungalow!"[46] Another mode of sending propaganda across —placing slips of paper extolling the virtues of General de Gaulle inside packets of French cigarettes to be smuggled across the border—did prove quite popular with African traders from the AOF.[47] One can assume that most such messages in these doctored cigarettes went up in smoke.

WHISPERING IN THE DARK

In mid 1941 a top secret memorandum from the Franck Mission headquarters in Lagos reviewed the matter of "Subversive. Verbal" propaganda directed at the Vichy colonies: "This requires great local knowledge and is carried out by the local officers attached to the Franck Mission and by frontier administrative officers. This requires no more than the most general direction, the details depending on local conditions and being left to the discretion of the local officers. They must, however, report to Headquarters that such and such a rumour has been circulated, and further as to its effects."[48] In the light of this directive, whispering campaigns were organized by district commissioners in border areas. No doubt demonstrating their classical educations, SOE members referred to these whispers as sibs, from the Latin *sibilare*, to hiss.[49] These became the prevailing method of disseminating rumors. The SOE operative in each district was charged with the organization of the campaign, seen as presenting the least risks to agents engaged in subversive activities. He was not to spread the rumors himself, but to appoint a "Chief Whisperer." This person, who must have the total confidence of his employer, would then, in turn, recruit subagents to whom the rumors would be passed. To guarantee the security of this campaign, the chief whisperer should not know any members of the SOE other than the man who had recruited him, the subagents should only know the chief whisperer, and so on down the line. Nothing should ever be written down, lest the chief whisperer or his agents be taken by the French. Should these agents have doubts about how to conduct a whispering campaign, helpful suggestions were given on the approved techniques:

> Whispering consists not in talking yourself, but in making other people talk. They will do this only if the whisper interests them and this is more important than that they should believe it. Whispers can be started in the following ways:
>
> 1. By sub-agents repeating the story by word of mouth.

Soldiers, Airmen, Spies, and Whisperers

2. By repeating the story in a loud voice in front of third parties . . . talking in front of servants, hair-dressers, waiters, etc, is often more effective than direct repetition, because the person over-hearing the story imagines "he is on to a good thing."

3. Jetsam—i.e. notes left in telephone boxes, letters sent to wrong addresses, waste-paper baskets in hotels, etc.

4. Faked Stop Press announcements in newspapers. . . . it is also easy to fake the printing of the Stop Press.

5. Talking on telephone wires known to be tapped.

6. Press and radio, where any control is exercised over these, may be used to support whispers but are not themselves to be regarded as whispering channels.

In all these methods it should be remembered that a story travels better if it is tied up with topical events—scandal, horror, or whatever it is people like to talk about.[50]

One can only imagine the amazement that this document, designed for SOE agents throughout the world, engendered in district commissioners like Miln and Wimshurst. Clearly this supposedly helpful advice, particularly the last four points, would be without much value in the towns and villages of the Colony, Asante, or the Northern Territories, nor conceivably of much use to chief whisperers working in the Côte d'Ivoire or Togo. It is unlikely that techniques of telephone tapping were in the repertoire of tricks possessed by the average British DC in Africa.

Nonetheless, the Ministry of Information in London, and the SOE's Political Warfare Executive (PWE), which had been created out of SO 1, began to produce large quantities of rumors and to distribute them to district commissioners in the Gold Coast. The instructions from FitzGerald of the Franck Mission were simple and certainly more realistic than those regarding the structure of the whispering campaign: "While there is no objection to whispers sent being sifted and ones which in the light of your local knowledge you consider unsuitable being discarded, those which you decide to circulate should not be altered in any way."[51] And what a selection of stories the district commissioners were being offered! Here is a very small sample of what the SOE hoped would be disseminated far and wide:

R/517. Germans make war on all the *Nas el Kitab* (People of the Book—Jews, Christians, Mohammedans). They have dealt with the Jews, they are dealing with the Christians, and next come the Mohammedans.

R/522. Three Germans died of snake bites in Dakar. The Snake Societies are watching.

R/523. Hitler's orders are to exterminate all secret Societies; German agents have been infecting cattle with the rinderpest because they are so short of hides.

R/564. Three pilgrims on their return from Mecca had a vision near Timbuktu of the Archangel Gabriel sharpening his sword.

R/606. A German and a French officer, who entered the country of the Bariba in Dahomey, were killed by lightning. The Bariba have a very powerful juju.[52]

Rumors that were dismissed even exceeded the above in the level of their credulity. The SOE's man on the western frontier, having received a new list of rumors deemed suitable for the Sunyani, Wenchi, and Bole area, found it included the nugget, "the German Armistice Commission are superintending the killing of negroes and shipping the corpses to Germany for pig fodder." It was presumably McGee who commented, "I think this one is too far fetched and likely to discredit our veracity." He could, however, still add, "but if you think otherwise use it by all means."[53]

In April 1942, DCs in all border districts of the Gold Coast, Asante, and the Northern Territories received a new list with the rumors divided by target areas. Rumor Q/246, for example, was to be whispered in the Côte d'Ivoire: "Near Grand Bassam the English have torpedoed a ship coming from France with 500 Germans on board. They intended to land in Liberia." For Senegal and Upper Volta, Rumor Q/280 had it that: "Of the 1,000 Moshis sent to work on the Saharan railway over half have died of the foul disease. The others ran away. They were driven into the desert where they perished. None will ever return." Rumor Q/277 was thought suitably gory for everyone: "When the order for the supply of 500 virgins came to a Chief of the Bambara tribe, his people burnt the courthouse and the house of the Commandant de Cercle, mutilated the messenger and sent him back on a bullock." Or, how about this one? "Beware of the Locusts: they are a warning. Thus the Germans may come."[54]

May's offerings were equally delicious. Ivoiriens were to be told that "the Commandants at Bobo Dioulasso and Ouagadougou have received secret orders for moving their garrisons to Abidjan, where they are to be shipped to France and the Russian front." One rumor intended for the coastal peoples of Togo and Dahomey was that "small pox has broken out in Kandi and Djougou where the German doctors have been." Whispers directed specifically at the Togo Ewe were heavily weighted by the belief that they lived in mortal terror of a return of the Germans, their old colonial masters. The entrance of the United States into the war gave new inspiration to the rumor mongers. Q/985, destined for West Africa, stated that, "during the round-up of spies in America, Hitler's plans were found for exterminating the negroes in Africa to make room for Germans. 100,000 trained American negro soldiers have asked for permission to fight in West Africa."[55]

The powers that be in the SOE clearly thought that what they called "propaganda whisper dissemination" was of great importance. A Mrs. Hale, presumably working in London, consulted "our propaganda rumour experts" and dispatched a memorandum to senior agents in the field. At Accra, the recipient was Lt. Col. N. Sutton of the PWE. The local fabrication of rumors was, however, allowed, but only under certain circumstances. The following passage in the Hale memorandum addressed this matter: "S.O.E. agents in West Africa will disseminate *local* propaganda rumours created by P.W.E., Accra, without reference to S.O.E. or P.W.E., London. This is in line with the present agreement that S.O.E. posts in the field may disseminate their own *local* propaganda rumours without reference to London. This agreement applies only to rumours of *purely local application.*" SOE agents were also required to spread rumors passed on to them by SOE London through PWE Accra. They were forbidden, however, without reference to London, to pass on rumors created by PWE New York, or any mission in Cairo or elsewhere. Significantly, Hale's memorandum stipulated that "P.W.E. Accra, has no power to create 'strategic deceit' rumours with any military application, since P.W.E., London has at present no such power. S.O.E. agents in West Africa will in no instance disseminate such rumours except on instruction from S.O.E. London. Such instructions will be sent direct to S.O.E. agents, and not routed through or divulged to, P.W.E. Accra."[56] Sutton, apparently having understood these mystifying instructions, signaled his acceptance of them to Mrs. Hale on 16 September 1942.

Close on the heels of the Hale document came further orders. PWE Accra was to be responsible for, among other things, "providing suitable personnel" to staff the traveling cinema vans and arranging the tours throughout the country. In return for this new chore they would, however, be permitted to divert the vans in order to carry out other less public activities of the SOE. Finally, all the costs of the propaganda drive, including salaries, were to be borne by the SOE itself, although the PWE would pay for such things as film projectors and all propaganda materials, but only after proper expense accounts were submitted.[57] In all, the understaffed Gold Coast Section of the SOE had quite a load to bear.

In Navrongo, one Mossi agent, a retired policeman, spent his days "talking" to groups of his countrymen from Haute Côte d'Ivoire. They sat under trees awaiting nightfall, when it would be safer for them to cross the French frontier with their smuggled goods. He was apparently a great success, helped along not only by his own authoritative manner of passing on inside information, but by the fact that no Europeans were present. He achieved all this for the British for the princely sum of £3 monthly. It was strongly suggested that all other frontier stations adopt this technique, given its twin advantages of simplicity and economy. Where contact had been made with chiefs considered friendly to the British cause, DCs were told to arrange a regular message service containing news and propaganda, although how anyone could distinguish between the two at this period of the war is questionable. These verbal messages were to be taken across the frontier by French Africans. In a memorandum of September 1941, Mothersill wrote, "it is easier for a French native to get across the frontier than for our own men." Presents (i.e., bribes), when considered appropriate, could be sent at the same time. These wonderful plans, utilizing French African smugglers, also put forward in Mothersill's memo, offered a solution to the current policy of sending Gold Coast Africans into French territory. "French restrictions on the frontier," he wrote, "are now such that it is impossible to spread propaganda by mouth and most of the written propaganda is discarded in the bush close to the frontier."[58] Clearly, it was only French African smugglers who had a strong enough financial motive to risk arrest by crossing the frontier.

Wimshurst, DC Wenchi, with his usual enthusiasm, immediately set about finding ways to disseminate the whispers provided by the SOE. "The idea was, you get an agent," he recollected in 1994, "a fellow selling something. You give him money. 'Wherever you go, you say this or this.' Next week you send another man to see who is saying what and what. It is a great way to upset the whole population. I had millions of francs in my safe in Wenchi. I used to give them money. Part of the work of propaganda is to try and upset any military organisations."[59] Earlier in the war, some traders from the Côte d'Ivoire had carried propaganda leaflets on their persons, although later claimed they had no idea what they were bringing in. One of them, Baba Camara of Bouna, remembered that "around that time [September 1940], they sent me with a package of something. I didn't know what was in it. It was for the commandant at Bouna. I came on my bicycle. There were Gaullist tracts, propaganda, in the package. The captain wasn't happy."[60] Another young Dyula trader in Bouna, Kangoute Katakie, remembered those who brought propaganda materials in from the Gold Coast. "There were some,

Soldiers, Airmen, Spies, and Whisperers

porters, or traders, who were already in Ghana when the Armistice came. They joined de Gaulle. The frontier was closely watched—all comings and goings were watched. Everyone was nervous in those times—here they were very upset. Some of them carried in papers from Ghana. There is one here. All we really knew then was that the war was on, not about de Gaulle."[61]

Border crossings, however provocative they might have been considered by General Giffard, were inevitable, should any success be expected from the propaganda machine. It was certainly dangerous for any individuals to cross the frontier for any subversive purpose, and indeed, as Holbrook as pointed out, any Gold Coast subjects found on the wrong side of the frontier were liable to receive harsh treatment from the French authorities.[62] The Gold Coast was already providing refuge for various dissident elements from the Côte d'Ivoire, and this was obviously regarded by the Vichy authorities as a threat to their interests. To prevent defections to the neighboring colony, French officials became zealous in reporting any signs of Gaullist, or pro-British, activity in their districts. A new service, the Comité pour la Répression des Menées Anti-Nationales, was created. According to British Intelligence its object was to deal "with Free French supporters on the lines followed by the Gestapo."[63]

Rumors, petty dislikes and suspicions, casual conversations, listening to British radio broadcasts, even the possession of American or English cigarettes by civilians, were all grist to the mill.[64] Even more strictly forbidden was attendance at any meeting with British officials, a directive aimed presumably at any French functionaries who had not broken off all contacts with their counterparts along the borders.[65] A new medal was devised to encourage informants, the Médaille du Mérite de l'Afrique Française Noire. It was to be awarded to "reward those in fighting those alien influences of which our colonies have been and are still the object."[66]

The whispering campaign continued throughout 1941 and 1942, although few in either the SOE or the Gold Coast government could have had much confidence in its success. Even Sir Frank Nelson of the SOE in London found the general level of propaganda materials destined for Africa to be appalling. Having dealt with a progress report on the SOE's operations in West Africa, Nelson then commented, "The one item of real interest which I think we should tackle at once is H. V.'s [Hanns Vischer] contempt for the propaganda which is putting out to the natives, for which he says we should immediately recruit scientists, anthropologists and zoologists etc., who have some knowledge of the natives, their customs, secret societies etc. in that part of the world, and seek to put propaganda into native hands rather than into the Vichy French who don't count anyway, so he says."[67] It is difficult to assess whether the content of the new lists of whispers produced by the SOE in the wake of Nelson's missive were any improvement. Certainly they do not appear to have been composed by Vischer's preferred professionals, thought to have a good understanding of the "natives." Whatever the case, by March 1942 a new set of ideas for leaflets destined for French territories was agreed upon by SOE personnel in the Gold Coast. Cartoons, in color, were to be used, and the message each conveyed was to be simple, "as if they were meant for children." The cartoonists were advised to portray all the Axis leaders as animals—but cautioned only to draw animals familiar to the residents of the target area (for, after all, the characteristics of a tiger or a kangaroo would not signify much to a inhabitant of Bouaké or Lomé.) As for representing French collaborators, presumably including men like Pétain and Pierre Laval, "special care should be taken," depending upon policy directives from on high.[68] In other words, it depended upon whether policy continued to treat Vichy personages kindly, as being potential allies, or vilely, as adherents of the Axis cause.

The thorny question of control over propaganda of all varieties was to plague the SOE throughout the war. It, and the Ministry of Economic Warfare, were constantly at loggerheads with the Foreign Office, Military Intelligence, MI 6, and the Ministry of Information over questions of jurisdiction, and indeed the battles of Hugh Dalton with the Ministry of Information over questions of propaganda led, eventually, to his removal from the MEW in February 1942.[69]

VICHY PROPAGANDA

The propaganda war was not, of course, one-sided. The Vichy government in the AOF was also active, although for obvious reasons unable to present much in the way of patriotic films extolling the military glories of France. Nor did it have the resources to send cinema vans throughout the vast reaches of its territory. The AOF did, however, have radio, and a propaganda department set up to "explain" the great benefits France would gain from its new alliance with Germany. Like the propaganda of their counterparts in the Gambia, Gold Coast, Sierra Leone, and Nigeria, two different types were produced. The first was designed to reassure its own population that under the benevolent leadership of the hero of Verdun, Marshal Pétain, France would again take her rightful place in the sun, albeit under a German parasol. The second, a much more modest operation, was aimed at Africans in the neighboring British colonies.

Propaganda designed for the home front was limited, as it was in the British colonies, by the paucity of radios among the population outside the capitals. As we have said, few Europeans, and even fewer Africans, owned sets. Indeed, in Dahomey, Africans had been prohibited from owning radios, presumably to prevent their access to Free French and British broadcasts.[70] The inability to import any technological equipment from Europe in order to set up anything like the subscription service introduced in the Gold Coast made domestic propaganda rely almost entirely on oral transmission. Notification of the dictates of new Vichy rules and regulations forbidding a large number of activities to Africans had to come almost exclusively from the local administrators, through, if necessary, their interpreters. The commandants de cercle were charged not only with rooting out any suspected British sympathizers, but also with making sure that all understood the penalties of not giving full support to the regime. The administration provided little or no information about either the scale or the consequences of the fall of France. For most Africans in the AOF there was little evidence that things had changed in their daily lives. They felt most immediately, of course, the disappearance of imported goods. But to balance that inconvenience, there was also a most welcome reduction in both military recruitment and forced labor quotas. Virtually all administrators stayed in their jobs, cash crops continued to be purchased by the government, and, for most of the people, little news of the outside world reached them. This is not to say that there was contentment, but since this had never been expected or received from their French masters in any case, the usual rhythm of life continued.[71] In the eyes of AOF officials, those who requested information over and above that provided by the Vichy press were regarded as potential troublemakers. Some Europeans were included in this category. So were prominent Muslim leaders, such as the grand marabout of French West Africa, Sheikh Nouridou Tal. And so were a number of important traditional rulers, the most notable being Moro Naba Kom II of the Mossi, whose authority extended over a wide area of Haute Côte d'Ivoire, and even over Mossi immigrants to the Gold Coast. To these must be added many members of the African elites, all of whom had summarily been deprived of their rights to be treated as Frenchmen under new Vichy legislation.[72]

In the AOF the focus of propaganda and press was on the peace now reigning in France, the benefits forthcoming from a new, purified motherland under Pétain, and, most especially, on the perfidy of the British and their new allies, the traitorous followers of Charles de Gaulle. Attacks on the British and Free French were most popular, for certainly they were the easiest targets. British Intelligence in West Africa monitored most of the broadcasts, and by the summer of 1941 was reporting that "Vichy broadcasts in Africa have recently increased in violence in their long tirades against the Free French Movement. The usual daily invectives against the British continue, coupled with the obviously German controlled policy of depicting France as European and Britain outside the European order of things."[73] Later in the year, British intelligence noted that "Anti-British propaganda increasing. CO [commanding officer] at Bouake supposed to have said that English to attack within 3 or 4 months. In Togo, spies report that pro-German feeling very strong. Deutscher Togo Bund reappearing, esp around Atakpamé and Kpalimé."[74]

Not to be outdone by the British, the AOF set up a special propaganda department aimed at Africans in the British colonies. It informed them of the virtual paradise now being enjoyed by their brothers and sisters in the Côte d'Ivoire as compared to the hardships they were undoubtedly suffering under British control. In what can only be regarded as the mother of all hypocrisy, the colonial power had conscripted over a hundred thousand West Africans for the Tirailleurs Sénégalais alone to fight in Europe, and had taken tens of thousands of others as forced laborers, yet the Vichy government produced this astonishing piece of propaganda:

> Moreover, we know that the Natives in French Equatorial Africa are compelled to enlist in the Native Forces and are being sent far away from their homes to fight for Great Britain's sake. The few Natives who had listened to the Gaullists' false promises and had left their villages have promptly gone back to their homes, in order to avoid their enrolment in the British army. The inhabitants of these colonies of French Equatorial Africa are thinking with regret of the happy times when they lived under the protection of France.[75]

Reports of the defeats suffered by Britain in Asia were printed, as was an article on British oppression of Hindus in India. In one of the few available Vichy propaganda tracts, a parable was offered to explain the current situation of the AOF. It began with the tale of how ancient China sought, but failed, to keep the banana tree from being grown outside its territory. It is of sufficient interest to quote at length.

> Reader, my friend, France may be compared to the banana-plant. In spite of all her trials, some of them having been inflicted upon her by her former friend, Great-Britain, France remains as strong and prosperous as ever. Under the wise and firm guidance of her venerable chef, Marshall Pétain, this coun-

Soldiers, Airmen, Spies, and Whisperers

try carries on productive work. She has withdrawn from the war and has no intention of attacking any other country, as it is sometimes falsely stated. She only wants to be left alone in peace and be respected.

The natives in the French colonies of West Africa live happy and satisfied under her protection. They are in good condition, plough their land, grow their cattle, go fishing or do trading as peacefully as ever. Remember, Reader, my friend, France and particularly the French colonies are, to-day, one of the only places in the world where war is not carried on, where men are not killed and where people do not suffer.

And, with your sensible mind, think over this question: what sense can there be in telling that the natives want to cross the boundary-line for joining the English colonies? What could they gain by it? They know that on the other side of the frontier they would be deprived of their freedom and compelled to enlist in the British army. They are equally well aware of the fact that the English with their customary selfishness, would not share with them the few supplies of clothing-materials they get, as it is known that they have denied sending any to the territories occupied by the Gaullists.

France and French West-Africa will continue living in complete union, in spite of Great-Britain's efforts and following with full confidence their unique chief: Marshall Pétain.[76]

France and Pétain were indeed unique, France being the only occupied country the legal government of which collaborated with the Nazis.

Other bulletins smuggled into Sokoto Province of Nigeria dealt at length with the cruelty of the British naval blockade of the French West African ports. "Britain does not care whether our women and children are starving and, regardless of those considerations, attacks our merchant ships and captures them with the whole cargo destined to the French People . . . maybe the blockade is a part of a British conspiracy whose darling object is the downfall of the French Empire, but, who has seen the agonies of mothers and children dying from starvation may but hate such a process."[77] These and other similar documents provide an interesting insight into the state of mind of Vichy officialdom. While the effect of AOF propaganda upon the peoples of British West Africa cannot easily be measured, the four colonial governments did become nervous. Their governors shared with the French, whether Vichy or Gaullist, fears about agitating the "natives."

Internal Vichy propaganda seemed to be effective in convincing the European population that Great Britain had once again become the enemy and had no chance whatsoever of stemming a German invasion, let alone achieving any military victory. It had, however, little impact on the Africans in French territory, an ineffectiveness it shared with the propaganda of the Free French. The U.S. Office of Strategic Services reported that the Gaullist propaganda leaflets that reached Bobo-Dioulasso had not only made an unfavorable impression, but contained very little that was not already public knowledge.[78] At the same time, it must be said that Governor-General Boisson did everything in his power also to keep German propaganda from entering the AOF. The postal service was ordered to seize any shipments of German brochures, and those Europeans suspected of being too ardent collaborators—in fact, Nazi sympathizers—were kept under police surveillance and, if convicted of espionage, were jailed by Boisson's courts.[79] However the bulk of the repression was reserved for supporters of the dissidents (i.e., the Free French).

One British missionary was arrested in Bobo-Dioulasso and sentenced to five years in prison simply for giving directions to a porter carrying Gaullist literature. Another simply refused to accept any parcels in case they should contain Free French leaflets. Any messengers caught with the material were arrested and forced to reveal to whom it was being sent. In turn, the addressee was arrested.

In one instance, the Free French in Accra sent a letter by one of their messengers to the Director of Education, also at Bobo-Dioulasso, asking him to undertake a particular mission for them. The man, reputed to be very pro-British, responded that it would be impossible for him to act, as he was under constant police watch by reason of his suspect loyalty. The Free French in Accra ignored his request to stop sending him literature and indeed sent more, which was intercepted. As a result, the man and his wife were arrested and taken to Dakar. They were only acquitted as a result of testimonials sent by "all the French all over the Ivory Coast."[80] This affair effectively ended any real assistance from Europeans in the Bobo-Dioulasso area, since even had they been pro-Gaullist, the conduct of the Free French representatives would have made it far too dangerous for them to be actively so.

The level of Free French sentiment in the Côte d'Ivoire was, in any case, minimal. After the first few weeks following the armistice of 22 June 1940, those Frenchmen in the colony who were sufficiently outraged by France's capitulation, left to join the British or de Gaulle. Those who remained took virtually no part in anti-Vichy activities, although at least seven Europeans were convicted of either consorting with Free French agents or giving them military information.[81] Meetings of all but Vichy-approved associations and clubs were banned, and one

British Intelligence report spoke of a corps of internal secret agents, fifty men and fifty women, whose sole task was to ferret out dissidents or identify those—Africans or Europeans—who could be labeled defeatists. (Locating "defeatists" must have occupied a great deal of the secret agents' time, since even the most diehard Vichyiste was unlikely to be predicting a French victory over the Germans!) "In Dahomey," the same report continued, "the authorities seem to have awoken to the dangerous susceptibility of the African to external propaganda and an intensive anti-British and anti-Free French campaign is being carried on by word of mouth. This is backed up by ceremonial parades at which the tricolour and portraits of Marshal Pétain are solemnly saluted and a band marches through the streets of Cotonou several times a week."[82] When it came to denigrating the intelligence of the African in the street, it was certainly a toss-up between the propagandists of Pétain's France and Churchill's Britain.

In June 1941 two British employees of the United Africa Company, MacDermott and Havelock, were permitted to leave Niger and crossed the border into Nigeria. They reported that the general feeling among the French of that colony was that the British were bound to lose and that "carrying it on is uselessly prolonging the agony and delaying France's hopes of recovery; that they have an unreasoning belief that Hitler will leave the French Empire alone in return for collaboration in the 'New Order,' and that they regard A.E.F. and the Cameroun as 'under British occupation.'"[83]

The successful invasion of the Levant by a combined British and Free French force in the spring of 1941 did little to increase the popularity of either among the Europeans of Vichy West Africa. Since there were no German forces in Syria or Lebanon, they could see no justification in this further humiliation of France. On the same subject, the WAPIC Bulletin of 18 July 1941 reported that Vichy leaflets sent into northern Nigeria contained strong statements to the effect that there are no Germans at Dakar or Cotonou, quoted Admiral Darlan's denial that German aircraft were making use of Syrian airfields, and suggested that false British propaganda was being promoted to cloak British and American designs on Dakar.[84] The conquest of the Levant by the Allies, however, did little to increase French confidence in the ability of the Vichy government to protect them, the French residents, in the event of a similar invasion in West Africa. For the most part, Europeans continued to accept the Vichy regime and simply hoped for the best. And, as Britain showed no sign of collapse and the Soviet Union and the United States were precipitated into the war, they awaited developments.

Such success that British propaganda achieved in engendering local enthusiasm for the war effort can probably be attributed as much to its entertainment value as to its content. There is little doubt, however, that the majority of Africans through-out the Northern Territories, Asante, and the Gold Coast Colony came whole-heartedly to support the struggle, "Hitler's war," against Germany. Nowhere was to this to be more evident than in the Gold Coast drive to purchase Spitfires for the defense of Great Britain. Although the emphasis in the colony had been on army recruitment and on defense of the borders, the authorities were not insen-sitive to the somewhat more glamorous image of the Royal Air Force. The idea of aerial warfare was by no means new to the people of the Gold Coast and Asante. Toward the end of World War I, a "Gold Coast" bomber squadron had been formed in Britain. There were, of course, neither Gold Coasters nor any other Africans in the unit, it was simply money that the colony was expected to pro-vide. The squadron was disbanded in June 1919. Resurrected in March 1936 as No. 218 Squadron, it saw service during the Battle of France.[85] But it was recog-nized that trying to raise funds for a bomber squadron, even one historically linked to the Gold Coast, might, granted the limited incomes of Africans, prove too dis-couraging for them. Far better to devise something that would produce tangible results in terms of the numbers of planes "bought" by Gold Coast residents, so inspiring them to ever greater efforts. To this end, in May 1940, the formation of a second Gold Coast Squadron, this time a fighter unit, was announced. It would, it was hoped, serve as a visible and highly popular symbol to encourage Africans to contribute to the purchase of the new and glamorous fighter aircraft, the Spitfire. This was the occasion of the launching of the Spitfires Fund.

In its first year the Spitfires Fund, under Hon. Treasurer Mr. F. A. B. John-ston, raised £65,000. The target for 1941 was £100,000. So enthusiastic was the re-sponse to the appeal that the entire sum had been raised by 19 June, £12,000 alone coming from the people of Kumasi.[86] In all, the men, women, and children of the Gold Coast responded with generous hearts to the various war drives. Over the course of 1941, the sums amassed for the war effort were truly amazing. Outright donations totaled £340,714, while another £205,000 was subscribed in war bonds and savings certificates.[87] But without question, the Spitfires Fund led the chari-table hit parade on the Gold Coast. T. E. Kyei, in his role as propagandist rather than Home Guardsman, commented, "The whole idea was to get the people aware —to contribute. . . . We called it the Spitfires Fund. We [the Asante people] were told that we weren't expecting the Germans to come here and land. We were expecting them to bomb. The Luftwaffe. And planes can be fought by planes. The British need to protect Kumasi and we could help by getting more Spitfires to fight. So we are to get money."[88]

Throughout the colony, dances, contests, and various other events were organized to drum up support for the fund. One group in Sunyani, for example, styling itself the Merry Makers, announced a "Konkomba Band Competition and Grand Evening Dress Dance," to be held on 2 August 1941. In a letter to a local dignitary, the Hon. Secretary of the Merry Makers asked the chief to encourage his people to attend, despite "the hard times." The function, he hoped, would include

> a large number of bands entering for the competition. The maximum number of players should be 24 and the entrance fee of 5/–; this amount is requested to be sent here by each competing band as early as possible. . . . The songs for the competition are:—
> "Bue me, opon bue me" (Blues)
> "Obi ne ne jolly, obra twa wu" (High Life).[89]

Stories of young lads bringing their hard-earned pocket money to district commissioners for the Spitfires Fund constantly appeared in local newspapers. A large "thermometer," beloved of fund-raisers worldwide, stood outside the General Post Office in Accra. On 19 October 1940, *West Africa* published a photograph of it, with the "temperature" already registering £35,000! While, indeed, there might have been internal competition among various cities, or even regions, as to who could raise the most money, the "Spitfires Fund—Give to It" was yet another institution cutting across ethnic and regional boundaries within the Gold Coast. So popular did the Fund become that members of the Gold Coast Brigade at war in East Africa started their own collection, using as a base £1,000 in captured Italian money.[90]

After the popular success of the fighter squadron, it was decided, in September 1941, to officially readopt the bomber squadron, and again it became known as No. 218 Gold Coast Squadron. Each member of the squadron was presented with a wooden cigarette box, which was greatly appreciated although the men found the taste of the cigarettes provided with it somewhat reminiscent of camel dung.[91] The exploits of both these units were regularly reported in the pages of *West Africa* and other publications directed to the empire. In addition to the nearly £2,000 being subscribed weekly to the Spitfires Fund, the people also donated generously to special funds set up for British and Allied causes. In 1942 the

Legislative Council of the Gold Coast Colony voted to provide an interest-free loan of £800,000 to the British government. All these efforts received great praise from white residents of the Gold Coast. Especially singled out for commendation was the paramount chief of Akyem Abuakwa in the colony. This was Sir Ofori Atta I, rather curiously described by *West Africa*'s columnist Vernon Cameron as "a man who, in the House of Lords or Commons, would be in the first score of its debaters, in the idiomatic English which he uses in the Council house at Accra."[92]

Popular enthusiasm, if possible, reached new heights when, in February 1941, Governor Hodson announced that it would now be possible for "suitable" African youths to join the Royal Air Force Volunteer Reserve. Local newspapers and magazines had been full of letters by Africans clamoring to be allowed to enlist for flight crews.[93] *West Africa*, one of the chief advocates of recruiting Africans for the air force, was exuberant at the news, and even offered advice to the RAF. It suggested that once large numbers of Africans had been taken in, the RAF would be "well advised" not only to put Africans in separate units, but to place them among their own "tribesmen." That way, its reporter advised, the RAF would benefit, "because a second's delay due to a misunderstanding might mean all the difference to the outcome of a fight."[94] Despite the implicit racism of this advice no exhortations to chiefs were necessary to attract large numbers of recruits for this most alluring of the armed forces. S. K. Boateng, who in the early 1950s was to be one of five founding members of the Asante National Liberation Movement, appreciated the advantages the air force provided:

> I was in Accra. I was a volunteer. I joined voluntarily by myself. . . . I thought it would serve me. . . . It is good. Discipline. You discipline your life. I was a stenographer then. I decided to join. In those days there were certain privileges with the army. You could take correspondence courses at half the rate. They had a big library. The army was the place for an ambitious young man. And I was ambitious. . . . You must understand. We had discipline. We were a unit with doctors, stenographers, teachers. There were a lot of non-tradesmen, men with no trade. Yes, illiterates. We had to name them something, so we called them magazine carriers. They had no skills so they carried the magazines, the ammunition for the planes. They carried the magazines and learned to shoot. My unit was records, personnel. I was in charge. There were the teachers who taught the illiterates. There were so many different units, ground crew, pilots, repair, so many different ones.[95]

S. K. Boateng may have joined for discipline and future prospects, but the popular press and many of its readers, while admitting that experience in the youngest arm of the military could be an "immense asset after the war," preferred to stress disinterest over self-interest in the motives of those who volunteered. As *West Africa* rhapsodized, "Enthusiastic is almost too weak a description. Not a shred of doubt could be left in the mind of any reader, of the writers' keen appreciation of the fact that to take part in the operations of R.A.F., is one of the highest honours that could come to any African or any other man, as regards not only his personal courage and endurance but also his privilege of helping to secure the conditions of human freedom and advancement."[96]

THE IMPACT OF THE PROPAGANDA MACHINE

Propaganda, as we have seen, included, on the one hand, its use to create dissatisfaction among the populations of Vichy territories and, on the other hand, its use on the home front to secure the loyalty of the peoples of the British colonies. On the efficacy of the first, the jury should perhaps remain out. Perhaps the most informed, if not necessarily the most objective, evaluation was that made by Miles Clifford, who ran the SOE's Frawest between the exit of Wingate and the entrance of Lumby. He thought that the quality of written propaganda being directed into the Vichy AOF was unsatisfactory, that its distribution was poor, and that its quantity was "too much," only a small part reaching its goal. "It is futile," he wrote by way of example, "to send over handsomely illustrated journals advertising our impregnable strength in Malaya which reach the reader some time after Singapore is in the hands of the Japanese. Generally speaking, large-size journals are useless, being difficult to transport or to conceal while the vigilance of the Vichy 'gestapo' is far keener than it used to be and those found in possession of our propaganda incur severe penalties." Clifford also thought that broadcasts beamed to the AOF were of questionable value since the number of serviceable sets in African hands was low, and Vichy jamming was fairly effective. He believed that external propaganda in general had the greatest impact when it was the least confrontational. It needed to command respect and understanding and to be friendly and objective. Factual material should be used—for example, British and U.S. production figures, the bombing of Cologne and Essen, the Free French victories in Libya, and so forth. Humorous pamphlets would be welcome, but they should not "point the finger of ridicule or shame at France or the Marshall" —that is, they should not make the readers feel guilty or unpatriotic for enjoying the joke.[97]

The position is clearer with regard to propaganda and fund-raising on the home front, for the British effort was undoubtedly successful in raising enthusiasm for the war effort and in reducing active dissent to a minimum. One of the few public pronouncements that might have been construed as manifesting less than total support for the British cause was that of the Asante lawyer Osafroadu Amankwatia, who wrote an article in the Asante national newspaper, the *Asante Pioneer*, in 1940. He argued the historical position that Asante had never technically been conquered by the British, that Britain therefore had no justification for its last two wars against Asante, and "thus Ashanti has the right to claim compensation."[98] Whether any censors thought this mildly subversive we do not know; but certainly no action seems to have been taken either to suppress the issue or to reprimand its editor. Interestingly, the Asantehene made an important speech in Kumasi only a few weeks later. Before a crowd of several thousand he referred to Hitler's harsh treatment of, inter alia, the Jews and the people of the occupied countries, and contrasted this with the benign attitude of the British toward their subjects. He spoke, in what seemed to be forgiving terms, of the banishment of his predecessor, Nana Agyeman Prempeh I, by the British and referred to the comfortable conditions provided for the exiles in the Seychelles.[99]

The wartime propaganda experience was to have long-term consequences for the Gold Coast as a whole. The Information Department's activities provided a future organizational model for the colony—one that would be useful for the postwar drive for greater opportunity particularly in the economic sector, for self-government, and finally, for independence. The new African politicians, launching the anticolonial struggle, were quick to use methods developed by the colonial administration. Political activists in the Gold Coast came to employ propaganda techniques to get their message across in a fashion every bit as sophisticated, if not more so, as those developed to mobilize the population for the war effort. Interestingly, Kwame Nkrumah, who was to lead the Gold Coast to independence as Ghana, had left the country for the United States in 1936 and had had no direct experience of his people at war. Nevertheless, he had seen an America resolutely isolationist transformed into one strongly committed to the overthrow of the Axis powers. Japan's attack on Pearl Harbor had been the catalyst of the remarkable change, but in a short space of time the American people, including most of those of German descent, had come to see themselves as engaged in a life-and-death struggle to build a new world that was free and democratic. Nkrumah could not have failed to appreciate the extent to which this remarkable transformation was accomplished through the power of media; through radio, press, and, not

Soldiers, Airmen, Spies, and Whisperers

least, Hollywood. On his return to the Gold Coast, in 1947, he was quick to draw personnel from the old wartime Information Department for the nationalist cause. As Holbrook has well put it, the wartime propaganda machine was "a valuable legacy to those charged with directing the territory's campaigns for national integration, education, and community development projects."[100] But that is another story.

7

The Crossing of the Gyaman

TRIUMPH OR EMBARRASSMENT?

ONE PEOPLE, TWO COLONIES: THE GYAMAN
OF CÔTE D'IVOIRE AND GOLD COAST

Free French intelligence and the Special Operations Executive were to score what was undoubtedly a major propaganda coup in early 1942.[1] The setting was one particular stretch of the Côte d'Ivoire–Gold Coast frontier, namely, that separating the Abron (or Gyaman) of the *Cercle* [i.e., District] of Bondoukou from the Bron (or Gyaman) of the North-West Province of Asante.[2] It was there, nineteen months after France had signed the armistice, that the ruler of the Abron of the Côte d'Ivoire led many of his people into the Gold Coast, thereby relocating the core of his state in British territory.

The history of Gyaman has been the subject of extensive study.[3] Of importance for present purposes are the relations between Gyaman and Asante. Gyaman was brought under the authority of the Golden Stool, and Gyamanhene Abo Kofi slain, probably in the decade 1730–40, and certainly during the reign of Asantehene Opoku Ware (ca. 1720–50).[4] In 1811, Gyamanhene Adinkra rebelled against Asante overlordship, and it was not until 1818–19 that Asantehene Osei Tutu Kwame launched the major invasion that ended Gyaman's brief period of independence. Half a century later, in the aftermath of their sack of Kumasi in 1874, the British attempted to woo the Gyamanhene. The rival powers, the Asante and the British, each sent missions to Gyaman, the former in an attempt to retain the Gyamanhene's allegiance, the latter to try to win it. The major Asante mission arrived in Gyaman in 1878. It was headed by the expatriate Carl Nielson, who sported the grand title of His Majesty's Commissioner and Headman for a Mission of Peace to the King of Gaman. The British immediately responded by sending a mission led by John Smith in 1879, and a much more high powered embassy conducted by Capt. R. LaT. Lonsdale between April and July 1882.[5] The situation, however, continued to be a confused one as the Gyamanhene certainly enjoyed being courted by both.

A decisive turn of events occurred in July 1893, when an agreement between Britain and France was signed that divided Gyaman between them, though leaving Gyamanhene Agyeman in the French sphere. Although the border agreement was at that time no more than a line on paper, neither power having any real presence in the area, nevertheless some substance was given it by Agyeman accepting the offer of French protection. He did so in the hope that the French would be of help to him against the Malinke warlord Samory, whose forces were then pressing into his territory. His hopes were unrealized, however, for in 1895 Samory's troops poured across Gyaman's northern frontier and occupied the Muslim-dominated town of Bondoukou. In response, Agyeman turned once again toward the British and Asante, seeking assistance from Governor Maxwell of the Gold Coast on the one hand, and Asantehene Agyeman Prempeh I on the other. Maxwell rejected the appeal on the grounds that the Gyamanhene had been associated with the French, the implication being that he was getting what he deserved. The emissary to Kumasi failed to get through, because of troubles on the main road between Kumasi and Bondoukou. Agyeman fled. To complete the circle, Samory then sent envoys to Kumasi to explain that he had invaded Gyaman only to open the trade routes and that he was prepared to help Asante defeat any rebellious chiefs, the Gyamanhene presumably included.[6] The Samorian-Asante contacts, as much as anything, occasioned the British invasion of Asante in 1896, when the Asantehene, the Queen mother, and many of the senior chiefs were taken into exile.

Asante was thus effectively removed from the power scene. Two years later, Samory was captured. Henceforth, the French and British were unhampered in making their claims to Gyaman a reality. Their respective spheres of influence were demarcated more or less on the basis of the Anglo-French Agreement of 1893. The greater part of Gyaman was incorporated into the Côte d'Ivoire, including its royal capitals of Zanzan and Yakasi, the four original territorial divisions of

Akyidom, Fumasa, Penango, and Siengi, and the important market town of Bon-doukou. A number of Gyaman's easterly districts, however, fell under the British administration of Asante and therefore under the authority of the governor of the Gold Coast.[7] British Gyaman, as it was known, included two powerful military divisions, Adonten, with its capital at Drobo, and Nifa, centered on Suma. The administration recognized Drobohene as paramount over British Gyaman, although the Sumahene disputed this, claiming that in the old Gyaman he was second only to the Gyamanhene.[8]

The establishment of the colonial border did not, of course, wipe out two centuries of history. The British Gyaman continued to regard the Gyamanhene in the Côte d'Ivoire as their (traditional) paramount. With the recognition of Osei Agyeman Prempeh II as Asantehene and the restoration of the so-called Ashanti Confederacy in 1935, the situation changed once again. Both Drobo and Suma found themselves once more serving an Asantehene. They now had two masters, one in a French colony, one in a British. As for the Gyamanhene, secure behind the colonial boundary, he could confidently style himself *roi des Abron,* and declared his rank equal to that of the Asantehene. In 1994 an elderly informant, Nana Yaw Kran—obviously a Gyaman patriot—recollected this:

> When France divided them, Nana Kofi Agyeman was the Bronhene and Prempeh was the Asantehene. In those days they were equals. Obviously in those days, Nana Kofi Agyeman was even greater than Prempeh II. His name —Agyeman—no chief had that name but he. Nana Kofi Agyeman—he and the Asantehene—they fought in the olden days. During that time—the time that brought about the demarcation—and that made Nana Agyeman remain on the French side because his city was on the French side. The remaining family, those who stayed, were left in Ghana. For example, Drobohene is in Ghana, but he used to be the Adontenhene to the Gyamanhene.[9]

For much of the colonial period there had been little impediment to the movement of people and produce across this frontier, though smuggling had flourished as a means of evading taxes imposed by one or other of the colonial powers. At times, when life under one master became intolerable, people might at least threaten to migrate, removing themselves to the jurisdiction of another. Suspicious of each other's territorial designs, the British and French generally reciprocated in refraining from offering any overt encouragement to the other's disaffected subjects. Thus, however *attractive* the idea of granting requests for asylum might be, realism dictated that the status quo should be maintained.

Soldiers, Airmen, Spies, and Whisperers

After the fall of France, any such tacit understanding no longer had force. When the Gyamanhene made known his desire to move his people into the Allied camp, literally by moving them across the border, it was difficult for the British to refuse them sanctuary.

THE GYAMAN UNDER VICHY

The French had considered Gyamanhene Kwadwo Agyeman one of their most loyal subjects. Immediately after the declaration of war in September 1939, he had demonstrated his wholehearted enthusiasm for the cause, assuring the then governor of the Côte d'Ivoire, Horace Crocicchia, that, "Facing these inhuman creatures who are bloodying France a second time, we, her children, sons of the Abron, at this moment of the defense of our dear motherland are ready to respond to her call and happy to die for her, being certain of victory."[10] "Prince" Kwame Adinkra, one of Kwadwo Agyeman's many sons, his Aduanahene, and his closest advisor, fully supported his father's pro-French stance.[11] Three other sons volunteered for the Tirailleurs Sénégalais, setting an example for general recruitment in the Bondoukou area. Indeed, over one thousand Gyaman were taken into the tirailleurs. During that first phase of the war, Agyeman claimed that he had raised half a million francs for the French Red Cross, as well as donating twenty-four tons of cocoa to provide chocolate bars for French soldiers. In recognition of their services to the war effort, both Agyeman and Adinkra were given medals by France.[12] Indeed, both men had prospered under the French and were among the wealthiest cocoa planters in the Côte d'Ivoire.

Precisely what happened to change this happy relationship between subjects and rulers is unclear. Certainly there is no evidence that the fall of France was seen as the occasion for instigating a rebellion against the colonial condition as such. Adolf Hitler was certainly not seen as a potential liberator of Africans from the colonial yoke. Why then did the Gyaman leaders decide to turn against France, now that it had become Vichy, and throw in their lot with Britain and the Free French? What made them willing to risk both their property and position? Much of the answer must lie in the intense hostility that had developed between them and Bondoukou's commandant de cercle. Some of the reasons are quite apparent. The commandant had been interfering in too many matters regarded as the prerogatives of the chiefs. He had apparently dissolved marriages when a wife came to complain about her husband. Gyaman chiefs had also been forced by the commandant to refund monies they had levied on their subjects for various transgressions.[13] That many of the Gyaman were profoundly unhappy under the straitened circumstances of the Vichy administration had been known to British intelligence for some months, and indeed had been brought to the attention of the British West African Governors' Conference during the summer of 1941. It had been learned "from a chief in Bondoukou, (less than halfway up the Gold Coast Border)," so the SOE informed the governors, that "a message had been received expressing dislike of the 'French Vichy Government' and complaining that they [the Gyaman] get no news of the war."[14] The governors also were given the news that "an intelligent African from the Ivory Coast declares that the natives believe that the French are helpless and fear the Germans—'The French Flag is a dead flag.'"[15]

News of these matters was brought over the border by agents employed by local district commissioners on behalf of the SOE, now in the shape of Frawest. We have already seen that the DC at Wenchi, H. V. Wimshurst, used a border policeman, Corporal Quarshie, stationed in the British Gyaman town of Sampa, to organize the flow of information from Vichy Bondoukou and beyond. In one of his weekly reports, Quarshie noted that the governor of the Côte d'Ivoire, now Hubert Deschamps, had received a letter of complaint from Kwame Adinkra concerning "the bad conduct towards himself and his father by the Commandant." Quarshie had also managed to learn the contents of Deschamps's reply, from which it is clear that the matter had to do with the commandant's unilateral decision to abolish their right to fine their subjects. The governor, he reported, "is preparing to come to Bondugu [Bondoukou] on trek to settle the misunderstandings between them. That the Commandant should collect back the money he forced Kwame Adinkra to refund and pay to him before his arrival at Bondugu."[16]

Things came to a head in November 1941. Relations between the Gyaman and their French overlords had so deteriorated that Kwadwo Agyeman dispatched a messenger to the Drobohene in British Gyaman, with instructions to have his letter writer prepare a document in English for the attention of the British authorities. The Drobohene, his linguist, and his clerk, together with the Gyaman messenger, traveled through the night to Wenchi. There they met Wimshurst. The importance of this letter, its urgent tone, and the atmosphere of the period it conveys, merit its reproduction in full. The messenger ("Ahenkwa"), coincidentally bore the same name as the Gyamanhene.

I, the undermarked Kojo Agyeman of Amanfe in French Ivory Coast near Buntuku hereby declare that I am Ahenkwa for Nana Kojo Agyeman the Jamanhene of Dabreyo in Buntuku and he and his son Prince Kwame Adinkra the Aduanahene of the whole Buntuku sent me to inform Nana Kofi Busiah the Drobohene as follows:

(a) That they want to serve the British Government so he Nana Drobohene may arrange with the D.C. Wenchi to fix a day to meet him the Aduanahene at a place on the boundary to see him personally and talk everything over.

(b) That they want the British Government to take possession of all their lands from Soko up to River Kumoi [Comoé].

(c) That they have more things to trade with and at present they might rebel but that may cost them lives and loss of properties so the D.C. must not waste anytime but report to the Governor at Accra and arrange everything at once.

(d) That even if there be any shooting all the native soldiers are prepared under their control to assist the English Government to safe them.

(e) That the Aduanahene wanted to come immediately to the D.C. or you the Drobohene in person but the French will not allow if he does it openly hence they sent me.

(f) That if you did not help them in time and this secret came to the hearing of the Frenchmen, they will get trouble that will cost them their lives and that of their subjects the Buntukuman; so they pray you in the Name of God the Almighty and the ghosts of their ancestors and their gods that you Nana Drobohene must give this immediate attention and see the D.C. Wenchi to communicate with the High Authorities for their immediate deliverance.

Dated at Drobo this 22nd day of November, 1941.

Kojo Agyeman—his mk.17

Convinced at once of the authenticity of the letter and impressed by the urgency it implied, Wimshurst telephoned the chief commissioner's office in Kumasi for advice. He then sent the messenger back to the Gyamanhene. "I would be prepared," replied Wimshurst, "to meet Nana Kojo Agyeman and his son Kwame Adinkra on the frontier and hear what he has to say. That I had already arranged to be in the Gyapekrom Sampa area from the 8th to 12th Dec. . . . That if Nana Kojo Agyeman and his son did a tour of his villages on their side of the border (as he frequently does) about this time and would send a message to D.C. Sunyani by Tues. or Wed. next week as to exact place and time, he could be at the frontier and the meeting could take place."[18]

Wimshurst immediately began scouting the frontier for all possible safe routes for a Gyaman exodus. Meanwhile, the news was passed on from Kumasi to the governor in Accra, who consulted with PERO. The question was one of considerable delicacy. On the one hand, the British had the pleasing prospect of a major propaganda coup. On the other hand, they ran the risk of provoking the Vichy French into resorting to military force. The Gold Coast administration had already been informed by London of the general policy toward those seeking refuge in the Gold Coast. The idea of mass immigration was "not to be encouraged or countenanced." However, it was conceded that where it was in line with policy, the government was prepared, "to encourage Chiefs to enter British territory but only if Government is satisfied that they can and will give direct assistance in the war effort. It is important that this should be kept in mind in any propaganda issued by or through District Commissioners."[19] The proposed exodus of the Gyamanhene and his principal chiefs seems not to have been regarded as "mass immigration," and therefore was to be allowed, if not encouraged. E. G. Hawkesworth, chief commissioner, Ashanti, laid out the guidelines in somewhat less than enthusiastic terms. At the border meeting Kwadwo Agyeman was to be told that there was "no objection to his coming on to English territory with stool etc. if he so desires." N. D. FitzGerald, the SOE section head in Accra, stated his intention of being present at the meeting whenever it could be arranged.[20] It will be remarked that no one seemed to feel it necessary to include any representatives of the Free French, although they would in time, of course, benefit if the operation succeeded.

Meanwhile, in the North West province of Asante, the DCs prepared for the meeting. Wimshurst, rather surprisingly in the circumstances, went on local leave to Winneba, leaving assistant DC Neil Ross to handle Quarshie and the agents. Malcolm Miln, the DC at Sunyani, by virtue of his seniority, temporarily took over local control of the operation. FitzGerald arrived from Accra. In late December 1941, Kwame Adinkra crossed the border to meet the three.[21] In 1996, Ross retained a clear recollection of the encounter: "Adinkra was charismatic. . . . He had sent messengers—would he be welcome in the Gold Coast?—to our clerks at Wenchi and Sunyani. Miln and myself met him at the boundaries of the Wenchi and Sunyani districts. There were fifty or a hundred people with him. There he asked, if he came across, would the reaction be positive? We said we'd find out from the chief commissioner quickly. . . . Adinkra was a real go-getter."[22] We may guess that Kwame Adinkra expressed some concern over the delay implicit in waiting for a reply from the chief commissioner. He presumably reported this to his father, for on 1 January, the Drobohene informed Miln that Kwadwo Agyeman wished the British to send a military force to Bondoukou that very day to "rescue him." This did not, however, deter him from also inquiring as to "the manner in

Soldiers, Airmen, Spies, and Whisperers

which he would be treated should he manage to get into the Gold Coast." Miln, not a man to be trifled with, described his reactions in a letter to FitzGerald: "I dealt with both matters in a verbal reply. I stated clearly, that in my opinion, indeed I felt very sure, the Gold Coast Government would not send a force to rescue Agyeman. So far as I know the British had no intention whatever of fighting their fallen comrades the French. The Germans were our real foes. But if Agyeman did get into the Gold Coast he and his people would be free and entirely unmolested. The Asantehene would, I believed, treat him personally, as an important guest."[23]

Miln was correct. There was no chance whatsoever that any British expedition would be allowed to cross the frontier. Even had troops been available, General Giffard would not have permitted their use. The problem was then to balance the propaganda value of the Abron's defection against the very real possibility of provoking the superior military might of the Vichy French troops. In other words, would the Vichy French launch an invasion of the Gold Coast with the object of bringing the Gyaman back? In the event, the British decided to take the risk.[24] They sought to minimize it, however, by choosing to relocate the refugees in Sunyani, some fifty miles from the border. Free French intelligence as well as FitzGerald of the SOE wanted the Gyamanhene and his people placed in Wenchi, but CCA Hawkesworth preferred situating them much further from the frontier.[25] An additional reason for choosing Sunyani, according to Ross, was the reality that roads and communications between that town and Kumasi were comparatively good.[26]

THE CROSSINGS OF THE GYAMAN

The night of 15 January 1942 was selected for the Gyaman exodus. It is very difficult to get a precise picture of how the operation was all arranged, undoubtedly because of the secrecy surrounding it. The crossings occurred between Sampa, in the north, and Domaa, some fifty-five miles to the south. This was a particularly wild stretch of country and no detailed account exists of the various points at which the Gyaman entered the Gold Coast, nor of the numbers involved. Miln described the arrival of the Gyaman in a letter to Wimshurst that has not been found. Fortunately, the faithful Corporal Quarshie, who was involved in transporting refugees from his station at Sampa to Sunyani, also wrote to Wimshurst. This handwritten communication, which he labeled his Intelligent Report, has miraculously survived:

Nana Agyeman with some of his Sub-Chiefs crossed the boundary to Bodaa and others at Sampa. The chiefs brought with them their black [ancestral] stools. Nana Agyeman brought in his black and the golden stools. Free transports were provided to them by the Gold Coast Government from Sampa and Bodaa to Sunyani.

On the 23rd inst; the D.C. Sunyani took Aduanahene Kwame Adinkra and some of the chiefs to Kumasi and greeted the C.C.A. and the Asantehene and returned in the evening.

On the 24th inst; Nana Agyeman and his followers arrived in Sunyani, were 583 excluded women and children. From the 24th to the 26th inst; about 100 more men arrived at Sunyani.

Information has been received that about 200 men, women and children have crossed the frontier and they are hanging [about!] at Kofi-Tia Krom, Zenera and Aduako. I have reported to the District Commissioner Sunyani and he has instructed me to find out from there and if that is true, I must convince them to travel to the motor road just to arrange for their conveyance to Sunyani.[27]

From this it will be apparent that at least a thousand people had arrived in, or were on the way to, Sunyani by 27 January 1942. Ross, at Wenchi, admitted he never counted them, but he estimated that around that number of Gyaman did indeed come with Agyeman. Governor Deschamps claimed in his apologia for having served the Vichy regime, that only a few hundred at most left.[28] In this, as in so many other of his comments about this period, he was wrong. F. J. Amon d'Aby, an Ivoirien historian, puts the number as high as ten thousand,[29] while Emmanuel Terray, somewhat vaguely, refers to la majorité des Abron as having crossed the frontier.[30] These last two estimates seem too high, and the truth of the matter is that no accurate figure can be reached on the available evidence.

Whatever the numbers involved, the identity of those leaders who did leave the Vichy-controlled area is known and is highly significant. Gyamanhene Kwadwo Agyeman was accompanied into exile by his son, Aduanahene Prince Kwame Adinkra; the Gyamanhemaa, or queen mother, Akosua Anima; four high divisional chiefs, namely Akyidomhene, Fumasahene, Penangohene, and Siengihene; and the lower-ranking Kerebiohene.[31] This entourage represented in effect the highest echelon of the Gyaman ruling class. There was a real sense in which the state itself had moved. Small wonder then that the entire operation was seen at the time as a major propaganda coup for the British.

The Gold Coast correspondent of West Africa reported the migration in the most purple of prose, seeming only to stop short of comparing the departure of the Gyaman to the exodus of Moses and the Hebrews from Egypt. However, his writing style should not obscure the fact that he appears to have obtained first-hand information about Kwadwo Agyeman's reactions. Accordingly, we reproduce the correspondent's own words.

Behind closed doors, men whispered and wondered what would happen next. One thing they felt certain of. What the French Administrator had been telling them about the wickedness of the British was untrue. Months rolled by. Slowly Koadio [Kwadwo Agyeman] was able to piece together the story of events. Not all Frenchmen gave the same account. Their leaders had apparently sold their country to the Germans, but others had joined the British and were still fighting Germany. In which direction then lay his own duty towards his own people and to France? Did he owe allegiance towards those who had betrayed France, who were letting German agents into the country? They would presently seize it and set about exploiting it and domineering everywhere. "A thousand times—No" answered Koadio's heated brain.

The day came when doubt hardened to certainty and bred decision to act. Time to make an end of cowardly opportunism favoured by French officials on the spot on pretexts which, in their hearts, they knew were false! Time to play a man's part in the struggle for liberty!

In the silence of the night, Koadio summoned his family and retainers on whose fidelity he could count. He bade them pack all they could carry. Land hallowed by the graves of ancestors, most precious of all possessions to Africans, homes and position—all these must be sacrificed for the cause. Danger of arrest by frontier guards must be faced.

Chief Koadio and his followers reached the Gold Coast safely to join Free France. They were given an enthusiastic reception. No living man has given greater proof of the strength of bonds which unite Britain, France and Africa. One might also say that here is an African who has more faith in France than Frenchmen now in power.[32]

While this and other reports of the period mention only the Gyamanhene, it was Prince Adinkra who now took center stage. On 23 January, even before Kwadwo Agyeman had arrived in Sunyani, Adinkra, so we have seen from Quarshie's "Intelligent Report," had traveled with Miln to Kumasi to pay his respects to the CCA, to Hawkesworth, and to Asantehene Osei Agyeman Prempeh II.[33] A popular account of this meeting was provided, in 1994, by the centenarian Kwadwo Bosompra, who had already been trading between Bondoukou and Kumasi in

1905: "When he [Adinkra] met the Asantehene, Prempeh II, he started to take his sandals off. But the Asantehene said, no, do not do that because you are a royal like me. Kwame Adinkra was a real prince. He was, more or less, the chief now. His father was not all that old, but Adinkra wanted to become the chief himself."[34] The next day, Kwadwo Agyeman, his subchiefs, and the rest of the Gyaman refugees arrived in Sunyani, all having been provided with transport from the border. It must have taken every vehicle in the district, but the government seems to have been intent on giving them as royal a welcome as Miln and the SOE could provide from the limited facilities available at Sunyani. There, quite a crowd had gathered to greet them. According to Nana Yaw Kran, "People from all the villages and subtowns came in to Sunyani. There were many many people. They knew. They knew. It was World War II that made them [the Gyaman] come. Because of that they came."[35] Kwadwo Bosompra, another eyewitness to the arrival, remembered, "We heard that Adinkra and his people were coming to Sunyani, so we went to see. They first landed at Sunyani. They sent a request to the English whites saying that the French whites did not treat them well. . . . I am telling you what I saw. I was there."[36]

Each chief and his family was assigned a house and given over to the care of a local dignitary. Their treatment during the nearly two years they were to remain in Sunyani mightily impressed the local inhabitants, as Nana Yaw Kran described it. The DC "gave them rice and British food, foreign food," he remembered, "and the chiefs here, in Sunyani, gave them food every day. The British in Accra sent each and every chief a car with a driver. All the drivers were paid for by the government. The DC paid them, but the money came from Accra, from headquarters. For each one."[37] Nothing like this had ever been seen in Sunyani, or indeed the whole region before, where such marks of respect and even deference by the British were generally reserved for the Asantehene alone.

The Gyaman chiefs had been in Sunyani for only a few weeks when they were confronted by Henry B. Cole. A Liberian exile in the Gold Coast, Cole had been commissioned by *Life* magazine to report on the refugees.[38] The assignment itself reflected the fact that American readers, depressed by Pearl Harbor and newly in the war, might be diverted and inspired by the flight to freedom of the Gyaman. Cole was received by Kwame Adinkra in Sunyani with great ceremony and taken to meet the Gyamanhene, who gave him a dramatic account of their flight. Cole wrote,

> It was a chilly 2 o'clock in the morning when the escape got under way. Not a bird chirped, not a beast growled as in that intense silence a long silhouetted

Soldiers, Airmen, Spies, and Whisperers

procession of men, women and children moved toward the Franco-British frontier. Because of his 70 years, Chief Nana Kojo [Kwadwo Agyeman] was secured in a hammock for the journey. At his side was Prince Adinkra. Then followed the Queen mother (none other than the sister of Nana Kojo). With them they carried their black stools and other royal properties. Toward the boundary some French guards attempted to stop them, but they were unable.

Cole adds one detail of considerable significance. As soon as they arrived on Gold Coast soil, Kwadwo Agyeman sent the following message to General de Gaulle: "We put ourselves at your service to continue war until victory and the liberation of France, our dear mother country. All chiefs and Africans of the Ivory Coast think as we do. Long live immortal France."[39]

SLICA personnel in Accra could scarcely have written it better themselves, although Cole owed much of his literary style to having successfully completed an American correspondence course titled "Fiction, Slick and Pulp!"[40] In fact, the Free French Mission in Accra, although not having been directly involved in the crossing of the Gyaman, were overjoyed at the enormous propaganda value of what had happened. Kwame Adinkra was immediately made a lieutenant in the French army. He became a frequent speaker on the Gold Coast Broadcasting Service, declaring that he and his people had joined the Allies for the liberation of Europe.[41] According to Nana Yaw Kran, the prince became the most important person in Sunyani and virtually dictated policy to his father:

There was Kwame Adinkra—his father was Kofi Yeboa, the one whose stool name was Kwadwo Agyeman. While they were here, you hardly saw Agyeman. It was Kwame Adinkra who was acting for his father. He took over the kingship from his father. He had his wives and children with him—and his dogs. He had a car and his driver, George, was a Nigerian. . . . At the time they were here, if you wanted to see Nana Agyeman and you did not go through his son, [you had to] have the permission of Kwame Adinkra. Agyeman would not do anything . . . He was a big, great man. . . . He was going to Accra all the time. With a government vehicle. They paid him well, very well. They paid for everything.[42]

Despite, or perhaps because of, this royal treatment, Kwame Adinkra's behavior soon ruffled the feathers of the Gyaman elders, particularly over the matter of British allowances.

In April 1942 the district commissioner of Sunyani was handed a written petition, signed by the queen mother, six chiefs, and other elders, protesting against their treatment by Adinkra. Sunyani's subinspector of police reported on the troubles to the police superintendent in Kumasi, C. S. Durity, who immediately passed it to the chief commissioner. "Their chief grievances," the subinspector reported, "are that Eduanahene Kwame Adinkra is very rude to them. He abuses them freely and always tells them that their stools are under his feet. Meaning that he is senior to them in rank. These Chiefs say this is incorrect. That they [the chiefs] and the people understood that the British Government had given them cloths, towels, soap and money but they do not see these things." Upon investigation, four of the chiefs—Fumasahene, Penangohene, Ankobiahene, and Akyidomhene—did admit to "receiving monthly payment of £6 each for the months of January, February, and March 1942," while the queen mother owned up to having been paid a total of £11 for the same period. The Adontenhene and Nkwantahene, on the other hand, insisted they had been given nothing since their arrival. Sunyani's DC had passed the petition on to the Free French Mission representative there, Commandant Raphael Beretta, who promised to look into the situation. Durity was pleased to end his report with the most important news: "the people are well behaved and the situation is quiet."[43]

Things may have been quiet, but the chiefs and the queen mother continued to insist that they were being neglected. It was decided that the Asantehene should hear the dispute. On 9 May the Gyaman elders, in the company of Beretta and Acting District Commissioner M. G. Hewson, traveled to Kumasi to meet with him. According to Hewson, who reported the proceedings to the CCA, the Asantehene "showed throughout to a marked degree the ability which he possesses in managing disputes concerning illiterate elders, and in dealing with their submissions in a manner at once firm, courteous, and dignified." In fact, the Asantehene had refused to become involved, saying that the Gyaman were his friends but not his subjects, and that the elders should return to Sunyani and apologize to the Gyamanhene. As for the matter of Adinkra's salary, he was entitled to receive this since none of the elders could do the work he did. Hewson was, of course, referring to Adinkra's propaganda forays on Free French radio broadcasts. Beretta clearly thought the advice good, especially since the Asantehene had stressed that the Gyaman were the responsibility of Beretta and should take any complaints to him. As a gesture of "his confidence in their future right behaviour," Beretta said he would pay their salaries directly. He then told them that he would proceed immediately to Accra and inform Colonel Ponton of the situation, after which he would return to Sunyani. Nonetheless, this dispute, so skillfully mediated by the Asantehene, must have mightily impressed Beretta, who, it will be remembered, had arrived in the Gold Coast from French Equatorial Africa, where he was un-

Soldiers, Airmen, Spies, and Whisperers

likely to have had any experience with African diplomatic procedures as sophisticated as those of the Asante. After the elders had departed with Beretta, the Asantehene told Hewson that he believed Adinkra to be largely to blame for the whole situation. The prince, he said, had ignored the elders, whose transgression was the result of ignorance rather than malice. Hewson was less sanguine. In his report to the CCA, he dismissed the elders as "not an impressive company, being especially interested in money," and maintained that Adinkra's main offense lay in his treatment of the queen mother.[44] It was not only the elders who looked askance at the privileges granted Adinkra, however, for at the same time the administration was querying his consumption of gasoline in March and April: 120 gallons.[45]

MEANWHILE, BACK IN THE CÔTE D'IVOIRE . . .

Quarshie's invaluable agents in Bondoukou reported in impressive detail the immediate aftermath of the exodus.[46] Showing every bit as much dramatic flair as one who had graduated from a course on "Fiction, Slick and Pulp," Quarshie described the commandant's actions upon learning of the Gyaman flight. He attempted to catch them. He failed. Then, "returning to Bondugu he cried bitterly saying that it is better to kill himself than to report the situation to the Governor at Abidjan." The commandant's despair must have been of short duration, for Quarshie tells us that immediately "he arrested the wives and a son of Nana Agyeman and one of the Aduanahene's [Adinkra's] wife. He took them to Bondugu and placed them in cell." He then apprised the governor of the disaster. Deschamps reacted in the time-honored manner of bureaucrats by blaming the underling responsible. The franc definitely stopped in Bondoukou. Deschamps swiftly dispatched his secretary (*chef du cabinet*) to Bondoukou. Arriving on 18 January 1942, the secretary conveyed the full extent of the governor's wrath. But Quarshie knew even more. He reported that the commandant was told in no uncertain terms that he was being held personally responsible for the disaster, that "in his [the governor's] opinion it must be the treatments given to them [the Gyaman] by the Commandant." The secretary's parting shot was to make it abundantly clear that the unfortunate official's future rested largely on his success in getting the Gyaman back. The secretary left for Abidjan at 1 P.M. that same day.[47]

By 30 January more reports on reactions in the Côte d'Ivoire to the exodus came in from a captured Tirailleur Sénégalais, Corporal Adou Kouadio. Assigned to border patrol and ordered to prevent any more Gyaman from crossing into British territory, Adou had himself crossed the frontier to the village of Zenera in pursuit of refugees. Arrested by the police and brought to Sampa, Adou Kouadio made a statement on recent developments in Bondoukou. It was taken down by Quarshie: "about 5 days today, about 30 European Officers arrived at Bondugu from Abidjan. 100 soldiers arrived at Bondugu with 2 European Officers from Bouna. These men brought in quantity of Magazine [machine] guns. There were 3 Magazine guns in the hand of the Soldiers at Bondugu. In my opinion and my experience in the Regiment, it appeared to me that the French Government means a war with the British Government in the Gold Coast. I can not state the date it shall be happened."[48]

Whatever plans the commandant might have had to effect the return of the Gyaman, the initiative was seized by the district commissioner in Sunyani. Miln apparently decided that tensions could be lowered, and reprisals against those Gyaman who had remained behind softened, if a meeting was arranged between the commandant of Bondoukou, Kwadwo Agyeman, and Kwame Adinkra. It is not known whether Miln acted on orders from Accra or not. In any case, it was agreed that the meeting would be held in Sunyani. The matter was obviously a highly sensitive one. Although Vichy France and Great Britain were still not, technically, at war, it was nevertheless quite unusual for a Vichy official to set foot in the Gold Coast. Certainly whatever documentation existed was either destroyed or locked up in secrecy, and I have been unable to locate any official account of the meeting. Fortunately, Kwadwo Bosompra was in Sunyani at the time, and half a century later was able to recollect the events, which he described as having taken place just "yesterday":

> The French whites fixed a day on which they came. The English whites met the French whites. It was the English whites who asked the French whites to meet them. There was one French white and his secretary. Only the two of them. He had a moustache. He had a beard as well. I know his name but I cannot remember it. It was the name of a dog. Before the French whites came, the English whites had prepared a reception for them in front of the DC's bungalow. They put down mats, local mats [kete], from the street to the reception place. The French white asked why they were getting this treatment. [The British whites said] you should walk on these mats, into the place. He wouldn't walk on it because he was annoyed. So he walked along the side of it. They would not even sit down. The French white was highly annoyed. He wouldn't sit down. He asked the English whites why they had sent for him. The English white said it was Adinkra and his people who had come to him.

The French white asked what Adinkra had been telling him [Miln] about him. He [Miln] said Adinkra and the other chiefs left because of the harsh treatment the French whites were giving them. And the French white said that if that is what they were saying, he would not sit down, but they should come back. He said that the English should let the Gyaman come back, but that he, Adinkra, should be brought in an airplane. Adinkra should be sent back in a plane. Adinkra understood the motive behind the honor. He [the commandant] wanted to arrest him. Adinkra refused the plane. He knew if he went back he would not come back. He told the French white point blank that he was not going back.[49]

Clearly the meeting could not be said to have been a success.

Governor Deschamps arrived in Bondoukou in person on 3 February, concerned that matters not get any worse. Quarshie's report offers the startling news that Deschamps told the remaining elders that he had "imprisoned the Commandant" for allowing the Gyamanhene to be "abducted." No doubt Deschamps might have wished to be able to do this, but it seems that he did no more than transfer him.[50] Deschamps spent four days in Bondoukou, laying down a conciliatory policy. He promised to request a suspension of that year's impôt.[51] He took immediate steps to improve the local economy. Shops in Bondoukou that had been virtually empty of cloth and other consumer goods, due to the almost complete absence of imports, were to be well stocked with all manner of merchandise, transferred on the governor's orders from stockpiles in Abidjan. All this, Deschamps hoped, would be interpreted as signs of Vichy's benevolent intentions toward its subjects and perhaps serve as an incentive to lure many of the Gyaman back to this sudden oasis of plenty.

The first goal was apparently reached, for six weeks later Quarshie reported that "everybody in the Bondugu and in the surrounding villages are now saying their livings coming into the old position and their Administration also changed to that of English."[52] Part of this largesse may be due to Deschamps's own feelings that the Gyaman were, in fact, led astray by the ambitions of Kwame Adinkra. Deschamps claimed in later years that the prince's motives in urging the Gyamanhene to decamp from the Côte d'Ivoire were entirely self-serving. He insisted that Adinkra, through his father, had demanded that the French administration acknowledge him as heir to the paramountcy. This the French refused to do, on the grounds that succession among the Gyaman, like all Akan peoples, was matrilineal. Thus, they argued, a son could never succeed his father (though it must be said that the French had seldom been deterred by such concerns of customary law when it served their own purposes). In any case, Deschamps's explanation may be reckoned equally self-serving, being at pains to portray the benevolent nature of his tenure, thereby attempting to justify how he, a socialist, could serve a fascist regime.[53] In any case, there was some success in the new policy, for some of the Gyaman did return to their farms in the Côte d'Ivoire. Conversely, however, other chiefs continued to cross into the Gold Coast to join Kwadwo Agyeman.[54]

Provisioning the shops and suspending the impôt were merely one side of Deschamps's policy. There was another, much harsher. Any Gyaman suspected of sympathizing or aiding the flight, or of collaborating with the British or Free French was summarily arrested. Among such were several elders, some of whom were tortured by the Bondoukou administrator to secure information. Several died in prison.[55] The homes of Agyeman, Adinkra, and the subchiefs who had accompanied them were burned.[56] Their cocoa and coffee plantations were destroyed.[57] French patrols did not hesitate to cross the border in search of Gyaman defectors. The British ordered the removal of all French Gyaman to at least ten miles behind the border, but there was considerable resistance to this policy. Many Gyaman continued to cross the frontier to visit their farms, check on their affairs, and, in some cases, engage in a bit of profitable smuggling, particularly of French cigarettes. When arrested on their return by the British, so the superintendent of police complained, each defendant offered much the same excuse, for example, "I had the cigarettes for sale in the French Ivory Coast before Nana Agyiman [Kwadwo Agyeman] had removed into the Gold Coast and as I followed him, I come into the Gold Coast with cigarettes."[58] A difficult political problem!

Miln, DC Sunyani, spent a good deal of his time dealing with the wanderings of his charges. On 22 June 1942 the police sent him a message that the Akyidomhene was in the process of decamping to the Côte d'Ivoire. Miln immediately investigated, only to discover that the chief had sent a gold-leafed message stick, two ceremonial cloths, and a box of assorted items to Bodaa, a tiny village on the Gold Coast side of the border. The Akyidomhene was sent for and lectured about the undesirability of trying to leave Sunyani without consulting the district commissioner. In fact, Miln assured him that should he return to French territory, he would most likely be murdered. "Such a project," the Akyidomhene said, "was not in his heart. He was sending his message stick to the pawnbrokers (at Bodaa) and his cloths and box to one of his wives."

No sooner had Miln dealt with this crisis than another erupted:

At about the same time, I was told by Madame Beretta—(M. Beretta was in Accra), she spoke in French, a language that I do not understand—that the Queen-mother of Jaman had left for the Ivory Coast. I enquired into this ex-

Soldiers, Airmen, Spies, and Whisperers

citing statement and ascertained that in fact Nana Akosua Nima had merely sent one of her maidservants to fetch her some meat from Nsoatre [about ten miles from Sunyani]. I then telephoned to Your Honour's secretary but the line was roaring and Mr. Bruton could not perfectly hear my message. I delayed my departure from Sunyani until the next morning and finally ordered the police to watch and to control all west-bound travellers. As I write the Jamanhene, all his sub-chiefs and their attendants are still in Sunyani.[59]

Despite these precautions, the reverse crossings continued, even after four Gyaman were arrested by the French in May. At least two, and possibly all, were executed in Bondoukou. Their crimes ranged from possession of English money to the suspicion of distributing Free French propaganda leaflets near the border.[60] In June, Beretta brought three of his agents to Miln. One of them, Kwaku Adinkra, claimed to have witnessed the murder of at least one of the men who had come to the Gold Coast with the Gyamanhene, and the torture of several more. Miln, who continued to harbor deep suspicions about Beretta, and the French in general, nonetheless believed what he had been told and passed a transcript of the man's account to the CCA in Kumasi. It was extremely graphic—full of details about the flogging of at least twenty naked men, beatings carried out not merely by two African policemen, but—so the account had it—by the commandant de cercle of Bondoukou. "This was inside the prison yard," Kwaku Adinkra recounted, adding, "Kofi Nketia Komde—Efi Yaw—and about 20 others. . . . They struck him more than ten times—after they had beaten him his belly swelled up—then they handed him over to his people—they took him home and he died in his home. I saw this with my own eyes. I heard the white man say: 'You, the Aduana-hene's [Prince Adinkra's] people who are still here; if I see you I will arrest and kill you then the Aduanahene will come back here. If we do this the Aduanahene will hear of it and will come back.' He spoke through an interpreter." Kwaku Adinkra also witnessed the arrest and torture of the Gyamanhene's drummer, Kwaku Num. Num was pushed into a fire by two policemen, horribly burned, and then put into a cell. Lagassama Kamati, another accused of collaboration with the refugees, was arrested one morning by six African policemen, the commandant, and the local doctor. Stripped naked, he was paraded before the people of the town and beaten. According to the informant, the DC then said that "if the relatives of those who had gone to the British did not go and fetch them back they would kill all those relatives." Kwaku Adinkra continued: "The next day I saw Lagassama Kamati dead. I saw rope marks on his neck—the body was then with his relatives. I got frightened and I went to the [French] D.C. I told him I

The Crossing of the Gyaman

could get my father to return. He gave me a paper to pass the frontier guard and here I am."[61]

Miln had little doubt of the truth of Kwaku Adinkra's statement, particularly as it had been substantiated by Ross, the acting DC at Wenchi. "Local Jaman reaction," Miln wrote, "to these typically German outrages, the nature and existence of which is confirmed by Mr. Ross, is, if the truth be told, 'let us again beg the British to send a British force to drive the French from our land.' They do not, with the single exception of Kwame Adinkra, understand what the Free French movement is."[62] In Miln's view, and indeed in that of most of British officials in the Gold Coast, the role of the Free French was to win the Vichy French over to their side, without disturbing the precarious calm on the frontier. Miln's exasperation with the continual Gyaman demands for British military intervention across the border can only serve to underline the Gold Coast government's determination to maintain the status quo by provoking the French as little as possible.

The Vichy administration of the Côte d'Ivoire continued its campaign of retribution. On the political front, Baba Ali, the imam of Bondoukou ("Alimamu Balie"), after assuring the local officials that he had known nothing about the plans of Kwame Adinkra and Kwadwo Agyeman, became, as Quarshie reported, "the right hand of the new Commandant. He is always with him in the day and night."[63] Within two months, new chiefs to replace the defectors were appointed. They were ordered to make new black stools. Kwaafohene Nana Jonah was asked by the commandant to produce a new stool for Bini Kofi, who was to be the new Akyidomhene. He did so, but immediately crossed the border with it and joined the exiles.[64]

Strong pressure to elect a new Gyamanhene was being applied to those elders who remained in the Côte d'Ivoire. Nana Kwadwo Agyeman, it was argued, was in effect "dead to his people," having taken his black stool to the Gold Coast, thus allowing the Asantes to "capture" it. Whether this fiction was believed is doubtful, but the Gyaman elders took the hint and, at a meeting held on 9 May 1942, agreed to name Kofi Yeboa as Gyamanhene. The only difficulty was that Kofi Yeboa had escaped to join Kwadwo Agyeman and was in Sunyani. In choosing an exile to succeed the Gyamanhene, the elders showed remarkable courage. The commandant, treading less heavily than was customary, agreed to their choice, but stipulated that if Kofi Yeboa should refuse to return, he would select Kofi Tarh of Tabange ("Tarban") as the next choice. A decision was postponed for several weeks while negotiations continued.[65] In the event, Kofi Yeboa declined to return to the Côte d'Ivoire, and Kofi Tarh was to be installed as Gyamanhene in June.

The degree of importance attached by the French to reasserting their control over the Gyaman situation was underlined by the decision to hold a large durbar at Bondoukou on or about 28 June 1942. The commandants of Abengourou, Bouaké, Abidjan, and even distant Bobo-Dioulasso arrived to celebrate the "funeral" of Kwadwo Agyeman, and the installation of Kofi Tarh. They were accompanied by at least one hundred soldiers and a military band. According to Corporal Quarshie, four kegs of gunpowder, an extremely scarce item in blockaded Côte d'Ivoire, were distributed. He also reported the speech given by Bondoukou's commandant to the assembled chiefs, who told them that

> the people who immigrated to the Gold Coast are classified as dead persons and would no more be allowed to come back to the Ivory Coast. The Commandant said he has given them fifteen days to bring down the Blackstools with the properties sent to the Gold Coast by Nana Agyeman, if not he would force them to make new stools. The new Jamanhene and his subchiefs have agreed and arranged that they would depute people to come to Sunyani and try so that they would get the stools back either by way of stealing or otherwise.

The commandant assured them that he had received a confidential letter from a European at Accra, to the effect that Kwadwo Agyeman would never return to the Côte d'Ivoire. Thus, he claimed, "there would be no war at Bondoukou," and the installation of the new Gyamanhene could proceed, for the land would be at peace. Whether or not this convinced the usurping chiefs is doubtful, but presumably having little choice about the matter, they accepted gifts of cows, guns, and money. Following the presentation, they swore an oath of allegiance to the commandant that, to follow Quarshie, "through rain and sunshine they would assist him to rule the land of Bondoukou." To underline the new peace, the wives of Kwadwo Agyeman, imprisoned since his flight, were released. Despite this impressive ceremony, however, and the swearing of loyalty oaths, the commandant was careful to remind them of his power. The commandant's right-hand man, Imam Baba Ali, also received gifts. The new Gyamanhene, lest he forget himself and not do his duty toward the commandant, was informed that "had he not come to occupy the stool, Alimamu Balie [Imam Baba Ali] would have been installed as Jamanhene because when the Jamanhene immigrated none of the subjects of Alimamu accompanied."[66]

During the summer of 1942, a military tribunal in Dakar tried (in absentia) both Kwame Adinkra and his father for treason, in that they had "left French territory to place themselves at the service of the Anglo-Gaullists in the Gold Coast, leading several frontier villages with them." Both were condemned to death and their property ordered to be confiscated.[67]

The reigns of the new chiefs were to be short. Five months after their installation and the "funeral" of Kwadwo Agyeman, the Anglo-American invasion of North Africa—Operation Torch—took place, and the AOF was shortly to move into the Allied camp. The "dead" chiefs returned to the Côte d'Ivoire and resumed their positions, being both grateful for their treatment by the British and aware of their importance to the cause of Free France. Both British and Free French, however, were sometimes to regret their involvement with the Gyaman. When chieftaincy disputes arose among the Gyaman of the Gold Coast, Kwadwo Agyeman was inclined to interfere, reminding the British of the debt the Allied cause owed him. In 1943, for example, Drobohene Kofi Busia of British Gyaman complained to Gyamanhene Kwadwo Agyeman that he had not received certain considerations promised him by the Gold Coast administration. The Gyamanhene immediately wrote to DC Wenchi to ensure that justice would be done:

> In spite of our separation by the frontier, this chief, who remained *chez vous,* has never ceased to be forever faithful and devoted to us, his former masters. Since the year 1940 [actually 1941], when we had decided to pass into the Gold Coast in order to ally ourselves with General de Gaulle, and throw ourselves against the Germans, this chief was eager to receive us and to serve as our guide in the interior [of Gold Coast]. . . . Finally, we returned to our country, grace of General de Gaulle, and the great reception given us by you, the British, I come, in the name of the entire Abron people, to bring to your attention the conduct and devotion of the Chief of Drobo, and to accord him a special place among your other native chiefs.[68]

Neil Ross, by this time DC Wenchi, forwarded the letter to the chief commissioner, with the comment that the Drobohene had already received substantial payments from PERO and thus "does not expect anything further."[69] Clearly the Drobohene did expect more, but optimistically so: the threat from the Côte d'Ivoire having disappeared, along with the largesse of the Gold Coast administration and the Free French, the normal parsimony of the colonial administration had resurfaced.

In 1944, Kwadwo Agyeman retired as Gyamanhene. The question of matrilineal succession was not raised by the current Gaullist governor, André Latrille, when Kwame Adinkra came to the throne. Few Gyaman, on either side of the border, objected. Nana Yaw Kran explained the situation:

There was no education in those days. Even though Kwame Adinkra never attended school, he had been moving with Europeans. He spoke very good French and the Europeans knew him well. He was good with the French and other Europeans. And he was the king after his father died. He became king even though he was an oheneba.[70] He had been to Paris; he had been to Parliament.[71] Kwame Adinkra had a chance to become the chief even when his father was alive. Yes, you are supposed to be a nephew, but he was acting as his father's deputy then. If it had been his uncle, he could not have stood in for him. But by our custom, being the son, he could. His father was old. He could have become the chief. Even if Agyeman was dead, he could have become chief. There is no taboo.[72]

Like his father, Adinkra had no hesitation in drawing on what he felt to be the obligations of the British toward himself and his people. Indeed, in a rather lengthy correspondence dealing with attempts by certain of the Drobo to destool the same Drobohene, Kofi Busia, the new Gyamanhene made a rather veiled threat to Asantehene Osei Agyeman Prempeh. On 23 July 1945, Adinkra sent a letter to the DC at Wenchi. He requested that this be passed on to the Asantehene, for "after I put every matter into amicable peace they [the malcontents and the Drobohene] will return to Gold Coast to serve the King and the Empire, with better frame of mind."[73] These communications provoked a flurry of messages passed between DC Wenchi, the chief commissioner in Kumasi, and the Asantehene. Now that the emergency in West Africa was over, argued DC Wenchi, "I consider that it is undesirable that the Jamanhene should take part in the affairs of British Jaman, and particularly so in the present case, where one of the leading malcontents is the Akwamuhene, who endeavoured some years ago to transfer his allegiance to the French Jamanhene."[74] Nevertheless, the next day, a further letter from Gyamanhene Adinkra arrived, reiterating his wish to mediate the same dispute. He asked the DC this time to forward two letters to the Asantehene, dealing with the list of charges compiled by the "malcontents" against the Drobohene. Speaking very much as equal to equal, Adinkra again asked to be allowed to mediate the dispute: "That, as the war is not yet over, it is my honest desire to assist both Nana, Asantehene, and the King. So that there might not be any further disturbances whilst the Great Empire is at war with Japan. Hence I am asking you most humbly permit me to bringing the people of Drobo into peaceful settlement. Not that the previous decision was erroneous far being from such intentions. I wish to promote peace or to reconcile them together in good spirit. As you kindly allowed me to settlement the dispute between Dwenim and Drobo land case."[75]

Ironically, in 1945 another Abron exodus was to occur, albeit on a smaller scale. The DC at Sunyani reported to the chief commissioner in Kumasi that the queen mother, Nana Akosua Anima, who had been one of the original Gyaman refugees with Nana Agyeman, had been driven from her home at Hwerebo by the new Gyamanhene, Kwame Adinkra. Along with several other members of the royal family and over two hundred followers, she was seeking refuge in the Gold Coast. Permission was apparently granted, as the French, in this particular instance, had for some reason no objections.[76] But, in general, the threat to the Gold Coast being long over, it was now time to put the colonial house in order and make it clear that the French Gyaman, having served their purpose, were again the problem of the French.

The 1942 Gyaman migration into the Gold Coast occurred during the governorship of Sir Alan Burns, who appears to have approved of the operation, but left it to be managed by other officers of his political administration, specifically CCA Hawkesworth and by DCs Miln, Ross, and Wimshurst. The extent to which SLICA was concerned in the planning and logistics of the exodus is quite unclear, although that organization was to claim it as a major triumph for the Free French. General Giffard would, of course, have deplored the whole exercise but, remarkably, seems not to have been made fully aware of its scope until it was a fait accompli. The Gold Coast Section of the SOE was certainly involved and came to regard it as one of its (regrettably) few successes. If General Giffard knew nothing about it, it is even more noteworthy that above the level of head of section, Gold Coast, the SOE also seems to have had no foreknowledge of it. Wingate, head of Frawest, makes no mention of it in any document I have seen. It was not until he had departed and his second in command and loyal ally, Miles Clifford, had temporarily taken over, that the matter of the Gyaman received comment. In a letter of 8 June 1942 to Hambro, the SOE's director of operations in London, Clifford, recommended that no similar undertaking should be encouraged in the future:

> In my own view, nothing is to be gained by persuading Chiefs and their followers to enter British territory where they only serve as a source of embarrassment to our own Administrators and to the Military and as a potential threat of Blackmail; if they don't find things exactly to their liking they will hop back over the frontier and the contra-propaganda of such a development would be exploited to the utmost. If an influential Chief on the other side is likely to be of use to us then it is much better, generally speaking, that he stays where he is and that his influence and services are available to us

Soldiers, Airmen, Spies, and Whisperers

when we need them; a Chief who vacates his territory will quite often lose his influence since rival factions are swift to spring up behind his back.[77]

Clifford reiterated his view in his handing over of notes to Lumby a month later. Chiefs such as the Gyamanhene, he felt, particularly if they are accompanied by a large following, "are a source of embarrassment to the Colonial Administration and present an unwanted security problem to the Area Commander."[78]

It appears to be the case that one of the most enterprising coups de théâtre of the Gold Coast's war was carried out by a combination of colonial administrators in Asante and the local section of the SOE, and this apparently without the knowledge of either the upper echelons of the SOE or the headquarters staff of the RWAFF in Achimota. Paradoxically, the measured decision of the Gyaman to move into the Gold Coast, and thereby into the Allied camp, proved inconvenient to just about everybody. However, the exodus was, if no more, undoubtedly a major propaganda triumph for the Allies at a time when any good news was at a premium.

8

The Beginning of the End

THE WAR MOVES ON

OPERATION TORCH: THE AOF DESERTS VICHY

In late September 1942 there was a flurry of activity in British West Africa that suggested that something consequential was afoot. Lord Swinton was asked by the War Cabinet to draw up plans for the administration of occupied Vichy territories. A War Office memorandum had been circulated that assumed that such responsibility would devolve on the British, with the Free French brought in at some undefined later stage. Swinton consulted General Giffard and found him to have much the same reactions to the proposal. Swinton produced a long memorandum, classified Most Secret, on the matter. He pointed out that there were many experienced administrators in the French missions in the four British colonies, adding that it was in any case likely that Gen. René Leclerc would insist on sending Free French forces in support of any Allied troops invading Vichy territory. It would prove highly embarrassing, if not impossible, to inform the Free French that their participation was neither welcome nor necessary. Swinton, with Giffard's agreement, thought the War Office memorandum thoroughly misguided for other reasons. It had contained the suggestion that the GOC-in-C would select British officers now serving with the RWAFF to establish military administrations in the AOF in the event of its invasion. Giffard, if nothing else the archetypal no-man, had strongly disagreed. Not only was he seriously understaffed, he pointed out, but he had few officers with the necessary qualifications for such jobs.

The War Office memorandum had also contemplated the swift replacement of these military administrators by ones supplied by the colonial governments. Swinton, for his part, let it be known that these administrations were also very short staffed, so many of their men having joined the army. Surprisingly, perhaps, Giffard agreed with the resident minister in recommending that the Free French should provide the administrations. Swinton proposed that, in conjunction with the governors, he should immediately begin working with the Free French toward an eventual takeover. He also suggested that the Free French should be asked to identify Vichy administrators who would be prepared to switch sides, surely an example of wishful thinking in light of the near-total devotion to Marshall Pétain evidenced by French administrators in the AOF since the summer of 1940. Nevertheless, Swinton and Giffard did have the example of French Equatorial Africa to hearten them, where the vast majority of administrators had elected to serve in de Gaulle's administration after the "rallying" of that federation in the autumn of 1940.[1] Indeed, they were probably justified in feeling that the nature of bureaucracy itself would contribute to the switching of sides—that bureaucrats tended to follow orders, in much the same way that soldiers did.

Swinton's memorandum shows that by the autumn of 1942 plans were in existence to attack the AOF. Invasions were to be launched through Dahomey, Togo, and the Conakry area of Guinea, and the newly occupied territories to be administered from Nigeria, the Gold Coast, and Sierra Leone respectively.[2] This memorandum shortly came to the attention of the Foreign Office, which, much in character, proposed that no action be taken for a month or two until the position was clearer. It seemed amenable to the idea of the Free French taking over from the military administrators, but caviled at the notion that the colonial governments should be involved. In a note of mandarinesque complexity, a high official of the Imperial General Staff commented: "I should hardly have thought that it would be a good idea to confide part of the French Colonial Empire to the administration of the British Colonial Empire." Paradoxically, however, he was much in favor of the Colonial Office in London assuming the burden so that, as he snidely remarked, "the cost of the administration would fall to that Office's Vote."[3] Be that as it may, it was quite obvious that something was in the air, and all the more so when, in October 1942, SOE London decided to send George Taylor ("AD") to the Gold Coast to review the state of the Frawest Mission.

It is unclear whether Taylor had been informed of the impending military initiatives in French North Africa before he left London. The Allied invasions, code-named Operation Torch, however, must have become known to him in Accra at the latest by 8 November—the day of the landings at Algiers and Oran, in Algeria, and Casablanca, in Morocco. It was headline news around the world and certainly figured prominently in radio broadcasts. But Operation Torch was not unopposed. British and America forces met considerable resistance from elements of the Armée d'Afrique and the Tirailleurs Sénégalais.[4] This was of much interest to those responsible for the defense of the Gold Coast, for we have seen that there were large numbers of well-trained tirailleurs in the Côte d'Ivoire. Moreover, on 9 November, Governor-General Pierre Boisson had made a speech from Dakar that gave no indication that Vichy authority in French West Africa might collapse. "American forces," said Boisson, "have attacked North Africa. Our turn will not be long in coming. I have carried out the Marshal's orders. For two years we have assisted France in the defeat; now we will defend her with arms."[5]

Meetings were convened in Achimota, bringing together the resident minister, Giffard's senior staff officers, Lumby of Frawest, and Taylor himself, who on 11 November summarized the discussions in a lengthy report to his superior, Hambro, in London. They had, Taylor wrote, considered the effects on the AOF should Operation Torch succeed: "There is at least the possibility, and if Metropolitan France is wholly occupied by the Germans, the probability that the remaining Vichy Colonies in Africa may rally fairly rapidly to the Allied cause. In this event, the principle raison d'être for the Frawest Mission would disappear, and the Mission itself could be reduced to skeleton form or even be withdrawn all together."[6] One of the options considered at the Achimota meetings was that Frawest should "mark time," and await developments in the AOF. All the participants were in agreement that this would be "the greatest possible mistake," and recommended that the SOE should continue its buildup. The army, Taylor pointed out, was already engaged in augmenting its strength, and that, he wrote, "should be a good guide for us. As long as there is need for a large military force to be tied up in this area, there is also need for a S.O.E. Mission. As long as that military force is here, they intend to behave as though they might have to go into action any day. We should do the same."[7] The problem was that no one in the Gold Coast knew exactly what the situation was in North Africa. This was not particularly surprising, since it was an extremely fluid one.

Within twenty-four hours of the Operation Torch landings, the Americans had entered into negotiations with the commander in chief of all Vichy French forces, Adm. François Darlan. The admiral, in fact, had only been in Algiers by chance, visiting his son there, who had contracted cerebral meningitis. He had, however, been detained by French civilians, who had taken over the city as they awaited the American forces. By indicating his willingness to cooperate with the Allies, Darlan convinced his captors to release him almost immediately. Although

Soldiers, Airmen, Spies, and Whisperers

insisting that he must await Pétain's orders to halt resistance, Darlan had called for a cease fire during the evening of 8 November.[8] It was, after a few tense days, obeyed, and the soldiers and sailors under his command shifted to the Allied cause. Algeria and Morocco were no longer "neutral." At 7 A.M. on 11 November all fighting ceased. On the same day the German Army swept into unoccupied France, so ending the mockery of Pétain's *l'état Français*, the truncated remainder of *la république Française*. Over the next few days, moreover, large numbers of German and Italian troops moved into Tunisia, and by 16 November were in occupation of the whole country. Clearly the war in North Africa was not entirely over.

On 13 November, Gen. Dwight D. Eisenhower had met with Admiral Darlan in Algiers. The occupation of Tunisia, however, now made cooperation with this protégé of Premier Pierre Laval, Vichy's most notorious pro-Nazi, a matter of strategic importance. How far could the admiral be trusted, particularly if the Axis forces were able to hold Tunisia, and then prepare to retake Morocco and Algeria? But if the position of Darlan was unclear, so too was that of Boisson. In the circumstances, no comparable build-up of Axis forces in the AOF was, of course, likely. In the two weeks following the launch of Operation Torch, however, Boisson indulged in his favorite pastime: sitting on the fence to determine which way the wind was blowing. He continued to report to Vichy, apparently unperturbed by its having being occupied by the Germans, but at the same time remained in touch with Darlan in Algiers. The admiral's decision to cooperate with the Allies, so he assured Boisson, was authorized by Pétain and had reached him before the events of 8 November. Boisson was skeptical, and Gen. Jean Marie Bergeret, Vichy's inspector general of air defenses, was sent to Dakar to convince him.[9] As a result, the governor-general then agreed to send a mission to Algiers to examine the elusive document. His envoys returned to Dakar and swore they had seen the message, which apparently gave Darlan the right to negotiate with the Allies should the Axis violate the terms of the armistice.[10]

On 23 November, Boisson, with the support of most of his military commanders, insisting he was only following Pétain's orders, decided to "join the United Nations."[11] The United States consul in Dakar, Fayette Flexer, made an interesting comment on the matter:

Popular and military reaction to the masterly American stroke in North Africa was immediate. A possible opportunity to arrest its [Boisson's administration's] declining prestige by riding the wave of popular enthusiasm was muffed, the Government in general standing aloof until the inevitable course in French North Africa had been definitely shaped. The decision to send a representative to Algiers, whilst maintaining communication with Vichy, was taken only when the investigations of special political agents had disclosed, if anything, that the population was overwhelmingly clamorous for joint action with the North African bloc against the Axis, and, most important of all, that the [AOF] defense forces were not dependable against the U.S. Army.[12]

The return to the Allied side of the AOF was greeted in the Gold Coast press with restrained enthusiasm. *West Africa* reported on the AOF's rejoining the fight under the headline "Dakar Decides to Line Up": "Two years' experience of Hitlerism had quickened the logical processes of communities willingly led by such men as M. M. Boisson and Chatel, Generals Barreau, Giraud and Nogues— all named, and their attitude unreservedly endorsed, by Admiral Darlan in his declaration that, henceforth, all French Africa is at one in acting 'boldly, with discipline and patriotism,' for the France that will always be."[13] There were many in the AOF, however, who resisted the about-face, who remembered the sinking of the French fleet at Mers el Kebir in July 1940, the Allied air and sea attack on Dakar of September 1940, the Anglo-Free French invasion of the Levant in March 1941, and no doubt other instances of *l'Albion perfide*. The most important of the skeptics was General Falvy, commander in chief of land forces in the AOF, who appears to have remained committed to a policy of Axis-leaning neutrality. Late in the afternoon of 23 November 1942, he issued an order to his troops. Paragraph 3, the only one reproduced by Consul Flexer, read: "I must add, to clarify for you that the negotiations that have been conducted rest upon the following conditions concerning our territories: (a) no foreign military occupation of any kind, land, naval, air, even the most minimal; (b) no fraternization with the British, and most strongly, the Gaullists—against whom we maintain our present attitude; (c) No base, no air strip will be put at the disposition of anyone, save in the most sparing case and only for the Americans." According to Flexer, this order was widely circulated, and met with "general stupefaction." Falvy, moreover, followed up this uncompromising order with the arrest, on 27 November, of one of his own officers for printing a pro-American leaflet for distribution among the troops. The comments of Foreign Office officials in London on political attitudes in the AOF made after studying a copy of Flexer's cable, ranged from "odd" to, "I should have thought that the lesson was that Boisson ought to go."[14]

The problem of Darlan vanished, when, on Christmas Eve 1942, Fernand Bonnier de la Chapelle, a member of a group of young anti-Nazis, assassinated him.[15] Two days later, de la Chapelle was executed by a French firing squad, although to *la Résistance*, he would forever be a hero. There remains considerable

Soldiers, Airmen, Spies, and Whisperers

speculation as to the part the SOE may have played in Darlan's assassination, particularly as de la Chapelle was one of its weapons instructors. Not only was he employed by the SOE, but he used a revolver supplied by the SOE operative David Keswick (who had been one of Louis Franck's men from the beginning of West African operations, and had recently arrived in North Africa from Nigeria.) One thing is clear, however: Darlan was generally detested by the British. An entry for 14 November 1942 in the diary of Sir Alexander Cadogan, permanent undersecretary of state at the Foreign Office, reads, for example: "We shall do no good till we've killed Darlan." Shades of Henry II and Thomas à Becket: "Will no one rid me of this turbulent priest?" We should not be surprised, that on 30 December, Cadogan was swift to deny any British complicity in the assassination.[16]

It is difficult to assess the impact of Darlan's death on the course of the war. In any case, the fighting in Tunisia was to rage for a further seven months. By the spring of 1943, sixty thousand French troops were fighting alongside the British and Americans. Fifteen thousand of them, including an unspecified number of tirailleurs, were to die before the last German units in Tunisia surrendered on 13 May 1943—and Africa was finally freed of an Axis presence.[17]

THE FATE OF FRAWEST

The fast moving events of November and December 1942 left the intelligence organizations in West Africa in somewhat of a quandary. Lumby, head of Frawest, received a cable from Hambro in mid-November. It made reference to an assumed "far reaching German organization in French West Africa." On 20 November, having consulted with Lord Swinton, Lumby replied to Hambro. Evidence to support this notion, Lumby wrote, has never been found. Boisson, he commented, "whose worst enemy would not call him pro German has consistently and we think successfully striven to keep Germans and German influence commercial or otherwise out of his area." Lumby (and Swinton) thought it unlikely that Boisson would long resist popular pressures for the material benefits that would come from joining the Allies. The European population of Vichy territory, they argued, was completely "apathetic," and there were few whose sympathy for the Axis would override their desire for a quiet life and improved economic conditions. In other words, Pétainist political ideals would come a distant second to the overarching goal of keeping the AOF quiescent. Nothing would be done to stir up the "natives." Lumby expressed his and Swinton's views that all Frawest subversive activities should be suspended and the training schools closed down. Covert propaganda would no longer be necessary, and the Political Warfare Executive should take over all overt activities. In effect, the whisperers should stop whispering, but the SOE should continue intelligence gathering, at least until the situation in the AOF became clearer.[18]

In the third week of November 1942, two telegrams originated from George Taylor in which he anticipated the "early liquidation" of Frawest, or its reduction to skeletal form.[19] A more activist view of the future role of the SOE came from the unidentified West African operative W.31, in a memo to Taylor. W.31 thought that, whatever the terms of the final agreement with the Vichy colonies, there was need to keep an eye on them in order to unearth any Axis elements. He cast his net wide to include German agents, pro-Vichy and anti-British or anti-American French functionaries (which certainly included most government officials in the Côte d'Ivoire), French businessmen, Syrian and African traders who may have been influenced by Axis sympathizers, Indian traders of doubtful loyalty in the large towns, and so forth. In addition, W.31 anticipated problems with such societies as the "Légion des anciens combattants," which he thought might form the nucleus of anti-Allied activity. To guard against these lurking perils, W.31 thought a mission should be established, staffed by hand-picked personnel with a good knowledge of both French and the French colonies. Its headquarters should be in Dakar, with subsections in other important cities of the AOF. W.31 was singularly cautious in not suggesting, at this stage, that this new mission should be a reconstituted Frawest.[20] By doing this, thereby he was no doubt trying to avoid raising the hackles of Giffard and Menzies of the SIS.

The discussion was continued in a cable from "CD" (Hambro) to Lumby, dated 26 November 1942. Hambro was not convinced that the course of events in West Africa had diminished the importance of Frawest. He was sure that, as he put it, "the Germans will leave many eggs behind in French territory." Rather optimistically, he supposed that the work of Frawest might become more rather than less important. He outlined his reasons:

A. Boisson may continue to sit on the fence and remain in some association with the puppet government in France.

B. In any case, all the pro-Axis elements in French West Africa will not suddenly change their views because of declaration by Darlan or Boisson.

C. Germany has through French firms with branches in French West Africa ready made cover for network of anti-Allied activities.

D. It probably will be months before situation North Africa finally clarifies in favour of United Nations.

Soldiers, Airmen, Spies, and Whisperers

E. U-boat activities will certainly continue.

F. Dissemination of propaganda to natives must continue.

G. Even if French West Africa "occupied" by United Nations, need for subversive organisation in this vast territory seems urgent.[21]

On 2 December, Taylor again took up the matter of Frawest's future. He argued that it was unlikely that Germany would allow the economic resources of the AOF—oil seeds, vegetable oils, rubber, and cotton—to pass under Allied control without making attempts to reduce production by subversive means. He conceded that Boisson had, indeed, successfully excluded large numbers of German officials from the AOF but thought it extremely improbable that the Germans had not built up a clandestine organization there. If not, they would start doing so. "Where German subversive elements are at work," he submitted, "there also should S.O.E. be at work." The SOE should abandon its programs of sabotage, but should involve itself more with counterespionage. However, Taylor envisaged a situation in which, despite the appearance of the AOF joining the Allies, "Governors, Secretaries General and officials are bribed and work secretly for the Axis." The upshot of this was that Taylor argued, "it should be the business of Frawest to see that the right people are appointed to influential offices; to see that the wrong people are excluded or dismissed; to make sure by bribes or pressure that the administration is pro-Allied and not pro-Vichy or pro-Axis." Taylor pressed home his point: "If this war has produced one lesson for us, it is that it [is] never safe to regard any territory as impregnable. We should therefore not eliminate from our calculations, a defeat in Libya or a successful German attack on Egypt through Syria and Palestine. It would be absurd to suppose that as a result of negotiations, the full effects of which are still not clear, that the whole of French West Africa will fall quietly into our hands and that all the pro-Vichy Frenchmen with anti-British bias will suddenly change their minds because of a proclamation by Boisson and a few economic advantages." The gist of his recommendations was, then, that albeit with a reduced staff, the SOE should be preparing themselves to work in the AOF as soon as the situation there was clarified. Interestingly enough, he strongly recommended that Lumby should be withdrawn on the grounds that he was "not well qualified to sell the subversive side of S.O.E." and did not "appear to have in mind the necessity of keeping an organisation alive as an insurance against future contingencies."[22]

Hambro set his seal on the new proposals in a coded telegram to Lumby on 14 December. All paramilitary operations were to be suspended and the work of propaganda was to be reevaluated in consultation with the head of the PWE. Hambro was particularly concerned with Lumby's direction of the SOE's intelligence collecting functions. This was where the great change was to occur. "I would prefer," Hambro wrote, "to call it a watching organisation of observers capable of watching the French colonies, infiltrating agents and with representatives in position to influence, bribe, and act subversively if called upon. I also think this should include secret W/T [Wireless/Telegraph] communications. If your staff are in position to carry this out, I believe that they would fulfill the proper S.O.E. role in unsatisfactory Allied territories."[23] It was not until 13 January 1943 that Lumby, having contemplated the new role he was being asked to play, steeled himself to respond to Hambro. "Selection and planting of watchers," he replied in code, "who will probably be found mostly from European commercial community will take time as also organization of communications. For latter I deprecate use of portable W/T sets at any rate till certain that French suspicious of individuals have been allayed so as not to dry up flow while watchers are being got into position. We must retain frame work of existing organization, mainly of African agents, working with added caution and limited objectives."[24]

We know little about the fate of this project. One may suspect that the records have been carefully cleansed. To spy on Vichy AOF was, it seems, one thing, to spy on Allied AOF was another. There are not even whispers of the records of the watchers. However, any threat to the Gold Coast was now over, and the Franck Mission, in all its various incarnations as PERO, Frawest, Neucols, and so forth, was wound down, and finally closed on 31 July 1944.[25] As for Louis Franck, after leaving West Africa he was assigned to the United States as British intelligence liaison officer. There he worked closely with that country's intelligence organization, the OSS, and with Hugh Stephenson, who was head of British Intelligence in North America, and had been given control over all British Secret Service operations there. In 1944, Franck's old associate David Keswick suggested that Louis Franck take over Special Operations Mediterranean. Major General Colin Gubbins, who had been appointed executive director of the SOE in September 1943, desperate for an experienced man, was in favor of the appointment. Franck's nationality, however, presented difficulties. It was felt that senior British military officers in the Mediterranean command would dislike working with a foreigner, albeit a "good" foreigner, particularly since Franck had a strong Belgian accent.[26] Gubbins went ahead nevertheless, and Franck once more proved a great success.[27] The not so grand finale for the SOE came on 15 January 1946, when it was given forty-eight hours to close by Labour Prime Minister Clement Attlee, who said, quite ridiculously, that he "had no wish to preside over a British Comintern, and that the network was to end immediately."[28]

And as for Pierre Boisson, governor-general of the AOF, he finally left Dakar in June 1943, having been fired by General de Gaulle and the Committee of National Liberation. He was not to escape a certain degree of retribution. He was arrested in December 1943, charged with endangering the security of the state. The investigation and the interrogations went on for two years. Eventually all charges of treason were dropped and Boisson was convicted simply of undertaking actions injurious to the national defense. He spent two years in prison, then, in 1947, due to his deteriorating health, was released. He died of heart failure on 20 July 1948 while still under house arrest.[29]

THE FATE OF THE SOLDIERS AND AIRMEN

From its foundation in late 1940, the Home Guard continued to train, patrol, and parade until late May 1944, when the decision was taken to disband it. The governor's final message to members of the Gold Coast Home Guard paid tribute to their contributions:

> Nearly three and a half years ago, when war clouds were darkening the sky over Africa and it appeared that this Colony might have to face up to enemy attack, an appeal was made for volunteers to form a Home Guard. The response was immediate. Hundreds of men in all parts of the Colony came forward, ready to do everything in their power to help in the defence of their homes, their towns, and their Country.
>
> In a very short space of time peace-loving men from all walks of life, African and European, were hard at work, side by side, training—for one grim purpose.... Tonight, on the occasion of your last parade, I wish to thank you all for your loyalty and for the sacrifices you have made during these difficult and anxious years.... A final word. I hope that the spirit of comradeship and discipline engendered by the training you have received in the Home Guard will be of enduring benefit to you.[30]

By contrast, the future of the Gold Coast Regiment was a guaranteed one. In the summer of 1942, 4 GCR had been sent to the Gambia to keep a wary eye on the Vichy French in Senegal. By October they had been joined by the First and Third Battalions of the regiment. Sometime in the autumn of 1942, 2 GCR had been sent to Sierra Leone with much the same purpose. The turnabout of the AOF in November 1942 ended any external threat to the Gold Coast. Despite this, there was no reduction in the strength of the Gold Coast Regiment. To the contrary, the battalions continued to recruit and train men in preparation for combat in other theatres. Their chance was soon to come, for in December 1942 General Giffard proposed to the War Office that two West African divisions be raised for service in Burma. On 1 January 1943 the War Office took up his offer and instructed GHQ West Africa to begin raising the first of these, the Eighty-First Division. It was formed on 1 March 1943, in Nigeria, and comprised the Fifth, Seventh, and Eighth, and auxiliaries, of the Gold Coast Regiment battalions, as well as units from the Gambia, Nigeria, and Sierra Leone. Two weeks later, orders were given for the other division, the Eighty-Second, to be raised. That month, the Gold Coast battalions marched overland, through northern Togo, now once again an "Ally," to Nigeria. In April 1943 the four battalions sent to Gambia and Sierra Leone returned to the Gold Coast and awaited their next mission. By that time, however, General Giffard had, with effect from 25 March, given up command of the RWAFF. He flew to India to become GOC-in-C of the Eastern Army.

While the Eighty-First and Eighty-Second Divisions of the West African Expeditionary Force were being formed and trained, an advance party sailed from Takoradi to India on 21 April 1943. It comprised staff officers, engineers, and medical personnel. The group of doctors and Queen Alexandra Nurses were charged with setting up special hospitals for the African troops. Broken only by four days at Capetown, the journey was exceedingly slow, and the party did not reach Bombay until 10 June 1943. The Eighty-First Division arrived there during August and September 1943. The Eighty-Second Division, which included the First, Second, and Third Battalions, GCR, and auxiliaries, disembarked in India three months later, during January 1944. Both divisions were to distinguish themselves in action in Burma.[31] Three battalions, the Fourth, Sixth, and Ninth, remained in the Gold Coast, continuing to expand and train men for needed reinforcements. These units, as well as garrison companies, were rightly considered more than sufficient to protect a colony once again surrounded by friendly territory.

As for Takoradi, it would continue to function as an assembly base for some months into 1943, now without fear of attack. However, with the increasing role being played by the Americans in the war, most ferry operations moved to the greatly expanded American Army Air Force base in Accra, the forerunner of Kotoko International Airport, which is now Ghana's main air link with the world.

Soldiers, Airmen, Spies, and Whisperers

Possible Futures

FANTASIES OF WAR

In a sense the Gold Coast had a war, but nobody came. There were no invasions from the surrounding Vichy territories and no bombardments from air or sea. The men of the Gold Coast went to war and fought well in East Africa and Burma, but no battle was fought, or needed to be fought, on Gold Coast soil. So, were all the steps taken for the defense of the Gold Coast in the end unnecessary? Or had these steps not been taken, would the probability of attack have been significantly higher?

One way, and perhaps the only way, of approaching such a problem is by the exploration of counterfactual situations, or of what have become more popularly known as what-ifs. In *Virtual History: Alternatives and Counterfactuals,* Niall Ferguson has brought together a collection of essays ranging from John Adamson's "What If Charles I Had Avoided the Civil War?" to Mark Almond's "What If Communism Had Not Collapsed?" In his introduction Ferguson remarks that there is

> a double rationale for counterfactual analysis. Firstly it is a *logical* necessity when asking questions about causation to pose "but for" questions, and to try to imagine what would have happened if our supposed cause had been absent. For this reason, we are obliged to construct plausible alternative pasts

on the basis of judgements about probability; and these can be made only on the basis of historical evidence. Secondly, to do this is a *historical* necessity when attempting to understand how the past "actually was"—precisely in the Rankean sense, as we must attach equal importance to all the possibilities which contemporaries contemplated before the fact, and greater importance to these than to an outcome which they did not anticipate.[1]

Another collection, titled *"What If?"* edited by Robert Cowley, is modestly subtitled, *The World's Foremost Military Historians Imagine What Might Have Been."*[2] It includes, for example, J. M. McPherson's "Robert E. Lee Humbles the Union, 1862"; J. Keegan's "The Drive for the Middle East, 1941"; and A. Waldron's "If Chiang Kai-shek Hadn't Gambled in 1946." Among the uses of what-ifs, Cowley argues, is to eliminate hindsight bias: "Much as we like to think otherwise, outcomes are no more certain in history than they are in our own lives. If nothing else, the diverging tracks in the undergrowth of history celebrate the infinity of human options. The road not taken belongs on the map." Planning, military or otherwise, has to take account of possible futures, only *one* of which will become the actual future. On 26 September 1942 a high-ranking SOE officer—probably Julius Hanau, code-named Caesar—produced a paper headed "S.O.E. Missions in West and East Africa." His object, he wrote, was "to review the position of the W. Section Missions in the light of experience gained since their foundation, to estimate the usefulness of their contribution to the war effort both present and future, and thus to make it possible to frame a balanced judgement of what their future policy should be." He referred to what he called "the waiting game," that is, the period of planning that precedes any decision. "Events in this war," he reflected, have shown

> that it is a game which must be played and played with skill and thoroughness. . . . S.O.E. is obliged to make elaborate and costly preparations to meet situations which may in the end never arise. The Frawest Mission is a case in point. The great effort of establishment, planning, and preparation . . . has to be undertaken, if only to enable us to guard against developments, military or political, in A.O.F. which cannot be foreseen. At the same time we should not, and do not, lose sight of the fact that the function of S.O.E. is not confined to this task of planning and preparing against the possibility of major military or political crises. S.O.E. is charged by H.M.G. with the conduct of a war of attrition against Axis nationals and sources of economic strength wherever they might be.[3]

Soldiers, Airmen, Spies, and Whisperers

A FIRST WHAT-IF: THE SOE TRIUMPHANT

The policies of the War Cabinet (as we have seen) were generally such as to allow General Giffard to feel justified in refraining from any form of aggressive action against the French territories. In other words, he was free to pursue his own little war against the SOE, blocking every plan that would have enabled the executive to carry out what was required of them by their own charter. But, what if the War Cabinet had specifically given the SOE the green light in late 1941 to conduct acts of economic sabotage in the AOF? The jubilant Wingate immediately carried out plans to attack railway lines and supply depots in the Côte d'Ivoire, blowing up warehouses filled with coffee, cocoa, latex, and other goods that were managing to find their way, by Atlantic convoys, to France and thence into German hands. Using African agents to plant incendiaries in the cargo holds of both French and neutral carriers but not, of course, in those vessels flying the American flag, ships lying offshore at Abidjan were put to the torch. Giffard viewed these activities with extreme trepidation, and what he feared came true. AOF Governor-General Boisson ordered reprisals, among them the long-anticipated and, in some quarters, much-feared land attack on the Gold Coast. Reinforcements bolstered the ranks of the Tirailleurs Sénégalais already based in Ouagadougou and Bobo-Dioulasso, and Vichy French troops crossed into the Northern Territories of the Gold Coast at Tumu, Navrongo, and Bawku. The few forces Giffard had at his disposal were unable to turn back the invaders, and the whole of the north was rapidly overrun. Now the tirailleurs, supported by artillery, began their long march southward, toward Kumasi and the coast.

Once the Vichy forces entered the heavily forested Asante country, the advance slowed up. Giffard, only too aware of dangers to the entire war effort should Takoradi be captured, concentrated most of his troops in the southwest. In Kumasi, only the training and supply depot stood in the path of the invaders. The Asantehene, Sir Osei Agyeman Prempeh II, combining his roles as occupant of the Golden Stool, Knight of the British Empire, and lieutenant colonel of the Home Guard, rallied the Asante on their own terms: how, he asked a crowd of many thousands, could they allow the Asanteman to be overrun by people from the north—*nnonkofo!*[4] Giffard hurriedly sent the regular troops he had available to support those who rallied to the Asantehene's call. Most of them were soldiers of the Gold Coast Brigade, who had just returned from the East African campaign. Instead of a well-deserved leave, they now found themselves facing thousands of combat-hardened tirailleurs, many of whom had fought in the European theatre of war. Giffard then ordered the demolition plans to be put into operation, and all over unoccupied Gold Coast, roads and bridges were destroyed.

Into the fray came the SOE. They struck at the tirailleurs' supply lines with much success. The demolition plans worked splendidly. The tirailleurs, soon deprived of ammunition and food supplies, pulled back. Within a week they were withdrawing from the Northern Territories, back into Haute Côte d'Ivoire. Giffard was of two minds about the whole business. One the one hand he felt that, despite his dire warnings, the SOE's activities had, in fact, precipitated the invasion of the Gold Coast. On the other hand, he had reluctantly to acknowledge that their operations against the invaders' supply lines had had much to do with saving the colony. Wingate and the Asantehene became war heroes. The Asante, in particular, compared them with the great warrior kings Opoku Ware and Osei Tutu. But the Asantehene emerged as more than a great war leader, more than a great traditional king. Indeed, in October 1954 the Convention People's Party decided that he, rather than Kwame Nkrumah, should become head of state of a future independent Ghana.[5]

A SECOND WHAT-IF: THE TAKORADI FERRY DISRUPTED

In March 1941 the German panzer divisions in North Africa were pushing vigorously eastward, toward Egypt, the Suez Canal, and beyond. However, there was one cloud on Rommel's horizon: the air superiority he had hitherto enjoyed was starting to be challenged. Reports from German agents in Vichy AOF and Brazil revealed that the Gold Coast port of Takoradi was being used as a base for assembling and ferrying aircraft from Britain and North America to North Africa, India, and the Middle East. The German high command gave Marshal Pétain the opportunity to prove his nation's loyalty to the Axis cause. Promised the support of German and Italian units, if necessary, field command of the operation was placed in the hands of AOF forces, now numbering over forty thousand men. A seaborne invasion was ruled out, since the waves of the South Atlantic were still ruled by the British. A land invasion through southeastern Côte d'Ivoire was deemed impractical due to the heavy forest cover and the virtually nonexistent communications. The decision was therefore taken to strike into the Northern Territories of the Gold Coast, putting the troops across the Black Volta at Vonkoro. Bobo-Dioulasso, where motorized units were being rapidly built up, was chosen as the base for the invasion. Vichy intelligence had discovered that Giffard had few troops capable of resisting a fast thrust of infantrymen supported by supply trucks. The tirailleurs passed through Kumasi, meeting only token resistance from the poorly equipped Home Guard. The invaders halted briefly at Tarkwa and blew up the main shaft at the mines there after looting the gold magazines. During these few hours, the Takoradi air base was heavily bombed by tactical bombers from Abidjan and its runways put out of action. The battalions of Tirailleurs Sénégalais then marched on Takoradi, overcoming the determined but inadequate resistance of the one and only company of the Gold Coast Regiment based there. The railway installations at Takoradi and the assembly plants were totally destroyed. It was to be nearly two months before even limited operations could be resumed. The effect upon the course of events was traumatic. The war in North Africa was lost even before Montgomery arrived.

A THIRD WHAT-IF: BOISSON BETWEEN AXIS AND ALLIES

Suppose that Boisson, with the ardent support of his commander in chief, had rallied the AOF to the Axis cause in late 1942, at the time of Operation Torch. This was a possible future that had to be explored by those responsible for the defense of British West Africa. We are privileged, in the case of this what-if, to sit back (a luxury we hope we have deserved) and sit in on the deliberations of those who had to do so. In November 1942, Resident Minister Lord Swinton, General Officer in Command Giffard, Governor Alan Burns of the Gold Coast, and the key SOE men in West Africa, Taylor and Lumby, met to discuss the matter of Boisson. They worked quite explicitly on the assumption that Boisson would not come out in support of the Allies.

Giffard knew that he might well be required to activate the plans to invade the AOF through Guinea, Togo, and Dahomey. He and his staff officers pored over whatever documents they could find about previous operations. The invasion of German Togo by the Gold Coast Regiment in 1914 attracted their attention. It had been a brief campaign, launched after the German administration in Lomé had, on 6 August, refused to surrender but retreated inland to Kamina and from there organized the defense of Germany's model colony. Moving northward, the GCR linked up with troops of their French allies, the Tirailleurs Sénégalais. The heaviest battle took place at Khra on 22 August. One British and one French officer, five WAFF soldiers, and seventeen tirailleurs died in the action. Three days later the Germans accepted terms of unconditional surrender.[6] Brilliant as this campaign was, however, it could scarcely be taken as an adequate model for an invasion of Vichy AOF in 1943.

Giffard readily acknowledged that an invasion of the AOF would require naval and air support. He was reluctant to allow that an organization such as the SOE had its share to contribute to a successful campaign. Now that military operations were finally being considered, however, he was obliged to moderate his views. He agreed that the SOE should not only be allowed to carry out acts of sabotage in Vichy territory, but that they should also create and train paramilitary forces. Those that were designated the up-country representatives of the SOE, with the cooperation of officers of the colonial political service—that is, district commissioners and the like—would recruit Africans for this force. They would be trained in special schools run by the SOE, and organized in bands under SOE officers. In the event of hostilities, saboteurs and paramilitaries would be placed at the disposal of Giffard's local military commanders, who would direct them to specific targets behind enemy lines. Finally, the SOE was to be used to build up networks of pro-Allied Frenchmen and women in major Vichy centers such as Abidjan and Lomé and to establish links with them by running "native agents" and by distributing secret radio transmitters. The Fighting French were to be involved in this operation, and Taylor commented on the great confidence the British had in Colonel Ponton, head of the Gold Coast French Mission.[7]

The problem facing Swinton, Giffard, Burns, Taylor, and Lumby was whether the sheer act of invasion, after nearly two years of delicate saber rattling, would be sufficient to induce Boisson into virtual surrender? Or would pressures from Boisson's own political administrators force him to fight to the last tirailleur? The five British officials thus grappled with what turned out to be a possible, but not an actual, future, for, as it happened, Boisson accepted the inevitable and, before any invasion could have been launched, came out in lukewarm support of the Allied cause.

A FOURTH WHAT-IF: DAKAR FALLS TO FREE FRANCE IN SEPTEMBER 1940

It was perhaps the sight of the naval force lying off Dakar, or perhaps the prospect of aerial bombardment that led Boisson to signal his willingness to meet with de Gaulle. They talked for a remarkably short space of time before Boisson intimated his readiness to throw the resources of the AOF into the continuing struggle

Soldiers, Airmen, Spies, and Whisperers

against the Axis powers. Churchill cabled his congratulations: "France is reborn, not only in Afrique Equatorial Française but now in Afrique Occidental Française. Together we shall face the future with confidence and equanimity." The Gold Coast found itself once again surrounded by friendly territories.

Granted this scenario, this book would not have needed to be written!

Notes

Chapter 1

1. For Ghana, see for example, R. B. Bening, "The Definition of the International Boundaries of Northern Ghana, 1888–1904," *Transactions of the Historical Society of Ghana* 14, no. 2 (1973): 229–61.

2. Public Record Office, London (hereafter PRO), WO 32\3515, "Secret Report on the Ivory Coast and a Part of French Guinea," by Captain R. M. Hall, [1925–27].

3. James Gamble, *West African Review,* April 1940.

4. Charles de Gaulle, *The Call to Honour 1940–1942,* vol. 1 of *War Memoirs,* trans. Jonathan Griffin (London: Collins, 1955), 11–12.

5. *West Africa,* 22 June 1940. For a detailed examination of Nazi Germany's African objectives, see Alexandre Kum'a N'Dumbe III, *Hitler voulait l'Afrique* (Paris: Editions d'Harmattan, 1980).

6. PRO, FO 371/28246, West African Political Intelligence Centre (hereafter WAPIC), bulletin no. 9, [late 1940], app. H, "Relations between the Government of the Gold Coast and Neighbouring French Colonies after the Collapse of France" (hereafter "Relations").

7. PRO, FO 371/28246, "Relations."

8. PRO, FO 371/28246, "Relations"; FO 371/28243, telegram, Colonial Office to Chairman, West African Governor's Conference, 1 January 1941.

9. PRO, FO 371/28246, "Relations."

10. Armand Annet, *Aux heures troublées de l'Afrique française, 1939–1943* (Le Mans: Editions du Conquistador, 1952), 25; PRO, FO 371/28246, "Relations." Major Hamilton is probably F. L. Hamilton, MC, veteran of WWI, who had arrived in the Gold Coast in 1921 to join the police and had achieved the rank of commissioner in 1927, a post he still held in 1937. He appears to be the person Annet refers to as the "*commandant des troupes de la Gold-Coast,*" but no one named Hamilton held this position at the relevant period.

11. PRO, FO 371/28246, "Relations."

12. Edmond Louveau, *"Au Bagne": Entre les griffes de Vichy et de la milice* (Bamako: Soudan Imprimerie, 1947), 2–4.

13. Ibid., 2–3.

14. PRO, FO 371/28246, "Relations."

15. A reserve captain in 1937, Le Mare had been called up from his post as collector of customs to join the RWAFF.

16. PRO, FO 371/28244, telegram to Secretary of State for the Colonies.

17. Theodore Draper, *The Six Weeks' War* (New York: Book Find Club, 1944), "text of proposal for French-British union," 331.

18. National Archives of Ghana (hereafter NAG)-Accra, ADM 12/1/214, telegram, Governor, Nigeria, to Governor, Gold Coast, 1 July 1940.

19. NAG-Accra, ADM 12/1/214, telegram, Consul General, Dakar, to Foreign Office, 4 July 1940.

20. Ibid., 1 July 1940.

21. Wendell Holbrook, "The Impact of the Second World War on the Gold Coast, 1939–1945" (Ph.D. diss., Princeton University, 1978), 72–73, citing NAG-Accra ADM 12/1/214, telegram, C-in-C, South Atlantic, to Governor, Gold Coast, 1 July 1940.

22. NAG-Accra, ADM 12/1/214.

23. NAG-Accra, ADM 12/11/214, Governor, Sierra Leone, to Governor, Gold Coast, 5 July 1940.

24. NAG-Accra, ADM 12/11/214, Governor, Nigeria, to Governor, Gold Coast, 19 July 1940.

25. Thirteen hundred French naval officers and men died as a result of the attack.

26. *West Africa,* 13 July 1940, 696.

27. PRO, FO 371/28246, "Relations."

28. NAG-Accra, ADM 12/1/214, telegram, Secretary of State, London to Governors, Nigeria and Gold Coast, 7 July 1940.

29. NAG-Accra, ADM 12/1/214, telegram, Secretary of State to Governor, Accra, 12 July 1940.

30. PRO, FO 371/28246, "Relations."

31. Louveau, *"Au Bagne,"* 2–4.

32. PRO, FO 371/28246, "Relations."

33. Ibid.

34. Ibid.

35. NAG-Accra, ADM 12/1/214, telegram, Secretary of State to Governor Hodson, 20 July 1940.

36. NAG-Accra, ADM 12/1/214, telegram, 26 September 1940.

37. PRO, FO 371/36200, encl. 2, Speaight to P. J. Dixon, Algiers, 13 January 1943.

38. NAG-Accra, ADM 12/1/214, de Gaulle to Bouillon, 12 July 1940.

39. A. C. Russell, *Gold Coast to Ghana: A Happy Life in West Africa* (Durham, England: Pentland Press, 1996), 50.

40. A. C. Russell, personal diary, 1940.

41. Robert Bourgi, *Le Général de Gaulle et l'Afrique noire, 1940–1969* (Paris: Nouvelles Editions Africaines, 1980), 53.

42. Interview with H. C. Norman, Bournemouth, 4–5 September 1998.

43. Interview with T. E. Kyei, Kumasi, 30 March 1994. Mr. Kyei passed away on 6 December 1999.

44. Interview with H. C. Norman, 4–5 September 1998; Norman to Lawler, 11 August 1998. At my request, Monty Norman checked his records and was able to tell me that the truck was a Hotchkiss six-cylinder, with the number plate AT 5775!

45. PRO, FO 371/28246, "Relations."

46. Jean-Noël Vincent, *Les Forces Françaises Libres en Afrique, 1940–1943* (Paris: Ministère de l'Armée de Terre, Service Historique, 1983), 47–48.

47. Bourgi, *Général de Gaulle*, 53.

48. PRO, WO 32/4140, War Office and Colonial Office memorandum, December 1937.

49. NAG-Accra, ADM 12/1/213, telegram, Secretary of State to Governor, Gold Coast, 31 August 1939.

50. A. H. W. Haywood and F. A. S. Clarke, *The History of the Royal West African Frontier Force* (Aldershot: Gale and Polden, 1964), 364.

51. NAG-Accra, ADM 12/1/214, Giffard to Hodson, 13 July 1940.

52. Ibid.

53. PRO, FO 371/28246, "Relations."

54. R. O. Paxton, *Vichy France: Old Guard and New Order, 1940–1944* (New York: Knopf, 1972), 37.

55. PRO, FO 371/28246, "Relations."

56. Desmond Dinan, *The Politics of Persuasion: British Policy and French African Neutrality, 1940–1942* (Boston: University Press of America, 1988), 54. Some of the themes treated in this chapter are also examined in Dinan's most useful work, which, however, focuses more on North, rather than West, Africa. The reader will remark that our interpretations are not always in agreement.

57. For the wider context of this, see Nancy Lawler, *Soldiers of Misfortune: Ivoirien Tirailleurs of World War II* (Athens: Ohio University Press, 1992), 124–25.

58. Charles de Gaulle, *The Complete War Memoirs of Charles de Gaulle*, vol. 1, trans. J. Griffin (New York: Simon and Schuster, 1968), 111.

59. See also, Maurice Martin du Gard, *La carte impériale: Histoire de la France outre-mer, 1940–1945* (Paris: André Bonne, 1949), 137–38.

60. John Kent, *The Internationalization of Colonialism: Britain, France and Black Africa, 1939–1956* (Oxford: Clarendon Press, 1992), 52–53.

61. De Gaulle, *Memoirs*, 115.

62. Of the many accounts of Operation Menace, as the Dakar attack was known, one has probably not received the attention it merits: John Williams, *The Guns of Dakar: September 1940* (London: Heinemann, 1976). See also, Emil Lengyel, *Dakar: Outpost of Two Hemispheres* (Garden City, N.Y.: Garden City Publishing, 1941), 81–104.

63. Kent, *Internationalization of Colonialism*, 45, 48–49.

64. PRO, FO 371/28243, telegram, Colonial Office to West African Governors Conference, 8 January 1941.

65. PRO, FO 371/28243, telegram, Colonial Office to Chairman, West African Governors' Conference, 1 January 1941.

66. Haywood and Clarke, *Royal West African Frontier Force*, 363.

67. Ibid., 370.

68. F. A. S. Clarke, "The Development of the West African Forces in the Second World War," *Army Quarterly,* October 1947, 70–71.

69. *Daily Telegraph,* 25 August 1999, obituary of Major the Rev. Richard Freeth, who, as a newly commissioned lieutenant in the Wiltshire Regiment, was among those who were picked up.

70. Lawler, *Soldiers of Misfortune,* 133–34.

71. Anthony Clayton, *France, Soldiers, and Africa* (London: Brassey's, 1988) 127–34. See also Myron Echenberg, *Colonial Conscripts: The Tirailleurs Sénégalais in French West Africa, 1857–1960* (Portsmouth, N.H.: Heinemann, 1991), 88.

72. Clayton, *France, Soldiers, and Africa,* 353–54.

73. PRO, FO 371/28243, Z204, War Cabinet notes, 16 January 1941. The note is typed, but I could not decipher the initials of the writer.

74. PRO, FO 371/28248, biographical note on Barrau prepared by Foreign Research and Press Service, Balliol College, Oxford, 14 December 1941.

75. Archives de l'Outre-Mer, Aix-en-Provence (hereafter AOM), DAM/91, "Note au sujet de la defense de l'AOF, 1 December 1940," 18 March 1942. I am grateful to Gregory Mann for securing copies of this file for me.

76. *West African Review,* check date and page, reference in *West Africa,* 25 January 1941, 62. Emphasis in original.

77. Archives Nationales de la Côte d'Ivoire (hereafter ANCI), "Rapport annuel de la Commission de Recrutement 1940," carton 339, dossier XIII–19–138/1085.

78. Lawler, *Soldiers of Misfortune,* 126–28.

79. David Killingray, "The Colonial Army in the Gold Coast: Official Policy and Local Response, 1890–1947" (Ph.D. diss., London University, 1982), 101.

80. Lawler, *Soldiers of Misfortune,* 133–36.

81. Interview with Zie Soro, Kolokpo, Côte d'Ivoire, 25 November 1985.

82. Sir Garnet Wolseley, "The Negro as a Soldier," *Fortnightly Review* 44 (1 December 1888): 691.

83. For the context of this campaign, see Ivor Wilks, *Asante in the Nineteenth Century: The Structure and Evolution of a Political Order* (London: Cambridge University Press, 1975), 207–42.

84. Killingray, "Colonial Army in the Gold Coast," 25.

85. See, for example, Haywood and Clarke, *Royal West African Frontier Force,* ch. 1, passim; Paul M. Mbayei, *British Military and Naval Forces in West African History, 1807–1874* (Lagos: NOK, 1978), 101–11; David Killingray, "Guarding the Extending Frontier: Policing the Gold Coast, 1865–1913," in *Policing the Empire,* ed. D. Anderson and D. Killingray (Manchester: Manchester University Press, 1991).

86. E. C. Lanning, "The Royal West African Frontier Force," *Newsletter of the Friends of the National Army Museum* 6, no. 2 (1995): 27–28. The publication of Lanning's *Regimental History of the Gold Coast Regiment* is eagerly awaited.

87. David Killingray, "The British Military Presence in West Africa," Oxford Development Records Project, report no. 3 (Oxford: Rhodes House Library, 1983), 92.

88. Lanning, "Royal West African Frontier Force," 27–28.

89. Nearly 165,000 Tirailleurs Sénégalais served in World War I; 134,000 were engaged in battle in Europe. Lawler, *Soldiers of Misfortune*, 21–22.

90. For example, see W. D. Downs, *With the Nigerians in German East Africa* (London: Methuen, 1919); Hugh Clifford, *The Gold Coast Regiment in the East African Campaign* (London: John Murray, 1920); Edmund H. Gorges, *The Great War in West Africa* (Plymouth: Mayflower Press, [early 1920s]); Byron Farwell, *The Great War in Africa, 1914–1918* (New York: Norton, 1986); Malcolm Page, *KAR: A History of the King's African Rifles* (London: Leo Cooper, 1998); Malcolm Page, ed., *Africa and the First World War* (New York: St. Martin's, 1987); and Haywood and Clarke, *Royal West African Frontier Force*, ch. 5, passim.

91. J. D. Amenyah, "Introduction Of Jacob Dosoo Amenyah An Ex-Service Man Bearing Regimental No. V124," Wilks Papers, Africana Library, Northwestern University, ms. Amenyah was indeed aboard the troopship, but this delightful recollection may be somewhat romanticized. I am hoping to edit this diary for publication.

92. Haywood and Clarke, *Royal West African Frontier Force*, 322.

93. W. R. Grigsby to E. C. Lanning, 16 April 1993.

94. David Killingray, "Military and Labour Recruitment in the Gold Coast during the Second World War," *Journal of African History* 23, no. 1 (1982): 83–85.

95. Haywood and Clark, *Royal West African Frontier Force*, 11.

96. Rhodes House Library, Oxford Development Records Project, MSS.Afr.s. 1734 (342); transcript of interview with General Sir Antony Read, GCB, CBE, DSO, MC, (1980) 10–11.

97. Interview with Professor Adu Boahen, Accra, 13 April 1994.

98. Edgar Wallace, *Sanders of the River* (London: Hodder and Stoughton, 1926).

99. Rhodes House Library, MSS.Afr.s. 1734 (342), Read, (1980) 2–4.

100. Haywood and Clark, *Royal West African Frontier Force*, 324–26. Emphasis in original.

101. Ibid., 325; E. C. Lanning, pers. comm, 17 November 1998.

102. Killingray, "Colonial Army in the Gold Coast," 35.

103. W. B. Ponting, typescript. "Gold Coast Regiment from 1935 to 1943," 9. I am grateful to Eric Lanning for kindly giving me access to this document. Ponting belonged to the Royal Scots Fusiliers, and had served with the Gold Coast Regiment since 1935.

104. PRO, WO 173/58, "War Diary" 1GCR, October 1939.

105. Killingray, "Military and Labour Recruitment," 84–85.

106. Interview with K. Attakora Gyimah, Kumasi, 1 April 1994. It is sad to report that Attakora Gyimah died in 2000.

107. Interview with H. C. Norman, Bournemouth, 4–5 September, 1998.

108. Several interviewees, who wish not to be cited by name on this issue, were unanimous in deploring the conduct of the Rhodesians toward the Africans and noted that they had objected strongly to being assigned to grass hut accommodation.

109. Ponting, "Gold Coast Regiment," 8–9.

110. Killingray, "Colonial Army in the Gold Coast," 35.

111. NAG-Accra, ADM 12/1/213, McDonald to Hodson, 5 September 1939.

112. NAG-Accra, ADM 12/1/213, Secretary of State, London, to Governor, Accra, 13 September 1939.

113. Gold Coast Government, *The Gold Coast Handbook, 1937* (London: Gold Coast Government, 1937), 131–32.

114. E. C. Lanning, pers. comm., 17 November 1998.

115. Interview with H. C. Norman, Bournemouth, 4 September 1998. Another of the many reservists called up was Agricultural Officer Allen Leeds. Leeds, *Long Ago and Far Away: Gold Coast Days, 1939–1958* (Upton upon Severn: Square One Publications, 1998), 16–25.

116. Letter 287 of E. H. Jacques, Tamale, 9 January 1940, Rhodes House Library, Oxford, xxx.

117. Letter 288 of E. H. Jacques, Tamale, 16 January 1940, and letter 290, Tamale, 28 January 1940, Rhodes House Library, Oxford, xxx.

118. F. A. S. Clarke, "Development of the West African Forces," 67. Emphasis in original.

119. NAG-Kumasi, 2755, annual report, Bekwai, 1941–42.

120. Almost without exception, Ivoirien veterans of the French Army told me that the food remained one of their best memories of the army. Their only complaint was that, unlike the French soldiers, they had no wine ration. Lawler, *Soldiers of Misfortune*, 56, 72.

121. Ponting, "Gold Coast Regiment," 11.

122. E. C. Lanning, pers. comm., 17 November 1998.

123. Ponting, "Gold Coast Regiment," 11–12.

124. Haywood and Clarke, *Royal West African Frontier Force*, 325–27.

125. NAG-Accra, ADM 12/1/214, Secretary of State to Governor, Gold Coast, 4 July 1940.

126. Ibid.

127. NAG-Accra, ADM 12/1/214, Governor to GCO West Africa, 12 July 1940.

128. PRO, WO 173/206, "4th Battalion, The Gold Coast Regiment, RWAFF, Progress Report no. 7. Feb. 1941." By Feb. 1941, 120 policemen remained in the battalion. They continued to be paid police wages, which were considerably higher than army rates of pay. According to the report this caused discontent among their peers.

129. Haywood and Clarke, *Royal West African Frontier Force*, 365; PRO, WO 173/25, "War Diary," Gold Coast HQ, October 1940.

130. An earlier project to attack Freetown on 8 July 1940, three days after the Royal Navy assault on the French fleet at Mers el Kebir, was called off: the official reason given was "bad weather." "Rapport annuel de l'Etat Major, troisième bureau, Troupes du groupe de l'AOF, 1940." Service Historique de l'Armée de la Terre, Vincennes, carton 3, dossier 02A2.

131. AOM, DAM/91, "Defense de l'AOF."

132. H. V. Wimshurst, pers. comm., 20 June 1994. Wimshurst died in 1995 at his home in South Africa.

Chapter 2

1. Denis Richards, *The Fight at Odds, 1939–1941*, vol. 1 of *Royal Air Force, 1939–1945* (London: HMSO, 1953), 247.

2. D. W. Ray, "The Takoradi Route: Roosevelt's Prewar Venture beyond the Western Hemisphere," *Journal of American History* 62 (September 1975), 341.

3. Richards, *Fight at Odds*, 247.

4. Jim Pickering, "The Takoradi Route," part 1, *FlyPast*, July 1997, 26. See also Richards, *Fight at Odds*, 247.

5. Robert McCormack, "The Politics and Economics of Air Transport Development in West Africa, 1919–1939," paper presented at the annual meeting of the Canadian Association of African Studies, York University, February 1975. For a general account of the development of the African routes, see Ernest Leslie Howard-Williams, *Something New Out of Africa* (London: Pitman and Sons, 1934).

6. Robert McCormack, "War and Change: Air Transport in British Africa, 1939–1946," *Canadian Journal of History* 24 (December 1989): 344–45.

7. Great Britain, Colonial Office, *Annual Report on the Social and Economic Progress of the People of the Gold Coast, 1938–39*, Colonial Reports Annual, no. 1919 (London: HMSO, 1939), 93–94.

8. Richards, *Fight at Odds*, 247.

9. Ibid., 248.

10. Pickering, "Takoradi Route," 1:26.

11. William Grigsby, pers. comm., 16 August 1998. The *Aska* was sunk on the return voyage. Elder Dempster & Co was created in 1852, and known as the African Steam Company, in order to carry mails from London to Madeira, the Canary Islands, and West Africa.

12. William Grigsby, pers. comm., 14 August 1998.

13. Interview with Otumfuo the Asantehene, Nana Opoku Ware II, Manhyia Palace, Kumasi, 2 April 1994. Otumfuo died in March 1999, after a reign of twenty-nine years. In early 1943, Matthew Poku was transferred to Axim, as officer in charge of the PWD there. His predecessor, an Englishman named A. T. Wood, had been killed when returning from leave when his ship was torpedoed by a German submarine. For further information on the Asantehene's early career, see Ivor Wilks, *A Portrait of Otumfuo Opoku Ware II as a Young Man* (Ghana: Anansesem Publications, 1995).

14. William Grigsby, pers. comm., 16 August 1998.

15. Richards, *Fight at Odds*, 248.

16. Pickering, "Takoradi Route," 1:28–29, July 1997, 2:34–35, August 1997.

17. Richards, *Fight at Odds*, 248–49.

18. Ibid., 249.

19. For example, interview with Brian Ellis, 7 July 1997.

20. NAG-Accra, ADM 12/1/214, Secretary of State, London, to Governor, Gold Coast, 29 September 1940.

21. Richards, *Fight at Odds*, 249.

22. Ray, "Takoradi Route," 341.

23. Gerry R. Rubin, *Durban 1942: A British Troopship Revolt* (London: Hambledon Press, 1992), 6–9.

24. *Daily Telegraph* (London), obituary of L. A. Harris, 30 June 1995.

25. NAG-Accra, ADM 12/1/214, telegram, Secretary of State for Colonies to Governor, 18 July 1940.

26. Lt. Col. A. F. Giles, "The History of the 5 Bn The Gold Coast Regiment, 1939–1945," Rhodes House, MSS. Afr. S. 1734 (150). I am grateful to E. C. Lanning for drawing my attention to this document.

27. Arthur William Tedder, *With Prejudice: The War Memoirs of Marshal of the Royal Air Force, Lord Tedder* (London: Cassell, 1966), 32–33.

28. McCormack, "War and Change," 348.

29. Tedder, *With Prejudice,* 32–33.

30. Pierre Clostermann, *Flames in the Sky,* trans. Oliver Berthoud (Harmondsworth: Penguin, 1958), 105–6.

31. Tedder, *With Prejudice,* 109. Air Vice Marshall G. G. Dawson had arrived in the Middle East in June 1940 and reorganized the maintenance and supply office.

32. Interview with Duncan Carmichael, Accra, 16 March 1994.

33. Interview with Brian Ellis, Ciliau Aeron, Wales, 14 May 1997.

34. Brian Ellis, pers. comm., 1 February 2000.

35. For a brief summary of the participation of South African pilots in the Takoradi Ferry, see J. A. Brown, *Eagles Strike: The Campaigns of the South African Air Force in Egypt, Cyrenaica, Libya, Tunisia, Tripolitania and Madagascar, 1941–1943* (Cape Town: Purnell, 1974), 3–4.

36. William Grigsby, pers. comm., 14 August 1998.

37. PRO, WO 173/208, "War Diary," 6 GCR.

38. "Canada 'Full Out' in the Air," *War Illustrated* 4, no. 76 (14 February 1941): 152.

39. Interview with Duncan Carmichael, Accra, 16 March 1994.

40. Pickering, "Takoradi Route," 1:28–29.

41. Interview with Brian Ellis, Ciliau Aeron, Wales, 7 July 1997.

42. Column in *British Homing World,* 4 August 1995, 32; Arthur Cogman, pers. comm., December 1995.

43. Interview with Jack Jones, Garreg, Wales, 6 June 1996.

44. PRO, WO 173/136, Brigadier Wood to Brigadier Clarke, [July 1941].

45. PRO, WO 173/137, "War Diary," Fortress Headquarters, Takoradi.

46. PRO, WO 173/138, "War Diary," Takoradi Fire Command, May–November 1941.

47. NAG-Kumasi, 2922, Traffic Superintendent to Broadcast Officer, Kumasi, 10 June 1941.

48. Interview with Duncan Carmichael, Accra, 16 March 1994.

49. Interview with Jack Jones, Garreg, Wales, 6 June 1996.

50. Brian Ellis, pers. comm., 1 February 2000.

51. Imperial War Museum, London "Secret Dossier, 1 January 1942," H. K. Thorold's "Report on the Formation and Development of the Royal Air Force Station, Takoradi,

and the West African Reinforcement Route, July, 1940–September, 1941." See Holbrook, "Impact of the Second World War," 79.

52. Ray, "Takoradi Route," 340–58.

53. Memorandum, 30 April 1941, Neutrality Act File, Oscar Cox Papers, Franklin D. Roosevelt Library, Hyde Park, cited in Ray, "Takoradi Route," 344.

54. Arthur Pearcy Jr., "Douglas Dakota MK I–IV," profile 220 (Windsor, Berkshire: Profile Publications, 1970), 209.

55. Ray, "Takoradi Route," 342–43.

56. Ibid., 350–51.

57. Ibid., 345–55.

58. PRO, WO 173/137, "War Diary," Fortress HQ, Takoradi.

59. AOM, DAM/91, "Défense de l'AOF."

60. PRO, WO 173/208, "War Diary," 6 GCR. A terse note in the diary indicates "special rations arrangements for this unit."

61. John Terraine, *The Right of the Line: The Royal Air Force in the European War, 1939–1945* (Ware, Hertfordshire: Wordsworth Editions, 1997) 305–6.

62. Great Britain, Colonial Office, *Annual Report on the Gold Coast, 1946*, Colonial Reports Annual (London: HMSO, 1946), 113.

63. Florence M. Bourret, *The Gold Coast: A Survey of the Gold Coast and British Togoland, 1919–1946* (London: Oxford University Press, 1949), 156.

64. PRO, WO 173/25, "War Diary," Gold Coast HQ, August–December 1940.

65. I am grateful to E. C. Lanning for many thoughtful reflections on this point. It will be appreciated that the usage differed from the more conventional one that distinguished between home forces; imperial forces, such as the Indian Army and the Transjordan Frontier Force; and colonial forces, drawn, as the name indicates, from the colonies.

66. PRO, WO 173/59, "War Diary," 4 GCR, October 1940.

67. Interview with H. C. Norman, Bournemouth, 5 September 1998.

68. H. C. Norman, pers. comm., 1 November 1999. Emphasis added.

69. E. C. Lanning, pers. comm., 19 October 1998; interview with E. C. Lanning, South Godstone, Surrey, 27 November 1998.

70. NAG-Accra, ADM 12/1/214, Richards to Governor, Gold Coast, 6 July 1940.

71. For these campaigns, see Haywood and Clarke, *Royal West African Frontier Force*, ch. 8, passim.

72. NAG-Kumasi, 2922, text of broadcast by Brig. S. S. Butler, 24 October 1940.

73. Ibid.

74. *West Africa*, 21 December 1940, 1325. Excerpts from governor's speech. The porcupine, or *kotoko,* was the traditional symbol of the Asante army.

75. Interview with E. C. Lanning, South Godstone, 27 November 1998.

76. NAG-Kumasi, 1282, Quarterly Report Obuasi, quarter ending 31 December 1940.

77. PRO, WO 173/209, "War Diary," 7 GCR.

78. NAG-Kumasi, 2755, annual report, Bekwai, 1939–1940.

79. E. C. Lanning, pers. comm., 25 October 2000.

80. National Army Museum Archives, London, Lt. W. N. Heaton, diary and tape recording. I am grateful to E. C. Lanning for this reference.

81. Interview with Nana Kofi Genfi II, Kumasi, 29 March 1994.

82. Ibid.

83. Ponting, "Gold Coast Regiment." Again, I am grateful to E. C. Lanning for material from this report.

84. Ibid.

85. *West Africa*, 5 July 1941, 647. Excerpts from speech to Gold Coast Legislative Assembly.

86. W. P. Holbrook, "The Impact of the Second World War on the Gold Coast: 1939–1945" (Ph.D. diss., Princeton University, 1978), 409–10.

87. Ponting, "Gold Coast Regiment." Emphasis in original.

88. Interview with K. Attakora Gyimah, Kumasi, 1 April 1994.

89. PRO, WO 173/25, "War Diary," Gold Coast HQ, 16 October 1940.

90. PRO, WO 173/25, "War Diary," Gold Coast HQ, 21 December 1940.

91. NAG-Kumasi, 2755, Annual Report Bekwai, 1939–1940. Indeed, in the National Archives, Kumasi, there are several copies of letters from RWAFF soldiers demanding compensation for their wives' adultery.

92. Interview with K. Attakora. Gyimah, Kumasi, 1 April 1994.

93. NAG-Kumasi, 2922, report of meeting of Joint Provincial Council, [early 1941].

94. Ibid.

95. Ibid.

96. Ibid.

97. *West Africa*, 27 September 1941, 1.

98. PRO, WO 173/25, "War Diary," Gold Coast HQ, 6 January 1941.

99. Dr. T. C. McCaskie, son of the late W. McCaskie, pers. comm., 11 May 1997.

100. Ibid.

101. Appeal by Price, reported by *West Africa*, 16 November 1940, 1191.

102. PRO, WO 32/9598, "Report from General Officer Commanding, West Africa," 24 June 1941.

103. *West Africa*, 30 August 1941, 1.

104. PRO, FO 371/28246, WAPIC bulletin no. 11, 28 June 1941, 5.

105. Colonial Office, *Annual Report on the Gold Coast, 1946*, 112–13. In 1942 eleven thousand recruits were enlisted, and a further ten thousand in 1943. Killingray puts the figure for numbers of Gold Coast men in the armed forces in World War II at forty-seven thousand as of July 1945. Killingray, "Military and Labour Recruitment," 83. This does not include any West Africans serving in units recruited in Britain, so the actual number is somewhat higher.

106. *West Africa*, 14 December 1940, 1298. Emphasis in original.

107. David Killingray, pers. comm., 15 September 2000. See also Killingray, "British Military Presence," 63–64.

108. For military recruitment and other administrative purposes, the northern

parts of British-mandated Togo were attached to the Northern Territories, and the southern sections to the Gold Coast Colony.

109. NAG-Kumasi, ARG 1/1/192, text of broadcast, 3 February 1941.

110. NAG-Kumasi, ARG 1/1/192, Acting DC to CCA, Kumasi, 27 March 1941.

111. Interview with K. Attakora, Gyimah, Kumasi, 1 April 1994.

112. United Africa Company, the wholesale and retail outlet of Unilever (Lever Brothers), the dominant firm throughout West Africa.

113. Interview with T. E. Kyei, Kumasi, 30 March 1994.

114. B. A. Akota, *Struggle against Dictatorship* (Kumasi: Payless Printing Press, 1992).

115. Interview with James Moxon, Kitase, Akwapim, Ghana, 17 March 1994. Moxon achieved no little fame when filmed by the CBS television program *60 Minutes,* in a segment titled "The White Chief of Ghana." James Moxon died in 1999, and was buried in Kitase.

116. Ibid.

117. Interview with T. E. Kyei, Kumasi, 30 March 1994. The blackout order and the alarm system was laid out in a government order of 10 June 1940, published in the *Gold Coast Gazette,* 15 June 1940.

118. Interview with T. E. Kyei, Kumasi, 30 March 1994.

119. Interview with James Moxon, Kitase, 17 March 1994.

120. NAG-Kumasi, 1/1/192, series of increasingly acrimonious letters on this issue, September 1942–October 1943.

121. NAG-Kumasi, ARG 1/1/192, "Training Instructions no. 2, 1941."

122. NAG-Kumasi, ARG 1/1/192, "Members of the Home Guard need Boots," *Ashanti Pioneer,* 26 June 1942.

123. NAG-Kumasi, ARG 1/1/192, Colonial Secretary to CCA, 9 July 1942.

124. NAG-Kumasi, ARG 1/1/192, letter to DC Bekwai, 25 March 1941.

125. Colonial Office, *Annual Report on the Gold Coast, 1946,* 113.

126. PRO, FO 371/28245, Mack to Hollis, 7 May 1941.

127. PRO, FO 371/28555, "Vichy French Action against Free French Territories in Africa," 1 June 1941.

128. PRO, FO 371/28555, "Possible Vichy Attack on Free French Colonies," 21 June 1941, report of a telegram from Lord Halifax on information received from Robert Murphy, FDR's personal representative to Vichy.

129. PRO, FO 371/28555, telegram from Parr to War Cabinet, 20 June 1941.

130. PRO, FO 371/28555, "Possible Attack on Free French Africa," 21 June 1941.

131. Speech by Sir Hugh Clifford, 28 October 1918. Gold Coast Colony, *Legislative Council Debates, 1918–1919* (Accra: Government Printing Department, 1940), 86. See also G. E. Metcalfe, *Great Britain and Ghana: Documents of Ghana History, 1807–1957* (Legon: University of Ghana, 1964), 569–70.

132. A. MacMillan, ed., *The Red Book of West Africa* (1920; reprint, London: Frank Cass, 1968), 172. F. & A. Swanzy became Swanzy and Miller during the war.

133. PRO, FO 371/28246, W. H. Grey to Lord Hankey, 16 May 1941.

134. PRO, FO 371/28247, WAPIC bulletin no. 12, 18 July 1941.

135. PRO, FO 371/28246, WAPIC bulletin no. 11, 28 June 1941.

136. PRO, FO 371/28247, WAPIC bulletin no. 12, 18 July 1941.

137. PRO, FO 371/28555, telegram from R. L. Speaight, 8 July 1941.

138. PRO, FO 271/28555, Halifax to War Cabinet, 14 October 1941.

139. PRO, CO 554/133/33819/1, WAWC, 2nd meeting, 14–15 August 1942; CO 968/82/14701/3, 1942. Cited in Killingray, "Colonial Army in the Gold Coast," 103–104.

140. PRO, WO 173/136, "Operation Instruction No. 5," 8 August 1941.

141. PRO, WO 173/136, "Appreciation," 6 April 1941.

142. PRO, WO 173/136, "Appreciation," 21 April 1941.

143. PRO, WO 173/136, "Appreciation," 6 April 1941.

144. PRO, WO 173/136, "Appreciation," 11 April 1941.

145. PRO, WO 173/136, "Memorandum on Defence of the Gold Coast," 21 April 1941.

146. PRO, WO 173/136, "Demolition Scheme, Gold Coast Area," 21 June 1941.

147. Dr. T. C. McCaskie, pers. comm., 11 May 1997.

148. PRO, FO 371/28248, WAPIC bulletin no. 14, 13 September 1941.

149. PRO, FO 371/28247, WAPIC bulletin no. 13, 13 August 1941.

150. PRO, WO 208/55, GHQ Weekly Military Review, no. 19, week ending 16 December 1941.

151. PRO, WO 208/55, GHQ Weekly Military Review, no. 22, week ending 7 January 1942.

152. PRO, WO 208/55, GHQ Weekly Military Review, no. 25, week ending 28 January 1942.

153. PRO, FO 371/28248, WAPIC bulletin no. 14, 13 September 1941.

154. AOM, DAM/91, "Defense de l'AOF," 18 March 1942.

155. Ibid.

156. Catherine Akpo-Vaché, *L'AOF et la Seconde Guerre mondiale (septembre 1939–octobre 1945)* (Editions Karthala: 1996), 22, 54. When, in the summer of 1942, Boisson categorically refused Vichy's request that German personnel be stationed in Dakar, Laval wanted to replace him as governor-general with Falvy. General Barrau intervened and Boisson kept his job.

157. AOM, DAM/91, "Defense de l'AOF," 18 March 1942.

158. PRO, WO 173/136, "Military Intelligence Summary no. 42," 28 November 1941.

Chapter 3

1. For a convenient account of these events, see Martin Gilbert, *Finest Hour: Winston S. Churchill, 1939–1941* (London: Heinemann/Minerva, 1983), 306–18.

2. Ben Pimlott, *Hugh Dalton* (London: Jonathon Cape, 1985), 276–77.

3. Ibid., 281–98.

4. Hugh Dalton, *The Second World War Diary of Hugh Dalton*, ed. Ben Pimlott (London: Jonathon Cape, 1986), xvi.

5. Kent, *Internationalization of Colonialism*, 54–56.

6. M. R. D. Foot, *SOE: An Outline History of the Special Operations Executive, 1940–46* (London: BBC, 1984), 4–26. For the most extensive survey of British covert operations, see F. H. Hinsley et al., *British Intelligence in the Second World War,* 5 vols. (London: HMSO, 1979, 1981).

7. Foot, *SOE: An Outline History,* 22.

8. Michael Howard, *British Intelligence in the Second World War,* vol. 5, *Strategic Deception* (London: HMSO, 1990), 51.

9. Richard Deacon, *British Secret Service,* rev. ed. (London: Grafton Books, 1991), 281; Foot, *SOE: An Outline History,* 21–22. It is often said that the D in Section D was short for *destruction,* but I am assured by Basil Davidson, himself a former SOE agent, that it was so called simply because it had been created after Section C.

10. B. Sweet-Escott, "Nelson, Sir Frank," in *Dictionary of National Biography, 1961–1970,* 788; Foot, *SOE: An Outline History,* 23; Deacon, *British Secret Service,* 286.

11. Foot, *SOE: An Outline History,* 23–24.

12. Ibid., 22.

13. Ibid., 28.

14. Dalton, *Second World War Diary,* xxi.

15. Most notably, Graham Greene, *The Heart of the Matter* (New York: Viking Press, 1948); John Bingley, *Mr. Khoury* (London: Constable, 1952); and John Harris, *A Funny Place to Hold a War* (London: Book Club Associates, 1984). All three authors had an involvement in West African affairs at the relevant time, and one wonders whether the operation of the Official Secrets Act led them to write of their experiences in fictionalized form.

16. Gaston Palewski will be known to many readers in a quite different context, as the great love of Nancy Mitford's life, appearing in her novels *Love in a Cold Climate* and *The Pursuit of Love,* as the thinly disguised duke in love with Linda Alconbury.

17. PRO, FO 371/24344, FO minute by W. Mack, 5 November 1940. It appears that Palewski managed to survive this initial encounter with the general, becoming a close political advisor, and even rating mention in de Gaulle's *Memoirs.*

18. NAG-Accra, ADM 12/1/214, draft telegram XAW 503/5, Secretary of State Accra to London, [late 1939].

19. Ronald Lewin, "Morton, Sir Desmond John Falkiner," *Dictionary of National Biography, 1971–1980,* 596–97.

20. Anthony Cave Brown, *"C": The Secret Life of Sir Stewart Graham Menzies, Spymaster to Winston Churchill* (New York: Macmillan, 1987). 272.

21. Foot, *SOE: An Outline History,* 351.

22. Ibid., 351–52.

23. PRO, HS 3/72, Fletcher to Morton, Sacombe House, Sacombe, Hertfordshire, 5 October 1940.

24. PRO, HS 3/72, Morton to Jebb, 10 Downing Street, 8 October 1940.

25. PRO, HS 3/72, Nelson to Jebb, 11 October 1940.

26. PRO, HS 3/72, notes by Fletcher, n.d., in Nelson's files.

27. PRO, HS 3/72, Nelson to Jebb, 11 October 1940.

28. PRO, HS 3/72, "SO Activities in West Africa," 24 October 1940.

29. M. R. D. Foot, pers. comm.

30. Franck's resignation was reported by the *Times*, 28 September 1939.

31. William Stevenson, *The Man Called Intrepid: The Secret War* (New York: Harcourt Brace Jovanovich, 1976).

32. PRO, HS 3/72, Nelson to Hall, 7 November 1940.

33. PRO, HS 3/72, telephone message from Nelson to Jebb, 26 November 1940.

34. SOE personnel were given British military rank, a practice that added to the general level of irritation more or less openly expressed by army officers, but was intended to protect agents captured in the field.

35. PRO, HS 3/72, CD to Jebb, 25 October 1940.

36. PRO, HS 3/72, CD to Hall, 29 October 1940.

37. PRO, HS 3/72, "Economic Mission to Gold Coast," 4 November 1940.

38. PRO, HS 3/72, Emery to CD, 6 November 1940. For Fletcher's extraordinary career with SOE later, in the Far East, see Foot, *SOE: An Outline History,* 351–52.

39. PRO, HS 3/72, CD to Hall, 7 November 1940.

40. Ibid.

41. PRO, HS 3/72, 13 November 1940.

42. PRO, HS 3/72, Minute Sheet, WSC, 21 November 1940.

43. Nigel West, *Secret War: The Story of SOE, Britain's Wartime Sabotage Organisation* (London: Hodder and Stoughton, 1992), 9.

44. PRO, HS 3/72, minute sheet, AD to CD, n.d.

45. PRO, HS 3/79, L. Franck, "The Franck Mission to West Africa," dictated end of November 1940.

46. PRO, HS 3/73, "The Franck Mission to West Africa," end of November 1940.

47. PRO, HS 3/72, telephone message from "CD," 26 November 1940; "CD" to "W," 28 November 1940.

48. PRO, HS 3/72, "CD" to Jebb, 30 November 1940; "CD" to "W," 4 December 1940.

49. PRO, HS 3/72, "CD" to Jebb, 30 November 1940.

50. PRO, HS 3/73, "Franck Mission to West Africa," end of November 1940.

51. If Sir Hanns Vischer was to be believed, Keswick patronized Franck, calling him "my young partner," and informing all who cared to listen that the Belgian "will do as I tell him." PRO, HS 3/73, CD to X, 10 June 1941.

52. PRO, HS 3/80, WO to GOC, 30 November 1940.

53. PRO, HS 3/72, "SO Activities in West Africa," 24 October 1940.

54. Stapledon went on to have a distinguished career in the Colonial Service, serving in both East and West Africa. Knighted in 1956, he became governor of the Eastern Region of Nigeria and, following that country's independence, did his final stint as governor of the Bahamas, 1960–64.

55. PRO, FO 371/28250, "Meeting of the Governors Conference held at Lagos on the 18th and 19th of December, 1940."

56. R. E. C. Wingate, *Not in the Limelight* (London: Hutchinson, 1959), 158–59.

57. PRO, FO 371/28250, "Meeting of the Governors' Conference held at Lagos on the 18th and 19th of December, 1940."

58. Kent, *Internationalization of Colonialism,* 64–66.

59. Robert Pearce, *Sir Bernard Bourdillon: The Biography of a Twentieth-Century Colonialist* (London: Kensal Press, 1987), 299–302.

60. PRO, FO 371/28250, "Meeting of the Governors' Conference held at Lagos on the 18th and 19th of December, 1940."

61. PRO, HS 3/72, Bourdillon to Secretary of State, 20 December 1940. The objectives of the conference were shortly worked out in great detail, and incorporated in a memorandum to the Colonial Office, copied to the Foreign Office, FO 371/28250, "Meeting of the Governors' Conference, 18–19 December 1940."

62. PRO, HS 3/72, Bourdillon to Secretary of State, 21 December 1940.

63. PRO, HS 3/72, Franck to Nelson, 21 December 1940.

64. For a very brief account of Hanau's activities in Romania, see Foot, *SOE: An Outline History,* 12–13.

65. Rodd, merchant banker, diplomat, and Saharan explorer, had obviously shown no reluctance in propounding his views to the MEW, and his name appears on documents to do with the stalled Hailey Mission.

66. PRO, HS 3/72, W to "AD" and Caesar, Lagos, 27 December 1940.

67. PRO, FO 371/28243, cipher telegram to chairman, West African Governors Conference, 3 January 1941.

68. PRO, HS 3/73, "CD" to X, 10 June 1941.

69. PRO, HS 3/73, "West Africa," [after July 1944].

70. PRO, HS 3/74, "SOE Missions in West Africa," 9 May 1942.

71. NAG-Sunyani, DAOW 1/5, CCA Hawkesworth to District Commissioners, Ashanti, 3 March 1941.

72. NAG-Sunyani, DAOW 1/5, Colonial Secretary Accra to CCA, Ashanti, 18 February 1941.

73. PRO, HS 3/96, "U" to "AD.3," "Recommendations for awards for former members of the PERO Mission in West Africa," 6 April 1944.

74. Glyn remained in West Africa until reassigned to Operation Torch. In October 1942, along with another officer, he was landed in North Africa ahead of the Allied Forces to set up the SOE station there. Following that stint, he became personal staff officer to the chief of SOE, returning to West Africa in 1944.

75. NAG-Sunyani, DAOW 1/5, "Memorandum on Franck Mission Reorganisation," Most Secret, 27 October 1941.

76. A. H. M. Kirk-Greene, *A Biographical Dictionary of the British Colonial Service, 1939–1966* (London: Hans Zell, 1991), 389.

77. NAG-Sunyani, DAOW 1/5, Colonial Secretary, Accra, to Chief Commissioner, Ashanti, 11 February 1941.

78. NAG-Sunyani, DAOW 1/5, Mothersill to DC Wenchi, 25 August 1941; "Memorandum on Franck Mission Reorganisation," 27 October 1941.

79. NAG-Sunyani, DAOW 1/5, Mothersill to DC Wenchi, Salaga, 7 April 1941.

80. NAG-Sunyani, DAOW 1/6, FitzGerald to DC Wenchi, 2 December 1941, citing letter from DC Sunyani.

81. Interview with Nana Yaw Kran, Okyeame, Sunyani, 6 April 1994.

82. Interview with Kofi Adinkra, Sunyani, 6 April 1994.

83. NAG-Sunyani, DAOW 1/6, Mothersill to DC Wenchi, 25 August 1941.

84. NAG-Sunyani, DAOW 1/5, "Memorandum on Franck Mission Reorganisation," 27 October 1941.

85. H. V. Wimshurst, pers. comm., 20 June 1994.

86. Dalton, *Second World War Diary,* 48.

87. Edward Spears, *Fulfilment of a Mission: The Spears Mission to Syria and Lebanon, 1941–1944* (Hamden, Conn.: Archon Books, 1977; London: Leo Cooper, 1977).

88. PRO, FO 371/32037, 1 May 1942.

89. Over the four years of its existence, L'Union des Français Libre, with its nucleus of French exiles, raised over £20,000 for the Allied war effort.

90. The background of the three is not yet known. "Rouillon," however, may possibly be a typing error: The reference may possibly be to the Bouillon already mentioned as crossing into the Gold Coast in July 1940. The difference in rank remains a problem.

91. PRO, FO 371/32078, de Larminat to Giffard, Brazzaville, 16 November 1940.

92. PRO, FO 371/32078, de Gaulle memorandum, Brazzaville, 1 November 1940.

93. NAG-Kumasi, ARG 1/1/188, Acting Colonial Secretary to CCA Hawkesworth, 30 June 1941.

94. NAG-Kumasi, ARG 1/1/188, Ponton to CCA Hawkesworth, 28 December 1941.

95. PRO, FO 371/28248, WAPIC bulletin no. 14, 13 September 1941.

96. PRO, FO 371/32078, telegram from Resident Minister Achimota to Secretary of State for the Colonies, 3 August 1942.

97. Ibid.

98. PRO, HS 3/79, "WF" to Caesar, 27 August 1942.

99. PRO, FO 371/32078, Swinton to Colonial Secretary, 24 August 1942.

100. PRO, FO 371/32078, de Gaulle, Personal Staff, Second Bureau, Military Missions, "Note on Military Missions Accra," encl. in de Gaulle to General Alan Brooke, 7 July 1942.

101. Ibid.

102. For more information on this aspect of the baroness's life, see *Variety,* 7–13 December 1988; see also *New York Times,* 2 December 1988; *Down Beat,* April 1989, 56.

103. NAG-Kumasi, ARG 1/1/188, Colonial Secretary's Office to CCA Hawkesworth, 7 April 1941. Emphasis in original.

104. Ibid. Emphasis in original.

Chapter 4

1. PRO, HS 3/73, Summary of Activities of Franck Mission, 1 March 1941, attached to document headed "West Africa," [after July 1944].

2. PRO, HS 3/73, "Further measures to be taken in West Africa . . . ," 2 May 1941.

3. NAG-Sunyani, DAOW 1/5, memorandum by Francis Glyn, 14 February 1941.

4. NAG-Sunyani, DAOW 1/5, Mothersill to DC Wenchi, 29 March 1941.

5. NAG-Sunyani, DAOW 1/5, Mothersill to DC Wenchi, 11 and 27 March, 1941.

6. NAG-Sunyani, DAOW 1/5, Mothersill to DC Wenchi, 7 April 1941.

7. PRO, HS 3/73, Franck to Chief Executive Officer et al., 15 July 1941, enclosing "most secret" memorandum of 12 July 1941.

8. Ibid.

9. David Stafford, *Britain and European Resistance, 1940–1945: A Survey of the Special Operations Executive, with Documents* (London: Macmillan, 1980), 26.

10. PRO, HS 3/73, W (Franck) to CD (Nelson), Lagos, 15 July 1941, enclosing "Most Secret Memorandum, Synopsis," Lagos, 12 July 1941.

11. PRO, HS 3/74, "SOE Missions in West Africa," unsigned memo, 9 May 1942; and "SOE in West Africa," undated and unsigned memo, notated, "Aide Memoire for Resident Minister."

12. Pimlott, *Hugh Dalton,* 307.

13. PRO, HS 3/73, anonymous high-level SOE document, 29 August 1941.

14. PRO, HS 3/74, "SOE Missions in West Africa," anonymous memo, 9 May 1942.

15. West, *Secret War,* 134–35.

16. NAG-Sunyani, DAOW 1/5, Wimshurst to Chief Commissioner, Ashanti, 8 October 1941.

17. NAG-Sunyani, DAOW 1/5, FitzGerald to Wimshurst et al., 17 October 1941.

18. NAG-Sunyani, DAOW 1/6, "Memorandum on Franck Mission Reorganization," 27 October 1941.

19. PRO, HS 3/74, "SOE Missions in West and East Africa," 26 September 1942; NAG-Sunyani, DAOW 1/5, FitzGerald to Wimshurst, 17 November 1941.

20. NAG-Sunyani, DAOW 1/6, [FitzGerald], "Memorandum on Franck Mission Reorganisation," 27 October 1941.

21. Ibid.

22. PRO, HS 3/79, undated doc. attached to WF to Caesar, 27 August 1942.

23. NAG-Sunyani, DAOW 1/5, FitzGerald to DC Wenchi, 22 December 1941, 5 January 1942.

24. PRO, WO 208/55, Weekly Military Review, no. 22, 7 January 1942.

25. PRO, WO 208/55, Intelligence Notes, no. 28, app. A, July 1942.

26. PRO, WO 208/55, Intelligence Notes, no. 55, October 1942.

27. PRO, WO 208/55, Intelligence Notes, no. 5, 5 May 1942.

28. PRO, WO 208/55, Intelligence Notes, no. 55, 19 November 1942.

29. PRO, WO 208/55, Intelligence Notes, no. 8, app. A, 16 May 1942.

30. NAG-Sunyani, DAOW 1/6, FitzGerald to DC Wenchi, 20 June 1942.

31. NAG-Sunyani, DAOW 1/6, Hedley-Denton to DCs et al., Accra, 22 July 1942.

32. NAG-Sunyani, DAOW 1/6, n.d.

33. PRO, FO 371/28245, WAPIC bulletin no. 7, 18 April 1941.

34. PRO, FO 371/28246, WAPIC bulletin no. 9, 24 May 1941.

35. PRO, FO 371/28246, WAPIC bulletin no. 11, 28 June 1941.

36. Jean Rouch, "Migrations en Gold Coast," *Journal de la Société des Africanistes* 26, nos. 1–2 (1956): 55; see also Edward Mortimer, *France and the Africans, 1944–1960: A Political History* (London: Faber and Faber, 1969), 46–47.

37. PRO, FO 371/28247, WAPIC bulletin no. 13, 13 August 1941.

38. For Kom II, see Lawler, *Soldiers of Misfortune,* 25–26, 134, 166.

39. PRO, WO 208/55, Weekly Military Review, week ending 18 November 1941.

40. PRO, WO 208/55, GHQ West Africa, Weekly Military Review, no. 22, 7 January 1942.

41. PRO, WO 208/55, GHQ West Africa, Weekly Military Review, no. 32, 14 March 1942.

42. PRO, WO 208/55, Weekly Military Review, no. 32, 21 March 1942. See also Salfo Albert Balima, *Genèse de la Haute-Volta* (Ouagadougou: Presses Africaines, 1969), 80.

43. Balima, *Genèse de la Haute-Volta,* 80–82.

44. PRO, WO 208/55, GHQ West Africa, Intelligence Notes, no. 28.

45. PRO, FO 371/28247, WAPIC bulletin no. 12, 18 July 1941.

46. PRO, HS 3/73, WP to AD/A, 17 October 1941.

47. For background to the clash between "C," head of SIS, and "M" (Gubbins, director of operations, SOE), see Stafford, *Britain and European Resistance,* 294–99.

48. As far back as mid-April 1941, it was proposed that a representative of SIS (MI 6) should work jointly with the Franck Mission and attend the Governors' Conference. This arrangement appears not to have come in force. PRO, HS 3/79, memorandum to CEO (Jebb) and copy to CD (Nelson), 15 April 1941.

49. PRO, HS 3/74, anonymous document headed "SOE Missions in West Africa," 9 May 1942.

50. PRO, HS 3/79, "Note on the Collection of Political and Economic Intelligence in West Africa and the Special Conditions which govern this," n.d.

51. PRO, HS 3/73: "The role of SOE Organization in West Africa," by WP, 31 October 1941.

52. PRO, HS 3/73, D/CD (Hambro) to CD (Nelson), AD (Taylor) and AD/W, 15 November 1941.

53. PRO, HS 3/73, Menzies to Hambro, 29 November 1941.

54. PRO, HS 3/73, W.29 to Caesar, M, and WE, 1 December 1941.

55. PRO, HS 3/73, Memorandum headed "Sabotage—AOF," 16 December 1941.

56. PRO, HS 3/79, 17 December 1941.

57. PRO, HS 3/73, AD to CEO, 19 December 1941.

58. PRO, HS 3/79, telegram no. 1405 to Lagos, 5 January 1942.

59. PRO 3/74, "Policy," 13 April 1942; see West, *Secret War,* 86–87.

60. PRO, HS 3/79, document headed "Sabotage—AOF Policy and Directives of Frawest Mission," 26 February 1942.

61. PRO, HS 3/80, Wingate to Hambro, 11 April 1942; HS 3/74, policy statement, 13 April 1942.

62. PRO, HS 3/74, D/CD (Hambro) to ADW, and Caesar, 23 March 1942.

63. PRO, HS 3/80, Wingate to Hambro, 11 April 1942.

64. PRO, HS 3/79, Caesar to D/CD, 6 March 1942.

65. PRO, HS 3/73, secret memorandum circulated by D/CD, 16 February 1942.

66. PRO, HS 3/74, "Note by Lieut. Col. R. E. C. Wingate," 6 April 1942.

67. PRO, HS 3/74, "SOE Missions in West Africa," anonymous memo, 9 May 1942.

68. PRO, HS 3/74, "SOE Missions in West Africa," 9 May 1942.

69. PRO, HS 3/80, W.29 to WE, "Memorandum on Sabotage Work in West Africa with respect to the Zaria Meeting 28th March, 1942," 31 March 1942; cipher telegram of the same date; W.32 to W.33, 1 April 1942.

70. PRO, HS 3/74, "SOE Missions in West Africa," 9 May 1942.

71. Wingate, *Not in the Limelight*, 154–82.

72. PRO, HS 3/79, letter to Brigadier C. S. Vaile, DDMI, War Office, 23 May 1942, and WS to A/D, 24 May 1942.

73. PRO, HS 3/79, GOC-in-C, West Africa, to War Office, 6 June 1942.

74. For Nelson's resignation as CD, see West, "Secret War," 59.

75. PRO, HS 3/74, WP to CD, 8 June 1942.

76. PRO, HS 3/79, cipher telegram, Secretary of State for the Colonies to Governors' Conference, 7 July 1942; cipher telegram to Frawest, Lagos, 9 July 1942, sender unidentified.

77. R. Wingate, *Not in the Limelight*, 181–82.

78. PRO, HS 3/79, telegram to Caesar, 25 May 1942; see also "Revised Directive for the General Officer Commanding-in-Chief, West Africa," leaked in Caesar to WF and W.4, 8 August 1942: "You will appreciate that this is a most secret document which is being sent to you against all rules and regulations."

79. See, for example, Charles Jeffries, *The Colonial Empire and Its Civil Service* (Cambridge: Cambridge University Press, 1938), 73–75, 203–4.

80. For a useful account of Swinton's work in West Africa, see Bourret, *Gold Coast*, 156–64.

81. *West Africa*, 19 September 1942, 915.

82. PRO, HS 3/79, AD/E to D/CD, AD, et al., 10 April 1942.

83. PRO, HS 3/73, W (Franck) to CD (Nelson), Lagos, 15 July 1941, enclosing "Most Secret Memorandum. Synopsis," Lagos, 12 July 1941.

84. Page, *KAR*, 173–75.

85. Wingate, *Not in the Limelight*, passim.

86. PRO, HS 3/79, AD/W to CD, 25 June 1942.

87. PRO, HS 3/74, memo, 13 April 1942.

88. PRO, HS 3/80, Giffard to War Office, 1 July 1942.

89. PRO. HS 3/79, summary of telegram, 9 July 1942.

90. PRO, HS 3/79, WP to AD/W, Frawest Lagos, 8 July 1942.

91. PRO, HS 3/79, "Handing over notes: WP to WF," 9 July 1942.

92. PRO, HS 3/79, WP to WS, 21 May 1942.

93. PRO, HS 3/79, WF to Caesar, 23 July 1942.

94. Personal communication, J. S. Harris, 21 December 1995. See also, Jack Harris, "Anthropologist, Secret Agent, Witch-Hunt Victim, Entrepreneur," in *Anthrowatch* 5, no. 2 (fall 1997), 8–14.

95. PRO, HS 3/79, telegram, WF to Caesar, 10 August 1942.

96. PRO, HS 3/79, AD to Caesar, 13 August 1942; telegram to WF, 15 August 1942.

97. PRO, HS 3/79, "Joint Intelligence Organisation in West Africa," memo, 21 August 1942.

98. PRO, HS 3/74, "Report on Frawest Mission," AD to CD, 11 November 1942.

99. A detailed account of the Olokomeji Training School is contained in PRO, HS 3/80, WA, response to WF, 5 August 1942.

100. PRO, HS 3/80, WP to WF, 11 August 1942.

101. PRO, HS 3/80, "The Nominal Role of Olokomeji Training School," in reply to CD's telegram of 29 July 1942.

102. PRO, HS 3/80, WA to M/T, 19 September 1942. The problems that had beset Olokomeji are obliquely referred to as "2 grps. Mut." (possibly, "2 groups mutinied").

103. PRO, HS 3/80, W.30 to WF, "Nanwa Training School," report dated 29 November 1942.

104. PRO, HS 3/74, AD to CD, "Report on Frawest Mission," 11 November 1942.

105. For an amusing account of the tension between Army and SOE in a middle eastern context, see Hermione Ranfurly, *To War with Whitaker: The Wartime Diaries of the Countess of Ranfurly 1939–1945* (London: Arrow Books, 1998), 70–100. "Maybe," she wrote from Cairo on 1 December 1940, "someone should remind GHQ that there is a war on—and that truth is important."

Chapter 5

1. PRO, HS 3/79, "Handing over notes: WP to WF," 9 July 1942.

2. H. V. Wimshurst, pers. comm., 15 July 1994.

3. The Escort Police were the rough equivalent of the French Gendarmerie, a paramilitary organization operating outside the cities. During the war, they were usually stationed along the borders. Quarshie reported directly to "His Worship," DC Wenchi.

4. NAG-Sunyani, DAOW 1/6, [Wimshurst to Superintendant of Police, Kumasi], n.d.

5. Interview with Neil Ross, Edinburgh, 15 April 1996.

6. Ibid.

7. NAG-Sunyani, DAOW 1/6, Ross to FitzGerald, Wenchi, 2 June 1942.

8. H. V. Wimshurst, pers. comm., 20 June 1994.

9. Little is known about Vichy's recruitment of agents, but Holbrook refers to an account in the *Ashanti Pioneer* (26 June 1941) of the role of African chiefs, including "he of Abengourou," in running agents into the Gold Coast to gather information on its defenses. Holbrook, "The Impact of the Second World War," 74.

10. NAG-Sunyani, DAOW 1/5, DC Wenchi, to Franck Mission, Accra, 18 November 1941.

11. NAG-Sunyani, DAOW 1/6, Quarshie to Acting DC Wenchi, N. Ross, 17 March 1942, and "Prices of market produce and goods sold in the market, Bundugu," 24 March 1942.

12. NAG-Sunyani, DAOW 1/6, Quarshie to Acting DC Wenchi, two letters from Sampa, both 9 April 1942.

13. NAG-Sunyani, DAOW 1/5, Wimshurst to FitzGerald, 21 and 23 November 1941.

14. NAG-Sunyani, DAOW 1/5, McGee to Wimshurst, Anomabu Fort, 10 December 1941.

15. NAG-Sunyani, DAOW 1/5, Wimshurst to Officer in Charge, Anomabu Fort, 14 December 1941.

16. NAG-Sunyani, DAOW 1/6, Ross to FitzGerald, Wenchi, 2 June 1942.

17. NAG-Sunyani, DAOW 1/6, n.d..

18. H. V. Wimshurst, pers. comm., 15 July and 16 September 1994. On 28 December 1994, M. Tetelman, a Northwestern University researcher, visited Wimshurst on my behalf, at his home near Capetown. Wimshurst expanded on his rifle initiative by adding, "I started off by offering ten thousand francs to bring a rifle. They said fifteen thousand."

19. NAG-Sunyani, DAOW 1/5, Mothersill to DC Wenchi, 5 July 1941.

20. ANCI, Carton 2798, dossier V–7–6/43.

21. F. J. Amon d'Aby, *La Côte d'Ivoire dans la cité africaine* (Paris: Editions Larose, 1951), 41.

22. PRO, FO 371/28246, WAPIC bulletin no. 9, 24 May 1941, 9. For an excellent study of resistance in the AOF, see Akpo-Vaché, *L'AOF et la Seconde Guerre mondiale*, ch. 5, passim.

23. PRO, WO 208/55, Intelligence Notes, no. 10, May 1942.

24. Virginia Thompson and Richard Adloff, *French West Africa* (Palo Alto: Stanford University Press, 1957), 294–96, 500.

25. PRO, WO 208/55, GHQ West Africa. Intelligence Notes, no. 13. It will be apparent that a number of the French acronyms defy the interpretation of the writer, at least in the form they have come to us via British intelligence.

26. PRO, WO 208/55, Intelligence Notes, no. 42, 5 September 1942.

27. Rouch, "Migrations en Gold Coast," 55–56.

28. Ibid., 55.

29. PRO, FO 371/32078, de Gaulle to Gen. Sir Alan Brooke, 7 July 1942, with encl. of the same date; Brooke to de Gaulle, 15 July 1942; and MO.4, War Office, to W. N. McG. Hogg, Foreign Office, 14 August 1942.

30. NAG-Kumasi, ARG 1/1/188. Robert Parr to Anthony Eden, 11 March 1942, and Acting Governor, Gold Coast, to WAGON, Lagos, 20 March 1942; PRO, HS 3/74, Burns to Secretary of State for the Colonies, 24 March 1942.

31. NAG-Kumasi, "The Free French in the Gold Coast," ARG 1/1/188, Miln to Hawkesworth, 28 July 1942.

32. NAG-Kumasi, "The Free French Mission in the Gold Coast," ARG 1/1/188, Hawkesworth to Sir George London, Col. Sec., Accra, 20 July 1942.

33. PRO, HS 3/79, WF to Caesar, 27 August 1942.

34. NAG-Sunyani, DAOW 1/5, "Memorandum on Economic and Financial Subversion in French Togoland, Dahomey and Ivory Coast," n.d.

35. PRO, HS 3/96, W.33 to W, 8 January 1943. Fortes came to be highly regarded by SOE, to the extent that he was moved temporarily to Accra to take over the running of the Gold Coast Section in the autumn of 1942. PRO HS 3/74, CD to AD, 11 November 1942.

36. PRO, WO 208/55, Weekly Military Review, nos. 22 and 24, 7 and 21 January 1942. Also, Intelligence Notes, no. 27, app. B, 22 July 1942. Also NAG-Sunyani, DAOW 1/5, "Extracts from a report on Information, Police and Surete in AOF," 14 January 1942.

37. PRO, WO 208/55, Weekly Military Review, no. 24, 21 January 1942.

38. Necklaces and bracelets of glass beads.

39. Interview with Mamourou Camara, Bouna, 14 June 1986. See Nancy Lawler, "Soldiers of Misfortune: The *Tirailleurs Sénégalais* of the Côte d'Ivoire in World War Two" (Ph.D. diss., Northwestern University, 1988), 1179–83.

40. Interview with Kwadwo Bosompra, Kumasi, 4 April 1994.

41. NAG-Kumasi, 1112, "The Extent of Smuggling in the Western Province of Ashanti," 27 April 1939.

42. Bourret, *Gold Coast*, 158.

43. PRO, HS 3/74, "Report on Frawest Mission," AD to CD, 11 November 1942.

44. PRO, HS 3/74, "SOE Missions in West and East Africa," anonymous, 26 September 1942.

45. NAG-Kumasi, "The Free French Mission in the Gold Coast," ARG 1/1/188, Hawkesworth to Sir George London, Col. Sec., Accra, 20 July 1942.

46. NAG-Kumasi, "The Free French Mission in the Gold Coast," ARG 1/1/188, Hawkesworth to DCs Sunyani and Wenchi, 22 April 1942.

47. NAG-Kumasi, "The Free French Mission in the Gold Coast," ARG 1/1/188, Hawkesworth to Sir George London, Col. Sec., Accra, 20 July 1942.

48. NAG-Kumasi, "The Free French Mission in the Gold Coast," ARG 1/1/188, Miln to Hawkesworth, 28 July 1942.

49. Ibid.

50. NAG-Kumasi, "The Free French Mission in the Gold Coast," ARG 1/1/188, Hawkesworth to Colonial Secretary, 31 July 1942.

51. NAG-Kumasi, "The Free French Mission in the Gold Coast," ARG 1/1/188, C. Butler, Secretariat, Accra to Hawkesworth, 14 August 1942.

52. NAG-Kumasi, "The Free French Mission in the Gold Coast," ARG 1/1/188, N. E. Hedley-Dent to Hawkesworth, 31 August 1942.

53. NAG-Kumasi, "The Free French Mission in the Gold Coast," ARG 1/1/188, Hawkesworth to Colonial Secretary, 31 July 1942.

54. PRO, FO 371/28247, WAPIC bulletin no. 13, 13 August 1941, 8.

55. PRO, HS 3/79, extract 2 in report, WF (Lumby) to Caesar (Hanau), 27 August 1942.

56. PRO, HS 3/79, extract 1 in report, WF to Caesar, 27 August 1942.

57. Ibid.

58. ANCI, carton 1440, dossier XVII–15–24.

59. PRO, HS 3/79, WF to Caesar, 27 August 1942, enclosing minute of 24 August 1942.

60. PRO, HS 3/79, Colonial Secretary to Chief Commissioners and Commissioners, 31 August 1942.

61. NAG-Kumasi, "The Free French Mission in the Gold Coast," ARG 1/1/188, deciphered telegraph from Colonial Secretary to DCs, 12 November 1942.

62. NAG-Kumasi, "The Free French Mission in the Gold Coast," ARG 1/1/188, Colonial Secretary to Hawkesworth, 21 November 1942.

Chapter 6

1. NAG-Kumasi, 2922, text of broadcast by Brig. S. S. Butler, 24 October 1940.
2. NAG-Kumasi, 2922, letter from John Duncan, Dept. of Information, Accra, to W. A. S. Cole, Secretary to CCA Ashanti, 27 January 1940.
3. Wendell Holbrook, "British Propaganda in the Gold Coast," *Journal of African History* 26, no. 4 (1985): 351–52. See Holbrook's footnote. NAG-Accra, Adm 1/2/272, dispatch from governor to Secretary of State for the Colonies, 8 November 1943.
4. NAG-Kumasi, 2922, Duncan to W. A. Cole, Secretary to the CCA, 18 January 1940.
5. NAG-Kumasi, 2922, Cole to Duncan, 23 January 1940.
6. NAG-Sunyani, DAOW 1/6, FitzGerald to DC Wenchi, 18 May 1942.
7. Interview with T. E. Kyei, Kumasi, 30 March 1994.
8. Interview with Rev. Christian Baeta, retired professor of religions at the University of Ghana, 11 April 1994, Accra.
9. Interview with James Moxon, 17 March 1994.
10. NAG-Sunyani, DAOW 1/5, DC (Franck Mission) Salaga to DC Wenchi, 21 May 1941. Presumably copies of this document were sent to all DCs in the Gold Coast.
11. PRO, WAPIC bulletin no. 8, para. 31, 1 May 1941.
12. PRO, FO 371/28245, Speaight to Bourdillon, 12 June 1941.
13. Interview with Tuo Lielourou, Napiédougou, Côte d'Ivoire, 11 December 1985, see Lawler, "Soldiers of Misfortune," 1988, 727–32.
14. NAG-Kumasi, 2922, P. H. Canham, News Officer, CCA's office, Kumasi, to Information Officer, Accra, 11 March 1941.
15. NAG-Kumasi, 2922, minutes of meeting of Kumasi Broadcasting Committee, 9 August 1941.
16. Gold Coast Colony, *Legislative Council Debates* (Accra: Government Printing, 1940), 20 March 1940, 157.
17. Ibid., 158–59.
18. NAG-Sunyani, DAOW 1/5, "Broadcasting," L. J. Mothersill, Franck Mission, Salaga, to DC Wenchi, 5 June 1941.
19. NAG-Kumasi, 1161, Weekly Report, Kumasi Information Bureau, 4 May 1940.
20. Ibid.
21. NAG-Kumasi, 1161, Weekly Report, Kumasi Information Bureau, 11 May 1940.
22. NAG-Kumasi, 1161, Weekly Report, Kumasi Information Bureau, 18 May 1940.
23. NAG-Kumasi, 1161, Weekly Report, Kumasi Information Bureau, 25 May 1940.
24. NAG-Kumasi, 1161, Weekly Report, Kumasi Information Bureau, 15 June 1940.
25. NAG-Kumasi, 1161, Weekly Report, Kumasi Information Bureau, 22 June 1940.
26. NAG-Kumasi, 1161, Weekly Report, Kumasi Information Bureau, 29 June 1940.
27. Interview with Nanlougo Soro, M'Bala, Côte d'Ivoire, 10 December 1985.
28. Bourret, *Gold Coast*, 154.
29. Holbrook, "British Propaganda," 355–56.
30. My treatment of the propaganda machine should be read in conjunction with

that by Holbrook, "Impact of the Second World War," 92–155. These complement rather than contradict each other. Holbrook obtained much useful detail from the Ministry of Information files in the PRO, which I did not consult.

31. NAG-Kumasi, 2922, Miln to CCA Kumasi, 1 October 1941.

32. NAG-Kumasi, 2922, Miln to CCA, 8 April 1941.

33. NAG-Kumasi, 2922, Stewart-Cole to Information Officer, Accra, 28 May 1941.

34. NAG-Kumasi, 2922, Effiduasehene and Krontihene to CCA, [1941].

35. NAG-Kumasi, 2922, Millar-Craig to Information Officer, Accra, 18 August 1941.

36. NAG-Kumasi, ARG 1/1/189, "Memorandum on Propaganda for French Africans," 27 September 1941.

37. For an excellent study of wartime propaganda in Nigeria, see Peter Clarke, "The Impact of Anti-German Propaganda on the Development of Nationalism in Nigeria during the Second World War," paper delivered at Conference on Africa and the Second World War, SOAS, University of London, 24–25 May 1984.

38. NAG-Kumasi, 2922. J. Wilson, Dept. of Information, Accra, to News Officer, Kumasi, 14 August 1940; PRO, FO 371/28504, WAGON to Governor, Gold Coast, 8 March 1941; PRO, FO 371/32174, Resident Minister, Accra, to Secretary of State for the Colonies, 7 December 1942.

39. Dinan, *Politics of Persuasion*, 53.

40. NAG-Kumasi, "Propaganda Directed at French Colonies," ARG 1/1/189, memo, 7 August 1941.

41. PRO, FO 371/28245, Parr to R. L. Speaight, 29 March 1941.

42. NAG-Sunyani, DAOW 1/6, FitzGerald to DC Wenchi, 2 December 1941. Emphasis in original.

43. NAG-Kumasi, "Propaganda Directed at French Colonies," ARG 1/1/189, memo, 7 August 1941.

44. PRO, FO 371/28247, WAPIC bulletin no. 13, 13 August 1941, 8.

45. PRO, FO 371/28504, Bourdillon to Hodson, 9 March 1941.

46. PRO, FO 371/28248, WAPIC bulletin no. 14, 13 September 1941.

47. NAG-Sunyani, DAOW 1/6, FitzGerald to DC Wenchi, 6 May 1942.

48. PRO, HS 3/73, most secret, Lagos, 12 July 1941.

49. Pimlott, *Hugh Dalton*, 323.

50. NAG-Sunyani, DAOW 1/5, "Notes for Agents entrusted with Rumour dissemination," 17 July 1941.

51. NAG-Sunyani, DAOW 1/5, FitzGerald to DC Wenchi, 13 November 1941. These instructions not to alter the rumors in any way were repeated with every new list that appeared.

52. NAG-Sunyani, DAOW 1/5, most secret, FitzGerald to DC Wenchi, 13 November 1941.

53. NAG-Sunyani, DAOW 1/5, Economy Sunyani to DCs Sunyani, Wenchi, Bole, 1 September 1941.

54. NAG-Sunyani, DAOW 1/6, most secret, "Rumours for West Africa," 9 April 1942.

55. NAG-Sunyani, DAOW 1/6, most secret, "Rumours for West Africa," 19 May 1942.

56. PRO, FO 898/125, "SOE's Position in Rumour Dissemination on Behalf of the PWE Propaganda Mission in West Africa," 12 September 1942. Emphasis in original.

57. PRO, FO 898/125, "Terms of Reference (Propaganda) for Head of PERO," 15 September 1942.

58. NAG-Kumasi, ARG 1/1/189, "Propaganda Directed at French Colonies," Mothersill to CCA, 27 September 1941.

59. H. V. Wimshurst, pers. comm., 28 December 1994.

60. Lawler, "Soldiers of Misfortune," 1988, 1085–86: interview with Baba Camara, Bouna, Côte d'Ivoire, 25 March 1986.

61. Ibid, 1080–84: interview with Kangoute Katakie, Bouna, Côte d'Ivoire, 25 March 1986.

62. Holbrook draws attention to the fact that the *Ashanti Pioneer* (26 June 1941) "editorialized against the Vichy treatment of Gold Coasters in French territories." Holbrook, "Impact of the Second World War," 73–74.

63. PRO, WO 208/55, Weekly Military Review, no. 2, 20 August 1941.

64. United States National Archives (hereafter USNA), carton 851T.0032, "Memorandum Dealing with General Conditions on French Ivory Coast," 5 February 1942.

65. NAG-Sunyani, DAOW 1/5, "Information, Police and Surete in AOF", 14 January 1942.

66. PRO, FO 371/28247, WAPIC bulletin no. 13, 13 August 1941, 7.

67. PRO, HS 3/73, CD to X, 10 June 1941

68. PRO, FO 898/125, confidential memo from KEM(?) to Lemond, Accra, 4 March 1942.

69. Dalton, *Second World War Diary,* xxi–xxii, 108.

70. PRO, FO 371/28245, WAPIC bulletin no. 6, 3 April 1941. For an excellent overview of AOF propaganda, see also Akpo-Vaché, *L'AOF et la Seconde Guerre mondiale,* 80–90.

71. For a general discussion of conditions in the Côte d'Ivoire during the Vichy era, see Lawler, *Soldiers of Misfortune,* ch. 6.

72. Ibid., 129–30.

73. PRO, WO 173/136, "Weekly Intelligence Summary," 15 August 1941.

74. PRO, WO 173/136, "Weekly Intelligence Summary," 7 November 1941.

75. ANCI, carton 2801, dossier V–15–9/151, Propaganda leaflet No. 113.

76. ANCI, carton 2801, dossier V–15–9/151. Several other examples of Vichy leaflets and propaganda messages in English.

77. PRO, FO 371.28245, WAPIC bulletin no. 8, app. A, "Extracts from French Bulletins," 1 May 1941.

78. USNA, 851t.00, OSS, report of interview with a South African missionary repatriated from Bobo-Dioulasso, 18 September 1942.

79. Daniel Chénet, *Qui a sauvé l'Afrique?* (Paris: l'Elan, 1949), 113.

80. USNA, 851t.00, OSS, report of interview with a South African missionary repatriated from Bobo-Dioulasso, 18 September 1942.

81. USNA, 851t.20/30, memo 166, American Consulate in Dakar to the Secretary of State. 11/09/42; also 851t.20/36, memo 185, 30/09/42.

82. PRO, FO 371/28245, WAPIC bulletin no. 8, 1 May 1941.

83. PRO, FO 371/28247, WAPIC bulletin no. 12, 18 July 1941.

84. Ibid.

85. *West Africa,* 6 September 1941, 863.

86. *West Africa,* 18 July 1941, 684.

87. Bourret, *Gold Coast,* 152.

88. Interview with T. E. Kyei, Kumasi, 30 March 1994.

89. NAG-Sunyani, DOAS 2/2, letter to "Nana," 17 June 1941. "High Life" was a style of dance music that developed in the Gold Coast between the wars.

90. *West Africa,* report of letter from Brig. C. E. M. Richards, Gold Coast Brigade, to F. A. B. Johnston, 26 July 1941, 718.

91. Mrs. M. Griffiths, Secretary of the 218 Gold Coast Squadron Association, pers. comm., 12 January 1999.

92. *West Africa,* 29 August 1942, 833.

93. *Gold Coast Gazette,* 22 February 1941, Gazette Notice no. 212.

94. *West Africa,* 22 February 1941.

95. Interview with S. K. Boateng, Kumase, 30 March 1994.

96. *West Africa,* 3 May 1941, 428.

97. PRO, HS 3/74, Clifford to CD, 8 June 1942; HS 3/79, "Handing over notes: WP to WF," 9 July 1942.

98. Osafroadu Amankwatia, "Ashanti Conquered—In What War?" *Ashanti Pioneer,* 16 February 1940.

99. See Holbrook, "Impact of the Second World War," 101–2, citing NAG-Accra, ADM 1/2/258, encl. in Governor to Secretary of State for the Colonies, 29 May 1940. Nana Sir Osei Agyeman Prempeh II was being very conciliatory. For the perfidious role played by the British in the overthrow of Nana Agyeman Prempeh I, see most recently, Ivor Wilks, "Asante at the End of the Nineteenth Century: Setting the Record Straight," *Ghana Studies* 3 (2000).

100. Holbrook, "British Propaganda," 359–60.

Chapter 7

1. An earlier and shorter version of the chapter appeared as Nancy Lawler, "The Crossing of the Gyaman to the Cross of Lorraine: Wartime Politics in West Africa, 1941–1942," *African Affairs* (1997): 96, 53–71.

2. French writers tend to prefer the form Abron, British writers, Brong. Gyaman, the name of the westernmost Abron or Brong state, often occurs in English sources as Jaman. Older French sources seldom refer to Gyaman but to the *royaume Abron.*

3. See esp. Emmanuel Terray, *Une histoire du royaume Abron du Gyaman: Des origines à la conquête coloniale* (Paris: Karthala, 1995; originally, doctorat d'état, Université de Paris, 5 vols., 1984).

4. Wilks, *Asante in the Nineteenth Century*, 22; Ivor Wilks, Nehemia Levtzion, and Bruce Haight, *Chronicles From Gonja* (Cambridge: Cambridge University Press, 1986), 126–27; Terray, *Histoire*, 427–39.

5. Wilks, *Asante in the Nineteenth Century*, 287–95, 621–26; Terray, *Histoire*, 879–908.

6. Wilks, *Asante in the Nineteenth Century*, 301–305.

7. Anglo-French agreement of 1893, modified by the Boundary Commission 1903.

8. Planning Committee, Accra, *Papers Relating to the Restoration of the Ashanti Confederacy* (Accra: Planning Committee, 1935; reprint, Kumasi: Planning Committee for the Celebration of the Golden Jubilee of the Restoration of Asanteman, 1984); Omanhene Kwami Busiah to DC Wenchi, Drobo, 23 September 1932, 92–93; Sumahene Kwabena Kwadu et. al to DC Wenchi, Sampa, June 1993, 95–96.

9. Interview with Nana Yaw Kran, Sunyani, 6 April 1994.

10. ANCI, report, 16 February 1940, carton 4018, dossier VI—13/3.

11. French documents of the period always used the form Kouadio, while British sources used Kojo for the Twi term Kwadwo. Adjoumani is used by the former for the Twi term Agyeman. In the same way, the French Kouame Adingra is the English Kwame Adinkra. I have taken the simple way out by following the practices of Terray (in *Histoire*); that is, by referring to them as Kwadwo Agyeman and Kwame Adinkra. Adinkra is usually styled Prince, a translation of the Twi *Oheneba*, meaning son (or daughter) of a king.

12. Henry B. Cole, "March of the Brongs," *Life*, 23 March 1942, 14–15.

13. NAG-Sunyani, DAOW 1/5, "Intelligent Report," Quarshie to Wimshurst, 27 January 1942.

14. PRO, FO 371/28248, WAPIC bulletin no. 14, 13 September 1941. Presumably the geographical insert as to Bondoukou's location was for the information of the other three West African Colonial governors!

15. Ibid.

16. NAG-Sunyani, DAOW 1/5, "Confidential Report from the Ivory Coast," 29 December 1941.

17. NAG-Sunyani, DAOW 1/5. The references to "the whole Buntuku" and to "the Buntukuman" are to the *cercle* of Bondoukou, of which Gyaman was part.

18. Ibid., draft of secret note written by Wimshurst, 25 November 1941.

19. NAG-Sunyani, DAOW 1/6, copy of letter from Acting Governor, Accra, to Chief Commissioner's Office Kumasi, 1 April 1941, forwarded to DC Wenchi. The original policy statement has not been found, but was presumably issued via the Colonial Office.

20. NAG-Sunyani, DAOW 1/5, letter to DC Wenchi, 19 December 1941.

21. NAG-Sunyani, RAO 2/14, Kwadwo Agyeman to DC Wenchi, 15 December 1943, recalling the circumstances of the earlier meeting.

22. Interview with Neil Ross, Edinburgh, 15 April 1996.

23. NAG-Sunyani, DAOW 1/5, Miln to FitzGerald, 5 January 1942.

24. PRO, WO 208/55, Weekly Military Review, no. 25, 28 Jan 1942.

25. NAG-Kumasi, "The Free French in the Gold Coast," ARG /1/1/188, letter, Colonial Secretary to CCA, 10 April 1942.

26. Interview with Neil Ross, 15 April 1996.

27. NAG-Sunyani, DAOW 1/5, "Intelligent Report," Quarshie to Wimshurst, 27 January 1942.

28. Hubert Deschamps, *Roi de la brousse: Mémoires d'autres mondes* (Paris: Berger-Levrault, 1975), 254–55.

29. Amon d'Aby, *Côte d'Ivoire*, 41.

30. Terray, *Histoire*, 8.

31. NAG-Sunyani, DAOW 1/5, Quarshie to Wimshurst, 27 January 1942; DAOW 1/6, Quarshie to Ross, 17 May 1942; interviews with Kwadwo Bosompra, Kumasi, 4 April 1994, and Nana Yaw Kran, Sunyani, 6 April 1994.

32. *West Africa*, 7 February 1942, 104. Another, slightly less fevered account of the departure may be found in *West Africa*, 4 April 1942, 304. In the latter, Koadio has been Akanized to Kojo.

33. NAG-Sunyani, DAOW 1/5, "Intelligent Report," Quarshie to Wimshurst, 27 January 1942.

34. Interview with Kwadwo Bosompra, Kumasi, 4 April 1994.

35. Interview with Nana Yaw Kran, Sunyani, 6 April 1994.

36. Interview with Kwadwo Bosompra, Kumasi, 4 April 1994.

37. Interview with Nana Yaw Kran, Sunyani, 6 April 1994.

38. Appointed undersecretary to Liberian President Barclay in 1939, he had been imprisoned in 1940, following rumors that the British, suspicious of Barclay's supposed pro-German sympathies, were behind a plot to overthrow the government. Cole appealed for help to British Consul General Arthur Ponsonby, sending him information of Nazi activities in Liberia. Able to buy himself out, Cole was released on Christmas Eve 1940 and managed to get to the Gold Coast. NAG-Accra, ADM/12/1/123, Cole to Governor Hodson, 28 May 1941, and Mogue to Hodson, 18 September 1941.

39. Cole, "March of the Brongs," 14–15.

40. NAG-Accra, ADM/12/1/123, Cole to Governor Hodson, 28 May 1941, and Mogue to Hodson, 18 September 1941.

41. Amon d'Aby, *Côte d'Ivoire*, 41.

42. Interview with Nana Yaw Kran, Sunyani, 6 April 1942.

43. NAG-Kumasi, ARG 1/1/188, Durity to Hawkesworth, 27 April 1942.

44. NAG-Kumasi, ARG 1/1/188, "The Free French Mission in the Gold Coast," Hewson to CCA, 10 May 1942.

45. NAG-Kumasi, ARG 1/1/188, "The Free French Mission in the Gold Coast," D. S. Mackay to CCA, 27 April 1942.

46. These agents included the mistress of the chief clerk in the commandant's office.

47. NAG-Sunyani, DAOW 1/5, "Intelligent Report," Quarshie to Wimshurst, 27 January 1942.

48. NAG-Sunyani, DAOW 1/5, "Suspect Cautioned Statement," 30 January 1942.

49. Interview with Kwadwo Bosompra, Kumasi, 4 April 1994.

50. NAG-Sunyani, DAOW 1/5, Quarshie to Superintendent of Police, 18 February 1942.

51. NAG-Sunyani, DAOW 1/6, "Confidential Report," Quarshie to Wimshurst, 10 February 1942.

52. NAG-Sunyani, DAOW 1/6, "Confidential Report," Quarshie to Wimshurst, 30 March 1942.

53. Deschamps, *Roi de la brousse,* 254–55.

54. NAG-Sunyani, DAOW 1/6, "Confidential Report," Quarshie to Wimshurst, 30 March 1942; "Bonduku Commandant escaped from gun shot." Quarshie to Ross, 26 April 1942.

55. Jean Loucou, "La deuxième guerre mondiale et ses effets en Côte d'Ivoire," *Annales de l'Université d'Abidjan,* 1, D (1980): 189.

56. NAG-Sunyani, DAOW 1/6, Quarshie to Ross, 26 April 1942.

57. USNA, 851T.20/30, memo no. 166 from American Consulate in Dakar, 11 September 1942.

58. NAG-Kumasi, ARG 1/1/188, "The Free French in the Gold Coast," Superintendent C. S. Durity to CCA, 27 April 1942.

59. NAG-Kumasi, ARG 1/1/188, "The Free French in the Gold Coast," Miln to CCA, 25 June 1942.

60. NAG-Sunyani, DAOW 1/6, Hawkesworth to Assistant Chief Commissioner, 27 April 1942; ACC to Wimshurst, 27 April 1942; Quarshie to Wimshurst, [early June 1942?].

61. NAG-Kumasi, "The Free French Mission in the Gold Coast." ARG 1/1/188, "Statement by Kwaku Adinkra of Kyenti in the Gold Coast," attached to DC Miln's report of 25 June 1942.

62. NAG-Kumasi, "The Free French Mission in the Gold Coast." ARG 1/1/188, Miln to CCA, 25 June 1942.

63. NAG-Sunyani, DAOW 1/6, Quarshie to Superintendent of Police, 18 February 1942.

64. NAG-Sunyani, DAOW 1/6, "Confidential Report," Quarshie to Wimshurst, 30 March 1942.

65. NAG-Sunyani, DAOW 1/6, Quarshie to Ross, 9 May 1942.

66. NAG-Sunyani, DAOW 1/6, Quarshie to Ross, 3 July 1942.

67. USNA, 851T.20/30, memo no. 166 from American Consulate in Dakar, 11 September 1942.

68. NAG-Sunyani, RAO 2/14, Kwadwo Agyeman to DC Wenchi, 15 December 1943.

69. NAG-Sunyani, RAO 2/14, Ross to CCA, Kumasi, 10 January 1944.

70. That is, "son of a king," and therefore in a matrilineal society such as the Gyaman unable by custom (despite Yaw Kran's observation) to succeed his father.

71. A slight case of telescoping. Adinkra indeed became a deputy in the French Assembly, but not until 1946.

72. Interview with NanaYaw Kran, Sunyani, 6 April 1942.

73. NAG-Sunyani, DOAS 2/2, Adinkra to DC Wenchi, 23 July 1945.

74. NAG-Sunyani, DOAS 2/2, DC Wenchi to CCA, 30 July 1945.

75. NAG-Sunyani, DOAS 2/2, Adinkra to Asantehene, 31 July 1945.

76. NAG-Sunyani, DOAS 2/2, Acting DC Sunyani to CCA, Kumasi, 4 September 1945.

77. PRO, HS 3/74, Clifford to Hambro, 8 June 1942.

78. PRO, HS 3/79, "Handing over notes: WP to WF," 9 July 1942.

Chapter 8

1. PRO, WO 32/16229, Swinton, "Occupied Enemy Territory Administration," 27 September 1942.

2. Ibid.

3. PRO, WO 32/16229, Vice Chairman, Imperial General Staff to Permanent Undersecretary, 29 October 1942; (illegible signature) to Permanent Undersecretary, 6 November 1942.

4. Lawler, *Soldiers of Misfortune,* 156–63.

5. *La Côte d'Ivoire Chrétienne,* 9 November 1942; and see Lawler, *Soldiers of Misfortune,* 163–64.

6. PRO, HS 3/74, AD to CD, "Report on Frawest Mission," 11 November 1942.

7. Ibid.

8. G. Ward Price, *Giraud and the African Scene* (New York: Macmillan, 1944), 123–24; M. R. D. Foot, *SOE in France* (Frederick, Md.: University Publications of America, 1984), 220–21.

9. For Bergeret's equivocal position vis-à-vis Vichy in this period, see Peter Tomkins, *The Murder of Admiral Darlan: A Study in Conspiracy* (New York: Simon and Schuster, 1965), 63–66.

10. See, for example, Lawler, *Soldiers of Misfortune,* 154–68.

11. PRO, WO 208/55, "West Africa Command Military Review," no. 13, 6 January 1943.

12. PRO, FO 371/36187, telegram from Flexer to State Department, Washington D.C., n.d., but a copy of relevant passages appeared in "Situation in French West Africa" report of 8 February 1943.

13. *West Africa,* 28 November 1942, 1151.

14. Ibid.

15. For a full account of the machinations involved in the assassination, see, for example, Tomkins, *Murder of Admiral Darlan.*

16. Nigel West, *Secret War: The Story of SOE, Britain's Wartime Sabotage Organisation* (London: Hodder and Stoughton, 1992), 135–36.

17. See Lawler, *Soldiers of Misfortune,* 156–67; also Charles Messenger, *The Tunisian Campaign* (Shepperton, Surrey: Ian Allen, 1982); and Anthony Clayton, *France, Soldiers, and Africa* (London: Brassey's, 1988), 137–45.

18. PRO, HS 3/74, coded telegram from Accra, 20 November 1942.

19. PRO, HS 3/74, coded telegram sent to Cairo, 27 November 1942.

20. PRO, HS 3/74, W.31 to AD.4, 25 November 1942. The reference to the *Légion des anciens combattants* is inaccurate. The correct name of this organization formed during the Vichy era was the Légion des Combattants et Volontaires. See Lawler, *Soldiers of Misfortune,* 130–31, 164.

21. PRO, HS 3/74, coded telegram sent to Cairo, 27 November 1942.

22. PRO, HS 3/74, AD.4 to ADU, 2 December 1942.

23. PRO, HS 3/74, CD to WF, 14 December 1942.

24. PRO, HS 3/96, WF to CD, 13 January 1943.

25. PRO, HS 3/73, summary of activities of Franck Mission, 1 March 1941, attached to document headed "West Africa," [after July 1944].

26. There is some question as to whether or not Franck did indeed have a strong accent. Basil Davidson, who had served in SOE and met Franck several times and was later to become a distinguished Africanist, laughed when I asked him about Franck's accent. He accused me of regarding Louis Franck as though he were Hercule Poirot.

27. Peter Wilkinson and Joan Astley, *Gubbins* (London: Leo Cooper, 1993), 201.

28. Foot, *SOE: An Outline History,* 245–46.

29. Académie des Sciences d'Outre-Mer, *Hommes et destins: Dictionnaire biographique d'outre-mer,* 10 vols. (Paris: Académie des Sciences d'Outre-Mer, 1975–1995), 4:81–87.

30. NAG-Kumasi, ARG 1/1/192, Governor's message, 23 May 1944.

31. For the complete story of the West African Expeditionary Force in Burma, see Haywood and Clarke, *Royal West African Frontier Force,* chs. 10, 11, 12, 13, passim.

Chapter 9

1. Niall Ferguson, ed., *Virtual History: Alternatives and Counterfactuals* (New York: Basic Books, 1999), 87. Emphasis in original.

2. Robert Cowley, ed. *"What If?" The World's Foremost Military Historians Imagine What Might Have Been"* (New York: Putnam, 1999), xii.

3. PRO, HS 3/74, "SOE Mission in West and East Africa," 26 September 1942.

4. In Twi, *nnonkofo* refers to people from the north of Ghana and beyond, and particularly to those practicing facial scarification. Many of the Tirailleurs Sénégalais were recruited from areas of the AOF that had such practices. In the context in which the Asantehene here used the term, it is derogatory.

5. See *Ghana Nationalist,* 20 October 1954. In October 1954 high officials of the CPP decided to suggest to the Asantehene that "he be made the Monarch of the Gold Coast."

6. Haywood and Clarke, *Royal West African Frontier Force,* 97–104.

7. PRO, HS 3/74, AD to CD, "Report on Frawest Mission," 11 November 1942.

Bibliography

Works Cited

Aboagye, Festus B. *The Ghana Army: A Concise Contemporary Guide to Its Centennial Regimental History, 1897–1999.* Accra: Sedco Enterprise, 1999.

Académie des Sciences d'Outre-Mer. *Hommes et Destins: Dictionnaire biographique d'Outre-Mer.* 10 vols. Paris: Académie des Sciences d'Outre-Mer, 1975–1995.

Akota, B. A. *Struggle against Dictatorship.* Kumasi: Payless Printing Press, 1992.

Akpo-Vaché, Catherine. *L'AOF et la Seconde Guerre mondiale (septembre 1939–octobre 1945).* Paris: Editions Karthala, 1996.

Amankwatia, Osafroadu. "Ashanti Conquered—In What War?" *Ashanti Pioneer,* 16 February 1940.

Amon d'Aby, F. J. *La Côte d'Ivoire dans la cité Africaine.* Paris: Editions Larose, 1951.

Annet, Armand. *Aux heures troublées de l'Afrique française, 1939–1943.* Le Mans: Editions du Conquistador, 1952.

Balima, A. S. *Genèse de la Haute-Volta.* Ouagadougou: Presses Africaines, 1969.

Bening, R. B. "The Definition of the International Boundaries of Northern Ghana, 1888–1904." *Transactions of the Historical Society of Ghana* 14, no. 2 (1973): 229–61.

Bingley, John. *Mr. Khoury.* London: Constable, 1952.

Bourgi, Robert. *Le Général de Gaulle et l'Afrique noire, 1940–1969.* Paris: Nouvelles Editions Africaines, 1980.

Bourret, Florence M. *The Gold Coast: A Survey of the Gold Coast and British Togoland, 1919–1946.* London: Oxford University Press, 1949.

Brown, Anthony Cave. *"C": The Secret Life of Sir Stewart Graham Menzies, Spymaster to Winston Churchill.* New York: Macmillan, 1987.

Brown, J. A. *Eagles Strike: The Campaigns of the South African Air Force in Egypt, Cyrenaica, Libya, Tunisia, Tripolitania and Madagascar, 1941–1943.* Cape Town: Purnell, 1974.

"Canada 'Full Out' in the Air." *War Illustrated* 4, no. 76 (14 February 1941).

Clarke, F. A. S. "The Development of the West African Forces in the Second World War." *Army Quarterly,* October 1947.

Clarke, Peter. "The Impact of Anti-German Propaganda on the Development of Nationalism in Nigeria during the Second World War." Paper delivered at the Conference on Africa and the Second World War, School of Oriental and African Studies, University of London, 24–25 May 1984.

———. *West Africans at War. 1914–18. 1939–45. Colonial Propaganda and its Cultural Aftermath.* London: Ethnographica, 1986.

Clayton, A. *France, Soldiers, and Africa.* London: Brassey's, 1988.

Clifford, Hugh. *The Gold Coast Regiment in the East African Campaign.* London: John Murray, 1920.

Clostermann, Pierre. *Flames in the Sky.* Trans. Oliver Berthoud. Harmondsworth: Penguin, 1958.

Cole, Henry B. "March of the Brongs." *Life* (23 March 1942): 14–15.

Cowley, Robert, ed. *"What If?" The World's Foremost Military Historians Imagine What Might Have Been.* New York: Putnam, 1999.

Dalton, Hugh. *The Second World War Diary of Hugh Dalton.* Ed. Ben Pimlott. London: Jonathon Cape, 1986.

Deacon, Richard. *British Secret Service.* Rev. ed. London: Grafton Books, 1991.

de Gaulle, Charles. *The Call to Honour 1940–1942.* Vol. 1 of *War Memoirs.* Trans. Jonathan Griffin. London: Collins, 1955.

———. *The Complete War Memoirs of Charles de Gaulle.* Trans. R. Howard. New York: Simon and Schuster, 1968.

Deschamps, Hubert. *Roi de la Brousse: Memoires d'autres mondes.* Paris: Berger-Levrault, 1975.

Dinan, Desmond. *The Politics of Persuasion: British Policy and French African Neutrality, 1940–1942.* Boston: University Press of America, 1988.

Downs, W. D. *With the Nigerians in German East Africa.* London: Methuen, 1919.

Draper, Theodore. *The Six Weeks War. France, May 10–June 25, 1940.* New York: Book Find Club, 1944.

Echenberg, M. *Colonial Conscripts: The Tirailleurs Sénégalais in French West Africa, 1857–1960.* Portsmouth, N.H.: Heinemann, 1991.

Farwell, B. *The Great War in Africa (1914–1918).* New York: Norton, 1986.

Ferguson, Niall, ed. *Virtual History: Alternatives and Counterfactuals.* New York: Basic Books, 1999.

Foot, M. R. D. *S.O.E.: An Outline History of the Special Operations Executive, 1940–46.* London: BBC, 1984.

———. *SOE in France.* Frederick, Md.: University Publications of America, 1984.

Gamble, James. Editorial in *West African Review,* April 1940.

Gilbert, Martin. *Finest Hour: Winston S. Churchill, 1939–1941.* London: Heinemann/Minerva, 1983.

Gold Coast Colony. *The Gold Coast Handbook, 1937.* London: Gold Coast Colony, 1937.

———. *Legislative Council Debates.* Accra: Government Printing Department, 1940.

Gorges, E. H. *The Great War in West Africa.* Plymouth: Mayflower Press, [early 1920s].

Great Britain. Colonial Office. *Annual Report on the Gold Coast, 1946.* Colonial Reports Annual. London: HMSO, 1946.

———. *Annual Report on the Social and Economic Progress of the People of the Gold Coast, 1938–39.* London: HMSO, 1939.

Greene, Graham. *The Heart of the Matter.* New York: Viking, 1948.

Harris, Jack. "Anthropologist, Secret Agent, Witch-Hunt Victim, Entrepreneur." *Anthro-watch* 5, no. 2 (1997): 8–14.

Harris, John. *A Funny Place to Hold a War.* London: Book Club Associates, 1984.

Haywood, A., and F. A. S. Clarke. *The History of the Royal West African Frontier Force.* Aldershot: Gale and Polden, 1964.

Hinsley, F. H., et al. *British Intelligence in the Second World War: Its Influence on Strategy and Operations.* 5 vols. London: HMSO, 1979.

Hitchcock, William J. "Pierre Boisson, French West Africa, and the Postwar *Epuration:* A Case from the Aix Files." *French Historical Studies* 24, no. 2 (2001): 305–41.

Holbrook, Wendell. "British Propaganda in the Gold Coast." *Journal of African History* 26, no. 4 (1985): 347–61.

———. "The Impact of the Second World War on the Gold Coast, 1939–1945." Ph.D. diss., Princeton University, 1978.

Howard, Michael. *British Intelligence in the Second World War.* Vol. 5, *Strategic Deception.* London: HMSO, 1990.

Howard-Williams, Ernest Leslie. *Something New Out of Africa.* London: Pitman and Sons, 1934.

Jeffries, Charles. *The Colonial Empire and Its Civil Service.* Cambridge: Cambridge University Press, 1938.

Kent, John. *The Internationalization of Colonialism: Britain, France, and Black Africa, 1939–1956.* Oxford: Clarendon Press, 1992.

Killingray, David. "The British Military Presence in West Africa." Oxford Development Records Project, report no. 3. Oxford: Rhodes House Library, 1983.

———. "The Colonial Army in the Gold Coast: Official Policy and Local Response, 1890–1947." Ph.D. diss., London University, 1982.

———. "Guarding the Extending Frontier: Policing the Gold Coast, 1865–1913." In *Policing the Empire,* ed. D. Anderson and D. Killingray. Manchester: Manchester University Press, 1991.

———. "Military and Labour Recruitment in the Gold Coast during the Second World War." *Journal of African History* 23, no. 1 (1982): 83–95.

Kirk-Greene, A. H. M. *A Biographical Dictionary of the British Colonial Service, 1939–1966.* London: Hans Zell, 1991.

Kum'a N'Dumbe, Alexandre, III. *Hitler voulait l'Afrique*. Paris: Editions d'Harmattan, 1980.

Lanning, E. C. "The Royal West African Frontier Force." *Newsletter of the Friends of the National Army Museum* 6, no. 2 (1995).

Lawler, Nancy Ellen. *Soldiers of Misfortune: Ivoirien Tirailleurs of World War II*. Athens: Ohio University Press, 1992.

———. "Soldiers of Misfortune: The Tirailleurs Sénégalais of the Côte d'Ivoire in World War II." Ph.D. diss., Northwestern University, 1988.

Leeds, Allen. *Long Ago and Far Away: Gold Coast Days, 1939–1958*. Upton upon Severn: Square One Publications, 1998.

Lengyel, Emil. *Dakar: Outpost of Two Hemispheres*. Garden City, N.Y.: Garden City Publishing, 1941.

Loucou, Jean. "La deuxième guerre mondiale et ses effets en Côte d'Ivoire." *Annales de l'Université d'Abidjan* 1, D (1980).

Louveau, Edmond. *"Au Bagne." Entre les griffes de Vichy et de la milice*. Bamako: Soudan Imprimerie, 1947.

MacMillan, Allister, ed. *The Red Book of West Africa: Historical and Descriptive, Commercial and Industrial Facts, Figures and Resources*. 1920. Reprint, London: Frank Cass, 1968.

Martin du Gard, Maurice. *La carte impériale: Histoire de la France outre-mer, 1940–1945*. Paris: André Bonne, 1949.

McCormack, Robert. "The Politics and Economics of Air Transport Development in West Africa, 1919–1939." Paper presented at the annual meeting of the Canadian Association of African Studies, York University, February 1975.

———. "War and Change: Air Transport in British Africa, 1939–1946." *Canadian Journal of History* 24 (December 1989).

Messenger, Charles. *The Tunisian Campaign*. Shepperton, Surrey: Ian Allen, 1982.

Metcalfe, G. E. *Great Britain and Ghana: Documents of Ghana History, 1807–1957*. Legon: University of Ghana, 1964.

Mortimer, Edward. *France and the Africans, 1944–1960: A Political History*. London: Faber and Faber, 1969.

Page, Malcolm. *KAR: A History of the King's African Rifles*. London: Leo Cooper, 1998.

———, ed. *Africa and the First World War*. New York: St. Martin's Press, 1987.

Paxton, R. O. *Vichy France: Old Guard and New Order, 1940–1944*. New York: Knopf, 1972.

Pearce, Robert. *Sir Bernard Bourdillon: The Biography of a Twentieth-Century Colonialist*. London: Kensal Press, 1987.

Pearcy, Arthur, Jr. "Douglas Dakota MK I–IV." *Profile 220*. Windsor, Berkshire: Profile Publications, 1970.

Pickering, Jim. "The Takoradi Route." *FlyPast*, part 1, July 1997: 26–29; part 2, August 1997: 34–37.

Pimlott, Ben. *Hugh Dalton.* London: Jonathon Cape, 1985.

Planning Committee, Accra. *Papers Relating to the Restoration of the Ashanti Confederacy.* Accra: Planning Committee, 1935.

Price, G. Ward. *Giraud and the African Scene.* New York: Macmillan, 1944.

Ranfurly, Hermione. *To War with Whitaker: The Wartime Diaries of the Countess of Ranfurly, 1939–1945.* London: Arrow Books, 1998.

Ray, D. W. "The Takoradi Route: Roosevelt's Prewar Venture beyond the Western Hemisphere." *Journal of American History* 62 (September 1975).

Richards, Denis. *The Fight at Odds.* Vol. 1, *Royal Air Force, 1939–1945.* London: HMSO, 1953.

Rouch, Jean. "Migrations en Gold Coast." *Journal de la Société des Africanistes* 26, nos. 1–2 (1956).

Rubin, Gerry R. *Durban 1942: A British Troopship Revolt.* London: Hambledon Press, 1992.

Russell, A. C. *Gold Coast to Ghana: A Happy Life in West Africa.* Durham, England: Pentland Press, 1996.

Spears, E. *Fulfilment of a Mission: The Spears Mission to Syria and Lebanon, 1941–1944.* Hamden, Conn.: Archon Books, 1977; London: Leo Cooper, 1977.

Stafford, David. *Britain and European Resistance, 1940–1945: A Survey of the Special Operations Executive, with Documents.* London: Macmillan, 1980.

Stevenson, William. *The Man Called Intrepid: The Secret War.* New York: Harcourt Brace Jovanovich, 1976.

Tedder, Arthur William. *With Prejudice: The War Memoirs of Marshal of the Royal Air Force Lord Tedder, 1939–1945.* London: Cassell, 1966.

Terraine, John. *The Right of the Line: The Royal Air Force in the European War, 1939–1945.* Ware, Hertfordshire: Wordsworth Editions, 1997.

Terray, Emmanuel. "Une Histoire du Royaume Abron du Gyaman: Des origines à la conquête coloniale." Doctorat d'état, Université de Paris, 1984. 5 vols. Reprint, Paris: Editions Karthala, 1995.

Thompson, Virginia, and Richard Adloff. *French West Africa.* Palo Alto: Stanford University Press, 1957.

Tomkins, Peter. *The Murder of Admiral Darlan: A Study in Conspiracy.* New York: Simon and Schuster, 1965.

Vincent, Jean-Noël. *Les Forces Françaises Libres en Afrique, 1940–1943.* Paris: Ministère de l'Armée de Terre, Service Historique, 1983.

Wallace, Edgar. *Sanders of the River.* London: Hodder and Stoughton, 1926.

West, Nigel. *Secret War: The Story of SOE, Britain's Wartime Sabotage Organisation.* London: Hodder and Stoughton, 1992.

Wilkinson, Peter, and Joan Astley. *Gubbins.* London: Leo Cooper, 1993.

Wilks, Ivor. "Asante at the End of the Nineteenth Century: Setting the Record Straight." *Ghana Studies* 3 (2000).

————. *Asante in the Nineteenth Century: The Structure and Evolution of a Political Order*. London: Cambridge University Press, 1975.

————. *A Portrait of Otumfuo Opoku Ware II as a Young Man*. Ghana: Anansesem Publications, 1995.

Wilks, I., N. Levtzion, and B. Haight. *Chronicles from Gonja: A Tradition of West African Muslim Historiography*. Cambridge: Cambridge University Press, 1986.

Williams, John. *The Guns of Dakar: September 1940*. London: Heinemann, 1976.

Wingate, R. E. C. *Not in the Limelight*. London: Hutchinson, 1959.

Wolseley, Sir Garnet. "The Negro as a Soldier." *Fortnightly Review* 44, 1 December 1888.

Schedule of Interviews

(Texts of all Lawler interviews are on deposit at the Melville J. Herskovits Memorial Library, Northwestern University, Evanston, Illinois.)

Name	Date of Interview	Location
Adinkra, Kofi	6 April 1994	Sunyani
Baba Camara	25 March 1986	Bouna, Côte d'Ivoire
Baeta, Rev. Christian	11 April 1994	Accra
Boahen, A. Adu	13 April 1994	Accra
Boateng, Sam K.	30 March 1994	Kumasi
Bosompra, Kwadwo	4 April 1994	Kumasi
Brown, Susan Drucker	18 April 1996.	Cambridge, England
Carmichael, Duncan	16 March 1994	Accra
Davidson, Basil	3 September 1998	North Wootton, Somerset
Ellis, Brian	14 May 1997	Ciliau Aeron, Ceredigion, Wales
Ellis, Brian	19 May 1997	Cribyn, Ceredigion, Wales
Genfi, Kofi	29 March 1994	Kumasi
Gyimah, K. Attakora	1 April 1994	Kumasi
Jones, Jack	6 June 1996	Garreg, Gwynedd, Wales
Kran, Nana Yaw	6 April 1994	Sunyani
Kyei, T. E.	30 March 1994	Kumasi
Lanning, Maj. E. C.	25 July 1998	South Godstone, Surrey
Lanning, Maj. E. C.	27 November 1998	South Godstone, Surrey
Mamourou Camara	14 June 1986	Bouna
McCaskie, T. C.	11 May 1997	Birmingham
McCaskie, T. C.	13 September 1998	Birmingham
Moxon, James	17 March 1994	Kitase, Akwapim

Name	Date of Interview	Location
Norman, H. C.	4 and 5 September 1998	Bournemouth
Opoku Ware II, Otumfuo	2 April 1994	Kumasi
Ross, Neil	15 April 1996	Edinburgh
Tuo Lielourou	11 December 1985	Napiédougou
Zie Soro	25 November 1985	Kolokpo

Index

51, 56–65, 76, 80, 87, 99, 113, 143, 161, 162, 172, 227, 228, 233
1 GCR, 28, 31, 32, 34
2 GCR, 28, 30, 31, 32, 34, 227
3 GCR, 32, 37, 227, 228
4 GCR, 37, 56, 227
5 GCR, 13, 37, 51, 56, 76
6 GCR, 49, 63
7 GCR, 51, 59, 60, 61, 63, 76
8 GCR, 37, 63
"Imperials," 56–57, 64
local forces, 26, 31
Territorials, 33
Gold Coast (fighter) Squadron. *See* Royal Air Force
Gold Coast (bomber) 218 Squadron. *See* Royal Air Force
Gonja, 156
Gonokrom, 154
Gourock, 48
Governors' Conference. *See* WAGON
Grand Bassam, 2, 178
grande rocade, 79, 80
Grandperrin, Lt., 12
Grant, Col. E. H.
Greece, 47
Greenock, 48
Grey, Maj. Gen. W .H., 73, 74
Grigsby, W. R., 29, 41–42
Groupe Mobile Coloniale. *See* Tirailleurs Sénégalais
Gubbins, Sir Colin, 123, 226
Guinea. *See* Guinée
Guinée, 40, 78, 107, 124, 219, 233
Gyaman (Abron, Bron, Brong), 106, 119, 142, 148, 153, chapter 7 *passim*
Gyamanhene. *See* Abo Kofi; Adinkra; Agyeman; Kwadwo Agyeman
Gyapekrom, 199

Hailey, Lord, 88, 90–91
Hale, Mrs., 179
Half Assini, 13
Halfaya Pass, 47
Halifax, Lord, 75
Hall, Noel, 86, 88–89
Hall, Capt. R. M., 2
Hambro, Sir Charles, 83, 122, 124, 126, 129, 133, 216, 220, 223–26
Hamilton, Maj. F. L., 5,
Hanau, Julius, 95, 122–24, 133, 136, 149, 158, 230

Hankey, Lord, 73
Harriman, Averell, 55
Harris, J. S., 135
Harrison, Ken, 162
Hausa, 142, 146, 162, 163, 265
Hausa Constabulary, 26
Haute Côte d'Ivoire. *See* Haute Volta
Haute Volta (now Burkina Faso), 74, 119
Havelock, Mr. (UAC), 187
Hawkesworth, E. G., 70, 98, 105, 106, 141, 148–49, 153–56, 161, 167, 200, 201, 203, 216
Hawkins, Coleman, 106
Hawkins, Major-Gen., 128
Hayes, Graham, 124
Hayes, Lt. Col. J. W. A., 32
Haywood, Col. A., 29
Heaton, Lt. W. N., 59
Hedley-Dent, N. E., 117
Helard, M., 10
Hewson, M. G., 206–7
Highland Princess, 48
Hitler, Adolf, 1, 18, 33, 36, 47, 61, 62, 66, 128, 152, 163–64, 168, 169, 178, 179, 187, 188, 192, 197
Ho, 99, 100
Hodson, Gov. Sir Arnold, 4, 7–8, 9–11, 15, 36–37, 45, 46, 57, 59, 60, 62, 92, 93, 152, 161, 167, 173, 175, 190
Holbrook, Wendell, 52, 61, 181, 193
Hollis, Col. L. C., 72
Home Guard, 65–71, 113, 161, 162, 163, 170, 188, 227, 231, 233
Hopkinson, H. L. d'A., 96
Hornsby, P. J. H., 70
Hudson. *See* aircraft
Hughes, A., 4–5, 6, 140
Huntziger, Gen. Léon, 3
Hurricane. *See* aircraft
Hwerebo, 216

Ibos, Lt., 155
Iehl, Lt., 15,
Imperial Airways, 40, 41, 46
"Imperials." *See* Gold Coast Regiment
India, 25, 63, 64, 70, 122, 132, 184, 228, 232
Indo-China, 22
Irish Free State (now Republic of Ireland), 53
Italy, 3, 7, 30, 35, 36, 39, 41, 44, 46, 47, 58, 60, 68, 78, 86, 189, 221, 232

Jacques, Lt. E. H., 34–35

Index